The Holt, Rinehart and Winston Accuracy Commitment:
From Manuscript to Bound Book

As a leading textbook publisher in foreign languages since 1866, Holt, Rinehart and Winston recognizes the importance of accuracy in foreign language textbooks. In an effort to produce the most accurate introductory foreign language program available, we have added two new stages to the development of *¡Atrévete!* — **double proofing** in production and a **final accuracy check** by experienced teachers.

The outline below shows the unprecedented steps we have taken to ensure accuracy:

Author	Writes and proofs first draft.
1st Round of Reviews	Review of first draft manuscript. Independent reviewers check for clarity of text organization, pedagogy, content, and proper use of language.
Author	Makes corrections/changes.
2nd Round of Reviews	Review of second draft manuscript. Independent reviewers again check for clarity of text organization, pedagogy, content, and proper use of language.
Author	Prepares text for production.
Production	Copyediting and proofreading. The project is **double-proofed** — at the galley proof stage and again at the page proof stage.
Final Accuracy Check	The entire work is read one last time by experienced instructors, this time to check for accurate use of language in text, examples, and exercises. The material is read word for word again and all exercises are worked to ensure the most accurate language program possible.
Final Textbook	Published with final corrections.

Holt, Rinehart and Winston would like to acknowledge the following instructors who, along with others, participated in the final accuracy check for *¡Atrévete!*: Kenneth Fleak, University of South Carolina; Donnie Richards, Georgia Southern University; Steve Rivas, California State University, Chico; Nancy Shumaker, Georgia Southern University; Asuncion Gomez, Florida International University; and Margarita Hidalgo, San Diego State University.

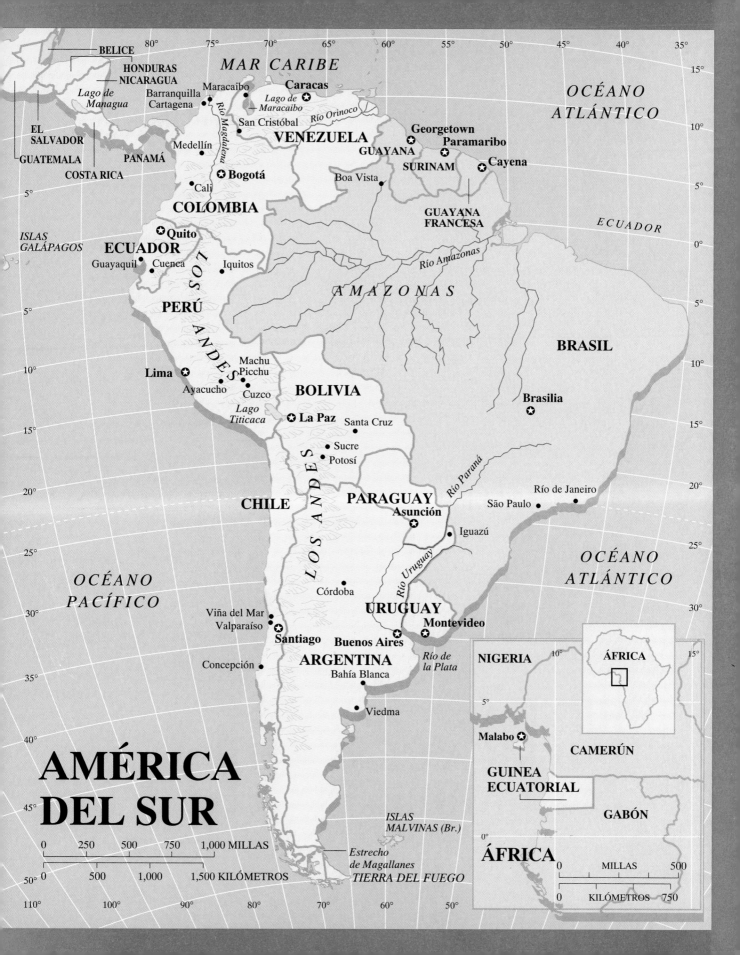

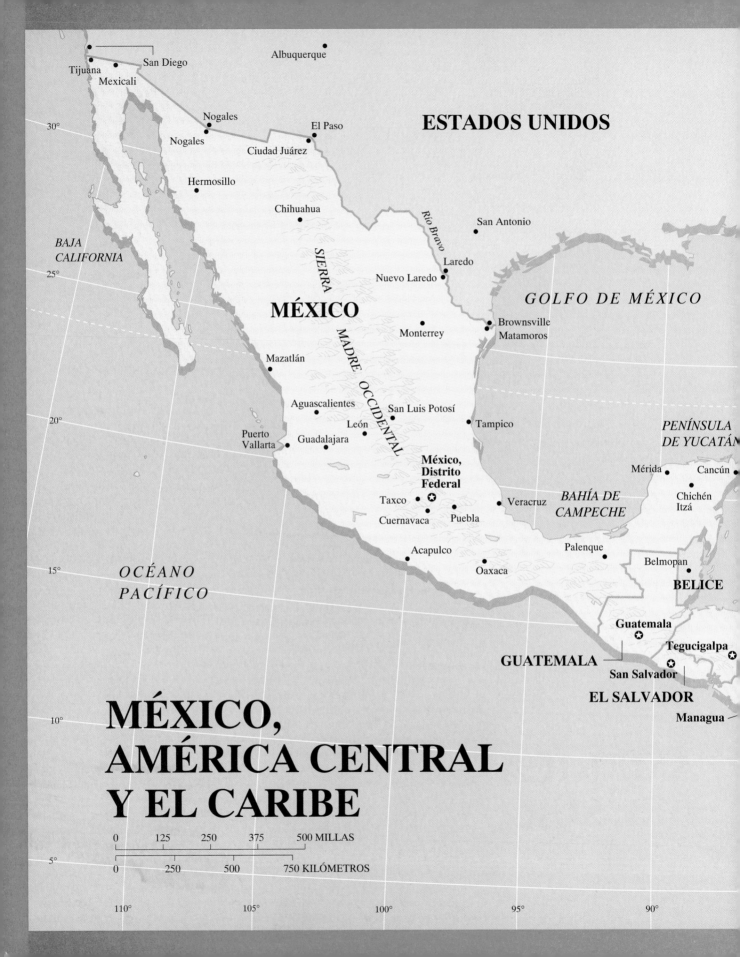

Tijuana
San Diego
Mexicali
Albuquerque

BAJA
CALIFORNIA

Nogales
Nogales
El Paso
Ciudad Juárez

ESTADOS UNIDOS

30°

Hermosillo

Chihuahua

Río Bravo

San Antonio

SIERRA

25°

MÉXICO

Laredo
Nuevo Laredo

GOLFO DE MÉXICO

Mazatlán

MADRE OCCIDENTAL

Monterrey

Brownsville
Matamoros

Aguascalientes

San Luis Potosí

20°

Puerto
Vallarta

León

Guadalajara

Tampico

PENÍNSULA
DE YUCATÁN

México,
Distrito
Federal

Mérida
Cancún

Chichén
Itzá

Taxco

Veracruz

BAHÍA DE
CAMPECHE

Cuernavaca

Puebla

OCÉANO
PACÍFICO

15°

Acapulco

Oaxaca

Palenque

Belmopan

BELICE

GUATEMALA

Guatemala

Tegucigalpa

GUATEMALA

San Salvador

MÉXICO,
AMÉRICA CENTRAL
Y EL CARIBE

EL SALVADOR

Managua

0   125   250   375   500 MILLAS

0   250   500   750 KILÓMETROS

5°

110°   105°   100°   95°   90°

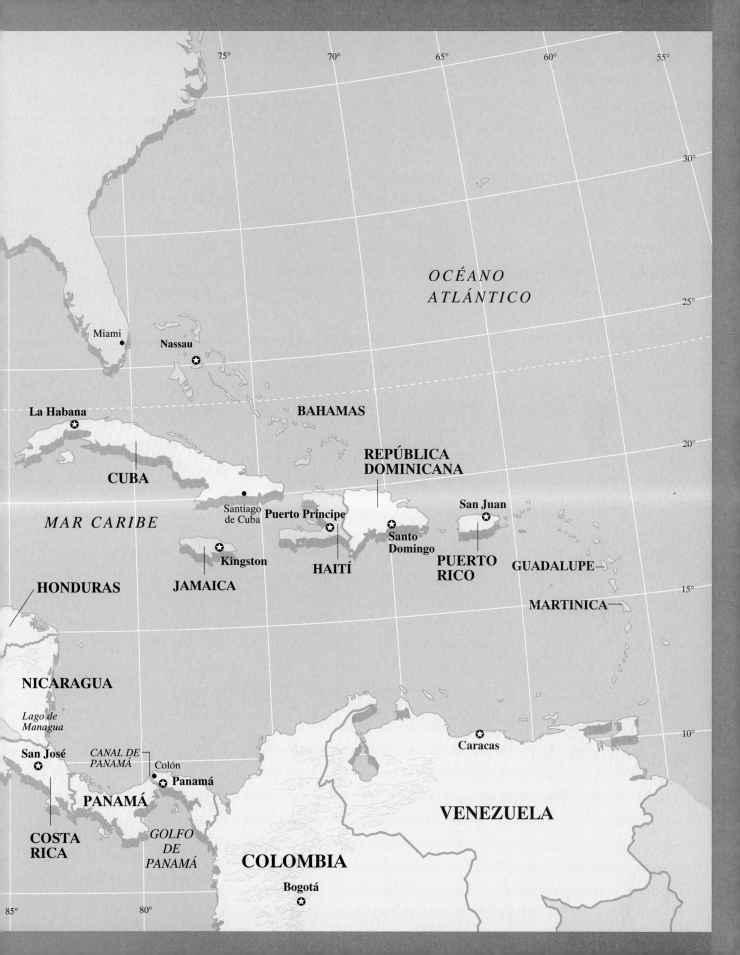

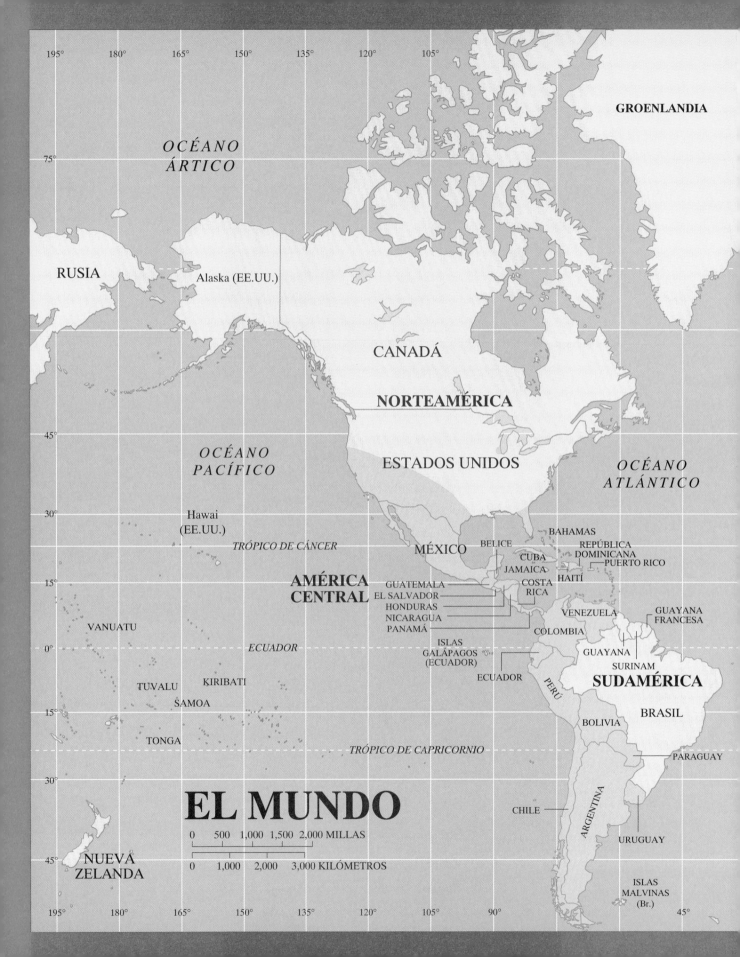

OCÉANO
ÁRTICO

GROENLANDIA

RUSIA

Alaska (EE.UU.)

CANADÁ

NORTEAMÉRICA

OCÉANO
PACÍFICO

ESTADOS UNIDOS

OCÉANO
ATLÁNTICO

Hawai
(EE.UU.)

TRÓPICO DE CÁNCER

MÉXICO

BELICE

BAHAMAS

REPÚBLICA
DOMINICANA
PUERTO RICO

CUBA

JAMAICA

AMÉRICA
CENTRAL

GUATEMALA

COSTA
RICA

HAITÍ

EL SALVADOR

HONDURAS

NICARAGUA

PANAMÁ

VENEZUELA

GUAYANA
FRANCESA

VANUATU

COLOMBIA

ECUADOR

ISLAS
GALÁPAGOS
(ECUADOR)

GUAYANA

SURINAM

ECUADOR

SUDAMÉRICA

TUVALU

KIRIBATI

PERÚ

SAMOA

BRASIL

BOLIVIA

TONGA

TRÓPICO DE CAPRICORNIO

PARAGUAY

EL MUNDO

ARGENTINA

CHILE

0   500   1,000 1,500 2,000 MILLAS

URUGUAY

0   1,000   2,000   3,000 KILÓMETROS

NUEVA
ZELANDA

ISLAS
MALVINAS
(Br.)

195°   180°   165°   150°   135°   120°   105°   90°   45°

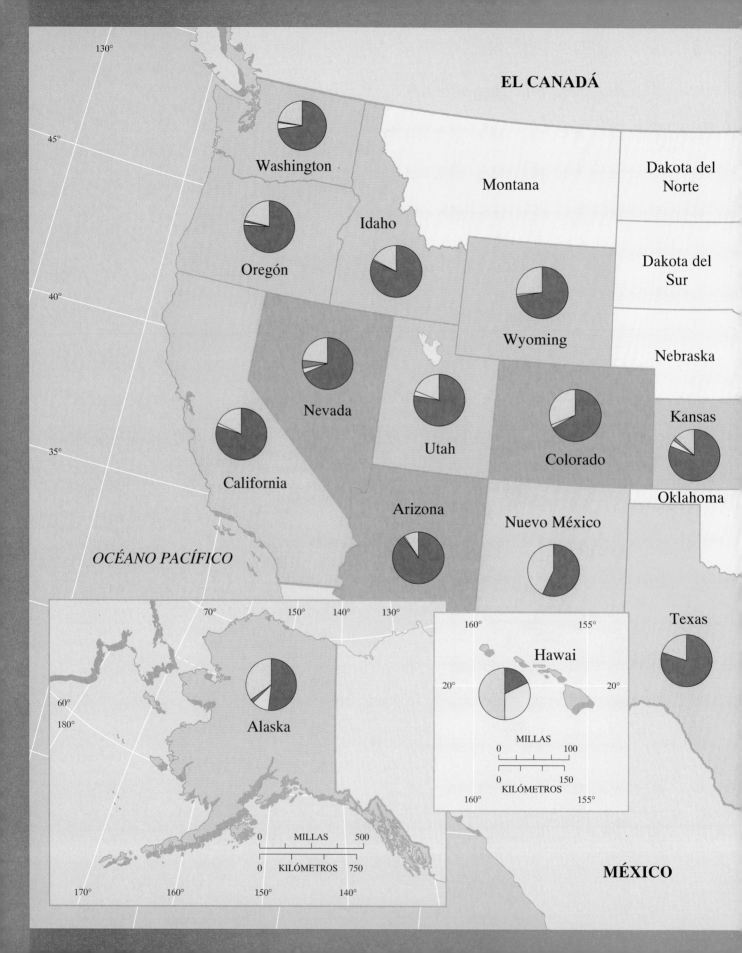

EL CANADÁ

Washington

Montana

Dakota del Norte

Oregón

Idaho

Dakota del Sur

Wyoming

Nebraska

Nevada

Utah

Kansas

California

Colorado

Oklahoma

Arizona

Nuevo México

OCÉANO PACÍFICO

Texas

Hawai

Alaska

MILLAS
0   100

KILÓMETROS
0   150

MILLAS
0   MILLAS   500

KILÓMETROS
0   KILÓMETROS   750

MÉXICO

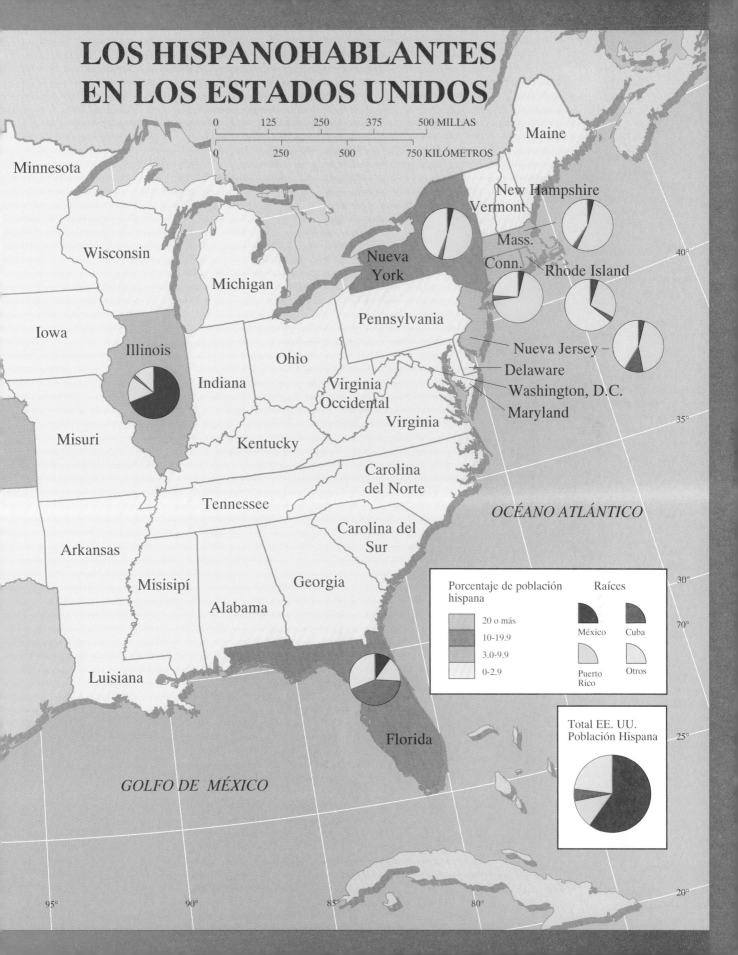

LOS HISPANOHABLANTES EN LOS ESTADOS UNIDOS

0   125   250   375   500 MILLAS

0   250   500   750 KILÓMETROS

Maine

Minnesota

New Hampshire
Vermont

Wisconsin

Mass.
Conn.

Nueva York

Rhode Island

Michigan

Iowa

Illinois

Pennsylvania

Nueva Jersey

Ohio

Delaware

Indiana

Washington, D.C.

Virginia
Occidental

Maryland

Misuri

Virginia

Kentucky

Carolina
del Norte

Tennessee

OCÉANO ATLÁNTICO

Arkansas

Carolina del
Sur

Misisipí

Georgia

Porcentaje de población
hispana

Raíces

Alabama

20 o más

10-19.9

México

Cuba

3.0-9.9

70°

0-2.9

Puerto
Rico

Otros

Luisiana

Total EE. UU.
Población Hispana

Florida

GOLFO DE MÉXICO

95°   90°   85°   80°

40°

35°

30°

25°

20°

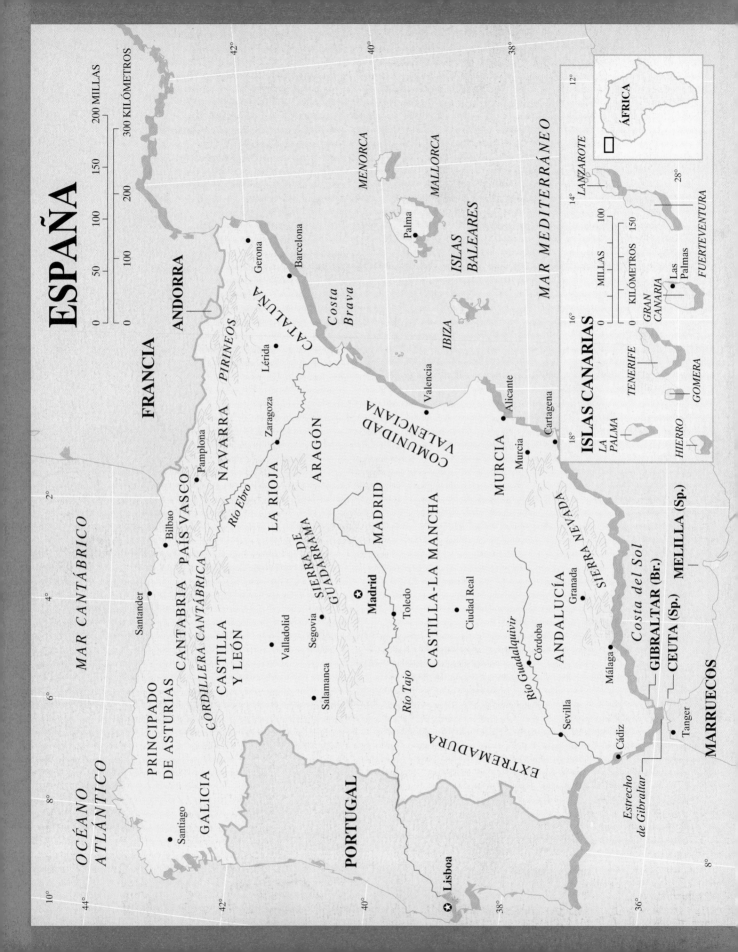

¡Atrévete!

Audrey L. Heining-Boynton
The University of North Carolina at Chapel Hill

Glynis S. Cowell
The University of North Carolina at Chapel Hill

Sonia S. Torres-Quiñones

HOLT, RINEHART AND WINSTON
HARCOURT BRACE COLLEGE PUBLISHERS

FORT WORTH   PHILADELPHIA   SAN DIEGO   NEW YORK   ORLANDO   AUSTIN   SAN ANTONIO

TORONTO   MONTREAL   LONDON   SYDNEY   TOKYO

Publisher	CHRISTOPHER CARSON
Market Strategist	KENNETH S. KASEE
Project Editor	LOUISE SLOMINSKY
Art Director	BURL DEAN SLOAN
Production Manager	CYNTHIA YOUNG

Cover photos: Tango dancers, D. Donne Bryant Stock Photography; Bullfighter, AP Wide World Photos; Women in hard hats, Super Stock; Soccer player, Uniphoto.

ISBN: 0-03-017358-2
Library of Congress Catalog Card Number: 98-72575

Address for Orders
Holt, Rinehart and Winston, 6277 Sea Harbor Drive, Orlando, FL 32887-6777
1-800-782-4479

Address for Editorial Correspondence
Holt, Rinehart and Winston, 301 Commerce Street, Suite 3700, Fort Worth, TX 76102

Web Site Address
http://www.hbcollege.com

Holt, Rinehart and Winston will provide complimentary supplements or supplement packages to those adopters qualified under our adoption policy. Please contact your sales representative to learn how you qualify. If as an adopter or potential user you receive supplements you do not need, please return them to your sales representative or send them to: Attn: Returns Department, Troy Warehouse, 465 South Lincoln Drive, Troy, MO 63379.

Printed in the United States of America

9 0 1 2 3 4 5 6 7   032   9 8 7 6 5 4 3 2

Holt, Rinehart and Winston
Harcourt Brace College Publishers

¡Atrévete!

To My Parents
Audrey L. Heining-Boynton

To John, Jack, and Kate
Glynis S. Cowell

To Mami, Ernesto, and Rafi
Sonia S. Torres-Quiñones

¡Atrévete! means *Take a chance! Go for it!* Learning a language is both exciting and challenging. What the authors of *¡Atrévete!* have done is provide you with a textbook that is innovative, creative, and supportive to help you meet your goals, to really *go for it!*

The innovative *¡Atrévete!* approach to learning Spanish is based on the American Council on the Teaching of Foreign Languages' (ACTFL) *Standards for Foreign Language Learning: Preparing for the Twenty-First Century. ¡Atrévete!* revolves around ACTFL's five organizing principles (the five Cs) of foreign language education: communication, cultures, connections, comparisons, and communities. The development of the *¡Atrévete!* program is the result of many years of teaching experience that guided the authors independently to make important discoveries about language learning, the most important of which center on the student.

The authors of *¡Atrévete!* believe that:

➤ All students can learn in a supportive environment where they are encouraged to take risks when learning another language.
➤ Instruction must begin where the learner is, and all students come to a learning experience with prior knowledge that needs to be tapped.
➤ A student-centered classroom is the best learning environment.
➤ Critical thinking is an important skill that must constantly be encouraged, practiced, and nurtured.
➤ Learners need to make connections with other disciplines in the Spanish classroom.

The authors have developed hundreds of creative and meaningful language-learning activities for the text and all of its supportive components with these beliefs in mind. Read the following material to learn how the entire *¡Atrévete!* program is meant to work for you. Enjoy and *go for it!*

ORGANIZATION OF *¡ATRÉVETE!*

Each chapter is divided into three **Etapas.** *Each* **Etapa** *is further divided into the following sections:*

¡Asómate!
The **¡Asómate!** sections visually introduce new vocabulary in **Etapa 1** and **Etapa 2** with four-color collages or black and white art. Activities follow that allow you to practice new vocabulary and to review previously introduced vocabulary.

¡Fíjate!
The **¡Fíjate!** sections in **Etapa 1** and **Etapa 2** introduce new grammar concepts with clear explanations in English. Many activities follow that allow you to practice the new grammar points.

¡ENTÉRATE!

Culture is presented in the many **¡Entérate!** sections in **Etapa 1** and **Etapa 2.** These cultural sections are always presented with critical thinking questions to help you relate Hispanic culture to your own culture.

RAFI Y EL SACRIFICIO FINAL

The reading section of **Etapa 3** is divided into the following five sections:

1. **Ya lo sabemos** helps you find out new information and organize what you already know.
2. **Estrategias de lectura** reading strategies help you become a more successful reader by making it easier to comprehend what you are reading.
3. **Rafi y el sacrificio final** mystery reinforce the vocabulary and grammar you have learned in the chapter.
4. **Comprensión** activities allow you to check your understanding of the story.
5. **Expansión** sections expand on the chapter episode through a variety of activities including discussions of the chapter debates, role plays, and writing exercises.

¡SÍ, SE PUEDE!

Review activities are provided to practice and synthesize the vocabulary, grammar, and culture presented in the chapter.

PARA RECORDAR

A checklist of the overall concepts introduced in the chapter is provided. You will be able to assess your knowledge of these concepts, checking off what you feel comfortable with and returning to review what you personally feel you have not yet mastered.

VOCABULARIO ACTIVO

A list of the chapter's active vocabulary appears at the end of each chapter in the **Vocabulario activo** section.

TAMBIÉN SE DICE...

To further personalize activities, additional vocabulary words are listed in Appendix A for your use while engaged in classroom activities with a partner or in a group.

VISUAL ICONS USED THROUGHOUT THE TEXT

 The *student note icon* points to useful explanations, study hints, notes about language learning, and handy cross-references to other parts of the textbook and to the *Manual de actividades.* In addition, in the first chapter, student notes explain the organization of the chapter and describe the function of each major chapter section.

The *listening icon* is positioned beside the **A mirar o escuchar** activity in **Etapa 3** of each chapter and reminds you to listen to the audio episode of the continuing Rafi story on the audio CD. You should consult the *Manual de actividades* for pre- and post-listening activities to enhance your understanding of the mystery.

 The *La Red icon* directs you to the Web site for *¡Atrévete!* and supplies you with Web activities linked to the cultural information relevant to the chapter.

The *writing icon* will highlight activities that offer you writing practice. Many of these activities are located in the **¡Sí se puede!** section of **Etapa 3.**

 The *Manual de actividades icon* is used to designate partner activities in your text that will be completed in the *Manual de actividades.* There, you fill in charts and grids that are a point of departure for compiling, sharing, and comparing information with classmates, thus sparking true communication. (These are also known as Information Gap Activities.)

STUDENT COMPONENTS AVAILABLE FOR PURCHASE

STUDENT TEXTBOOK WITH FREE AUDIO CD
¡Atrévete! comes packaged with a free audio CD when a new textbook is purchased from the college bookstore.

MANUAL DE ACTIVIDADES
The organization of the *Manual de actividades* parallels that of the main text. This manual will provide you with activities to practice vocabulary and grammar. Listening exercises for the **A mirar o escuchar** section of the student textbook are found in this manual, which provides true–false, multiple choice, fill-in-the-blank, completion, and writing questions.

MANUAL DE VIDEO
This manual is to be used when you are listening to and viewing the **Rafi y el sacrificio final** mystery video on VHS cassette. The exercises provided vary from true–false, multiple choice, and completion to writing. This manual can be purchased alone or packaged with a copy of the video.

IBM AND MACINTOSH TUTORIAL SOFTWARE
You can practice the vocabulary and grammar presented in each chapter at your own pace and get instantaneous feedback through self-scoring exercises.

Student's Home Page at http://www.hrwcollege.com
¡Atrévete! offers an interactive Web site where you can discover additional cultural and language activities. You will also be encouraged to communicate with other *¡Atrévete!* users by recording data obtained in class while engaged in activities with a partner or group.

Video Program on VHS Cassette
The *¡Atrévete!* video presents additional episodes of the **Rafi y el sacrificio final** story. This is unique to *¡Atrévete!* because these episodes provide information about the **Rafi y el sacrificio final** mystery not presented in the text. This motivates you to listen to and view the additional information to help solve the mystery.

Dual-Platform CD-ROM for PC or MAC
The CD-ROM has the additional **Rafi y el sacrificio final** mysteries as well as activities that incorporate listening, reading, speaking, and writing skills.

To purchase any of these components that were not available in your college bookstore, please call or write:

    Holt, Rinehart and Winston College Division Sales Office
    200 Academic Way
    Troy, MO 63379
    1-800-237-2665

Also, feel free to write to us with comments about or suggestions for *¡Atrévete!* at:

    Holt, Rinehart and Winston
    World Languages Editorial and Marketing Department
    301 Commerce Street, Suite 3700
    Fort Worth, TX 76102

ACKNOWLEDGMENTS

Many individuals have been involved with the development and production of the *¡Atrévete!* program, and the author team acknowledges their contributions. Jim Harmon, our initial acquisitions editor, recognized and understood the potential of the project and provided invaluable advice from its inception.

Harriet Dishman, developmental editor, comprehended from the beginning the unique direction of the authors and their ideas. She guided, and when necessary, gently corralled the team for an end result that reflects their vision. Among her greatly appreciated skills were her expertise, insight, compassion, and interpersonal *savoir faire*.

Burl Sloan, senior art director, conceived a design that showcases the excitement and beauty of the project. He also selected artists who rendered images that make the pages come to life, duplicating what was in the mind's eye of the authors. Kudos to Stephanie O'Shaughnessy for her masterful, delightfully whimsical illustrations that enhance instruction, and to Faith DeLong and Glen Caldwell for their artistically rendered maps. Other artists and illustrators who assisted in bringing life to the pages were Terry Rasberry, James Kranefeld, and Brenda Chambers; they also deserve many thanks for their contributions. Additionally, Susan Friedman, photo editor, deserves high praise for the abundant selection of photographic images that grace the pages.

Louise Slominsky, senior project editor, managed the words, design, and images with aplomb and great care. Her talent, skills, and experience as an editor shone during the demanding production schedule.

We appreciate Ken Kasee, market strategist, for his enthusiastic reception and support during the production stage. We also thank Chris Carson, publisher; Pam Hatley, project manager; Terri Rowenhorst, acquisitions editor; Rosemarie Console, vice president for market intelligence; as well as Debra Jenkin and Cynthia Young, senior production managers, for their important contributions. Sincere thanks and appreciation go to Rolando Hernández, senior vice president of market systems, for his constant support and belief in the project.

We would also like to thank David Heining-Boynton, who served as our technology manager and researcher, for his important contributions. Finally, we wish to give our deepest thanks to our families, friends, colleagues, and students who continue to encourage, support, inspire, motivate, and nurture us.

In addition, we recognize the cogent, eye-opening comments of our reviewers:

Carmen J. Coraeides   *Scottsdale Community College, Arizona*
Vilma Concha-Chiaraviglio   *Brandeis University, Massachusetts*
Alan Garfinkel   *Purdue University, Indiana*
Sonja G. Hokanson   *Washington State University, Washington*
Roma Hoff   *University of Wisconsin–Eau Claire*
Alvin L. Prince   *Furman University, South Carolina*
Joan F. Turner   *The University of Arkansas–Fayetteville*
Patricia Rush   *Ventura College, California*
Estelita Calderón-Young   *Collin County Community College, Texas*

Audrey L. Heining-Boynton
Glynis S. Cowell
Sonia S. Torres-Quiñones

Contents

Capítulo 8   A viajar 237

Welcome to **¡Atrévete!** The word **¡Atrévete!** means *Try it!*; *Take a chance!*; or *Go for it!* You are about to begin the exciting journey of studying the Spanish language and learning about Hispanic culture. Research indicates that successful language learners are willing to take risks and experiment with language. Learning a language is a skill much like learning to ski or learning to play the piano. Developing these skills takes practice. In the beginning, perfection is not expected. What is essential in learning Spanish is to keep trying and risk making mistakes, knowing that the practice will garner results.

Para comenzar

By the end of this chapter you will be able to:

- understand some of the important reasons for studying another language
- list nationally and internationally famous Hispanics
- greet people and introduce them to someone else
- use some basic classroom expressions with your instructor
- say the Spanish alphabet
- state the subject pronouns in Spanish
- know when to use the Spanish forms of *you,* which are "tú" and "Ud."
- use the verb "ser" *(to be)*

¡ENTÉRATE!
Los hispanos en los Estados Unidos

¡Atrévete! is based on the premise that language and culture are inextricably intertwined. Therefore, while you learn to understand, speak, read, and write Spanish, you will also explore the culture of a vast, diverse, and fascinating people. At the same time, you will have the opportunity to reflect on what constitutes culture in the United States.

Mexican Americans form nearly 63 percent of the U.S. Hispanic population. The majority of Mexican Americans live in Texas, New Mexico, Colorado, Arizona, Nevada, and California. Twelve percent of the Hispanic population is Puerto Rican, living principally in New York, New Jersey, and Chicago. Cuban Americans make up 5 percent of the Hispanic population, the majority of whom reside in Florida, particularly in Miami.

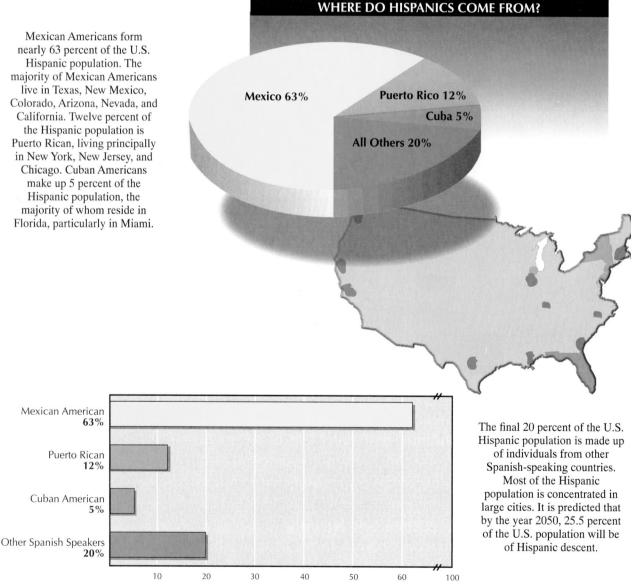

WHERE DO HISPANICS COME FROM?

Mexico 63%

Puerto Rico 12%

Cuba 5%

All Others 20%

Mexican American
63%

Puerto Rican
12%

Cuban American
5%

Other Spanish Speakers
20%

10 20 30 40 50 60 100

United States Percentage of Hispanic Population

The final 20 percent of the U.S. Hispanic population is made up of individuals from other Spanish-speaking countries. Most of the Hispanic population is concentrated in large cities. It is predicted that by the year 2050, 25.5 percent of the U.S. population will be of Hispanic descent.

¿Qué te parece?

1. How many countries can you name where Spanish is spoken? Where are the countries located?
2. How did these countries become Spanish speaking? How did the United States become English speaking? What conclusions can you draw?
3. It is said that English is the international language. If so, why is it important to learn Spanish or any other foreign language?

¡ENTÉRATE!
Algunos hispanos conocidos en los Estados Unidos

The following photographs represent some famous Hispanics well known in the United States.

In 1990, Antonia C. Novello, born in Fajardo, Puerto Rico, became the first woman appointed to the post of surgeon general of the United States.

Oscar Hijuelos was born in New York City to Cuban American parents. Hijuelos is the first Hispanic to win the Pulitzer Prize in literature for his work *Mambo Kings Play Songs of Love* (1989).

Gloria Estefan is a Cuban American singer and composer. She has enjoyed a very successful recording career, recording songs in both English and Spanish.

Walt Disney, or José Luis Guirao, was born in Mojácar, Spain, and later adopted by Elias and Flora Disney of Chicago. His 1928 film, *Steamboat Willy,* was the first of many classic films. During his career he won thirty-two Academy Awards.

¿Qué te parece?

Many Hispanics have become prominent not only nationally but internationally. With a partner, list three other Hispanics who have made a positive impact in the United States. Where can you go to find out about others?

¡ASÓMATE! 1
Los saludos y las despedidas

This section introduces common greetings and farewells.

Otros saludos y otras despedidas

¡Hola!	*Hi!; Hello!*
Soy _____.	*I'm _____ .*
¿Cómo te llamas?	*What is your name? (familiar)*
¿Cómo se llama usted?	*What is your name? (formal)*
Me llamo...	*My name is . . .*
Encantado. / Encantada.	*Nice to meet you.*
Igualmente.	*The same to you.*

The expressions **¿Cómo se llama usted?** and **¿Cómo te llamas?** both mean *What is your name?*, but the latter is used among students and other peers. You will learn about the differences later in this chapter. Note that **Encantado** is said by a male, and **Encantada** is said by a female.

Spanish uses special punctuation to signal a question or an exclamation. An upside-down question mark begins a question and an upside-down exclamation point begins an exclamation, as in **¿Cómo te llamas?** and **¡Hola!**

1. **¿Cómo te llamas?**   Introduce yourself to three classmates.

   Modelo   Soy _____. ¿Cómo te llamas?

Más saludos y despedidas

¿Cómo está?	*How are you? (formal)*
Así, así.	*So, so.*
Más o menos.	*So, so.*
Bastante bien.	*Just fine.*
Muy bien.	*Really well.*
Regular.	*OK.*
¿Y tú?	*And you? (familiar)*
¿Y usted?	*And you? (formal)*
Chao.	*Bye.*
Hasta luego.	*See you later.*
Hasta pronto.	*See you soon.*
Que tenga(s) un buen día.	*Have a good (nice) day.*
Igualmente.	*You too.; The same to you.*

2. **Saludos y despedidas.**   Respond appropriately to each of the following greetings and farewells.

   1. Adiós.
   2. ¿Qué tal?
   3. ¿Cómo te llamas?
   4. Hasta mañana.
   5. Que tengas un buen día.

3. **¡Hola! ¿Qué tal?**   Greet five classmates, ask them how they are, and then tell them how you are. After you are comfortable with one greeting, try a different greeting.

4. **Encantado, mucho gusto.**   Imagine that you are in a receiving line at a university reception. The entire class stands, and in groups of five, the first student (**Estudiante 1**) greets the next student in line (**Estudiante 2**), introducing himself or herself and asking how he or she is. **Estudiante 2** replies and then introduces **Estudiante 3** to **Estudiante 1.** Then **Estudiante 3** turns to **Estudiante 4** and starts the process over again. Repeat until your entire group has been through the line. Vary your greetings and responses.

Modelo	ESTUDIANTE 1:	Hola, buenos días. Soy Kay.
	ESTUDIANTE 2:	Buenos días, Kay. Soy Tom. ¿Cómo estás?
	ESTUDIANTE 1:	Muy bien, Tom. ¿Y tú?
	ESTUDIANTE 2:	Bien, gracias. Kay, quiero presentarte a Brad.
	ESTUDIANTE 1	Mucho gusto. / Encantado. / Encantada...
	AND ESTUDIANTE 3:	

¡ENTÉRATE!
Cómo se saluda la gente

When Spanish speakers meet, they greet each other and ask each other how they are doing, and respond appropriately when asked, using phrases like the ones you just learned. In most of the Spanish-speaking world, men usually shake hands when greeting, although close friends may greet each other with an **abrazo** *(hug)*. Between female friends, the usual greeting is a **besito** *(little kiss)* on one or both cheeks (depending on the country) and a gentle hug. While conversing, Spanish speakers may stand quite close to each other.

¿Qué te parece?

1. How can you tell that the party in the previous picture is taking place in a Spanish-speaking country?
2. What common greetings are used in the United States? What types of greetings are being used in the drawing? Are they similar?
3. Think about other social situations and how you greet others. Are there different greetings that you use for different people?

¡ASÓMATE! 2
Expresiones útiles para la clase

To learn Spanish faster, you should attempt to speak only Spanish in the classroom. The following list provides useful expressions that you and your instructor will use frequently.

Preguntas y respuestas

¿Cómo?	*What?; How?*
¿Cómo se dice _____ en español?	*How do you say _____ in Spanish?*
¿Cómo se escribe _____ en español?	*How do you write _____ in Spanish?*
¿De dónde _____?	*From where _____?*
¿Qué significa? / ¿Qué es?	*What does it mean?*
¿Quién?	*Who?*
¿Qué es esto?	*What is this?*
Comprendo.	*I understand.*
No comprendo.	*I don't understand.*
Lo sé.	*I know.*
No lo sé.	*I don't know.*
No.	*No.*
Sí.	*Yes.*

Mandatos para la clase

Abra(n) el libro en la página...	*Open your book to page . . .*
Cierre(n)...	*Close . . .*
Conteste(n).	*Answer.*
Escriba(n).	*Write.*
Escuche(n).	*Listen.*
Lea(n).	*Read.*
Repita(n).	*Repeat.*
Vaya(n) a la pizarra.	*Go to the board.*

Expresiones de cortesía

De nada.	*You're welcome.*
Gracias.	*Thank you.*
Por favor.	*Please.*

In Spanish, commands (**mandatos**) can have two forms. The singular form (**abra, cierre, conteste, etc.**) is directed to one person, while the plural form (those ending in **-n: abran, cierren, contesten, etc.**) is used with more than one person.

5. Más práctica.   With a partner, practice being the instructor and the student. The "instructor" either tells the "student" to do something or asks the student a question; the student responds appropriately. Practice with at least five sentences or questions, utilizing the new expressions, then change roles.

Modelo	**INSTRUCTOR:**	Abra el libro.
	ESTUDIANTE:	*(Student opens the book)*
	INSTRUCTOR:	¿Cómo se dice «*hello*»?
	ESTUDIANTE:	Se dice «hola».

¡FÍJATE! 1
El alfabeto

Letter		Examples	Letter		Examples
a	a	**a**diós	**ñ**	eñe	ma**ñ**ana
b	be	**b**uenos	**o**	o	có**m**o
c	ce	**c**lase	**p**	pe	**p**or favor
d	de	**d**ía	**q**	cu	**q**ué
e	e	**e**spañol	**r**	ere	seño**r**a
f	efe	por **f**avor	**rr**	erre	pe**rr**o
g	ge *(hay)*	lue**g**o	**s**	ese	**s**aludos
h	hache	**h**ola	**t**	te	**t**arde
i	i	señor**i**ta	**u**	u	**u**sted
j	jota	**j**ulio	**v**	ve	nue**v**e
k	ka	**k**ilómetro	**w**	doble ve	**W**ashington
l	ele	**l**uego	**x**	equis	e**x**amen
m	eme	**m**adre	**y**	i griega	**y**o
n	ene	**n**oche	**z**	zeta	pi**z**arra

The letter **rr** is considered a single letter in Spanish. In books and documents that predate 1994, you will also see **ch** and **ll** treated as separate letters.

6. En español.   Pronounce the following common abbreviations in Spanish.

1. CD	6. ABC	11. MCI
2. IBM	7. CBS	12. UPS
3. BMW	8. NBC	13. ESPN
4. CNN	9. M&M	14. WWW
5. MTV	10. AT&T	

7. **¿Qué es esto?**   Spell the following words for a partner, who will say the spelled word without looking at the book.

1. hola
2. mañana
3. usted
4. quiero

5. buenos
6. igualmente
7. encantada
8. *your own last name*

¡FÍJATE! 2
Los pronombres personales

Subject pronouns are used for clarification or for emphasis. These subject pronouns are listed in the following box.

Singular		Plural	
yo	*I*	nosotros, nosotras	*we*
tú	*you (familiar)*	vosotros, vosotras	*you (plural, SPAIN)*
él, ella, usted	*he, she, you (formal)*	ellos, ellas, ustedes	*they, you (plural)*

Spanish has several equivalents for *you*. Generally speaking, **tú** *(you, singular)* is used for people with whom you are on a first-name basis, such as family members and friends. **Usted,** abbreviated **Ud.,** is used with people you do not know well, or with people with whom you are not on a first-name basis. **Ud.** is also used with older people, or with those to whom you want to show respect.

Spanish shows gender more clearly than English. **Nosotros** and **ellos** are used to refer to either all males or to a mixed group of males and females. **Nosotras** and **ellas** refer to a group of all females.

Languages are constantly evolving. Words are added and deleted, words change in meaning, and the use of language in certain situations changes. For example, in Spanish, the use of **tú** and **Ud.** is changing dramatically. **Tú** may now be used more freely in situations where **Ud.** was previously used. For example, in some Spanish-speaking countries, it is now acceptable for a shopper to use **tú** with a young store clerk. Only a few years ago, it was strictly **Ud.** Nevertheless, throughout the Western Hemisphere, a more traditional use of **tú** and **Ud.** still exists. When traveling to Spanish-speaking countries or meeting Spanish-speaking people in the United States, you should listen to the language used in a variety of social situations. Regarding the use of **tú** or **Ud.,** a good rule of thumb is: *When in doubt, be more formal.*

There are a few regional differences in the use of pronouns. Spanish speakers in Spain use **vosotros** when addressing more than one person with whom they are on a first-name basis *("you all")*. **Ustedes,** abbreviated **Uds.,** is used throughout the rest of the Spanish-speaking world. Spanish speakers in Costa Rica, Argentina, and other parts of Latin America use **vos** for **tú.** Yet, **tú** and **ustedes** would be understood perfectly in these countries.

¿Qué te parece?

To understand how Spanish is changing, consider what has happened to English over the years.

1. What new words have been added to the English language in the past twenty years? In the past century?
2. What are some words and expressions that we do not use anymore in English? Are there any English words that have changed or added meanings?
3. What are some regional language differences in the United States? What differences in language occur between the United States and England? What differences in language occur between the United States and Canada? Can the British, Canadians, and Americans understand each other?

8. **¿Tú o Ud.?**   When speaking with the following people, would you use **tú** or **Ud.** if you lived in a Spanish-speaking country?

   1. your sister
   2. your mom
   3. your professor
   4. your grandfather
   5. your best friend's father
   6. a clerk in a department store
   7. a gas station attendant
   8. the mail carrier
   9. someone you have just met who is older
   10. someone you have just met who is your age
   11. a child you have just met

9. **¿Cómo se dice?**   How would you express the following in Spanish?

   1. they (men and women)
   2. they (just women)
   3. they (just men)
   4. they (fifty women and one man)
   5. we (all women)
   6. we (all men)
   7. we (men and women)

¡FÍJATE! 3
El verbo ser

In English, there are different verb forms for different subjects. Consider the forms of *to be,* for example.

	to be		
I	*am*	we	*are*
you	*are*	you	*are*
he, she, it	*is*	they	*are*

Spanish verbs behave in a similar way. Look at the verb **ser,** *to be.*

		ser		*to be*			
yo	**soy**	*I am*	nosotros, nosotras	**somos**	*we are*		
tú	**eres**	*you are*	vosotros, vosotras	**sois**	*you are*		
él, ella, Ud.	**es**	*he, she, it is*	ellos, ellas, Uds.	**son**	*they, you are*		

10. **Vamos a practicar.** With a partner, practice the verb **ser** with the following pronouns.

Modelo   nosotros   ⇒   **nosotros somos**

1. nosotras
2. Ud.
3. yo
4. él

5. ellas
6. tú
7. Uds.
8. ella

11. **«Ser o no ser...»**   Take the following forms of **ser** and change them to plural if they are singular and vice versa.

Modelo   yo soy   ⇒   **nosotros somos**

1. usted es
2. nosotros somos
3. ella es

4. ellos son
5. tú eres

Para recordar

In this preliminary chapter you learned to:

☑ understand some of the important reasons for studying another language

☑ list nationally and internationally famous Hispanics

☑ greet people and introduce them to someone else

☑ use some basic classroom expressions with your instructor

☑ say the Spanish alphabet

☑ state the subject pronouns in Spanish

☑ distinguish between **tú** and **Ud.** and know when to use them

☑ use the verb **ser** *(to be)*

VOCABULARIO ACTIVO

Los saludos *Greetings*

Así, así.   *So, so.*
Bien.   *Fine.*
Bastante bien.   *Just fine.*
Muy bien.   *Really well.*
Buenas noches.   *Good evening.; Good night.*

Buenas tardes.   *Good afternoon.*
Buenos días.   *Good morning.*
¿Cómo estás?   *How are you? (familiar)*
¿Cómo está?   *How are you? (formal)*
¡Hola!   *Hi!; Hello!*

Más o menos.   *So, so.*
¿Qué hay?   *What's new?; What's up?*
¿Qué tal?   *How's it going?*
Regular.   *OK.*
¿Y tú?   *And you? (familiar)*
¿Y usted?   *And you? (formal)*

Las despedidas *Farewells*

Adiós.   *Good-bye.*
Chao.   *Bye.*
Hasta luego.   *See you later.*

Hasta mañana.   *See you tomorrow.*
Hasta pronto.   *See you soon.*

Que tenga(s) un buen día.   *Have a nice day.*

Las presentaciones *Presentations*

¿Cómo te llamas?   *What is your name? (familiar)*
¿Cómo se llama usted?   *What is your name? (formal)*
Encantado. / Encantada.   *Nice to meet you.*

Igualmente.   *The same to you; You too.*
Me llamo...   *My name is . . .*
Mucho gusto.   *How do you do? / Nice to meet you.*

Quiero presentarte a _____.   *I would like to introduce you to _____.*
Soy _____.   *I'm _____.*

Preguntas y respuestas *Questions + Responses*

¿Cómo?   *What? / How?*
¿Cómo se dice _____ en español?   *How do you say _____ in Spanish?*
¿Cómo se escribe _____ en español?   *How do you write _____ in Spanish?*

(No) comprendo.   *I (don't) understand.*
¿De dónde...?   *From where . . . ?*
Lo sé.   *I know.*
No lo sé.   *I don't know.*
No.   *No.*
Sí.   *Yes.*
¿Qué es esto?   *What is this?*

¿Qué significa? / ¿Qué es?   *What does it mean?*
¿Quién?   *Who?*

Also Say it again for class

Mandatos para la clase

Abra(n) el libro en la página...
Open your book to page . . .
Cierre(n)... *Close . . .*

Conteste(n)... *Answer . . .*
Escriba(n). *Write.*
Escuche(n). *Listen.*
Lea(n). *Read.*

Repita(n). *Repeat.*
Vaya(n) a la pizarra. *Go to the board.*

Expresiones de cortesía Expressions of courtesy

De nada. *You're welcome.*

Gracias. *Thank you.*

Por favor. *Please.*

Los pronombres personales Personal pronouns

él *he*
ella *she*
ellos, ellas *they*
nosotros, nosotras *we*

tú *you (familiar)*
usted *you (formal)*
ustedes *you (plural)*

vosotros, vosotras *you (plural, SPAIN)*
yo *I*

Verbos Verbs

ser *to be*

soy	yo	I am
eres	tú	you are
es	el/ella/ud.	he/she/it is
somos	nostros/nosotras	we are
son	ellos/ellas/uds.	they are

Hay - there is
there are

yo
tu
él/ella/ud.
nosotros/nosotras
ellos/ellas/uds.

~~He~~
~~Has~~
~~Ha~~
~~Hamos~~
~~Han~~

Extended families are very important in the Spanish-speaking world. Frequently, several generations live in the same household or next door to each other: parents, their married sons and daughters and their families, grandparents, aunts and uncles, and so on. Elderly people are treated with great respect, and often adult children willingly take on the responsibility for the care of their aged parents. Even if they do not live in the same household, adult children provide for their parents by sending money and food and by arranging for their basic needs to be met.

¿Qué te parece?

1. Do you have (or have you had) people other than the nuclear family (e.g., mom, dad, children) living under your roof? If so, who?
2. What are the rewards of this kind of living arrangement? What are some challenges?

Al conocernos

By the end of this chapter you will be able to:

ETAPA 1 ¡Sígueme!
- [ ] talk about your family
- [ ] discuss various aspects of Hispanic families

ETAPA 2 ¡Dime más!
- ◆ describe yourself and others
- ◆ discuss important facts about Puerto Rico

ETAPA 3 ¡Cuéntame!
- ● meet some of the characters from the continuing mystery story: Rafi, his family, and his best friend Chema

ETAPA 1

¡Sígueme!

Each chapter is divided into three sections, called **Etapas** (Levels *or* Stages), *which will take you progressively through the chapter.* **Etapa 1, ¡Sígueme!** (Follow me!) *begins each chapter.*

¡Atrévete! is committed to presenting the Spanish language based on five organizing principles: *communication, cultures, connections, comparisons,* and *communities.* While you learn to *communicate* in the language, you will gain an insight into the broad Spanish-speaking *culture,* make *connections* with other disciplines such as sociology and business, *compare* and gain insights into the nature of language and culture, and come to realize the importance of working together in local or global *communities.*

¡ASÓMATE! 1
La familia de Rafael

The **¡Asómate!** (Take a look! *or* Check it out!) *sections of* **¡Atrévete!** *present high-frequency vocabulary for you to practice and incorporate into your Spanish vocabulary.*

La familia

el abuelo / la abuela	*grandfather / grandmother*
los abuelos	*grandparents*
el esposo / la esposa	*husband / wife*
el hermano / la hermana	*brother / sister*
los hermanos	*brothers and sisters; siblings*
el hijo / la hija	*son / daughter*
los hijos	*sons and daughters; children*
la madre / la mamá	*mother / mom*
el padre / el papá	*father / dad*
los padres	*parents*
el primo / la prima	*cousin (masc. / fem.)*
los primos	*cousins*
el sobrino / la sobrina	*nephew / niece*
el tío / la tía	*uncle / aunt*
los tíos	*aunts and uncles*

[handwritten notes]

el marrido
companero
companera

padrastro → step
madrasta
hermanastra → step
hermanastro

gemala → twin
gemalo → twin

16

abuela
Rosario Jiménez de Martín

abuelo
Rafael Martín Acosta

tía
Teresa Ávila
de Martín

tío
Enrique Martín Jiménez

padre
Manuel Jesús Martín Jiménez

madre
Francisca Lara de Martín

tío
Pedro Lara Torres

prima
Sonia Martín Ávila

Rafi
(Rafael Martín Lara)

hermana
Carmen Soledad
Martín Lara

hermano
Antonio Martín Lara

cuñada
Pilar Saborío
de Martín

sister
in
law

sobrina
Gabriela Martín Saborío

17

For additional vocabulary words related to family relationships, for example, stepmother **(la madrastra)** *or* stepfather **(el padrastro),** *see the section called* **También se dice...** *(One also says . . .) in Appendix A.*

1 **La familia de Rafi.**   Look at Rafi's family tree. How are the following people related to Rafi?

> **Modelo**   Antonio es su...   ➡   **hermano**

1. Francisca es su...
2. Carmen Soledad es su...
3. Enrique es su...
4. Manuel es su...

5. Pedro es su...
6. Rosario es su...
7. Sonia es su...
8. Rafael Martín Acosta es su...

2 **Mi familia.**   Sketch out and label three or four generations of your own family tree. Prepare five oral sentences to share with a partner. Finally, write your five sentences. Follow the model.

Vocabulario: Mi mamá es...; mi papá es...; mi...

> **Modelo**   **Mi mamá es Katrina. Mi papá es Russ. Bill es mi hermano.**
> **Candace es mi hermana. Wendy es mi abuela.**

Save the sketch of your family because you will use it in a later activity.

¡ENTÉRATE!
nicknames   *Last names*
Los nombres, apodos y apellidos

The **¡Entérate!** *sections, which mean* Take note! *or* Become aware!*, present interesting cultural information about the Spanish-speaking world.*

The following list introduces some common Spanish first names and their nicknames.

Hombres *Men*

Nombre	Apodo *nick name*
Antonio	Toño, Toni
Francisco	Paco, Pancho, Cisco
Guillermo	Memo, Guillo
Jesús	Chu, Chuito, Chucho
José María	Chema
Manuel	Manolo, Mani
Rafael	Rafi, Rafa

Mujeres *women*

Nombre	Apodo
Antonia	Toñín, Toña, Toñita
Concepción	Concha, Conchita
Guadalupe	Lupe
María Soledad	Marisol
María Teresa	Maite, Marité
Pilar	Pili
Rosario	Charo

El sábado diecisiete de junio
en la Iglesia Discípulos de Cristo
en Río Piedras
se reunieron en matrimonio

Carmen Torres López

y

Ricardo Colón Montoya

El enlace tuvo como padrinos
a Carlos Colón, Sonia García,
María Martínez y a Manuel Caballero

In Spanish-speaking countries, it is customary for people to use both paternal and maternal last names (surnames). For example, Rafi's father is **Manuel Jesús Martín Jiménez** and his mother's maiden name is **Francisca Lara Torres.** Rafi's first last name would be his father's first last name (**Martín**); Rafi's second last name would be his mother's first last name (**Lara**). Therefore, Rafi's full name would be **Rafael Martín Lara.** In most informal situations, though, Rafi would use only his first last name, or **Rafi Martín.**

A woman may still retain the surname of her father upon marriage in some Hispanic countries, while giving up her mother's surname. She will take her new husband's last name preceded by the preposition **de** *(of).* When Rafi's mother, for example, married his father, her name became **Francisca Lara de Martín.** Therefore, if a woman named **Carmen Torres López** married a man named **Ricardo Colón Montoya,** her name would then become **Carmen Torres de Colón.**

¿Qué te parece?

1. Do you have a nickname? If so, where does it come from? Do you know what your name would be in Spanish? If you do not know, ask your instructor if there is a translation or equivalent for your name in Spanish.

2. Hispanic last names may seem very long to you. Are there any other equivalents in the United States? Can you think of any international equivalents?

3. Can you think of any advantages to using both the mother's and the father's last names?

4. What is your own name in the Spanish style? Write it out, then write the names of five family members or friends **a la española.** For example, Gail Parker's mother's maiden name is Smith. Her name **a la española** would be *Gail Parker Smith.*

5. Bring the wedding announcement page of a newspaper to class. With a partner, decide what the names of five new brides would be **a la española** if they take their new husbands' last names. (Remember, the groom's name will not change, only the bride's.)

¡FÍJATE! 1
El verbo tener

¡Fíjate! *sections, which mean* Notice!; Look!; *or* Imagine that!, *present important grammar points and concepts.*

You learned the present tense forms of the verb **ser** in **Capítulo preliminar.** Another very common verb in Spanish is **tener** *(to have)*. The present tense forms of the verb **tener** follow.

[handwritten annotations: "Present/Indicative", "irregular verb", "infinitive verb — it has "to" in front of it"]

tener	*to have*		
yo **tengo**		nosotros, nosotras	**tenemos**
tú **tienes**		vosotros, vosotras	**tenéis**
él, ella, Ud. **tiene**		ellos, ellas, Uds.	**tienen**

3 **Practica conmigo.** With a partner, practice the different present tense forms of **tener,** taking turns giving the subject pronouns. Practice until you can do the forms quickly without errors.

Modelo   nosotras   ➡   **nosotras tenemos**

1. tú	6. ellas
2. Uds.	7. él
3. yo	8. ellos
4. nosotros	9. Ud.
5. ella	10. tú y yo

4 **¡Apúrate!** Work in groups of at least four students. One person makes a ball out of a piece of paper, says a subject pronoun, and tosses the paper ball to someone in the group. That person catches the ball and must give the corresponding form of **tener.** If the form is correct, he or she receives a point. After finishing **tener,** review the forms of **ser.**

Modelo   **yo… tengo; ella… tiene**

5 **De tal palo, tal astilla.** Work in groups of three. Refer to the family tree you sketched for **actividad 2,** page 18, to tell a partner about your family. Create three sentences, using the verb **tener.** After listening to you, your partner will share what you told him or her with another classmate. To say what you do not have, say **no tengo...** Use the article **un** *(a / an)* with a masculine noun and **una** with a feminine noun.

Vocabulario: 2 = **dos,** 3 = **tres,** 4 = **cuatro,** 5 = **cinco,** 6 = **seis,** 7 = **siete,** 8 = **ocho,** 9 = **nueve,** 10 = **diez**

Modelo   ESTUDIANTE 1 *(ALICE)*:   Tengo un hermano, Scott. No tengo abuelos. Tengo dos tíos, George y David.

ESTUDIANTE 2 *(JEFF)*:   Alice tiene un hermano, Scott. No tiene abuelos. Tiene dos tíos, George y David.

Sigue ▸

¡Dime más!
¡Dime más!

Etapa 2 *of every chapter is called* **¡Dime más!** (Tell me more!). *This middle section in the chapter provides additional information and concepts on vocabulary, grammar, and culture, building on what you learned in* **Etapa 1.**

¡FÍJATE! 2
Cómo acentuar las palabras

In Spanish, written accents are used to distinguish word meaning, or when a word is "breaking" a pronunciation rule. Here are the basic rules of Spanish pronunciation and accentuation.

1. Words ending in a vowel, or in the consonants **-n** or **-s,** are stressed on the next-to-last syllable; that is, the stress of your voice falls on the next-to-last syllable.

   her<u>ma</u>na, her<u>ma</u>no, <u>gran</u>de, <u>tie</u>nen, a<u>bue</u>los, no<u>so</u>tros, <u>e</u>res

2. Words ending in consonants other than **-n** or **-s** are stressed on the last syllable.

   te<u>ner</u>, us<u>ted</u>, Rafa<u>el</u>, ciu<u>dad</u>, <u>ser</u>, Gabri<u>el</u>, fe<u>liz</u>

3. All words "breaking" rules 1 and 2 need a written accent on the stressed syllable.

   televisión, lápiz *(pencil),* **teléfono, papá, Ramón, lápices** *(pencils)*

4. Accents are used on all interrogative words and exclamatory words.

   ¿Cómo?; ¿Qué?; ¿Cuándo? *(When?);* **¿Quién?; ¿Cuántos?** *(How many?);*
      ¿Dónde?; ¡Qué bueno! *(How nice!)*

5. Accents are used to differentiate meaning of certain one-syllable words.
   él *(he)* versus **el** *(the)*   **sí** *(yes)* versus **si** *(if)*
   mí *(me)* versus **mi** *(my)*   **tú** *(you)* versus **tu** *(your)*

¡FÍJATE! 3
Grammar

El singular y el plural

To make singular forms of Spanish nouns and adjectives plural, follow these simple guidelines.

1. If the word ends in a vowel, add **-s.**

   hermana ➡ **hermanas**   **abuelo** ➡ **abuelos**
   día ➡ **días**   **mi** ➡ **mis**

2. If the word ends in a consonant, add **-es.**

   usted ➡ **ustedes**   **ciudad** ➡ **ciudades**
   televisión ➡ **televisiones**   **joven** ➡ **jóvenes**

   Note that words ending in **-ión,** such as **televisión,** lose their accent in the plural because the stress falls naturally on the next-to-last syllable. The plural of **joven** is **jóvenes,** which adds an accent to retain the stress on the syllable **jo.**

3. If the word ends in a **-z,** change the **z** to **c,** and add **-es.**

   lápiz ➡ **lápices**   **feliz** ➡ **felices**

1 **¿Sí o no?** Write the following words in Spanish and tell why they do or do not need written accents.

   1. the telephone   3. Who?   5. sisters
   2. yes   4. Joe

2 **Te toca a ti.** Make the following singular nouns plural.

   Modelo   primo ➡ **primos**

   1. padre   3. taxi   5. abuela
   2. tía   4. nieta   6. joven

23

¡FÍJATE! 4
El masculino y el femenino

In Spanish, all nouns (people, places, and things) have gender; they are either masculine or feminine. Use the following rules to help you determine the gender of nouns. If you encounter a noun that does not belong to any of the following categories, you must memorize the gender as you learn the noun.

1. Most words ending in **-a** are feminine: **la hermana, la hija, la mamá, la tía.**

   Some exceptions: **el día** *(day),* **el mapa** *(map),* **el papá** *(dad),* **el problema** *(problem),* **el programa** *(program)*

2. Most words ending in **-o** are masculine: **el abuelo, el hermano, el hijo, el nieto.**

   Some exceptions: **la foto** *(photo),* **la mano** *(hand),* **la moto** *(motorcycle)*

3. Words ending in **-ción** and **-sión** are feminine: **la discusión, la recepción, la televisión.**

4. Words ending in **-dad** or **-tad** are feminine: **la ciudad, la libertad, la universidad.**

Words that look alike and have the same meaning in both English and Spanish are known as *cognates,* such as **discusión** and **universidad.** Use them to help you decipher meaning and to form words. For example, **prosperidad** looks like what English word? What is its gender?

 Successful foreign language learners make educated guesses about the meaning of unknown words in the new language.

3 **Para practicar.** Decide whether the following cognates are masculine or feminine, then give their English equivalents.

1. guitarra
2. teléfono
3. computadora
4. selección
5. cafetería

¡FÍJATE! 5
Los artículos definidos e indefinidos

Words that are used with nouns, for example, articles and adjectives, mirror their gender (masculine or feminine) and number (singular or plural). For example, articles and all other words referring to a singular masculine noun must also be singular and masculine.

Just as in English, Spanish has two kinds of articles: definite (e.g., *the*), and indefinite (e.g., *a, an, some*). Note the forms in the following charts.

Los artículos definidos			
el hermano	*the brother*	los hermanos	*the brothers / the brothers and sisters*
la hermana	*the sister*	las hermanas	*the sisters*

Definite articles are used to refer to a specific person, place, or thing.

must agree in gender + number

Los artículos indefinidos			
un hermano	*a / one brother*	unos hermanos	*some brothers / some brothers and sisters*
una hermana	*a / one sister*	unas hermanas	*some sisters*

Indefinite articles are used to refer to a nonspecific person, place, or thing.

4 **Vamos a practicar.** With a partner, practice the correct forms of the definite article with the following nouns.

Modelo   tías   ➡   **las tías**

1. tío
2. padres
3. mamá
4. papá
5. hermanas
6. hijo
7. abuela
8. primo

5 **Una vez más.** Repeat **actividad 4,** and precede all of the nouns with the correct form of the indefinite article.

Modelo   tías   ➡   **unas tías**

6 **Una concordancia.** Demonstrate your understanding of number and gender by matching the articles from **Columna a** correctly with the family members from **Columna b.** Note that you can use each noun from **Columna b** twice.

Columna a
el
la
los
las
un
una
unos
unas

Columna b
hijo
hermanas
tía
primas
abuelos
nieta

Los adjetivos posesivos

When talking about their family, people often refer to *my* dad, or *his* sister, or *our* cousins. Look at the chart below to see how to personalize talk about your family using possessive adjectives.

Los adjetivos posesivos			
mi, mis	*my*	**nuestro (a, os, as)**	*our*
tu, tus	*your (familiar)*	**vuestro (a, os, as)**	*your*
su, sus	*your (formal); his, her, its*	**su, sus**	*your, their*

Possessive adjectives agree with the person, place, or thing possessed. They show number (singular or plural), and in addition, **nuestro** and **vuestro** show gender (masculine or feminine).

<u>nuestro</u> papá	<u>our</u> dad	<u>nuestros</u> papás	<u>our</u> dads / <u>our</u> parents
<u>nuestra</u> mamá	<u>our</u> mom	<u>nuestras</u> mamás	<u>our</u> moms
<u>vuestro</u> papá	<u>your</u> dad	<u>vuestros</u> papás	<u>your</u> dads / <u>your</u> parents
<u>vuestra</u> mamá	<u>your</u> mom	<u>vuestras</u> mamás	<u>your</u> moms

7 ¿Quién pertenece a quién?   Work with a partner. Take turns telling each other how you would express the following in Spanish.

Modelo   my cousins   ➡   **mis primos**

1. his grandfather
2. her mother
3. their father
4. our grandfather
5. your female cousin *(familiar)*
6. my grandparents
7. her daughters
8. your brothers and sisters *(familiar)*

8 La familia de Rafi.   Work in groups of four. Refer back to Rafi's family tree on page 17. Two students will assume the identities of two of Rafi's family members, and talk to the two other members of your group about "their" family, making at least five sentences. Then switch roles as the other two members of the group assume identities of Rafi's family members. If you prefer, describe other families.

Modelo   CARMEN: Rafi y Antonio son mis hermanos. Nuestros abuelos son Rafael y Rosario. Mis tíos son Pedro, Enrique y Teresa. Tengo una prima, Sonia.

RAFAEL: Rosario es mi esposa. Manuel y Enrique son nuestros hijos. Mi esposa no tiene hermanas.

For additional vocabulary words, see the **También se dice...** *section in Appendix A.*

¡ASÓMATE! 2
Hombres y mujeres

el niño / la niña
Carlitos / Anita

el chico / la chica
el muchacho / la muchacha
Felipe / Patricia

el joven / la joven
Javier / Constanza

el amigo / la amiga
Manolo / Pepita

el novio / la novia
Roberto / Beatriz

el hombre / la mujer
Ángel / Ángela

el señor / la señora / la señorita
el señor Martín / la señora Torres / la señorita Sánchez

El hombre and **la mujer** are general terms for *man* and *woman*. The words **señor,
señora,** and **señorita** are often used as titles of address; in that case, they may also be abbreviated as **Sr., Sra.,** and **Srta.,** respectively.

Buenos días, señor Martín.	*Good morning, Mr. Martín.*
¿Cómo está Ud., Srta. Sánchez?	*How are you, Miss Sánchez?*

9 **¿Cómo se llama?** Answer the following questions.

Modelo   ¿Cómo se llama el hombre?   ➡   **El hombre se llama Ángel.**

1. ¿Cómo se llama la joven?
2. ¿Cómo se llama el niño?
3. ¿Cómo se llaman los novios?
4. ¿Cómo se llama la señora?

¡FÍJATE! 7
Los adjetivos

Adjectives are words that describe nouns and pronouns. In English, adjectives usually come before the words they modify, but in Spanish they usually follow the nouns or pronouns. Also, adjectives agree with the noun in number (singular or plural) and in gender (masculine or feminine).

Carlos es un chico simpático.	*Carlos is a nice boy.*
Él es simpático.	*He's nice.*
Adela es una chica simpática.	*Adela is a nice girl.*
Ella es simpática.	*She's nice.*
Carlos y Adela son (unos) chicos simpáticos.	*Carlos and Adela are (some) nice children.*
Ellos son simpáticos.	*They're nice.*

Adjetivos útiles

alto / alta
tall

bajo / baja
short

delgado / delgada

skinny

gordo / gorda

fat

débil

weak

fuerte

strong

guapo / guapa

handsome / pretty

inteligente

intelligent

estupido / stupid

viejo / vieja

old

joven

young

pobre

poor

rico / rica

rich

Otros adjetivos

antipático / antipática ≠ simpático / simpática	*unpleasant ≠ nice*
bonito / bonita	*pretty*
bueno / buena ≠ malo / mala	*good ≠ bad*
cómico / cómica	*funny, comical*
feo / fea	*ugly*
grande ≠ pequeño / pequeña	*big ≠ small*
interesante ≠ aburrido / aburrida	*interesting ≠ boring*
paciente	*patient*
responsable	*responsible*
tonto / tonta	*silly, dumb*
trabajador / trabajadora ≠ perezoso / perezosa	*hardworking ≠ lazy*

¡ASÓMATE! 3
Las nacionalidades

alemán / alemana
Hans / Kassandra

Germany

canadiense
Eugene / Karen

cubano / cubana
Rolando / Pilar

español / española
Rodrigo / Marisol

francés / francesa
Émile / Brigitte

inglés / inglesa
Ben / Gwenyth

japonés / japonesa
Yasu / Takako

mexicano / mexicana
José Manuel / Milagros

nigeriano / nigeriana
Ngidaha / Yena

norteamericano / norteamericana
(estadounidense)
Bob / Rhonda

puertorriqueño / puertorriqueña
Ernesto / Sonia

In Spanish, adjectives of nationality are not capitalized when they appear within a sentence. Note that some adjectives of nationality have a written accent in the masculine form, but not in the feminine, for example, **inglés, inglesa** and **francés, francesa.**

Mi abuelo es <u>inglés</u> y mi abuela es <u>francesa.</u>

My grandfather is <u>English</u> and my grandmother is <u>French.</u>

16 **¿Cuál es tu nacionalidad?**   Work with a partner. Look at the drawings and give the names of the people who match the nationalities below. Make complete sentences using either **es** or **son.** Follow the model.

Modelo   japonesa   ⇨   **Takako es japonesa.**

1. puertorriqueño
2. francesa
3. japoneses
4. norteamericano
5. canadiense
6. mexicanos
7. inglesa
8. alemán
9. cubanos
10. española

17 **¿Qué son?**   Work with a partner. Look at the drawings again, and tell what nationality the following people are. Use either **es** or **son** in your sentence. Follow the model.

Modelo   Pilar   ⇨   **Pilar es cubana.**

   Marisol y Rodrigo   ⇨   **Marisol y Rodrigo son españoles.**

1. Bob
2. Takako
3. Kassandra
4. Rolando y Pilar
5. Brigitte
6. Ben y Gwenyth
7. Rhonda
8. Hans
9. Karen y Eugene
10. Émile

18 **¿Cómo se escribe?**   Role-play this scenario with a partner. You work in the admissions office of a major university in the Spanish-speaking world. Dozens of calls come in daily from around the world requesting information about courses for foreigners. Prospective students have requested that you mail them information. Verify the spelling of their names. Spell the names from the previous activity and then add new names to the list. **¿Cómo se escribe <u>tu nombre</u>?**

¡ASÓMATE! 4
Los números de 0 a 30

0	cero	11	once	22	veintidós
1	uno	12	doce	23	veintitrés
2	dos	13	trece	24	veinticuatro
3	tres	14	catorce	25	veinticinco
4	cuatro	15	quince	26	veintiséis
5	cinco	16	dieciséis	27	veintisiete
6	seis	17	diecisiete	28	veintiocho
7	siete	18	dieciocho	29	veintinueve
8	ocho	19	diecinueve	30	treinta
9	nueve	20	veinte		
10	diez	21	veintiuno		

Handwritten:
40 quartente
50 siguente
60 sisente
70 sitente
80 ochente
90 novente
100 cien

19 **¿Qué viene después?** First tell a partner what number follows each number below, then what number precedes it. Reverse roles.

1. 2   4. 11   7. 20
2. 5   5. 15   8. 23
3. 8   6. 17   9. 24

20 **¿Cuál es la secuencia?** Read aloud the number pattern to a partner and fill in the missing numbers.

1. 1, 3, 5, _____, 9, _____, 13, _____, _____.
2. 2, 4, _____, 8, _____, 12, _____, 16, _____,
   20, _____.
3. 3, _____, 9, _____, 15, _____, 21, _____, 27, _____.
4. 1, 3, 6, _____, 15, _____, 28.
5. 1, 4, 5, _____, 9, 12, _____, _____, 17, _____,
   21, _____, _____, _____.

*The final ¡**Entérate!** of every chapter concludes each **Etapa 2**. Each of these ¡**Entérate!** sections focuses on a Spanish-speaking country or region that relates directly to the chapter. For example, in this chapter you will discover why Puerto Rico is important to Rafi, the main character of the mystery story. Your **Manual de actividades** (Student Activities Manual) also features fascinating information about the region in the ¡**No me digas!** (You don't say!) sections, as well as additional sources in the **Para explorar** (To explore) sections of your **Manual de actividades** so that you can discover more about the featured country or region. After finishing the course, you will be able to reflect on the varied cultures within the Spanish-speaking world and perhaps decide on future visits, either in person or vicariously, traveling via books, videos, cassettes, CD-ROM, or the Internet. Enjoy the journey! Let's start by going to the Caribbean!*

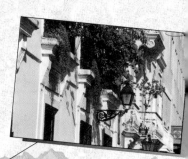

OCÉANO ATLÁNTICO

El Morro

SAN JUAN

Arecibo

CORDILLERA CENTRAL

PUERTO RICO

El Yunque

Ponce

MAR CARIBE

the enchanted island

El Yunque is the only tropical rain forest in North America.

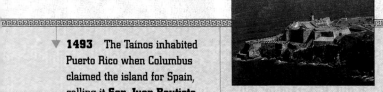

1493 The Taínos inhabited Puerto Rico when Columbus claimed the island for Spain, calling it **San Juan Bautista**.

1539–1587 El Morro was built by the Spaniards; its eighteen-foot walls helped protect the Bay of San Juan from pirate attacks.

1898 As a part of the Spanish-American War, Spain ceded the island to the United States.

1952 Puerto Rico became a commonwealth of the United States with its own constitution. Subsequent votes in 1967, 1991, and 1998 revisited the commonwealth decision.

1917 Puerto Rico's people were granted U.S. citizenship.

Puerto Rican foods reflect a variety of ethnic backgrounds, including Spanish, Indian, and African. Popular dishes include **arroz con pollo** (rice and chicken), **paella** (rice, chicken, seafood, and vegetables), **arroz con gandules y pernil** (rice with pigeon peas and roasted pig), and foods made with **plátanos** (plantains). Seafood and tropical fruits are also common in the diet of Puerto Ricans.

Merengue and **salsa** are highly popular types of music with all ages in Puerto Rico. **Merengue** music comes from the Dominican Republic, and **salsa** music comes from Puerto Rico.

Since World War II, industrialization on the island has transformed the once-poor country into one of the countries with the highest per capita income in Latin America. Major industries or products on the island are pharmaceuticals, electronics, and tourism.

¿Qué te parece?

1. What were other dangers that the Spaniards faced besides pirates?

2. What does it mean to be a commonwealth of the United States? What rights and privileges come with this distinction? Does the United States have any other commonwealth territories?

3. Why would Puerto Rican food have the influences that it does? What nationalities are suggested by the foods you eat? *Indian Spanish African*

4. What types of music are enjoyed by a range of age groups where you live?

1981 The Luis A. Ferré Center for Performing Arts opened in San Juan and has attracted world-famous performers ever since.

1979 Puerto Rico launched the Pan-American games.

1993 Law Number 1 declared both English and Spanish as joint official languages, overturning an island-wide vote in 1991 that made Spanish the only official language.

LA RED ¡Navega la Internet!

To discover more information on the culture of this chapter, check the Holt Web site and other suggestions listed in your **Manual de actividades.**

http://www.hrwcollege.com/

●ETAPA 3

¡Cuéntame!

Etapa 3 ¡Cuéntame! (Tell me!), *the third and final* **Etapa** *of every chapter, contains the continuing mystery story of* **Rafi y el sacrificio final.** *The episodes of the mystery tie in closely and reinforce what you have learned already in the chapter regarding grammar, vocabulary, and culture. It is a wonderful opportunity for you to observe at the end of each chapter how much your language ability has increased.*

Ya lo sabemos

Ya lo sabemos (We already know it) *sections activate your prior knowledge about the mystery and its characters. Some sections deal with familiar topics and what you know about life in general.*

Preguntas

Repasemos el árbol geneológico de Rafael Martín Lara en la página 17.

1. ¿Cómo se llaman los padres de Rafi? ¿sus hermanos?
2. ¿Cómo es Rafael? (descripción)

Estrategias de lectura
Cognates

Estrategias de lectura (Reading strategies) *provide you with strategies for becoming a successful reader.*

In the first episode of the mystery story **Rafi y el sacrificio final** you learn that Rafi, who appears to be happy and successful, is struggling with some interesting questions.

You are not expected to understand every word in the passage. First, keep in mind the topic of the episode, our new friend Rafi. Then, concentrate on the words that you *do* know and on cognates—the Spanish words that look similar to words you know in English. Read the passage quickly, underlining all cognates. Share your list of cognates with your classmates. What percentage of the passage is made up of cognates?

Now your instructor will guide you through the reading. You should be pleased at how much you understand!

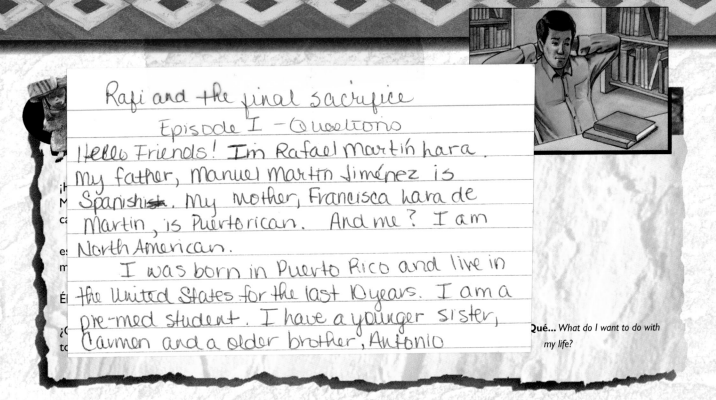

Rafi and the final sacrifice

Episode I - Questions

Hello Friends! I'm Rafael Martín hara. My father, Manuel Martín Jiménez is Spanishish. My mother, Francisca hara de Martin, is Puertorican. And me? I am North American.

I was born in Puerto Rico and live in the United States for the last 10 years. I am a pre-med student. I have a younger sister, Carmen and a older brother, Antonio

Qué... What do I want to do with my life?

Comprensión

*The **Comprensión** (Comprehension) sections after each episode help you check your understanding of the episode you read.*

1. Complete the following chart with information from the episode.

	Nombre	Nacionalidad
Rafael	Rafi o Rafael	Norte americano
Su padre	Español →	Manuel Martín Jiménez
Su madre	puertoreguena →	Francisca hara de martin
Su amigo	mexicano →	Chema

2. Complete the following sentences.

   a. Rafael es estudiante de ___pre medicina___

   b. Rafael y Chema son voluntarios en ___una escuela primaria___

3. Discuss with a partner the following questions related to **Rafi y el sacrificio final.**

   a. With what questions is Rafi struggling? Have you or anyone you know struggled with similar questions? Have you or anyone you know struggled with questions of identity, not necessarily concerning origin or nationality? How did you / she / he react? What did you / she / he do to try to resolve those issues?

   b. Reread about the Hispanics in the United States on pages 2–3. Do you think that young people of Hispanic origin in the United States, or of any other different cultural background, may have similar questions as Rafi? Why?

c. What problems may a person face who experiences one culture at home and perhaps in the neighborhood, and another culture away from home such as at school or work?

d. What can we do to make people of other cultures feel more comfortable in this country?

Expansión

The **Expansión** *(Expansion)* *sections expand on this chapter's episode of* **Rafi y el sacrificio final** *through a variety of activities, including discussion questions, debates, role-plays, and writing exercises.*

(1) With a partner, play the roles of Rafi and Chema. It is your first day as volunteers in the elementary school class. Introduce yourselves to the children and briefly tell them about your respective families (2–3 minutes).

(2) With a partner, play the roles of Rafi and Chema. Develop a short Spanish lesson (3–4 minutes) to teach the elementary school children one of the following:

- ◆ greetings and farewells
- ◆ numbers 0 to 30
- ◆ useful classroom expressions

A mirar o escuchar

(3) View the video or listen to the audio CD to find out what happens next to Rafi and his friends. Consult the pre- and post-listening comprehension activities in your **Manual de actividades.**

¡Sí, se puede!

The purpose of **¡Sí, se puede!** *(Yes, you can!) is to help you review the chapter and to synthesize what you have learned and apply it in a meaningful way.*

1.

Write five different facts (language and culture) that you have learned in this first chapter. Give an example for each one that you mention.

Modelo *(Introduce myself)*
Hola. Me llamo _____.

2.

As Rafi and Chema are leaving the elementary school where they are volunteers, they meet Isabel, a very nice young woman, who is completing her student teaching practicum at the same school. They go for coffee to a nearby café. Create a conversation like the following in which they are getting to know each other. If you need help, use the first episode entitled **Preguntas** of **Rafi y el sacrificio final** as a model.

Modelo

RAFI: Bueno, Isabel, ¿de dónde eres?

ISABEL: Soy de Puerto Rico, pero ahora soy estudiante aquí en la universidad. ¿Y Uds.?

CHEMA: Yo _____ pero también *estudiante* vivo en _____. Yo *mexico* _____ estudiante en la *yo* universidad también *(as well, too)*.

RAFI: Isabel, mi padre _____ y *Manuel* mi madre _____. ¿Y yo? *Francesca* Soy _____. *dos hermanos*

ISABEL: ¿Tienen familias grandes?

RAFI: Yo sí. Además *(Besides)* de mis padres, tengo dos abuelos, dos hermanos y una sobrina.

CHEMA: Mi familia también es grande. Yo _____. ¿Y tú, Isabel?

ISABEL: No. Mis padres no tienen hermanos así que *(so that)* yo no tengo _____. Pero, tengo _____.

CHEMA: ¿Cómo son tus hermanos?

ISABEL: *Sí*.

RAFI: ¿Cómo se llaman?

ISABEL: _____.

3. In groups of three, create a dialogue in which you all meet, introduce yourselves, and begin to get to know each other. Use the conversation above as a guideline. When you are finished, present the dialogue to the class.

4. Write a paragraph about your best friend. Use the following questions as a guide: What is his or her name? What is he or she like? Give a description. Describe his or her family.

5. Refer to your own family tree that you created for your classmates. In groups of three, *introduce* at least two members of your family, explaining their relationship to you and your parents. Then, tell at least one interesting thing about each person.

6. In groups of three or four, brainstorm about various aspects of Hispanic culture that you learned about in this chapter. Together, jot down as much information as you can remember about each topic, without looking back in the book or referring to your notes. Your instructor will provide an example for you. After brainstorming, discuss what information each of you found most interesting and why.

7. Individually, choose three important names, key words, or key phrases from the **¡Asómate!** sections. Then, in groups of eight to ten students, take turns playing Hangman with those words or phrases.

Para recordar

Each chapter ends with a **Para recordar** *(For remembering) checklist that you can use as a measure of what you have learned in the chapter. Check off the topics you feel you know, and review the other topics that you feel you need to practice more.*

In this chapter you have learned to:

Etapa 1 ¡Sígueme!

☑ discuss the concept of the extended family

☑ recognize some Hispanic names and nicknames

☑ describe how Hispanic last names are formed

☑ use the verb **tener**

Etapa 2 ¡Dime más!

☑ accentuate words

☑ identify number and gender of nouns

☑ use definite and indefinite articles

☑ employ possessive adjectives

☑ describe yourself and others (using adjectives and nationalities)

☑ use the numbers 0 through 30

☑ list at least three important facts about Puerto Rico

Etapa 3 ¡Cuéntame!

☑ learn to identify cognates to enhance reading comprehension

☑ describe Rafi, his family, and his best friend Chema

VOCABULARIO ACTIVO

The **Vocabulario activo** (Active vocabulary) *section lists alphabetically by theme all the vocabulary from the chapter that you should know by the end of the chapter.*

La familia

el abuelo / la abuela
grandfather / grandmother
los abuelos *grandparents*
el esposo / la esposa
husband / wife
el hermano / la hermana
brother / sister

parientes = relatives

los hermanos *brothers and sisters,
siblings*
el hijo / la hija *son / daughter*
los hijos *sons and daughters;
children*
la madre / la mamá *mother, mom*
el padre / el papá *father, dad*

padrastro = step father
hermanastro > step
hermanastra

los padres *parents*
el primo / la prima *cousin
(masc. / fem.)*
los primos *cousins*
el sobrino / la sobrina *nephew / niece*
el tío / la tía *uncle / aunt*
los tíos *aunts and uncles*

Hombres y mujeres

el amigo / la amiga *friend
(masc. / fem.)*
el chico / la chica *boy / girl*
el hombre *man*
el joven / la joven
young man / young woman

el muchacho / la muchacha *boy / girl*
la mujer *woman*
el niño / la niña *little boy / little girl*
el novio / la novia
boyfriend / girlfriend
el señor (Sr.) *man, gentleman, (Mr.)*

la señora (Sra.) *woman, lady, (Mrs.)*
la señorita (Srta.) *young woman,
(Miss)*

Los adjetivos

aburrido / aburrida *boring*
alto / alta *tall*
antipático / antipática
unpleasant
bajo / baja *short*
bonito / bonita *pretty*
bueno / buena *good*
cómico / cómica *funny, comical*
débil *weak*
delgado / delgada *thin*

feo / fea *ugly*
fuerte *strong*
gordo / gorda *fat*
grande *big, large*
guapo / guapa *pretty, handsome*
inteligente *intelligent*
interesante *interesting*
joven *young*
malo / mala *bad*
paciente *patient*

pequeño / pequeña *small*
perezoso / perezosa *lazy*
pobre *poor*
responsable *responsible*
rico / rica *rich*
simpático / simpática *nice*
tonto / tonta *silly, dumb*
trabajador / trabajadora *hard-
working*
viejo / vieja *old*

Las nacionalidades

alemán / alemana *German*
canadiense *Canadian*
cubano / cubana *Cuban*
español / española *Spanish*
estadounidense *American*

francés / francesa *French*
inglés / inglesa *English*
japonés / japonesa *Japanese*
mexicano / mexicana *Mexican*
nigeriano / nigeriana *Nigerian*

norteamericano / norteamericana
North American
puertorriqueño / puertorriqueña
Puerto Rican

Verbos

tener *to have*

tengo tenemos
tienes tienen
tiene

Otras palabras útiles

muy *very*

(un) poco *a little*

ESTADOS UNIDOS

GOLFO DE
MÉXICO

MÉXICO

OCÉANO PACÍFICO

México D.F.

CENTROAMÉRICA

The majority of universities throughout the Spanish-speaking world tend to be public—charging minimal tuition, if any. Students must pass rigorous admissions exams in order to attend a university. In many countries, the exams they take or the scores they receive determine what career they may choose. From their first year, college students begin to take courses in their major area; for example, future doctors begin taking medical courses immediately. Public universities generally have vast numbers of students. The **Universidad Nacional Autónoma de México (UNAM)** currently has over 150,000 students enrolled.

¿Qué te parece?

1. How large is your college or university? What are the advantages of studying at a college or university of this size? Are there any disadvantages?
2. What are some advantages and disadvantages of the mega-universities of some Spanish-speaking countries?
3. When do you begin taking courses in your major? What are the advantages of beginning immediately? What are the advantages of waiting until the third year or after receiving an undergraduate degree to begin your specialized studies, such as law, in the United States?

La vida estudiantil

By the end of this chapter you will be able to:

ETAPA 1 ¡Sígueme!

- talk about your school and your life as a student
- consider university life in Spanish-speaking countries

ETAPA 2 ¡Dime más!

- ◆ tell friends where you will be and when and ask them the same
- ◆ share the sports and pastimes you like and dislike
- ◆ explore the diverse and colorful world of our southern neighbor, Mexico

ETAPA 3 ¡Cuéntame!

- ● learn more about tío Pedro and Rafi's concerns for his uncle

ETAPA 1

¡Sígueme!

¡ASÓMATE! 1
La vida universitaria

courses

Las materias y las especialidades

1. la arquitectura
2. el arte
3. la biología
4. la ciencia
5. el derecho *law*
6. los idiomas *language*
7. la informática *Computer Science*
8. la literatura
9. las matemáticas
10. la medicina
11. la música
12. los negocios *business*
13. la pedagogía *education*
14. el periodismo *journalism*
15. la psicología *(psychology)*

Otras palabras útiles

difícil	*difficult*		más	*more*
fácil	*easy*		menos	*less*

If the meaning of any of the vocabulary words is not clear, verify the definition in the **Vocabulario activo** *at the end of this chapter. Also, if your personal favorites are not among those presented in* **¡Asómate! 1,** *go to Appendix A of the textbook, to the* **También se dice...** *section, for an expanded list of majors.* **También se dice...** *includes additional vocabulary and regional expressions for all chapters. Although not exhaustive, the list will give you an idea of the variety and richness of the Spanish language.*

1 **¿Cuál es tu especialidad?** With a partner, decide what the major of the following people might have been in college.

Modelo Picasso ➡ **El arte es su especialidad.**

1. Bill Gates
2. Agatha Christie
3. Marie Curie
4. Frank Lloyd Wright
5. Katie Couric / Barbara Walters
6. Dave Barry / Mike Lupica / William Randolph Hearst
7. Celine Dion / Johann Sebastian Bach / Kenny G
8. El presidente de IBM
9. Sigmund Freud
10. Supreme Court Justice Sandra Day O'Connor

2 **¿Cuál es más fácil...?**   Whether we admit it or not, we all have our own personal rankings of how we feel about certain majors. Express your feelings by filling in the **Etapa 1, actividad 2** chart in **capítulo 2** of your **Manual de actividades.**

3 **Los estereotipos.**   List the college majors that you feel stereotypically exhibit the following characteristics.

Los estereotipos	Los estudiantes de...
1. Son ricos.	
2. Son simpáticos.	
3. Son trabajadores.	
4. Son cómicos.	
5. Son responsables.	
6. Son pacientes.	
7. Son interesantes.	
8. Son japoneses.	

Compare your list with that of a partner. On how many do you agree? Did your partner think of some that had not occurred to you? Do you think these stereotypes exist just at your university, or do you think they are found throughout the United States?

¡ENTÉRATE!
Los estereotipos

The first definition that the *American Heritage Dictionary* lists for stereotype is "a conventional, formulaic, and usually oversimplified conception, opinion, or belief." Something not mentioned is that often stereotypes are hurtful and mean-spirited.

When you learn about the Spanish-speaking world, remember that it is comprised of a vast group of individuals united by the same language. Making generalizations about the Spanish-speaking world is as difficult as making generalizations about the English-speaking world.

¿Qué te parece?

1. What are stereotypes that foreigners hold about the United States?
2. Are there any stereotypes about your college or university? Are there any stereotypes about your town?
3. Have you ever experienced any untrue, unkind stereotypes? How did you feel?
4. How do stereotypes begin? How can they be stopped?

¡ASÓMATE! 2
La sala de clase

En la sala de clase

1. los apuntes *(pl.)*
2. el bolígrafo *pen*
3. el borrador *eraser*
4. el compañero / la compañera de clase
5. el cuaderno
6. el escritorio *desk*
7. el estudiante / la estudiante
8. el examen
9. el lápiz
10. el libro
11. el mapa

12. la mesa *table*
13. la mochila *bookbag*
14. el papel
15. la pared *wall*
16. la pizarra
17. el profesor / la profesora
18. la puerta *door*
19. la sala de clase *classroom*
20. la silla *chair*
21. la tarea *homework*
22. la tiza *chalk*

Otras palabras útiles

con	*with*	pero	*but*
demasiado	*too much*	también	*too, also*
hay	*there is, there are*	y	*and*
mucho	*a lot*		

4 **¿Cómo es tu sala de clase?**   With a partner, describe your classroom. Indicate the number of items that you encounter so that you can practice the numbers 0 through 30. You and your partner should each say at least five sentences following the model.

Modelo   **Hay veinticinco mochilas.**

5 **¿Qué tiene?**   Raúl is running late for class—again. He has remembered some things and forgotten others. Tell a classmate five things he has and does not have for class, using the verb **tener.** To say what Raúl does *not* have, put a **no** in front of the verb to make the sentence negative; for example, **Raúl no tiene...**

Modelo   **Raúl tiene sus apuntes.**

             Raúl no tiene su libro de matemáticas.

6 **¿Qué tienen tus compañeros?**   With a partner, take turns identifying three class-mates and describe them. List five things each classmate has and does not have for class. Use the **Etapa 1, actividad 6** chart in **capítulo 2** of your **Manual de actividades.**

7 **Asociación libre.** The following list presents words associated with school. In Spanish, tell your partner the first word that comes to your mind that you associate with each word in the list. What comes to your partner's mind?

Modelo mochila ➡ **los libros**

1. los apuntes
2. el lápiz
3. la pizarra
4. la silla
5. el profesor / la profesora
6. la literatura
7. la tarea
8. el estudiante
9. la tiza
10. el cuaderno

¡ENTÉRATE!
El español, lengua diversa

Spanish is spoken by more than 400 million people throughout the world; 346 million of those are native speakers and the rest have learned the language through study or travel. Like English, the Spanish language is not always uniform and has a variety of ways to express the same thing. For example, what English word do you use when referring to "soft drinks?" Some people in the United States say *soda,* others say *pop,* and still others use *Coke* as a generic term for all brands and flavors of soft drinks. There are also some differences between English, as spoken in the United States, and British English. What words do Americans use for *lift* and *flat?*

The point is, despite some regional or national differences, especially with vocabulary, Spanish is still Spanish, and you should have little trouble understanding or making yourself understood. You will have to make some adjustments, but that is part of the intrigue of learning a language.

¡FÍJATE! 1
Los verbos regulares del presente del indicativo

There are three classes of verbs in Spanish that are categorized by the ending of the infinitive. An infinitive is expressed in English by the word *to: to have, to be,* and *to speak* are all infinitive forms of English verbs. Spanish infinitives end in **-ar, -er,** or **-ir.** Look at the following infinitives.

Los verbos de -ar

comprar	*to buy*	necesitar	*to need*
contestar	*to answer*	preparar	*to prepare; to get ready*
enseñar	*to teach; to show*	regresar	*to return*
entrar	*to enter, to go in*	terminar	*to finish, to end*
esperar	*to wait for; to hope*	tomar	*to take; to drink*
estudiar	*to study*	trabajar	*to work*
hablar	*to speak*	usar	*to use*
llegar	*to arrive*		

Los verbos de -er

comer	*to eat*	creer	*to believe*
correr	*to run*	leer	*to read*

Los verbos de -ir

escribir	*to write*	vivir	*to live*
recibir	*to receive*		

In order to talk about daily activities or actions that are in progress, you need to use the present indicative. To form the present indicative, drop the **-ar, -er,** or **-ir** endings from the infinitive, and add the appropriate ending.

Follow the simple patterns highlighted with all regular verbs. Remember that the subject pronouns (**yo, tú, él, ella,** etc.) do not have to be expressed because they are usually clear from the verb ending: (**tú**) **trabaj<u>as</u>.**

habl<u>ar</u>	*to speak*		
yo	habl**o**	nosotros, nosotras	habl**amos**
tú	habl**as**	vosotros, vosotras	habl**áis**
él, ella, Ud.	habl**a**	ellos, ellas, Uds.	habl**an**

Habl<u>as</u> demasiado.   *<u>You</u> talk too much.*

	comer	to eat	
yo	como	nosotros, nosotras	com**emos**
tú	com**es**	vosotros, vosotras	com**éis**
él, ella, Ud.	com**e**	ellos, ellas, Uds.	com**en**

Com<u>emos</u> a la una.   *<u>We</u> eat at one.*

	vivir	to live	
yo	viv**o**	nosotros, nosotras	viv**imos**
tú	viv**es**	vosotros, vosotras	viv**ís**
él, ella, Ud.	viv**e**	ellos, ellas, Uds.	viv**en**

Viv<u>en</u> en la residencia estudiantil.   *<u>They</u> live in the dormitory.*

The **-ar** group is the largest group of verbs, and whenever new verbs are added to the Spanish language they usually are **-ar** verbs. Several examples are **reciclar** *(to recycle)* and **faxear** *(to fax).*

Spanish is often a wonderfully compact language; that is, in some cases one Spanish word is the equivalent of several English words. One of the best examples is the present tense. The word **estudio,** *for example, expresses one of three notions:*

estudio   { *I study*
            I do study
            I am studying

8 **Vamos a practicar.**   With a partner, practice the following new verbs. Quickly say their correct forms using the following ten nouns and pronouns listed with each of these six verbs: **estudiar, hablar, comer, correr, escribir, vivir.**

1. tú
2. nosotros
3. Marco
4. Ud.
5. Uds.

6. Juan y Eva
7. yo
8. ellas
9. Mariela
10. ella

Remember that the subject pronouns such as **yo, tú,** *and* **Uds.** *are optional; the verb ending tells you who the subject is. You may use the pronouns for emphasis or for clarification.*

9 **Más práctica.**   Practice with a partner. Take ten small pieces of paper and write a different pronoun (**yo, tú, él,** etc.) on each one. Then take another five small pieces of paper and write five new infinitives, one for each piece of paper. Taking turns, draw a piece of paper from each pile. Give the correct form of the verb you selected to match the pronoun you picked from the pronoun pile. Each person should say at least five verbs in a row correctly.

10 **¿Cierto o falso?** You know how it goes . . . rumors, hearsay, and grossly exaggerated statements. So, what is the truth according to you? Indicate whether you feel the following statements are **cierto** *(true)* or **falso** *(false).* Then compare your answers with a partner's. Where do you agree? Disagree?

	Cierto	Falso
1. Los estudiantes de pedagogía estudian menos que *(less than)* los estudiantes de ciencias políticas.	✓	(✓)
2. Los estudiantes de medicina compran más libros que los estudiantes de arquitectura.	✓	
3. Los estudiantes de informática usan más computadoras que los estudiantes de música.	✓	
4. Los estudiantes de literatura escriben menos que los estudiantes de derecho.	✓	

11 **¿A quién conoces que...?** Who exhibits the following characteristics? Fill in the **Etapa 1, actividad 11** chart in **capítulo 2** of your **Manual de actividades,** following the model.

Modelo	**ESTUDIANTE 1:**	¿Quién habla poco?
	ESTUDIANTE 2:	Mi hermano Tom habla poco *(little).*

¡FÍJATE! 2
Formación de preguntas y palabras interrogativas

Yes / No Questions

In English, questions are formed in a variety of ways. A yes / no question is formed by taking a statement and preceding it with a form of the auxiliary *to do.*

> *<u>Do</u> you like jazz?*
> *<u>Does</u> Mary know Roger?*
> *<u>Did</u> she really arrive on time?*

Spanish yes / no questions are even easier — you simply add question marks to the statement. Therefore, to ask *Do you speak Spanish?* you would say **¿Hablas español?** As in English, your voice goes up at the end of the sentence. Remember that written Spanish has an upside-down question mark at the beginning of a question.

Answering questions is also like English; for example, to answer the question **¿Hablas español?** you could say:

<u>Sí</u>, hablo español.	<u>Yes</u>, I speak Spanish.
<u>No, no</u> hablo español.	<u>No</u>, I <u>don't</u> speak Spanish.

Notice that in the negative response to the question above, both English and Spanish have two negative words.

Information Questions

Information questions begin with interrogative words such as **¿Qué?** or **¿Quién?.**

<u>¿Qué</u> estudias este semestre?   *What are you studying this semester?*

Study the list of question words in the following box.

Las palabras interrogativas			
¿Adónde?	*To where?*	¿Dónde?	*Where?*
¿Cómo?	*How?; What?*	¿Por qué?	*Why?*
¿Cuál?, ¿Cuáles?	*Which?*	¿Qué?	*What?*
¿Cuándo?	*When?*	¿Quién?, ¿Quiénes?	*Who?, Whom?*
¿Cuánto(a / os / as)?	*How much?; How many?*		

Otra palabra útil

porque   *because*

Look at the interrogative words that were just presented and answer the following questions:

1. What does every interrogative word need?
2. Why do you think **¿Cuánto?, ¿Cuál?,** and **¿Quién?** have more than one form?

12 **¿Cómo se dice?**   What questions would elicit the following responses?

Modelo   Estudio <u>las</u> <u>matemáticas</u>.   ⟱   **¿Qué estudias?**

1. Estudio <u>con música.</u>
2. Estudia <u>en</u> <u>la</u> <u>sala</u> <u>de</u> <u>clase.</u>
3. Estudiamos español <u>porque</u> <u>es</u> <u>interesante.</u>
4. Estudian <u>entre</u> <u>las</u> <u>7:00–10:00</u> de la noche.
5. <u>Susana</u> <u>y</u> <u>Julia</u> estudian.

¡FÍJATE! 3
El verbo estar

Another verb that expresses *to be* in Spanish is **estar. Estar,** like **tener** and **ser,** is not regular; that is, you cannot simply drop the **-ar** from the infinitive and add the endings.

	estar	*to be*	
yo	estoy	nosotros, nosotras	estamos
tú	estás	vosotros, vosotras	estáis
él, ella, Ud.	está	ellos, ellas, Uds.	están

Ser and **estar** are not interchangeable because they are used differently. Two uses of **estar** are:

1. To describe the location of someone or something

   Manuel <u>está</u> en la sala de clase.   *Manuel is in the classroom.*
   Nuestros padres <u>están</u> en México.   *Our parents are in Mexico.*

2. To describe how someone is feeling or to express a change from the norm

   <u>Estoy</u> muy bien, gracias. ¿Y tú?   *I'm fine, thanks. And you?*
   <u>Estamos</u> tristes hoy.   *We are sad today. (Normally we are upbeat and happy.)*

The following page presents more adjectives to help you describe yourself and others. These descriptive adjectives are commonly used with the verb **estar.**

Unos adjetivos

aburrido / aburrida

cansado / cansada

contento / contenta; feliz

enfermo / enferma

enojado / enojada

nervioso / nerviosa

preocupado / preocupada

triste

???

13 **¿Cómo están?** Look at the above drawing and describe how the following people are feeling. Watch out for agreement!

Modelo **Silvia está triste.**

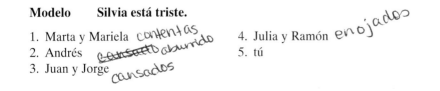

1. Marta y Mariela contentas
2. Andrés ~~cansado~~ aburrido
3. Juan y Jorge cansados
4. Julia y Ramón enojados
5. tú

14 **La gente que conozco.** Think about five people you know, such as family members, roommates, or friends and tell how they are (or probably are) today.

Modelo **Mi amiga Sonia está contenta.**

◆ETAPA 2

¡Dime más!

¡ASÓMATE! 3
En la universidad

Los lugares

1. el apartamento
2. la biblioteca
3. la cafetería
4. el centro estudiantil
5. el cuarto
6. el edificio

7. el estadio
8. el gimnasio
9. el laboratorio
10. la librería
11. la residencia estudiantil
12. la tienda

Otras palabras útiles

cerca (de)   *close, near*
entre   *between*
lejos (de)   *far, far away*

Las cosas en la residencia

1. la calculadora
2. la carta
3. las cintas (pl.)
4. el compañero / la compañera de cuarto
5. la composición
6. la computadora
7. el curso

8. el despertador
9. el dinero
10. los discos compactos (pl.)
11. el estéreo
12. el horario (de clases)
13. el radio / la radio
14. el reloj
15. el semestre

1 ¿**Dónde estarán?** Say where the following people might be. Give as many possibilities as you can.

Modelos La profesora Sánchez ➡ **La profesora Sánchez está en la sala de clase.**
necesita enseñar. **La profesora Sánchez está en el laboratorio.**

1. Chris necesita estudiar.
2. Louise necesita comprar bolígrafos y cuadernos.
3. Gregorio y David necesitan terminar su tarea de matemáticas.
4. Ken y Phyllis necesitan comer.
5. José y Martín necesitan escribir una carta a sus padres.

2 **¿Dónde están?** **Cerca** and **lejos** are very relative terms. Based on your point of view, tell whether the following places are **cerca** or **lejos.** Follow the model. Do you agree with your classmates?

Modelo   *(Your destination / Where you are now)*
la biblioteca / tu salón de clase de español   ➡   **La biblioteca está lejos.**

1. la biblioteca / donde vives
2. tu residencia estudiantil (o apartamento) / la librería de la universidad
3. un laboratorio de computadoras / donde vives
4. el gimnasio / tu residencia
5. la biblioteca / la cafetería
6. donde vive tu familia / donde tú vives
7. las tiendas / el estadio

3 **Datos personales.** You are a foreign exchange student in Mexico, and you are living with a family. One of your new Mexican "brothers" is a six year old who is fascinated by you, and he wants to know everything about you! Answer his questions, which follow, then ask a classmate these same questions.

1. ¿Cómo te llamas?
2. ¿De dónde eres?
3. ¿Qué estudias?
4. ¿Dónde estudias?
5. ¿Cómo estudias?
6. ¿Dónde comes?
7. ¿Dónde vive tu familia?
8. ¿Qué necesitas para tu clase de español?
9. ¿Qué necesitas para una clase de matemáticas?
10. ¿Qué tienes en tu mochila?

¡ASÓMATE! 4
La hora

Es la medianoche.   Es el mediodía.   Es la una de la mañana.

Son las tres y cuarto
de la tarde.

Son las seis y media
de la tarde.

Son las nueve menos cuarto
de la mañana.

Son las nueve y treinta y
cinco de la noche.

La hora

¿Qué hora es?	*What time is it?*
Es la una. Son las (dos).	*It's one o'clock. It's (two) o'clock.*
A la... / A las...	*At . . . o'clock.*
¿A qué hora...?	*At what time. . . ?*
de la mañana	*in the morning*
de la tarde	*in the afternoon*
de la noche	*in the evening*

In the Spanish-speaking world, **de la tarde** tends to mean from noon until 7:00 or 8:00 P.M. Note that the singular article **la** is used with **una (a la una)** and **las** for hours greater than one (**a las ocho**).

4 **¿Qué tiene Gloria?** Gloria's boyfriend, Burl, calls at 8:00 A.M., but she has not arrived yet for work in the library. She left her schedule on her desk so you are able to tell him when and where he can find her today.

Modelo **A las 7:30 Gloria está en la cafetería con Julia.**

Mi horario

7:30	Comer con Julia en la universidad
8:00	Trabajar en la biblioteca
9:30	Terminar los ejercicios para la clase de matemáticas
11:00	Preparar un experimento para la clase de psicología
12:30	Comprar libros para mi clase de literatura
5:00	Regresar a mi cuarto

5 **Dime quién, dónde y cuándo.** Look at the chart in **Etapa 2, actividad 5** in **capítulo 2** of your **Manual de actividades.** With a pen, connect one item from each column, a pronoun to an activity and then to a time, creating five sentences.

6 **¿Conoces a tu profesor o profesora?** How well do you know the schedule of your Spanish instructor? Take the quiz below.

¿A qué hora...?	A la / A las...
1. Llega a la universidad	
2. Enseña su primera clase	
3. Come	
4. Toma un café	
5. Tiene su última clase	
6. Regresa a casa	
7. Lee unas composiciones o tareas	
8. No trabaja más	
9. Habla por teléfono	

Now — the moment of truth — your instructor will tell you the correct answers. How close were your estimates?

7 **Mi horario personal.** Do you keep your schedule in your head or do you write down all of your appointments and things to do and then cross off everything that you complete? Create your personal schedule for today in the **Etapa 2, actividad 7** chart in **capítulo 2** of your **Manual de actividades.**

¡ASÓMATE! 5
Los días, los meses y las estaciones

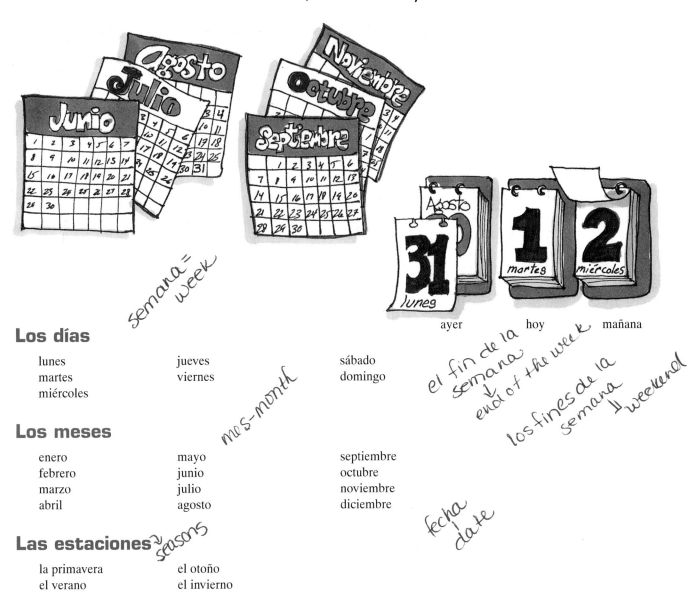

semana = week

mes = month

el fin de la semana ↓ end of the week

los fines de la semana = weekend

fecha ↓ date

ayer   hoy   mañana

Los días

lunes   jueves   sábado
martes   viernes   domingo
miércoles

Los meses

enero   mayo   septiembre
febrero   junio   octubre
marzo   julio   noviembre
abril   agosto   diciembre

Las estaciones *↓ seasons*

la primavera   el otoño
el verano   el invierno

 Note that, unlike English, the days of the week and the months of the year are not capitalized.

Expresiones

¿Cuál es la fecha de hoy?   *What is today's date?*
Hoy es el 1 (primero) de septiembre.   *Today is September first.*
Mañana es el 2 (dos) de septiembre.   *Tomorrow is September second.*

El viernes means *on Friday.* To say *on Fridays* (repeated occurrences), you would say **los viernes.** By itself, **mañana** means *tomorrow.* Preceded by a preposition, **mañana** means *morning.* For example, **mañana por la mañana** is *tomorrow (in the) morning.*

8 ¿**De qué programa hablas?**   Think of five television programs. Give your partner three clues so that he or she can guess the TV programs you have in mind. Leave the most obvious clue until the end, then change roles.

Modelo Hay una mujer alta. Trabaja en la televisión y en el periodismo. Tiene muchas secretarias que son horribles. ⮕ **Es Murphy Brown. Es los miércoles a las nueve.**

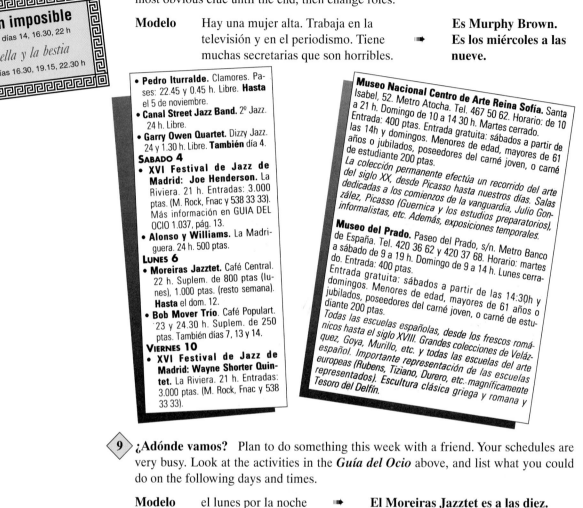

Misión imposible
Todos los días 14, 16.30, 22 h
La bella y la bestia
Todos los días 16.30, 19.15, 22.30 h

- **Pedro Iturralde.** Clamores. Pases: 22.45 y 0.45 h. Libre. **Hasta** el 5 de noviembre.
- **Canal Street Jazz Band.** 2º Jazz. 24 h. Libre.
- **Garry Owen Quartet.** Dizzy Jazz. 24 y 1.30 h. Libre. **También** día 4.

SÁBADO 4
- **XVI Festival de Jazz de Madrid: Joe Henderson.** La Riviera. 21 h. Entradas: 3.000 ptas. (M. Rock, Fnac y 538 33 33). Más información en GUIA DEL OCIO 1.037, pág. 13.
- **Alonso y Williams.** La Madriguera. 24 h. 500 ptas.

LUNES 6
- **Moreiras Jazztet.** Café Central. 22 h. Suplem. de 800 ptas (lunes), 1.000 ptas. (resto semana). **Hasta** el dom. 12.
- **Bob Mover Trío.** Café Populart. 23 y 24.30 h. Suplem. de 250 ptas. También días 7, 13 y 14.

VIERNES 10
- **XVI Festival de Jazz de Madrid: Wayne Shorter Quintet.** La Riviera. 21 h. Entradas: 3.000 ptas. (M. Rock, Fnac y 538 33 33).

Museo Nacional Centro de Arte Reina Sofía. Santa Isabel, 52. Metro Atocha. Tel. 467 50 62. Horario: de 10 a 21 h. Domingo de 10 a 14.30 h. Martes cerrado. Entrada: 400 ptas. Entrada gratuita: sábados a partir de las 14h y domingos. Menores de edad, mayores de 61 años o jubilados, poseedores del carné joven, o carné de estudiante 200 ptas.
La colección permanente efectúa un recorrido del arte del siglo XX, desde Picasso hasta nuestros días. Salas dedicadas a los comienzos de la vanguardia, Julio González, Picasso (Guernica y los estudios preparatorios), informalistas, etc. Además, exposiciones temporales.

Museo del Prado. Paseo del Prado, s/n. Metro Banco de España. Tel. 420 36 62 y 420 37 68. Horario: martes a sábado de 9 a 19 h. Domingo de 9 a 14 h. Lunes cerrado. Entrada: 400 ptas.
Entrada gratuita: sábados a partir de las 14:30h y domingos. Menores de edad, mayores de 61 años o jubilados, poseedores del carné joven, o carné de estudiante 200 ptas.
Todas las escuelas españolas, desde los frescos románicos hasta el siglo XVIII. Grandes colecciones de Velázquez, Goya, Murillo, etc. y todas las escuelas del arte español. Importante representación de las escuelas europeas (Rubens, Tiziano, Durero, etc..magníficamente representados). Escultura clásica griega y romana y Tesoro del Delfín.

9 ¿**Adónde vamos?**   Plan to do something this week with a friend. Your schedules are very busy. Look at the activities in the *Guía del Ocio* above, and list what you could do on the following days and times.

Modelo el lunes por la noche ⮕ **El Moreiras Jazztet es a las diez.**

1. el sábado por la tarde
2. el miércoles por la mañana
3. el domingo por la tarde

4. el viernes por la noche
5. el martes por la tarde

¡FÍJATE! 4
Gustar y los verbos como gustar

The verb **gustar** is used to express likes and dislikes.

¿Les gusta el libro?   *Do they like the book?*
— No, no les gusta.   *—No, they don't like it.*
¿Te gustan tus clases?   *Do you like your classes?*
— Sí, me gustan.   *—Yes, I like them.*

Gustar, which means *to like* or *to be pleasing to,* behaves differently from other verbs you have studied so far. The person, thing, or idea that is pleasing is the *subject* of the sentence, and the person to whom it is pleasing is the *indirect object.* Study the previous interchanges between two people, then the grammar boxes below. How many different forms of **gustar** do you see?

(A mí)	**me**	gusta la clase.	*I like the class.*
(A ti)	**te**	gusta la clase.	*You like the class.*
(A él)	**le**	gusta la clase.	*He likes the class.*
(A ella)	**le**	gusta la clase.	*She likes the class.*
(A Ud.)	**le**	gusta la clase.	*You like the class.*
(A nosotros, nosotras)	**nos**	gusta la clase.	*We like the class.*
(A vosotros, vosotras)	**os**	gusta la clase.	*You (all) like the class.*
(A ellos, ellas)	**les**	gusta la clase.	*They like the class.*
(A Uds.)	**les**	gusta la clase.	*You (all) like the class.*

The words in parenthesis in the chart above are optional. They are used for clarification or emphasis. Clarification of **le gusta** or **les gusta** is especially important since **le** and **les** can refer to several people. You will learn more about indirect object pronouns in chapter 6.

Me	gustan las clases.	*I like the classes.*
Te	gustan las clases.	*You like the classes.*
Le	gustan las clases.	*He, she, you like the classes.*
Nos	gustan las clases.	*We like the classes.*
Os	gustan las clases.	*You (all) like the classes.*
Les	gustan las clases.	*They, you (all) like the classes.*

Use the plural form **gustan** when the person, thing, or idea that is liked is plural**.**

Several other verbs behave like **gustar.**

Unos verbos como gustar

encantar	*to love, delight*	Me **encanta** leer.
fascinar	*to fascinate*	A Juan le **fascina** enseñar.
hacer falta	*to need; to be lacking*	¿Te **hacen falta** tus libros?
molestar	*to bother*	Nos **molestan** las personas que hablan mucho.
importar	*to matter; to be important*	Me **importa** recibir buenas notas.

Note that if the thing liked is an action expressed by an infinitive, **gustar** and verbs like **gustar** are used in the singular, for example, **me encanta leer** or **me importa recibir buenas notas.**

10 **¿Qué te gusta?**   Decide whether or not you like the items below.

Modelo	la biología	⇒	**No me gusta la biología.**
	los viernes	⇒	**Me gustan los viernes.**

1. la cafetería
2. los lunes
3. estudiar
4. las matemáticas
5. el profesor / la profesora de la clase de español (¡Ojo!)
6. el centro estudiantil
7. correr
8. la residencia estudiantil o el apartamento

11 **Te toca a ti.** Now change the cues from **actividad 10** into questions, and ask your partner to answer them.

Modelos   la biología   ➡   **¿Te gusta la biología?**

los viernes   ➡   **¿Te gustan los viernes?**

Remember, if you answer negatively, you will need to say no twice. If you need to review, check **¡Fíjate! 2, Formación de preguntas** *on page 55.*

12 **En mi opinión...** What really bugs you about your campus? What do you really love? What does your campus need? Fill in the **Etapa 2, actividad 12** chart in **capítulo 2** of your **Manual de actividades** with your top three answers in each category.

¡ASÓMATE! 6
Los deportes y los pasatiempos

bailar

montar en bicicleta (correr)

hacer ejercicios (aeróbicos)

jugar al básquetbol

jugar al béisbol

jugar al fútbol

jugar al fútbol americano

mirar la televisión

nadar

patinar

Otros deportes y pasatiempos

caminar	*to walk*
escuchar música	*to listen to music*
ir de compras	*to go shopping*
jugar al golf	*to play golf*
jugar al tenis	*to play tennis*
tocar un instrumento	*to play an instrument*
tomar el sol	*to sunbathe*

Otras palabras útiles

a menudo	*often*
a veces	*sometimes; from time to time*
nadie	*no one*
nunca	*never*
siempre	*always*
la cancha de tenis	*tennis court*
el equipo	*team*
la pelota	*ball*
la piscina	*swimming pool*

13 **¿Te gusta?** What activities do you enjoy in your spare time? Look at the **Etapa 2, actividad 13** chart in **capítulo 2** of your **Manual de actividades.** Rank the sports and pastimes by placing a check mark in the column that best describes your feeling toward the sport or pastime. What do you suppose **¡Lo odio!** means?

14 **Tus preferencias.** Select your three favorite and then your three least favorite from the sports and pastimes illustrations. Fill in the **Etapa 2, actividad 14** charts in **capítulo 2** of your **Manual de actividades** and then tell a partner your preferences. Follow the model. Are there any similarities? How are the charts different?

15 **¿Eres activo?** Just how active are you? How do you spend your time? What do you do frequently? What do you do occasionally? What should you do more of? Look at all of the sports and pastimes of **¡Asómate! 6.** Fill in the chart in **Etapa 2, actividad 15** in **capítulo 2** of your **Manual de actividades.**

16 **¿En qué mes te gusta...?**   Make a list of the top three sports or pastimes you enjoy in the months listed below. How do they compare and contrast with your classmates' lists?

enero	mayo	julio	octubre
1.	1.	1.	1.
2.	2.	2.	2.
3.	3.	3.	3.

Modelo   En enero me gusta patinar.

After you compare your findings with your class, go to the *¡Atrévete!* Web site to report your preferences. Do you see any national trends? Can you generalize by regions of the country?

¡ENTÉRATE!
Los deportes en el mundo hispano

Fútbol (soccer) is the most popular sport overall in the Spanish-speaking world. The fans (mostly males) are extremely passionate. They usually support one team and faithfully follow their team's season.

In Venezuela, Puerto Rico, the Dominican Republic, Cuba, and Nicaragua, baseball is the number one sport. Many U.S. baseball teams have benefited by players coming from these countries to play baseball.

An **espectáculo** (show) originating in Spain is the **corrida de toros** (bullfight). Although mainly popular in Spain among the older generation, there are also **plazas de toros** (bullfight arenas) in some Spanish-speaking countries of this hemisphere.

Other spectator sports that are big attractions include horse racing, boxing, auto racing, track and field, wrestling, and bicycle racing. Volleyball, golf, and tennis are also popular throughout the Hispanic world.

Some famous Hispanic athletes are El Cordobés, a Spanish matador born in 1937; Miguel Induraín, a multiple winner of the Tour de France and other bicycle racing events who was born in Spain in 1964; Omar Vizquel, a baseball player who won the 1996 Gold Glove award for best shortstop; Arantxa Sanchez Vicario, a tennis player and 1994 winner of the U.S. Open, born in Spain in 1971; and Severiano Ballesteros, a golfer and winner of the Masters Tournament in 1980 and 1983, who also was born in Spain, in 1957.

¿Qué te parece?

1. Do you have a favorite sport that you enjoy playing or watching? Are you a fan of a certain team? Do you enjoy other pastimes?
2. Since what time have sports been a part of our culture? Why were they important? Are they more or less important now?
3. List at least three similarities between Spanish-speaking countries and the United States in the area of sports.

¡ASÓMATE! 7
Los números de 30 a 100

30	treinta		39	treinta y nueve
40	cuarenta		42	cuarenta y dos
50	cincuenta		57	cincuenta y siete
60	sesenta			
70	setenta			
80	ochenta			
90	noventa			
100	cien			

When reading off a long series of numbers, such as phone numbers or serial numbers, Spanish speakers often pair the numbers in groups of two, especially in Mexico. For example, if there are seven numbers, then the first number is said alone and the remainder would be read as three two-digit numerals. Thus, the phone number 919–4827 in Mexico would be 9–19–48–27, said as follows: **nueve, diecinueve, cuarenta y ocho, veintisiete.**

LOPEZ GARCIA DE ALBA ALMA
AVENIDA LABNA L105 MANZ 2 CASA 45 SN TROPEZ 84-4545
CP 77500 ....
LOPEZ GARCIA DEL CASTILLO SUSANA
ACAPULCO SM 31 MZA 3 EDF 15 DEP 12 CP 77508 84-5408
LOPEZ GARCIA JORGE DANIEL
MAYAPAN33 L7 M33 SM59 CP 77500 86-4247
LOPEZ GARCIA JOSE LUIS
AVENIDA COMALCALCO Y ACANCEH Z IND CP 77535 86-6434
86-6435
LOPEZ GARCIA ROSA MARIA
AVENIDA NADER NUM 32 EDIF PERLA DEPTO 001 87-3729
CP 77500 ....
LOPEZ GARCIA SALVADOR ELIODORO
AVENIDA MIGUEL HIDALGO LOTE 28 NUM 831 M34 88-6919
CP 77517 86-6027
LOPEZ GARCIA SARA
MANZANA 101 EDIF 6 DEPTO 302 RES ISLAS CP 77534 87-0855
LOPEZ GATELL JOSE MARIA
HUACHINANGO NUM 11 CP 77500 84-5516
LOPEZ GOMEZ ANGEL SILVINO
L 16Y17 DEP 5C MZA 10 SM63 CP 77513 88-2566
LOPEZ GOMEZ FANNY LETICIA
CALLE 22 PTE NUM 425 MANZ 16 CP 77500 83-2068
LOPEZ GOMEZ IVONNE
BOULEVARD KUKULCAN QUETZAL L 31 CASA 7 ZT 82-0047
CP 77500 ....
LOPEZ GOMEZ ROGELIO
JAVIER RIJI GOMEZ 37 MANZ 5 CP 77560 84-9377
LOPEZ GONGORA ANDREA
PRIVADA EFRAIN C LARA 9 SM26 M4 INFONAVIT 88-7897
CP 77500 ....
LOPEZ GONGORA ISABEL
CALLE 38 PTE M-6 L-20 NO 718 CP 77500 88-2387
LOPEZ GONZALEZ ABELARDO
CALLE 42 PTE REG91 M6 L9 CP 77500

SANTOS SANTOS JAIME -SIERRA 12 L12 M11 SM 3 CP 77500 84-0661
SANTOS SANTOS JAVIER
SAUCE L1 Y 12 M10 SM43 PEDREGAL CP 77500
SANTOS SEGOVIA FREDDY
CALLE 45 NTE 468 MANZ 34 LTE 3 COL F VILL CP 77528 80-5138
SANTOS SEGURA ALBA ROSA
COL LEONA VICARIO M 8 L 14 SM 74 CP 77500 80-2242
SANTOS SOLIS FELIPE
CALLE 20 OTE NO 181 SM 68 M 12 L 28 CP 77500 80-0861
SANTOS VELAZQUEZ MARIA JESUS
CALLE 3 MZA 12 LOTE 24 PUERTA DEL SOL CP 77500 80-1330
SANTOS VILLANUEVA ARMINDA
CALLE 46 PTE MANZ 20 LTE 16 4 CP 77510 86-6949
SANTOS WUY JOSE E
CALLE 33 Y 38 OTE 171 L 14 M 25 SM 75 CP 77500 88-3999
SANTOSCOY LAGUNES ELIZABETH
CERRADA FLAMBOYANES 2 SM23 M40 RET2A L1 80-1175
CP 77500 ....
SANTOYO ADELAIDA
CALLE 75 NTE DEPTO 7 EDIF 2 MZ 22 SM 92 CP 77500 87-6204
SANTOYO BETANCOURT PEDRO ARIEL
HDA NUM 12 MANZ 61 REG 93 CP 77517 88-6875
SANTOYO CORTEZ ADELAIDA A
EDIFICIO QUETZAL DEPTO C-1 SM 32 FUENTES CP 77500 88-7941
SANTOYO MARTIN AIDA MARIA
NANCE DEP 5 MZA 21 NUM 13 87-4875
87-3799

17 **¿Qué número es?** Look at the pages from an Acapulco telephone book. Say the phone numbers for the following people.

1. José Luis López García
2. Felipe Santos Solís
3. La doctora Pilar Hernández Acevedo
4. Ángel Silvino López Gómez
5. Adelaida A. Santoyo Cortez

18 **¿Quiere dejar algún recado?** Choose a partner. You work in a busy office and your partner will leave a call-back message with the following numbers. Write down the numbers your partner tells you. How accurate were you? Change roles. When it is your turn to leave a message, select five new phone numbers from the Acapulco phone book pages in **actividad 17** and give them to your partner. Put a mark by them so your partner can verify his or her answers.

1. 8–54–79–08
2. 15–95–63
3. 71–49–00
4. 4–14–44–15
5. 7–61–38–20

The number of digits in a phone number in Spanish-speaking countries will vary. It often depends on the size of the city or town.

Los Estados Unidos Mexicanos

Tijuana

Ciudad Juárez

ESTADOS UNIDOS

Río Grande

SIERRA MADRE OCCIDENTAL

SIERRA MADRE ORIENTAL

MÉXICO

GOLFO DE MÉXICO

OCÉANO PACÍFICO

Iztaccíhuatl

Guadalajara

Popocatépetl

MÉXICO D.F.

Veracruz

Acapulco

CENTROAMÉRICA

Mexico's tourist industry is highly developed.

1300s The Mayans, a highly organized and prosperous society, disappeared.

2000 B.C. The **Olmecas** are considered the first inhabitants of the area. Archaeological findings suggest they lived around this era.

1519 The Aztecs, last of the great indigenous empires, were conquered by the Spanish.

1820 Miguel Hidalgo, a Mexican priest, began a drive for Mexico's independence from Spain and in 1824, a constitution was adopted and independence was gained.

1855 Santa Ana, who came to power in 1833 and ruled as a dictator, resigned and Benito Juárez became president.

Mexico City
is one of the largest cities in the world.

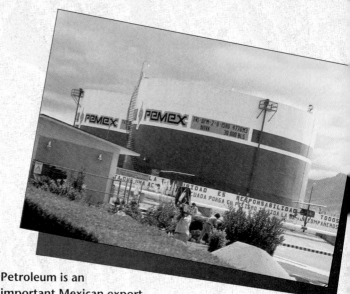

Petroleum is an
important Mexican export.

Diego Rivera and
Frida Kahlo are
two important
twentieth-century
Mexican artists.

¿Qué te parece?

1. What are the names of some Native American nations that inhabited the area where you live? Is their culture still present?

2. Mexico, like the United States, is divided into states. Considering the problems that the U.S. federal government faces in serving its states, what might be some problems that Mexico faces?

3. Consider why U.S. cities increase and decrease in population. Is **México D.F.'s** increase in population similar? Why?

1900s Mexico's contemporary artists and authors make internationally recognized contributions.

1993 El Tratado Norteamericano de Libre Comercio (NAFTA) was signed by Mexico, Canada, and the United States.

1968 Mexico hosts the Summer Olympics.

LA RED ¡Navega la Internet!

To discover more information on the culture of this chapter, check the Holt Web site and other suggestions listed in your **Manual de actividades.**

http://www.hrwcollege.com/

●ETAPA 3

¡Cuéntame!

Ya lo sabemos

In this episode you will learn more about Rafi and

- ◆ his favorite uncle
- ◆ one of his preoccupations
- ◆ how he and Chema spend an afternoon together

Preguntas personales

1. How do you and your best friend typically spend your time together?
2. Do you have a close relationship with one of your relatives? If so, describe that person and your relationship. How often do you see each other? What do you like to do together?

Estrategias de lectura
Skimming

Skim, or read quickly, the first paragraph of this episode. Try to capture the main points. Practice with skimming helps you learn to focus on key points and main ideas in your reading. Successful reading in Spanish will require that you read the episodes more than once. It is helpful to skim the passage for the first reading and then ask yourself what key information you have discovered. After skimming the first paragraph of this episode, write what you consider to be the two or three key points of information. Verify those with your instructor. Finally, see if you can answer the following questions without looking back at the passage.

1. Where is Rafi?
2. To whom is he writing a letter?
3. What is Rafi's emotional state at this moment?

Now skim the remaining paragraphs and write a main idea for each paragraph. Reread the entire episode, this time more carefully, in order to add details to those main ideas. Do not forget to take advantage of cognates like **sacrificio** and **jovial** to boost your comprehension.

Rafi and the final sacrifice
Episode 2: The uncle Pedro

Rafi is in the library of the university. It is 2:00 *while he waits for* Chema he writes an electronic card to his uncle Pedro. Pedro is his favorite uncle and and they speak a lot on the telephone. Pedro always helps Rafi with his questions and problems. But recently Rafi is preoccupied *(worried)*. When they talk, his uncle is very distracted. When Rafi questions what is the matter, Pedro only responds: no, no, it's nothing. And yesterday when he called, Pedro

muy jovial. Siempre está contento y ¡parece que tiene la energía de cinco personas! Cuando Rafi y él juegan al tenis, parece que su tío no se cansa.°

Por fin,° llega Chema. Los dos amigos pasan la tarde jugando al tenis y visitando en la residencia estudiantil. También hablan y preparan actividades para los niños de la escuela primaria en donde son voluntarios.

Se despiden° a las nueve de la noche, y al regresar a su cuarto, Rafi mira para ver si tiene una respuesta° del tío a su carta. Está ansioso por saber° lo que significa —«Roma, sacrificio final».

He is anxious to know the meaning of the "Final sacrifice" (Roma)

while

helps
parece... *seems very distracted*

brunette

se... *gets tired*
Por... *Finally*

Se... *They say good-bye*
answer / **ansioso...** *anxious to know*

Comprensión

1. Why is Rafi in the library?
2. Why is Rafi worried about his uncle?
3. What is Pedro like?
4. List three things that Rafi and Chema do together that afternoon.

Expansión

1 With a partner, invent and act out a brief conversation in Spanish between Rafi and Chema about one of the following topics (2 to 3 minutes).

◆ el tío de Rafi
◆ el trabajo voluntario con los niños
◆ cómo pasan ellos los días

2 You are Rafi. Write the first paragraph of your e-mail letter to Uncle Pedro, in which you share how you are spending your days this semester. Invent any information you wish, but be sure to include what you and Chema typically do together. Start your letter with **Querido tío Pedro:**

A mirar o escuchar

3 View the video or listen to the audio CD to find out what happens next to Rafi and Chema. Consult the pre- and post-listening activities in your **Manual de actividades.**

¡Sí, se puede!

1. Make a list in Spanish of eight questions to interview a classmate. Be sure to include questions about his or her family, classes, professors, daily schedule, or favorite sports and pastimes. Pay attention to correct spelling and punctuation.

2. With a partner, take turns interviewing each other, using the questions you wrote for the previous activity. Your instructor will call on several students to report their findings to the class.

3. As a class, decide on three of your favorite questions. Then form groups of three students. Within your group of three, **Estudiante 1** will ask each of you the class's favorite questions, **Estudiante 2** will record your group's answers, and **Estudiante 3** will compile and report your responses. Then combine the information as a class. What have you discovered? Do you see any trends?

4.   Revise and refine your list of interview questions, making them as interesting and informative as possible. Next, interview a friend or an acquaintance who is also taking a Spanish class this semester, then write your findings in the form of a paragraph based on the interview with that person. Be sure to use the third-person form of the verbs.

Modelo   Joseph Martin es estudiante de la universidad de Virginia. Es de Kentucky y tiene veinte años. Este semestre tiene clases de filosofía, cálculo, geografía, inglés y español. Joseph estudia mucho. Su clase favorita es español porque el profesor es muy interesante. Tiene muchos amigos y le gusta jugar al fútbol americano con ellos.

5. In groups of three or four students, prepare answers for the following *Jeopardy* categories and then the appropriate "questions."

Categorías

la vida estudiantil, las materias y las especialidades, las matemáticas *(math problems / equations)*, los deportes y los pasatiempos, México

Modelos

Categoría:	la vida estudiantil
Respuesta:	la residencia estudiantil
Pregunta:	**¿Dónde viven los estudiantes?**

Categoría:	los deportes / pasatiempos
Respuesta:	Michelle Kwan
Pregunta:	**¿Quién patina bien?**

Assign point values to the answers and present them to your instructor; he or she will be Alejandro or Alejandra Trebek. **¡Buena suerte!** *(Good luck!)*

Para recordar

Having completed this chapter you are now able to:

Etapa 1 ¡Sígueme!

❐ talk about your school and your life as a student

❐ discuss diversity and stereotype issues regarding learning languages

❐ describe your classroom

❐ use regular **-ar, -er,** and **-ir** verbs in the present tense

❐ formulate questions

❐ use the verb **estar**

Etapa 2 ¡Dime más!

❐ talk about your life as a university student

❐ tell time

❐ know the days of the week and months of the year

❐ tell what you like and do not like, using **gustar**

❐ share information about your favorite and not-so-favorite pastimes and sports

❐ list some sports and pastimes of the Hispanic world

❐ use the numbers 30 through 100

❐ share three facts about Mexico that you find interesting

Etapa 3 ¡Cuéntame!

❐ describe tío Pedro and how Rafi and Chema spend their afternoon and evening

VOCABULARIO ACTIVO

Las materias y las especialidades

la arquitectura *architecture*
el arte *art*
la biología *biology*
la ciencia *science*
el derecho *law*
el idioma *language*

los idiomas *languages*
la informática *computer science*
la literatura *literature*
las matemáticas *(pl.)* *mathematics*
la medicina *medicine*
la música *music*

los negocios *business*
la pedagogía *education*
el periodismo *journalism*
la psicología *psychology*

En la sala de clase

los apuntes *(pl.)* *notes*
el bolígrafo *ballpoint pen*
el borrador *eraser*
el compañero / la compañera
　　de clase *classmate*
el cuaderno *notebook*
el escritorio *desk*
el estudiante / la estudiante *student*

el examen *exam*
el lápiz *pencil*
el libro *book*
el mapa *map*
la mesa *table*
la mochila *book bag, knapsack*
el papel *paper*
la pared *wall*

la pizarra *chalkboard*
el profesor / la profesora *professor*
la puerta *door*
la sala de clase *classroom*
la silla *chair*
la tarea *homework*
la tiza *chalk*

Los verbos

el sacapuntas – pencil sharpener

comer *to eat*
comprar *to buy*
contestar *to answer*
correr *to run*
creer *to believe*
enseñar *to teach; to show*
entrar *to enter, to go in*
escribir *to write*

esperar *to wait for; to hope*
estar *to be*
estudiar *to study*
hablar *to speak*
leer *to read*
llegar *to arrive*
necesitar *to need*
preparar *to prepare; to get ready*

recibir *to receive*
regresar *to return*
terminar *to finish, to end*
tomar *to take; to drink*
trabajar *to work*
usar *to use*
vivir *to live*

Unos verbos como gustar

llavanta – to wear; to take, carry

encantar *to love, to delight*
fascinar *to fascinate*

gustar *to like*
hacer falta *to need; to be lacking*

molestar *to bother*
importar *to matter; to be important*

Las palabras interrogativas

¿Adónde? *To where?*
¿Cómo? *How?; What?*
¿Cuál?, ¿Cuáles? *Which?*
¿Cuándo? *When?*

¿Cuánto (a / os / as)? *How much?; How many?*
¿Dónde? *Where?*
¿Por qué? *Why?*

¿Qué? *What?*
¿Quién?; ¿Quiénes? *Who?; Whom?*

Unos adjetivos

aburrido / aburrida *bored (with **estar**)*
cansado / cansada *tired*
contento / contenta *content, happy*

enfermo / enferma *ill, sick*
enojado / enojada *angry*
feliz *happy*

nervioso / nerviosa *upset, nervous*
preocupado / preocupada *worried*
triste *sad*

Los lugares

el apartamento *apartment*
la biblioteca *library*
la cafetería *cafeteria*
el centro estudiantil *student union*

el cuarto *room*
el edificio *building*
el estadio *stadium*
el gimnasio *gymnasium*

el laboratorio *laboratory*
la librería *bookstore*
la residencia estudiantil *dormitory*
la tienda *store*

Las cosas en la residencia

la calculadora *calculator*
la carta *letter*
la cinta *cassette tape*
el compañero / la compañera
    de cuarto *roommate*
la composición *composition*

la computadora *computer*
el curso *course*
el despertador *alarm clock*
el dinero *money*
los discos compactos *(pl.)* *compact disks*
el estéreo *stereo*

el horario (de clases) *schedule*
el radio / la radio *radio*
el reloj *clock; watch*
el semestre *semester*

La hora

A la... / A las... *At . . . o'clock.*
¿A qué hora? *At what time?*
de la mañana *in the morning*

de la noche *in the evening*
de la tarde *in the afternoon*

Es la... / Son las... *It's . . . o'clock.*
¿Qué hora es? *What time is it?*

Los días

lunes *Monday*
martes *Tuesday*
miércoles *Wednesday*

jueves *Thursday*
viernes *Friday*

sábado *Saturday*
domingo *Sunday*

Los meses

enero *January*
febrero *February*
marzo *March*
abril *April*

mayo *May*
junio *June*
julio *July*
agosto *August*

septiembre *September*
octubre *October*
noviembre *November*
diciembre *December*

Las estaciones

el invierno *winter*
la primavera *spring*

el otoño *autumn, fall*

el verano *summer*

Los deportes y los pasatiempos

bailar *to dance*
caminar *to walk*
escuchar música *to listen to music*
hacer ejercicios (aeróbicos) *to do
    (aerobics) exercises*
ir de compras *to go shopping*
jugar al básquetbol *to play
    basketball*

jugar al béisbol *to play baseball*
jugar al fútbol *to play soccer*
jugar al fútbol americano *to play football*
jugar al golf *to play golf*
jugar al tenis *to play tennis*
mirar la televisión *to watch TV*
montar en bicicleta (correr) *to bikeride*
nadar *to swim*

patinar *to skate*
tocar un instrumento *to play an
    instrument*
tomar el sol *to sunbathe*

Otras palabras útiles

la cancha de tenis *tennis court*
el equipo *team*
la pelota *ball*
la piscina *swimming pool*
a menudo *often*
a veces *sometimes, from time to
    time*
ayer *yesterday*
cerca (de) *close, near*
con *with*
demasiado *too much*

difícil *difficult*
entre *between*
fácil *easy*
hay *there is, there are*
hasta *until*
hoy *today*
lejos (de) *far, far away*
mañana *tomorrow*
más *more*
menos *less*
mucho *a lot*

nadie *no one*
nunca *never*
pero *but*
porque *because*
siempre *always*
también *too, also*
y *and*

ISLAS CANARIAS

MARRUECOS

PORTUGAL

FRANCIA

Madrid

ESPAÑA

MAR MEDITERRÁNEO

OCÉANO ATLÁNTICO

Hispanic architecture is as varied as the people who speak Spanish, ranging from the most modern of skyscrapers and twenty-first century structures, to Spanish colonial styles, to architecture that models designs of the indigenous populations. **En los países hispanohablantes,** *(Spanish-speaking)* **hay de todo.**

¿Qué te parece?

1. Why is Spanish architecture so prevalent throughout North, Central, and South America? Why can French influence be seen in Mexico?
2. Architects will tell you that any building design is a product of form and function. Which comes first, do you think, form or function?
3. What other factors must be considered when constructing homes? Is your style home found in any other region of the United States? Why or why not?

Capítulo 3

Hogar, dulce hogar

By the end of this chapter you will be able to:

ETAPA 1 ¡Sígueme!
- describe your house and the things you do (or need to do) around your house
- discuss the changing role of Hispanic women and their impact on society

ETAPA 2 ¡Dime más!
- use a variety of common expressions
- list at least three interesting facts about Spain

ETAPA 3 ¡Cuéntame!
- discover what mysterious object Rafi finds and where he encounters the mysterious object

¡Sígueme!

¡ASÓMATE! 1
La casa

En la casa

1. el armario
2. el baño
3. la cocina
4. el comedor
5. el dormitorio, la alcoba
6. la escalera
7. el garaje
8. la guardilla
9. el jardín
10. la oficina
11. el piso
12. la sala
13. el suelo
14. el techo
15. la planta baja
16. el primer piso
17. el segundo piso

The *first floor,* or *ground floor,* is generally called the **planta baja**; **primer piso** actually refers to the *second floor.* What is the *third floor* called?

1 **¿Dónde están?**   Mira el dibujo *(drawing)* de la casa. ¿Dónde están los cuartos siguientes *(following)*?

Modelo   **El garaje está en la planta baja.**

	En la planta baja	En el primer piso	En el segundo piso
la sala			
el baño			
el dormitorio			
la cocina			
la oficina			

2 **¿Y tu casa... ?**   Con un compañero, compara tu casa con la casa del dibujo. Usa el modelo para ayudar a crear por lo menos *(at least)* cinco frases *(sentences)*.

Modelo   En la casa del dibujo, la sala está en la planta baja y mi sala está en la planta baja también. En la casa del dibujo, el dormitorio está en el segundo piso, pero mi dormitorio está en la planta baja. No tenemos guardilla...

¡FÍJATE! 1
Hay

To say *there is* or *there are* in Spanish you use **hay.** The irregular form **hay** comes from the verb **haber,** which you will learn more about in a later chapter.

<u>Hay</u> un baño en mi casa.	*There is one bathroom in my house.*
<u>Hay</u> cuatro dormitorios.	*There are four bedrooms.*
¿<u>Hay</u> tres baños en la casa?	*Are there three bathrooms in the house?*
No, no <u>hay</u> tres baños.	*No, there aren't three bathrooms.*

3 **¿Qué hay?**   Dile *(Tell)* a tu compañero cuántas de las siguientes cosas encuentras en tu sala de clase. Si no estás seguro, trata de calcular aproximadamente.

Modelo   escritorios   ➡   **Hay 30 escritorios.**

1. puertas
2. libros de español
3. mochilas
4. cuadernos
5. estudiantes contentos
6. estudiantes cansados
7. computadoras
8. estudiantes a quienes les gusta jugar al fútbol
9. estudiantes a quienes les gusta ir a fiestas
10. estudiantes a quienes les gusta estudiar

4 **¿Cómo somos?**   In groups of four, assign a number to each student (**Estudiante 1, Estudiante 2,** etc.) and turn to the **Etapa 1, actividad 4** chart in **capítulo 3** of your **Manual de actividades.** First, fill in the column that corresponds to your number. Then, take turns describing yourselves to your classmates, following model A. While your classmates describe themselves, complete the chart for each student by checking each item that applies. Count the responses, verify the findings, and take turns reporting the findings to your class, following model B.

Modelo A   Yo soy Phyllis, la estudiante 3. Soy inteligente y joven. No soy aburrida.

Modelo B   En nuestro grupo, hay cuatro personas interesantes. También, hay dos personas pacientes y dos personas que *(that)* no son pacientes.

¡ASÓMATE! 2

Unas cosas y unos aparatos en la casa

En la sala y el comedor

1. la alfombra
2. el estante de libros
3. la lámpara
4. la mesa
5. los muebles

6. la silla
7. el sillón
8. el sofá
9. el televisor

En la cocina

10. la estufa

11. el lavaplatos

12. el microondas

13. el refrigerador

En el baño

14. la bañera

15. la ducha

16. el inodoro

17. el lavabo

En el dormitorio

18. la cama

19. la frazada

20. el tocador

Otras palabras útiles en la casa

el árbol	*tree*	la cosa	*thing*
el baúl	*trunk, chest*	el cuadro	*picture*
la caja	*box*	la flor	*flower*
el coche / el carro /		la planta	*plant*
el auto	*car*	la ventana	*window*

Otras palabras útiles

a la derecha	*to the right*
a la izquierda	*to the left*

Verbos

desear	*to want, to desire*
se encuentra(n)	*one finds, you find*

5 **¿Qué hay en tu casa?** Dile a un compañero cuáles de las cosas de la lista se encuentran en tu casa y cuántas hay.

Modelo	**ESTUDIANTE 1:**	¿Hay un sillón en tu casa?
	ESTUDIANTE 2:	Sí, hay cinco sillones. Y, ¿en tu casa hay un sillón?
	ESTUDIANTE 1:	No, en mi casa hay diez sillas, pero no hay un sillón.

1. un sillón
2. un lavaplatos
3. unas lámparas
4. unas alfombras
5. un inodoro

6. una guardilla
7. un jardín grande
8. un armario
9. tres alcobas
10. dos pisos

6 **Tengo una casa que tiene...** Form a group of at least four people. **Estudiante 1** says **Tengo una casa que tiene...** and inserts something that his or her house has. **Estudiante 2** says the phrase, inserting what his or her own house has, and then repeats what **Estudiante 1** has. Keep on going to see how many rooms or things in a house you can add.

Modelo	**ESTUDIANTE 1:**	Tengo una casa que tiene un microondas.
	ESTUDIANTE 2:	Tengo una casa que tiene una estufa y un microondas.
	ESTUDIANTE 3:	Tengo una casa que tiene tres camas, una estufa y un microondas.

7 **¡Escucha bien!** Describe a room of your house to your partner in three sentences. When you finish, your partner will repeat what you said, then switch roles. How good a listener are you?

Modelo	**ESTUDIANTE 1:**	En mi dormitorio hay una cama, una lámpara y un tocador. También hay dos ventanas. No hay una alfombra. ➠
	ESTUDIANTE 2:	**En tu dormitorio hay...**

8 ¿**Qué encuentras?** Tienes tres minutos para llenar la gráfica **Etapa 1, actividad 8,** en **capítulo 3** de tu **Manual de actividades.** Piensa en todas las cosas que puedas encontrar *(can find)* en estos *(these)* cuartos. Puedes usar la misma *(same)* palabra más de una vez pero las respuestas deben de ser lógicas. Repasa *(Review)* y usa palabras del capítulo 2 también.

9 ¿**Deseas una casa estupenda?** You have received a grant to study abroad in the Spanish-speaking country of your choice for the summer! You decide to sublet your house or apartment here at home. Write an ad for the local newspaper that incorporates five enticing things about your home.

Gran apartamento nuevo de alto diseño en la mejor zona de Barcelona, con vistas espectaculares sobre el mar y al horizonte de la ciudad. El apartamento de 250m², consta de tres dormitorios, cuatro baños, cocina, comedor y salón con chimenea.

Precio:
280.000 ptas. mensuales
Tel. 93 790 2233

Casa moderna de 150 m² con jardín a media hora al norte de Madrid. Construída en 1985, con dos dormitorios, tres baños, cocina y salón.

Precio: 225.000 ptas. mensuales
Tel. 91 859 9213

10 **Y ahora, ¿dónde quieres vivir?**   In **actividad 9** you made arrangements to sublet your house or apartment, and now you need a place to live in the Spanish-speaking country. Look at the two house ads on the previous page and select one of them. Give your partner at least three reasons why it is just the place for you! Use expressions like **Me encanta(n)...** ; **Me gusta(n)...** ; **Tiene un / una...** ; or **Hay...** Be creative!

Modelos   **¡Me encantan las vistas sobre el mar!**

Me gusta el salón con chimenea.

¡FÍJATE! 2
Algunos verbos irregulares

Look at the present tense forms of the verbs. Notice that all of the verbs follow the same patterns that you learned to form the present tense of regular verbs, *except* the **yo** form.

dar	*to give*		
yo	**doy**	nosotros, nosotras	damos
tú	das	vosotros, vosotras	dais
él, ella, Ud.	da	ellos, ellas, Uds.	dan

caer	*to fall*		
yo	**caigo**	nosotros, nosotras	caemos
tú	caes	vosotros, vosotras	caéis
él, ella, Ud.	cae	ellos, ellas, Uds.	caen

conocer	*to know*		
yo	**conozco**	nosotros, nosotras	conocemos
tú	conoces	vosotros, vosotras	conocéis
él, ella, Ud.	conoce	ellos, ellas, Uds.	conocen

→ a person
Be familiar with (a place)

hacer	*to do; to make*		
yo	**hago**	nosotros, nosotras	hacemos
tú	haces	vosotros, vosotras	hacéis
él, ella, Ud.	hace	ellos, ellas, Uds.	hacen

The verbs **ofrecer** *(to offer)* and **parecer** *(to appear, to seem)* behave like **conocer.**

	poner	*to put, to place*	
yo	**pongo**	nosotros, nosotras	ponemos
tú	pones	vosotros, vosotras	ponéis
él, ella, Ud.	pone	ellos, ellas, Uds.	ponen

	traer	*to bring*	
yo	**traigo**	nosotros, nosotras	traemos
tú	traes	vosotros, vosotras	traéis
él, ella, Ud.	trae	ellos, ellas, Uds.	traen

	ver	*to see*	
yo	**veo**	nosotros, nosotras	vemos
tú	ves	vosotros, vosotras	veis
él, ella, Ud.	ve	ellos, ellas, Uds.	ven

	salir	*to leave*	
yo	**salgo**	nosotros, nosotras	salimos
tú	sales	vosotros, vosotras	salís
él, ella, Ud.	sale	ellos, ellas, Uds.	salen

Five other irregular, but very common verbs, follow. Practice saying their forms with your instructor and / or with a partner. Include **estar, ser,** and **tener** in your practice.

	poder	*to be able to*	
yo	puedo	nosotros, nosotras	podemos
tú	puedes	vosotros, vosotras	podéis
él, ella, Ud.	puede	ellos, ellas, Uds.	pueden

	querer	*to want; to love*	
yo	quiero	nosotros, nosotras	queremos
tú	quieres	vosotros, vosotras	queréis
él, ella, Ud.	quiere	ellos, ellas, Uds.	quieren

decir	*to say*		
yo	digo	nosotros, nosotras	decimos
tú	dices	vosotros, vosotras	decís
él, ella, Ud.	dice	ellos, ellas, Uds.	dicen

oír	*to hear*		
yo	oigo	nosotros, nosotras	oímos
tú	oyes	vosotros, vosotras	oís
él, ella, Ud.	oye	ellos, ellas, Uds.	oyen

venir	*to come*		
yo	vengo	nosotros, nosotras	venimos
tú	vienes	vosotros, vosotras	venís
él, ella, Ud.	viene	ellos, ellas, Uds.	vienen

11 **La ruleta.** Use either a die that you have brought to class or put the numbers one through six on small pieces of paper. Number 1 = **yo;** 2 = **tú;** 3 = **él, ella;** 4 = **Ud.;** 5 = **nosotros, nosotras;** 6 = **ellos, ellas, Uds.** Form groups of two to four students. The first person rolls the die (or selects a numbered piece of paper). Give the correct form of the verbs that follow, matching the number you rolled. Other group members must verify your answer. Pass the die after you say the verb form correctly. Keep practicing until the forms come quickly and automatically.

1. traer
2. hacer
3. oír
4. querer
5. conocer
6. dar
7. decir
8. venir
9. poder
10. caer

Repeat the activity with different verbs and include **estar, ser,** and **tener.** Remember, **¡Sólo con la práctica se llega a la perfección!** (*Practice makes perfect!*)

12 **Oraciones.**   First, combine elements from columns a, b, and c to write one complete sentence for each verb. Then, in groups of three, take turns reading your sentences to your classmates and correcting each other's sentences. Finally, select three sentences to share with the rest of the class.

Modelo   **Nosotros hacemos la tarea todos los días.**

Columna a	Columna b	Columna c
yo	(no) hacer	estudiar ciencias
tú	(no) oír	a clases tarde
él, ella, Ud.	(no) querer	la tarea todos los días
nosotros, nosotras	(no) salir	mis libros a clase
vosotros, vosotras	(no) traer	temprano de la universidad los viernes
ellos, ellas	(no) venir	a mis abuelos los domingos
Uds.	(no) ver	mucho trabajo
el profesor		ruidos *(noises)* por la noche
mamá y papá		

13 **Confesiones.**   Time for true confessions! With a partner, take turns asking each other how often you carry out the following activities. Use **siempre, a menudo, a veces,** or **nunca** in your answers.

Modelo   (venir al dormitorio durante el día)

ESTUDIANTE 1:   ¿Vienes al dormitorio durante el día?

ESTUDIANTE 2:   Nunca vengo al dormitorio durante el día.

1. querer estudiar
2. oír lo que *(what)* dice tu profesor o profesora
3. venir a tus clases tarde
4. poder contestar las preguntas de tu profesor o profesora de español
5. darles tus apuntes a tus amigos (¿Les das tus...?)
6. hacer preguntas tontas en la clase
7. traer tus libros a tus clases
8. salir temprano de tus clases
9. querer comer en la sala para ver la televisión
10. caerte bien *(to get along well)* tus compañeros de cuarto

Make a note of your answers and compare them with a partner's. How are you similar? How are you different? Review question formation in chapter 2, if necessary.

14 **Entrevista.** Part of the fun of learning another language is getting to know other people. Pair up with a classmate you do not know, and ask that person the following questions, then change roles. When you both have finished, be prepared to share a few of the things you have learned about your classmate with the class.

1. ¿Qué deporte puedes hacer muy bien?
2. ¿Qué deporte no sabes hacer muy bien?
3. ¿Haces ejercicios todos los días?
4. ¿Qué te dice tu mamá siempre?
5. ¿Siempre traes todo lo que debes a tus clases?
6. ¿Sales los fines de semana? ¿Con quién(es) sales?
7. ¿Qué quieres ser (o hacer) en el futuro?
8. ¿Conoces a una persona famosa?
9. ¿Qué pones en tu mochila los lunes? ¿Los martes?
10. ¿Vienes a la clase de español todos los días?

¡ASÓMATE! 3
Los quehaceres que se hacen en y alrededor de la casa

Los quehaceres de la casa

1. arreglar
2. ayudar
3. cocinar, preparar una comida
4. guardar
5. hacer la cama
6. lavar los platos
7. limpiar
8. pasar la aspiradora
9. poner la mesa
10. sacar la basura
11. sacudir

Otras palabras útiles

acabar de	*to have just*	limpio / limpia	*clean*
antes (de)	*before*	prometer	*to promise*
después (de)	*after*	sucio / sucia	*dirty*

15 **¿Quién hace qué?**   Work with a partner. Who does what in your household? Create a chart like the one below, including yourself and roommates or family members. List who does each of the household chores in the preceding list. Who has to do the most chores? Who does the least? Share your finished list with a partner.

Modelo   **Mi compañero de cuarto pasa la aspiradora.**

Yo	?	?	?
1.	1.	1.	1.
2.	2.	2.	2.
3.	3.	3.	3.
4.	4.	4.	4.
5.	5.	5.	5.

16 **¿Qué tienes que hacer?** ¿Cuáles son los quehaceres que tienes que hacer? ¿Cuándo necesitas hacerlos en tu apartamento o casa? ¿Cuánto tiempo necesitas para hacerlos? Termina la gráfica **Etapa 1, actividad 16,** en **capítulo 3** de tu **Manual de actividades,** siguiendo *(following)* el modelo allí.

¡ENTÉRATE!
Las mujeres en el mundo hispano

The roles of women in the Spanish-speaking world have changed dramatically in the past decades. Their quest for emancipation began somewhat later than the movement in the United States. Now it is more common for Hispanic women worldwide to work outside the home, own their own businesses, and have positions of responsibility, influence, and power. **El movimiento de las mujeres** is further along in the more industrialized Spanish-speaking countries.

Now read about several Hispanic women who have achieved international recognition.

Rigoberta Menchú (n. 1959)
En 1992, Rigoberta Menchú recibe el Premio Nóbel de la Paz. Es famosa internacionalmente por ser la primera persona indígena que recibe ese premio. Menchú, guatemalteca, es una activista de los derechos humanos. En el año 1991, crea una fundación para luchar por los derechos humanos y la educación de la gente indígena de las Américas.

Gabriela Mistral (1885–1957)
Gabriela Mistral es poetisa y prosista chilena famosa. En 1945, es la primera persona latinoamericana en recibir el Premio Nóbel de Literatura. Entre sus versos más famosos se encuentran ***Ternura*** (1925) y ***Lagar*** (1954). En 1909, debido al *(due to)* suicidio de su primer novio, escribe tres poemas titulados «Sonetos de la Muerte». En 1914, gana un premio chileno de poesía muy prestigioso por los sonetos y el reconocimiento de su pueblo.

Dolores Huerta (n. 1930)

Dolores Huerta es activista mexicana-americana en derechos sociales y líder del movimiento de trabajadores. Trabaja para fomentar la inscripción para votar y organizar a la comunidad mexicoamericana. Mientras trabaja para la organización de Servicios de la Comunidad en California, conoce a César Chávez. Juntos en 1963, fundan la Asociación de Trabajadores de Finca que luego llega a ser *(becomes)* la Unión de Trabajadores Unidos.

Frida Kahlo (1907–1954)

Frida Kahlo es una gran artista mexicana. Sus pinturas se caracterizan por sus colores brillantes. En 1990, una de sus pinturas se vende por más de un millón de dólares. Es la primera persona de Latinoamérica en recibir esta distinción. Kahlo estuvo casada *(was married)* dos veces con el famoso muralista mexicano Diego Rivera.

Ellen Ochoa (n. 1959)

Ellen Ochoa es la primera mujer hispana que es astronauta. En 1990, NASA la selecciona para recibir entrenamiento en el Centro Espacial Johnson en la ciudad de Houston, Tejas. Su doctorado es en ingeniería eléctrica.

¿Qué te parece?

1. ¿Quiénes reciben los Premios Nóbel? ¿Para qué?
2. ¿Quién estudia muchas ciencias probablemente?
3. ¿Quién expresa su talento en una manera artística visual?
4. ¿Quiénes son otras mujeres hispanas famosas?

¡ASÓMATE! 4
Los colores

Unos colores

1. amarillo / amarilla
2. anaranjado / anaranjada
3. azul
4. beige
5. blanco / blanca
6. café, marrón
7. gris
8. morado / morada
9. negro / negra
10. rojo / roja
11. rosado / rosada
12. verde

Colors are descriptive adjectives, and like descriptive adjectives, they must agree with the noun in number and gender. Adjectives ending in **-o** have four forms; for example, **rojo, roja, rojos, rojas.** Adjectives ending in a vowel other than **-o,** or in a consonant, have two forms; for example, **verde, verdes** and **azul, azules.**

¿Tu <u>coche</u> nuevo es <u>rojo</u>?	*Your new car is red?*
Necesito comprar <u>dos cuadernos</u> <u>azules.</u>	*I need to buy two blue notebooks.*

How would you say *a black refrigerator, a white sofa, a yellow kitchen, yellow chairs?**

---

*Un refrigerador negro, un sofá blanco, una cocina amarilla, unas sillas amarillas

17 **Mi color favorito.** ¿Cuáles son tus tres colores favoritos? Escríbelos en un papel. Ahora, observa tu salón de clase. Haz una lista de todo lo que está en tu salón de clase de tus colores favoritos. Luego, compara tu lista con un compañero. ¿Tienen los mismos *(same)* colores favoritos?

Modelo	ESTUDIANTE 1:	Hay veinte escritorios amarillos y...
	ESTUDIANTE 2:	Sí, y también hay una puerta amarilla.

18 **La rueda de colores.** Work with three classmates. One person (**Estudiante 1**) selects a color and identifies something in the classroom with that color. The next person (**Estudiante 2**) has to name something in Spanish that is the same color. If a person cannot, they are "out." The last person left can choose the next color. Follow the model.

Modelo	ESTUDIANTE 1:	Veo una mochila roja.
	ESTUDIANTE 2:	Veo un cuaderno rojo.

Were some colors easier than others for your group? If so, which colors were easier?

19 **Mi casa ideal.** ¿Cómo es tu casa ideal? Termina las frases siguientes para explicar tu casa ideal.

Modelo   Deseo una casa con...   ➠   **Deseo una casa con una cocina amarilla.**

1. una alfombra...
2. una bañera...
3. un inodoro y un lavabo...
4. un refrigerador...
5. un comedor...
6. unos sillones...

20 **¿Qué tal tu memoria?** Bring in colorful pictures of a house or rooms in a house. Select one picture and take a minute to study it carefully. Turn it over and tell a partner as much detail as you can remember about the picture. Then listen to your partner talk about his or her picture. Who remembered more? Who has the better photographic memory?

21 **Yo soy diseñador / diseñadora.**   Lucky you! You have just been selected by *House Beautiful* to do a spread for their next issue. You must select the colors for the living room that you envision and prepare a written list for the editor. List all of the furniture or appliances that you envision and indicate their color. After you have finished your project, get together with the person in your class who knows you best. Take turns guessing which colors you each chose.

Modelo   **ESTUDIANTE 1:**   ¿Usas los colores rojo y azul para el sofá?

               ESTUDIANTE 2:   Sí, uso rojo y azul.

22 **¿Se parecen o no?**   Acabas de recibir la foto de arriba de tu amigo Luis; es una foto de su dormitorio. Describe su dormitorio y luego tu dormitorio. Usa los verbos **hay, ser** y **tener.** Sigue los **modelos.**

Modelos   En el dormitorio de Luis hay estantes blancos. En mi dormitorio tengo estantes blancos.

                              (o)

               Luis tiene estantes blancos en su dormitorio y yo también tengo estantes blancos.

                              (o)

               Los estantes de Luis son blancos y mis estantes son blancos.

¡Dime más!

¡ASÓMATE! 5
Unas expresiones con *tener*

The verb **tener,** besides meaning *to have,* is used in a variety of expressions where in English various verbs are used.

Expresiones con tener

tener... años	*to be . . . years old*
tener calor	*to be hot*
tener cuidado	*to be careful*
tener éxito	*to be successful*
tener frío	*to be cold*
tener ganas de + *(infinitive)*	*to feel like + (verb)*
tener hambre	*to be hungry*
tener miedo	*to be afraid*
tener prisa	*to be in a hurry*
tener que + *(infinitive)*	*to have to + (verb)*
tener razón	*to be right*
tener sed	*to be thirsty*
tener sueño	*to be sleepy*
tener suerte	*to be lucky*

1 **Describe lo que pasa.** Mira el dibujo y haz frases para cada persona. Usa expresiones con **tener.** Puedes inventar nombres para cada persona si quieres.

Modelo **Beatriz tiene miedo.**

2 **¿Qué tengo yo?** Expresa cómo te sientes *(you feel)* durante los tiempos siguientes. Usa las expresiones con **tener.** Compara tus respuestas con las de un compañero.

Modelo antes de tener un examen ➡ **Antes de tener un examen tengo miedo.**

1. en la mañana
2. los lunes
3. los viernes
4. en la noche
5. antes de comer

6. en el verano
7. en el invierno
8. durante *(during)* la semana de los exámenes
9. cuando recibes una A en un examen
10. cuando lees un libro muy misterioso

3 **Pobre Jorge.**   Poor Jorge is having one of those days! Retell his story using **tener** expressions.

> **Modelo**   El despertador de Jorge no funciona.   ➡   **Jorge tiene prisa.**
> Tiene una clase a las 8:00 y está tarde.
> Sale de la casa a las 8:10.

1. Es invierno y Jorge no tiene su chaqueta.
2. Jorge recibe su examen. Tiene un 60%.
3. Jorge ve que no tiene dinero para comer.
4. Jorge está en casa y quiere una Coca Cola. Va a su refrigerador y no hay ninguna *(none)*.
5. Jorge recibe la oferta *(offer)* de un trabajo increíble.

4 **Información personal.**   Contesta las preguntas siguientes y comparte tus respuestas con un compañero.

1. ¿Cuántos años tienes?
2. ¿Cuándo tienes hambre?
3. ¿Qué tienes que hacer hoy?
4. ¿Tienes ganas de hacer algo *(something)* diferente? ¿Qué?
5. ¿En qué clase tienes sueño?
6. ¿En qué clase tienes mucha suerte?
7. ¿Siempre tienes razón?
8. ¿Cuándo tienes sueño?
9. Cuando tienes sed, ¿deseas una Coca Cola o una cerveza *(beer)*?

¡ASÓMATE! 6
El tiempo

España	Máx.	Mín.
Barcelona	15	9
Ciudad Real	14	12
Córdoba	16	15
Coruña, La	16	14
Madrid	17	9
Mallorca	21	6
Murcia	24	14
Palmas, Las	25	18
Pamplona	9	−1
Salamanca	11	9
Sevilla	15	14
Valencia	22	12

Sol   Nubes   Lluvia   Nieve   Viento

Expresiones del tiempo

¿Qué tiempo hace?   *What's the weather like?*
Hace buen / mal tiempo.   *It's nice / bad weather.*
Hace calor.   *It's hot.*
Hace frío.   *It's cold.*
Hace sol.   *It's sunny.*
Hace viento.   *It's windy.*

Está húmedo.   *It's humid.*
Está nublado.   *It's cloudy.*
Está seco.   *It's dry.*

Llueve.   *It's raining.*
Nieva.   *It's snowing.*

Otras palabras útiles

llover   *to rain*
la lluvia   *rain*
nevar   *to snow*
la nieve   *snow*
la nube   *cloud*
el sol   *sun*
la temperatura   *temperature*

5 ¿Qué es típico de tu región? ¿Qué tiempo es típico de tu región? Llena la gráfica según tu región.

Modelo   **En el otoño hace sol. No llueve.**

	¿Qué es típico?	¿Qué no es típico?
1. En el otoño		
2. En el invierno		
3. En la primavera		
4. En el verano		

6 ¿El tiempo te controla? Muchas veces el tiempo nos controla. ¿Qué tiempo hace cuando haces las actividades siguientes? Luego comparte tu lista con un amigo.

¿Qué tiempo hace cuando...

1. haces ejercicios?
2. limpias la casa?
3. lees un libro?
4. nadas?
5. montas en bicicleta?

7 La meteorología. Mira el mapa en la página 104 y contesta las preguntas siguientes.

1. ¿Qué tiempo hace en Mallorca?
2. ¿Qué tiempo hace en el norte de España?
3. ¿Dónde no llueve?
4. ¿Dónde hay nieve?
5. ¿Dónde hace viento?

¡ASÓMATE! 7
Los números de 100 a 100.000.000

100	cien	1.000	mil
101	ciento uno	1.001	mil uno
102	ciento dos	1.010	mil diez
116	ciento dieciséis	2.000	dos mil
120	ciento veinte	30.000	treinta mil
200	doscientos / doscientas	100.000	cien mil
201	doscientos uno	400.000	cuatrocientos mil
300	trescientos / trescientas	1.000.000	un millón
400	cuatrocientos / cuatrocientas	2.000.000	dos millones
500	quinientos / quinientas	100.000.000	cien millones
600	seiscientos / seiscientas		
700	setecientos / setecientas		
800	ochocientos / ochocientas		
900	novecientos / novecientas		

Note the following:

1. **Cien** is used before **mil** and **millones** and before any noun; for example, **cien dólares.**
2. Periods are used instead of commas to group three digits together; for example, **1.000.000 de árboles** *(1,000,000 trees).*
3. The conjunction **y,** which is used to connect tens and ones, does not follow **ciento, mil,** and so on; for example, **ciento uno** (101), **ciento doce** (112), but **ciento treinta y cinco** (135).
4. Multiples of **cientos** agree in gender with nouns; for example, **doscientos hombres y trescientas mujeres.**

Many Spanish-speaking countries have experienced dramatic inflation over the past decade; therefore, large numbers are useful because the cost of an item in U.S. dollars may be equivalent to a very large number in the foreign currency. Learning the numbers, especially the larger ones, will help you be a successful consumer in the Spanish-speaking world.

8 **¿Cuánto es?**   Look at the catalog items pictured on pages 87–88 and tell your part-ner which of the following items you like and how much they cost. Follow the model.

Modelo   la mesa   ➡   **Me gusta la mesa de $350.000 pesetas.**

1. la lámpara
2. el sillón
3. la frazada
4. la cama
5. el estante

POBLACIÓN EN MILES			
PAÍS	1996	2010	2020
Argentina	34.673	39.947	43.190
Canadá	28.821	32.534	34.753
Colombia	36.813	44.504	49.266
España	39.181	40.398	39.758
Estados Unidos	265.563	298.026	323.052
Honduras	5.605	7.643	9.042
México	95.772	120.115	136.096
Paraguay	5.504	7.730	9.474
Uruguay	3.239	3.582	3.811

9 **¿Cuál es su población?** Mira la gráfica y di *(say)* las poblaciones de los países siguientes en los años indicados.

1. España, 2010
2. México, 1996
3. Paraguay, 2020
4. Honduras, 1996 y 2020
5. Argentina, 2010

10 **¿Qué compras?** Your rich Spanish uncle left you an inheritance with the stipulation that you use the money to furnish your house. (Remember, he saw your under-furnished student housing!) Once again, refer to the pictures on pages 87–88 to spend 350.000 pesetas on your house. What would you buy? Assign prices to those items without tags.

11 **Vamos a adivinar.** Are you familiar with the TV show *The Price Is Right?* Contestants must guess the price of objects. Bring in five ads and cover the prices of the objects. In groups of three or four, have your classmates guess the prices in U.S. dollars. The person who comes the closest without going over the price wins the article!

Modelo   **Creo que el coche cuesta** *(costs)* **veintidós mil dólares.**

¡FÍJATE! 3
Los pronombres de los complementos directos

Direct objects receive the action of the verb and answer the questions *What?* or *Whom?*
Note these examples:

A: I need to do *what?*

B: You need to pay *the bills* by Monday.

A: Yes, I do need to pay *them.*

A: I have to call *whom?*

B: You have to call *Gary.*

A: Yes, I do have to call *him.*

In order to avoid the repetition of a noun, speakers of English and Spanish frequently
replace a noun with a pronoun.

¿Tienes <u>el libro</u>?	Sí, <u>lo</u> tengo.
¿Tienes <u>la mochila</u>?	Sí, <u>la</u> tengo.
¿Tienes <u>los libros</u>?	Sí, <u>los</u> tengo.
¿Tienes <u>las mochilas</u>?	Sí, <u>las</u> tengo.

In Spanish, direct object pronouns agree in gender and number with the nouns they
replace. The chart below lists the direct object pronouns.

Los pronombres de los complementos directos			
me	*me*	**nos**	*us*
te	*you (familiar, singular)*	**os**	*you (familiar, plural)*
lo, la	*him, her, it, you (formal, singular)*	**los, las**	*them, you (formal, plural)*

The direct object pronoun precedes a conjugated verb. Direct object pronouns can
also be attached to infinitives.

¿Tienes <u>los apuntes</u>?	Sí, <u>los</u> tengo.
Tengo que hacer <u>la tarea</u>.	<u>La</u> tengo que hacer. **(o)** Tengo que hacer<u>la</u>.
Tiene que lavar <u>los platos</u>.	<u>Los</u> tiene que lavar. **(o)** Tiene que lavar<u>los</u>.

12 **¿Estás listo / lista para la clase?** ¿Estás preparado / preparada para la clase de español? Contesta las preguntas usando **lo, la, los, las.**

Modelo   ¿Tienes tu libro?   ➠   **Sí, lo tengo.**

1. ¿Traes tu mochila?
2. ¿Siempre haces la tarea?
3. ¿Traes tus bolígrafos?
4. ¿Tienes tu cuaderno?
5. ¿Escuchas a tu profesor / profesora?
6. ¿Preparas los ejercicios?

13 **¿Qué tienes que hacer?** George es un estudiante extranjero *(foreign)* en Costa Rica y vive con una familia costarricense. George pregunta a su «hermano» Manuel qué tiene que hacer como quehaceres. Contesta las preguntas como Manuel las contestaría.

Modelo   **GEORGE:**   ¿Tienes que limpiar tu dormitorio?

   MANUEL: **Sí, tengo que limpiarlo.**

1. ¿Tienes que sacar la basura?
2. ¿Tienes que limpiar el garaje?
3. ¿Tienes que hacer tu cama?
4. ¿Tienes que lavar los platos?
5. ¿Tienes que arreglar la sala?
6. ¿Tienes que sacudir los muebles en tu dormitorio?
7. ¿Tienes que limpiar tu baño?

14 **¿Me prometes? Sí, ¡palabra!** Deb, your fourteen-year-old cousin, has just done something *really* stupid and her parents have grounded her. She promises her mom and dad to do the following in order to get back into their good graces. Repeat what Deb said. Follow the model.

Modelo   **LOS PADRES:**   ¿Prometes limpiar el baño cada semana?

   DEB: **Sí, prometo limpiarlo cada *(each)* semana.**

1. ¿Prometes limpiar la cocina?
2. ¿Prometes arreglar tu cuarto?
3. ¿Prometes lavar los platos?
4. ¿Prometes guardar tus cosas?
5. ¿Prometes lavar los pisos?
6. ¿Prometes sacudir los muebles?
7. ¿Prometes hacer las camas?
8. ¿Prometes cocinar la comida?
9. ¿Prometes poner la mesa?

¡FÍJATE! 4
La a personal

Spanish speakers make a distinction between direct objects referring to things and those referring to people. Compare the pairs of sentences below.

Things

Ve <u>la casa</u>.

Conocemos <u>la Ciudad de Nueva York</u>.

Necesita <u>una casa nueva</u>.

People

Ve **a** <u>Marta</u>.

Conocemos **a** <u>sus padres</u>.

Necesita **a** <u>Guillermo</u>.

The personal **a** precedes a direct object noun that refers to a person. When the definite article **el** precedes a direct object that is a person, **a + el** contracts to become **al;** for example, **Vemos al señor.**

15 **Haz una frase.**   Haz frases con las palabras siguientes. Pon atención *(Pay attention)* si se necesita la **a** personal. Sigue el modelo.

Modelo   Yo / no / ver / David   ⟶   **Yo no veo a David.**

1. nosotros / necesitar / mochila / nuevo
2. él / esperar / padres
3. ¿tú / conocer / hermanas / de Pepe?
4. yo / no escribir / cartas
5. el profesor / enseñar / dos clases
6. mi mamá / ayudar / hermano menor *(younger)* / con su tarea

16 **¿La necesita o no?**   Decide si las frases siguientes necesitan la **a** personal o no. Luego, contesta las preguntas con **lo, la, los, las,** cuando sea posible. Finalmente, pregúntalas a un compañero.

Modelo   ¿Escribes la carta?   ⟶   **Sí, la escribo.**

1. ¿Terminas _____ la tarea?
2. ¿Hablas _____ español y francés?
3. ¿Conoces _____ el presidente de los Estados Unidos?
4. ¿Siempre escuchas _____ tu mamá cuando te habla?
5. ¿Siempre traes _____ tus libros a la clase?

¡FÍJATE! 5
Un repaso de *estar* y *ser*

You have learned two Spanish verbs that mean *to be* in English. These verbs, **estar** and **ser,** are contrasted below.

Estar is used:

◆ To describe a physical or mental condition that can change or to indicate a change in condition
La cocina <u>está</u> sucia.
María <u>está</u> muy bien.
Jorge y Julia <u>están</u> tristes.

◆ To describe the location of people or places
<u>Estamos</u> en Boston este fin de semana.
Mi dormitorio <u>está</u> en el segundo piso.

Ser is used:

◆ To describe physical or personality characteristics
Jorge <u>es</u> inteligente.
Yanina <u>es</u> guapa.
Su cocina <u>es</u> amarilla.
Las casas <u>son</u> grandes.

◆ To tell time, or to tell when or where an event takes place
¿Qué hora <u>es</u>?
<u>Son</u> las ocho.
Mi clase de español <u>es</u> a las ocho y <u>es</u> en Peabody Hall.

◆ To tell where someone is from and to express nationality
<u>Somos</u> de los Estados Unidos. <u>Somos</u> estadounidenses.
Ellos <u>son</u> de Bolivia. <u>Son</u> bolivianos.

Compare the two sentences below. Why do you use **ser** in the first sentence? Why do you use **estar** in the second sentence?

1. Su hermano <u>es</u> simpático.
2. Su hermano <u>está</u> enfermo.

You will learn several more uses for **estar** and **ser** by the end of *¡Atrévete!*

17 **¿Conoces a Isabel?** Isabel es una estudiante en tu universidad. Llena los blancos con la forma correcta de **estar** o **ser** para conocerla *(to know her)* mejor.

(1) _____ las siete de la mañana. Isabel (2) _____ cansada pero tiene que correr porque su clase de física (3) _____ a las ocho. ¿Me dices que no la conoces? Pues, (4) _____ una mujer alta, inteligente y muy simpática. Le gusta estudiar. (5) _____ de Cleveland, y sus padres (6) _____ allí *(there)* todavía *(still)*. Ellos (7) _____ orgullosos *(proud)* de ella. Bueno, ya (8) _____ las ocho. Isabel, como siempre *(always)*, llega a tiempo a su clase; no le gusta llegar tarde *(late)*.

18 **A conocerte aún más.** Contesta las preguntas siguientes. Luego, pregúntaselas *(ask them)* a un compañero.

1. ¿De dónde eres?
2. ¿A qué hora son tus clases?
3. ¿Cómo es tu casa?
4. ¿Dónde está tu casa?
5. ¿Cómo es tu dormitorio?
6. ¿Dónde está tu dormitorio?
7. ¿De qué color es tu casa?
8. ¿Cuál es tu color favorito?
9. ¿Cómo es tu novio / novia (esposo / esposa) (amigo / amiga)?
10. ¿Dónde está él / ella ahora *(now)*?
11. ¿Cómo eres tú?
12. ¿Cómo estás tú hoy?

19 **¡A jugar!** Make two columns on your paper. Label one **ser** and the other **estar.** Your instructor will give you three minutes to write as many sentences with **ser** and **estar** as you can. After you have finished writing, form groups of four to check your sentences and your uses of the verbs. How many correct sentences did you have?

20 **Luces, cámara, acción.** You are getting a screen test! The director has sent you the script, but some lines are difficult to read. Your best friend also received a copy of the script, but he or she has different parts that are difficult to read. Help each other decipher the missing stage directions and set descriptions by asking each other questions until you uncover all the information you are lacking. Use the "stage directions" in the **Etapa 2, actividad 20,** in **capítulo 3** of your **Manual de actividades.** Follow the model.

Modelo **Estudiante 1:** ¿Qué hora es?

      Estudiante 2: Son las ocho y cuarto. ¿De qué color es la alfombra?

      Estudiante 1: La alfombra es roja.

Your instructor attempts to pair you each class period with a different partner. This enables you to help and learn from a variety of your peers, an important and highly effective learning technique. Equally important is the fact that working in small groups, rather than as a large class, gives you more opportunities and time to practice Spanish, as well as to realize how similar you and your fellow classmates really are as you get to know each other better.

21 **Somos iguales.** Your instructor will give you and your partner a sheet of newsprint. Draw a big circle in the center of the paper. In that circle, using **ser** or **estar,** you will write sentences about things that you have in common. For example, your first sentence could be **Nuestro color favorito es _____.** Continue to look for things that you have in common.

As you look for these commonalities, you will also discover things that set the two of you apart, that make each of you unique. For example, you might say to your partner, **"Hoy, estoy nerviosa. ¿Cómo estás tú hoy?"** and your partner might answer **"Hoy estoy cansado."** Draw another circle and connect it to the big one with a line. Inside that circle you will write all of the things that make you unique, and that you do not have in common with your partner, as in the following drawing.

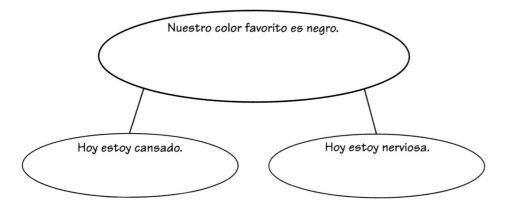

Nuestro color favorito es negro.

Hoy estoy cansado.

Hoy estoy nerviosa.

Share your drawings with your class when the groups are finished. You may also want to develop and draw an icon or symbol that represents you and your partner, and then one that represents just you. What are some of the things that all of your classmates have in common?

¡ENTÉRATE! España

FRANCIA

Andorra

PIRINEOS

CORDILLERA CANTÁBRICA

Pamplona

ESPAÑA

Barcelona

⭐ MADRID

Toledo

Valencia

Islas Baleares

PORTUGAL

Guadalquivir

SIERRA NEVADA

Sevilla

Granada

Islas Canarias

MARRUECOS

Toledo,
ciudad de El Greco

Sevilla,
la catedral y la Giralda

711 Moors from Northern Africa invaded.

1492 Union of the kingdoms of Fernando and Isabel. Expulsion of the Moors. Financing of Columbus' first voyage.

1500s Age of exploration.

1898 Spain lost the Spanish American War and its territories: Cuba, Puerto Rico, and the Philippines.

Barcelona, el Barrio Gótico

La Plaza España y sus estatuas de Cervantes, Don Quijote y Sancho Panza

Granada, la Alhambra

Madrid, el Palacio Real

La Sagrada Familia, catedral de Gaudí

¿Qué te parece?

1. The Moors ruled Spain for over 700 years. What effect did that have on Spanish culture?

2. Why was Spain so successful during the age of exploration?

3. What caused Spain to lose its colonies after 300 years of possession?

1969 Franco named Juan Carlos de Borbón y Borbón as his eventual successor.

1939 General Francisco Franco victorious. The Spanish Civil War ended.

1936 Spanish Civil War began.

1992 Barcelona hosted the Summer Olympics. Sevilla hosted the World's Fair.

1986 Spain joined the European Union.

LA RED

¡Navega la Internet!

To discover more information on the culture of this chapter, check out the Holt Web site and other suggestions listed in your **Manual de actividades.**

http://www.hrwcollege.com/

ETAPA 3

¡Cuéntame!

Ya lo sabemos

Rafi invites Adriana to spend the weekend with him at his parents' home. In this episode you will

◆ get to know a bit about the house in which Rafi's parents live
◆ learn more about Uncle Pedro's strange behavior

Preguntas personales

1. ¿Cómo es la casa de tus padres? Con un compañero, describe tu casa mientras él / ella la dibuja *(sketches it)*. ¿Es correcto el dibujo? Ahora cambia de papel *(Now switch roles)*.
2. ¿Qué te gusta más de la casa de tus padres? ¿Qué no te gusta?
3. ¿Qué sabemos ya *(already)* del tío Pedro?

Estrategias de lectura
Scanning for Information

When you read in English, do you often scan (or search) the passage for specific information? Scanning is another strategy to help you focus on key information in your reading. With skimming, you read quickly to get the gist of the passage for the main ideas. With scanning, you already know what you need to find out, so you concentrate on searching for that information.

1. Read the first two paragraphs of this episode, looking for the following specific information:
   a. the season of the year
   b. the weather on this day
   c. the two characters mentioned
2. Now reread the first paragraph to determine what the relationship is between Rafi and Adriana. In your opinion, are they just friends?

Finish reading the episode. First skim the remaining paragraphs and write the main idea of each. Then reread, this time scanning for specific information to support those main ideas. Remember to pay attention to cognates to boost your comprehension.

Rafi y el sacrificio final

Episodio 3: El misterio empieza

El otoño llega y con el viento y el frío también llegan los colores brillantes. Rafi está muy feliz porque hace un mes que sale con Adriana. Le encanta Adriana. Es peruana, inteligente, simpática y también muy bonita.

Rafi invita a Adriana a pasar el fin de semana con él en la casa de sus padres. Viven en un pueblo pequeño, a dos horas de la universidad. En los meses de octubre y noviembre la ruta a su casa parece una tarjeta postal con todos los colores de los árboles.

Rafi y Adriana llegan a las cinco de la tarde y ya hace frío. Es una casa blanca y grande al estilo victoriano. Los señores Martín los reciben con entusiasmo. La señora Martín le enseña la casa a Adriana mientras Rafi habla con su papá en su oficina. La oficina del señor Martín tiene muebles antiguos muy buenos que hacen un contraste muy interesante con la computadora y el sistema electrónico moderno. Las paredes están adornadas con fotos de la familia y hay figurines y otros objetos de arte, todos regalos del tío Pedro de sus viajes.

—Papá, ¿qué pasa con el tío Pedro? ¿Cómo está?

—No sé —le contesta el señor Martín. —Se comporta° misteriosamente. Hace dos meses que nos manda° muchas cosas para poner en la guardilla.

—¿Qué tipo de cosas? —le pregunta Rafi.

—Cosas como un baúl y...

En ese momento, Adriana y la señora Martín entran en la oficina. —¿De qué hablan? —les pregunta la señora Martín.

—Nada, Mamá, nada. —le contesta Rafi. Para cambiar la conversación Rafi le pregunta a Adriana, —¿Te gusta la casa?

Se... *He's behaving*

nos... *he's been sending us*

Comprensión

1. ¿Dónde está la casa de la familia de Rafi?
2. ¿Los padres están contentos al ver a Rafi y a Adriana? Explica.
3. ¿De qué clase socioeconómica es la familia Martín Lara? Explica.
4. ¿De qué hablan Rafi y su padre?
5. ¿Por qué le dice el señor Martín a Rafi que el tío «se porta misteriosamente»?

Expansión

1. In pairs, prepare and then act out the scene of Mrs. Martín showing Adriana the house (2 to 3 minutes).

2. In groups of three or four, speculate on what Uncle Pedro has been sending to Rafi's parents. Share your speculations with the other groups.

3. On the way back to the university, Rafi and Adriana stop for gas. While at the station, Adriana buys a postcard of the area. The first thing she does when she gets to her apartment is write the postcard to her parents. Complete the message for her on page 118.

Queridísimos padres:
¡Tengo un amigo nuevo! Se llama
—————— . El es ——————.
También conozco a sus padres. Ellos
son —————— . Viven en
—————— . Esta postal es de la
región donde ellos viven. Bueno, es
todo por ahora. Pronto les
escribo una carta.
    ¡Los quiere un montón!
     Adriana

SELLO
POSTAL

P-8

A mirar o escuchar

4 View the video or listen to the audio CD as Rafi and Adriana are about to discover Uncle Pedro's old trunk. Consult the pre- and post-listening activities in your **Manual de actividades.**

¡Sí, se puede!

1. **Veo, veo.** In groups of four or five students, take turns playing "I Spy" with items in your classroom.

  Modelo **Veo, veo algo rojo.**

2. 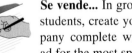 **Se vende...** In groups of three or four students, create your own realty company complete with name. Write an ad for the most spectacular house that your company has to offer. Provide a detailed description of the house and the selling price. You may use the ads on page 90 as your model. For maximum appeal, include at least five items about each house. After you finish, your instructor will read the ads to the class. Each student votes for (1) the house he or she would most like to buy and (2), the best buy. Be prepared to share the reasons for your choices. Did many of you choose the same houses?

3. **¡B-I-N-G-O!** On separate pieces of paper, create *two* Bingo sheets using the following model:

  Modelo

B	I	N	G	O
30–39	90–99	450–459	870–879	1,500–1,509

  Your instructor will call out numbers and keep track of all those named. You will mark through the spaces, containing the numbers called, that appear on your sheets.

4. **¡Qué buen precio!** In groups of three or four students, choose three pieces of furniture or other household items. Sketch them and on the back of each drawing determine a price and write a description of the item, including the color. Groups take turns presenting items while the other groups guess the prices.

Groups alternate guesses up to three tries. The group with the closest guess without going over "wins" the item!

Modelo   el sofá verde   ➡   **$300 (trescientos dólares)**

5. **Tengo una casa...** In groups of two or three students, play the roles of a homeowner selling his or her home and two prospective buyers. The seller begins by describing the house, while pretending to give a tour. The prospective buyers will ask lots of questions, as well as talk about the kind of house they want (e.g., **Deseamos una casa de un solo piso**).

6. **¡Necesito ayuda!** With a partner, play the roles of a homeowner looking for a housekeeper and a person inquiring about the position. The homeowner names the tasks that he or she expects the housekeeper to perform (e.g., **Necesita pasar la aspiradora cada día**) while the prospective housekeeper clearly states what he or she does and does not do on the job (e.g., **Yo no lavo las ventanas**).

7.   **¡He ganado la lotería!** Congratulations! You have just won the new homeowner's contest sponsored by a local bank! You have been provisionally awarded $25,000. Now you must write a brief essay describing how you plan to spend the money. The stipulations are that you must spend the money on purchases for your home, and that you mention each purchase you plan to make and why. For example, the item you want to replace is old, broken (**roto / rota**), or you simply don't have one and you explain why it is needed.

8.   **Se vende una casa.** Write a detailed real estate ad to sell your house or the house of a close friend, including at least five of the house's outstanding features.

9. **El correo electrónico.** Answer an e-mail message that you have just received from your new pen pal in Spain in which she has inquired about the household responsibilities of teenagers in the United States. Discuss when they usually begin to do household chores and the kinds of chores they are given. Also mention the things you do to help out around the house when you are home. Tell your new pen pal at least five things.

Para recordar

Having completed this chapter, you are now able to:

Etapa 1 ¡Sígueme!

❑ describe the types and styles of homes in the Spanish-speaking world

❑ share facts about your house and the things you find in it

❑ use the verb form **hay**

❑ use new verbs that have an irregular **yo** form

❑ talk about what you do or should do around your house

❑ discuss the changing role of Hispanic women, and list at least three Hispanic women who have made an impact on society

❑ make your world more colorful by using colors to describe things

Etapa 2 ¡Dime más!

❑ use idiomatic expressions with the verb **tener** to express physical and emotional states

❑ talk about the weather

❑ use numbers from 100 to 100,000,000

❑ use direct object pronouns in your speaking and writing

❑ know what the personal **a** is and when to use it

❑ review uses of **ser** and **estar**

❑ list at least three facts about **España**

Etapa 3 ¡Cuéntame!

❑ describe Rafi's and Adriana's visit with his parents and what Rafi discovers about Uncle Pedro

 You can practice concepts from this and earlier chapters by doing the ¡Recuérdate! sections in your Manual de actividades.

VOCABULARIO ACTIVO

En la casa

el armario   *closet*
el baño   *bathroom*
la cocina   *kitchen*
el comedor   *dining room*
el dormitorio, la alcoba
      bedroom

la escalera   *staircase*
el garaje   *garage*
la guardilla   *attic*
el jardín   *garden*
la oficina   *office*
el piso   *floor, story*

la planta baja   *ground floor*
el primer piso   *second floor*
la sala   *living room*
el segundo piso   *third floor*
el suelo   *floor*
el techo   *roof*

En la sala y el comedor

la alfombra   *rug, carpet*
el estante de libros   *bookcase*
la lámpara   *lamp*

la mesa   *table*
los muebles   *furniture*
la silla   *chair*

el sillón   *armchair*
el sofá   *sofa*
el televisor   *television*

En la cocina

la estufa   *stove*
el lavaplatos   *dishwasher*

el microondas   *microwave*
el refrigerador   *refrigerator*

En el baño

la bañera   *bathtub*
la ducha   *shower*

el inodoro   *toilet*
el lavabo   *sink*

En el dormitorio

la cama   *bed*

la frazada   *blanket*

el tocador   *dresser*

Otras palabras útiles en la casa

el árbol   *tree*
el auto   *car*
el baúl   *trunk, chest*
la caja   *box*

el carro   *car*
el coche   *car*
la cosa   *thing*
el cuadro   *picture, painting*

la flor   *flower*
la planta   *plant*
la ventana   *window*

Los quehaceres de la casa

arreglar   *to straighten up*
ayudar   *to help*
cocinar   *to cook*
guardar   *to put away, to keep*
hacer la cama   *to make the bed*

lavar los platos   *to wash the dishes*
limpiar   *to clean*
pasar la aspiradora   *to vacuum*
poner la mesa   *to set the table*
preparar una comida   *to cook*

sacar la basura   *to take out the garbage*
sacudir   *to dust*

Verbos

acabar de *to have just*	hacer *to do, to make*	salir *to leave*
caer *to fall*	oír *to hear*	traer *to bring*
conocer *to know*	poder *to be able to*	venir *to come*
dar *to give*	poner *to put, to place*	ver *to see*
decir *to say*	prometer *to promise*	
desear *to want, to desire*	querer *to want; to love*	

Expresiones con *tener*

tener... años *to be . . . years old*	tener ganas de + *(infinitive) to feel like* + *(verb)*	tener que + *(infinitive) to have to* + *(verb)*
tener calor *to be hot*	tener hambre *to be hungry*	tener razón *to be right*
tener cuidado *to be careful*	tener miedo *to be afraid*	tener sed *to be thirsty*
tener éxito *to be successful*	tener prisa *to be in a hurry*	tener sueño *to be sleepy*
tener frío *to be cold*		tener suerte *to be lucky*

Unos colores

amarillo / amarilla *yellow*	café *brown*	rojo / roja *red*
anaranjado / anaranjada *orange*	gris *gray*	rosado / rosada *pink*
azul *blue*	marrón *brown*	verde *green*
beige *beige*	morado / morada *purple*	
blanco / blanca *white*	negro / negra *black*	

Expresiones del tiempo

Está húmedo. *It's humid.*	Hace mal tiempo. *It's bad weather.*	Nieva. *It's snowing.*
Está nublado. *It's cloudy.*	Hace sol. *It's sunny.*	la nieve *snow*
Está seco. *It's dry.*	Hace viento. *It's windy.*	la nube *cloud*
Hace buen tiempo. *It's nice weather.*	llover *to rain*	¿Qué tiempo hace? *What's the weather like?*
Hace calor. *It's hot.*	Llueve. *It's raining.*	el sol *sun*
Hace frío. *It's cold.*	la lluvia *rain*	la temperatura *temperature*
	nevar *to snow*	

Los números de 100 a 100.000.000

cien *100*	quinientos / quinientas *500*	mil *1.000*
doscientos / doscientas *200*	seiscientos / seiscientas *600*	cien mil *100.000*
trescientos / trescientas *300*	setecientos / setecientas *700*	un millón *1.000.000*
cuatrocientos / cuatrocientas *400*	ochocientos / ochocientas *800*	cien millones *100.000.000*
	novecientos / novecientas *900*	

Otras palabras útiles

antes (de) *before*	a la izquierda *to the left*	sucio / sucia *dirty*
a la derecha *to the right*	limpio / limpia *clean*	
después (de) *after*	se encuentra(n) *one finds, you find*	

MÉXICO

BELICE

MAR CARIBE

GUATEMALA HONDURAS

Ciudad de Guatemala ✪

EL SALVADOR

OCÉANO PACÍFICO

Travel and telecommunications have made our globe much more accessible to the masses. Even people without the time or the economic means to visit distant lands can be armchair visitors via books, magazines, television, or the Internet, experiencing pictorial and word images of people who may be continents away. The photo on these two pages represents one aspect of the diversity of the Spanish-speaking world.

¿Qué te parece?

1. What is your ethnic background? What nationality are your parents? What nationality are your grandparents? How far back can your family be traced?

2. What companies make use of advertising based on multiculturalism? What is the message they are trying to convey?

3. What are the benefits of having many cultures in the same country? What are the challenges?

4. What are the results of visitors (both temporary and permanent) to a culture?

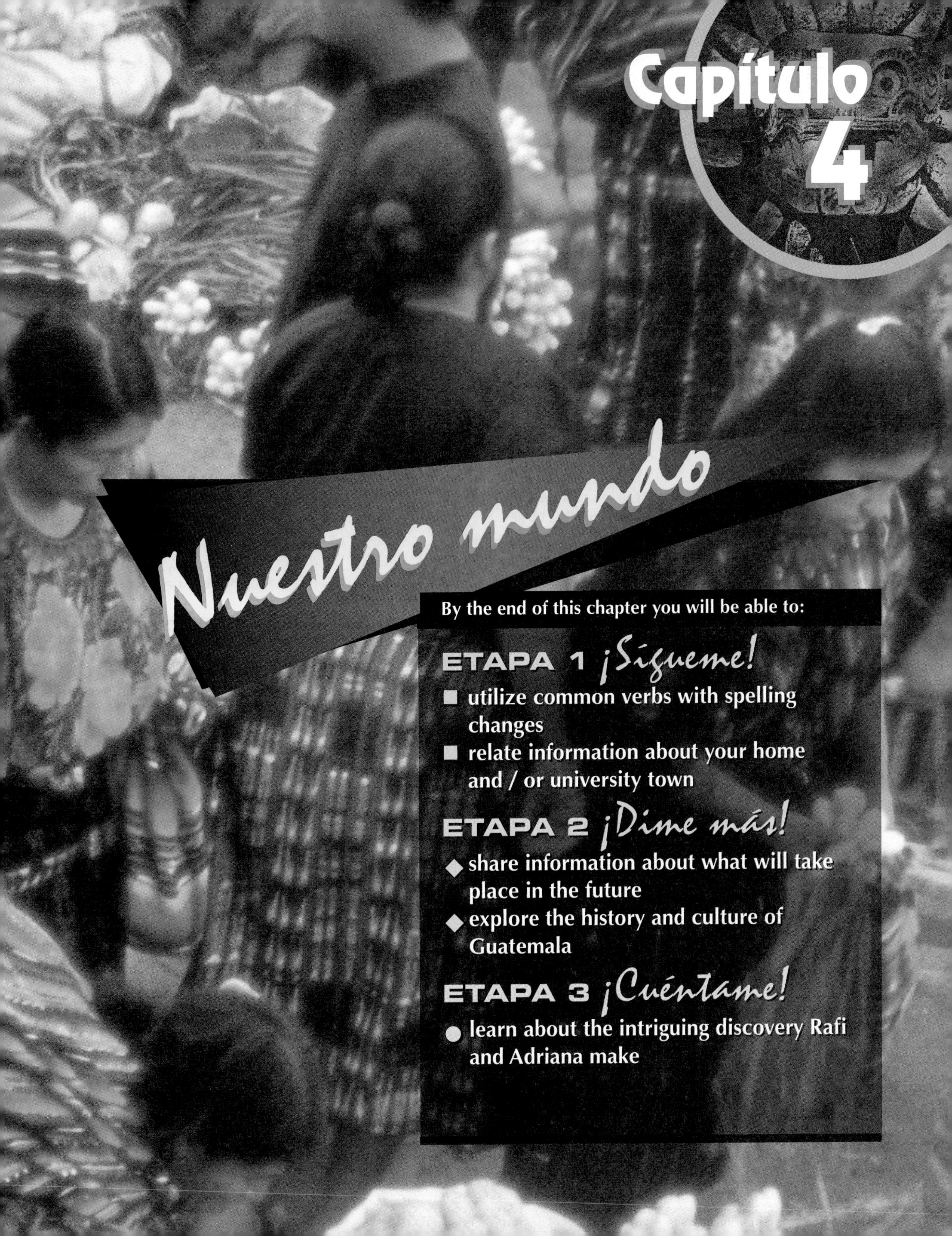

Capítulo 4

Nuestro mundo

By the end of this chapter you will be able to:

ETAPA 1 ¡Sígueme!

- utilize common verbs with spelling changes
- relate information about your home and / or university town

ETAPA 2 ¡Dime más!

- share information about what will take place in the future
- explore the history and culture of Guatemala

ETAPA 3 ¡Cuéntame!

- learn about the intriguing discovery Rafi and Adriana make

ETAPA 1

¡Sígueme!

¡ASÓMATE! 1
Tiene que...

¿Qué tiene que hacer?

1. almorzar *to have lunch*
2. cerrar *to close*
3. comenzar *to begin*
4. costar *to cost*
5. dormir *to sleep*
6. encontrar *to find*
7. entender *to understand*
8. mostrar *to show*
9. pedir *to ask for*
10. pensar *to think*
11. perder *to lose; to waste*
12. preferir *to prefer*
13. querer *to want; to love*
14. recordar *to remember*
15. repetir *to repeat*
16. seguir *to follow; to continue*
17. servir *to serve*
18. volver *to return*

1 **Asociación libre.** Which infinitive, from the list of new verbs depicted, do you associate with each of the following?

Modelo regresar ➡ **volver**

1. Tengo hambre.
2. ¿Cuánto es?
3. desear
4. ¿Tienes sueño?
5. creer
6. gustar más
7. Una cerveza, por favor.

2 **Tic-tac-toe.** Make a tic-tac-toe grid on a sheet of paper. Write a different verb from **¡Asómate!** 1 in each of the nine boxes. Do not show your grid to your partner. Take turns guessing the words your partner has selected. Each time you guess correctly, your partner marks an X over the word. Who can get tic-tac-toe first?

Modelo **ESTUDIANTE 1:** ¿Tienes «pensar»?

ESTUDIANTE 2: Sí, tengo «pensar».

(o)

No, no tengo «pensar».

3 **Los quehaceres.**   Completa las siguientes frases con lo que tú tienes que hacer.

Modelos   Tengo que encontrar...   ➡   **Tengo que encontrar un libro para mi clase de inglés.**

Tengo que pensar más en...   ➡   **Tengo que pensar más en mi clase de español.**

1. Tengo que dormir... 5
2. Tengo que almorzar... 1
3. Tengo que comenzar... 3

4. Tengo que recordar... 7
5. Tengo que volver a... 14
6. Tengo que encontrar... 6

¡FÍJATE! 1
Los verbos de cambios radicales

Look at each of the following drawings. Which verb forms look like the infinitive? Which ones have a spelling change that differs from the infinitives?

These stem-changing verbs are also known as *shoe verbs.* Note the three major groups of shoe verbs and the other verbs that follow the same pattern.

Change e ➞ ie

	cerrar	*to close*	
yo	**cie**rro	nosotros, nosotras	cerramos
tú	**cie**rras	vosotros, vosotras	cerráis
él, ella, Ud.	**cie**rra	ellos, ellas, Uds.	**cie**rran

Other verbs like **cerrar (e ➞ ie)** are:

comenzar	*to begin*
empezar	*to begin*
pensar	*to think*
recomendar	*to recommend*
entender	*to understand*
perder	*to lose; to waste*
mentir	*to lie*
preferir	*to prefer*

Change e ➞ i

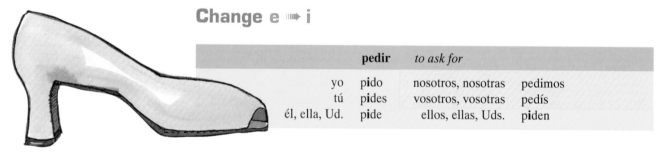

	pedir	*to ask for*	
yo	**pi**do	nosotros, nosotras	pedimos
tú	**pi**des	vosotros, vosotras	pedís
él, ella, Ud.	**pi**de	ellos, ellas, Uds.	**pi**den

Other verbs like **pedir (e ➞ i)** are:

repetir	*to repeat*
seguir	*to follow; to continue (doing something)*
servir	*to serve*

Note that the **yo** form of **seguir** is **sigo.**

Change o ➡ ue

	encontrar	*to find*	
yo	enc**ue**ntro	nosotros, nosotras	encontramos
tú	enc**ue**ntras	vosotros, vosotras	encontráis
él, ella, Ud.	enc**ue**ntra	ellos, ellas, Uds.	enc**ue**ntran

Other verbs like **encontrar (o ➡ ue)** are:

almorzar	*to have lunch*
costar	*to cost*
mostrar	*to show*
recordar	*to remember*
volver	*to return*
dormir	*to sleep*
morir	*to die*

Look at the following infinitives. What other infinitives does each one look like? What are the present tense forms for each infinitive?

demostrar	*to demonstrate*
encerrar	*to enclose*
devolver	*to return (an object)*
perseguir	*to chase*

Verbos de cambios radicales that you already know are **poder** and **querer.** Another common irregular verb with a stem change is given below.

	jugar (u ➡ ue)	*to play*	
yo	**jue**go	nosotros, nosotras	jugamos
tú	**jue**gas	vosotros, vosotras	jugáis
él, ella, Ud.	**jue**ga	ellos, ellas, Uds.	**jue**gan

4 | **Qué tipo de verbo es?** With a partner, write on individual slips of paper the stem-changing verbs that were just presented. Next, make a chart with three categories: **e ➡ ie, e ➡ i, o ➡ ue.** Join another group of two students. When your instructor says **¡Empieza!**, place the verbs under the correct category of either **e ➡ ie, e ➡ i,** or **o ➡ ue.** Do several rounds of this activity, playing against different doubles partners.

5 **¡Córrele!**   Form teams of equal size with at least four people, but no more than six people. Team members sit in a row, one behind the other, facing the chalkboard. The first team member writes the subject pronouns *out of order* on the left side of a piece of paper as in the model. Your instructor will write a stem-changing verb on the board. The first team member in each row writes the **tú** form of the verb next to the pronoun and quickly passes it to the team member behind them. The next team member has to write the **nosotros** form and pass the paper to the next person, and so on. Any team member may correct any of their teammates' previous answers if they are incorrect. The first group to get all of the verb forms correct gets five points, the second group gets four, and so forth. So, **¡En sus marcas, listos, fuera!**

Modelo

tú			
nosotros			
ella			
yo			
Uds.			
ellos			

6 **¿Quién...?**   ¿A quién conoces que hace las siguientes cosas? ¿Alguien de tu familia — tu hermano o tu hermana? ¿Tu tío o tu tía? ¿Tus padres? ¿Tus amigos o tus amigas? ¿Tu compañero o tu compañera de cuarto? ¿Tu novio o tu novia? Escribe los nombres de las personas y la relación que tienen contigo. Después, comparte la información con un compañero en frases completas. Sigue el modelo.

Modelo   preferir dormir hasta   ➡   **Mi hermano Bill prefiere dormir**
              el mediodía   **hasta el mediodía.**

1. preferir dormir hasta el mediodía
2. pensar ser doctor
3. almorzar en McDonalds a menudo
4. querer visitar Sudamérica
5. siempre perder la tarea
6. poder jugar al tenis muy bien
7. no poder bailar muy bien
8. volver a casa tarde a menudo
9. nunca tener dinero y siempre pedirlo
10. nunca encontrar sus cosas
11. no entender las direcciones
12. pensar que hay un Santa Claus
13. nunca mentir

7 **¿Quién es?**   Contesta las siguientes preguntas en una hoja de papel aparte. Pon *(Put)* las respuestas en forma de párrafo. Cuando termines, dale la hoja a tu profesor o profesora. El profesor o la profesora va a leerle los párrafos a la clase mientras los estudiantes adivinan *(guess)* quién los escribió *(wrote)*.

Primer párrafo

1. ¿Cómo eres?
2. ¿Qué clases tienes este semestre?
3. ¿Qué clase prefieres? ¿Por qué?
4. ¿A qué hora empieza tu clase preferida?
5. ¿Cuándo termina?
6. ¿Dónde es tu clase preferida?

Segundo párrafo

1. ¿Qué coche manejas?
2. ¿Cómo vienes a la universidad?

3. ¿Te gusta tu universidad?
4. ¿Qué quieres ser / hacer en el futuro?

Tercer párrafo

1. ¿Qué deporte prefieres?
2. ¿Lo juegas o lo miras en la televisión?

3. Normalmente, ¿cuándo juegas?
4. ¿Con quién juegas?
5. ¿Qué otros deportes te gustan?

¡FÍJATE! 2
Los pronombres de los complementos indirectos

To indicate *to whom* or *for whom* actions are done, you use indirect object nouns and pronouns. Look at the sentences in the following box.

Los pronombres de los complementos indirectos		
Arturo	**me**	escribe muchas cartas.
Arturo	**te**	escribe muchas cartas.
Arturo	**le**	escribe muchas cartas a Mariela.
Arturo	**nos**	escribe muchas cartas.
Arturo	**os**	escribe muchas cartas.
Arturo	**les**	escribe muchas cartas a Beto y Chucho.

In each of the above sentences, who is writing the letters? Who is receiving the letters? Where are the words in bold type in relation to the verb?

All of the boldface words in the previous box are *indirect object pronouns*. Indirect objects answer the questions *to whom* and *for whom*. Therefore, what is the direct object in each of the previous sentences?

Like direct object pronouns, indirect object pronouns precede the conjugated verb and can also be attached to infinitives.

Based on the previous examples, how would you say the following in Spanish:

1. Arturo writes him a lot of letters.
2. Arturo writes you *(singular, formal)* a lot of letters.
3. Arturo writes you *(plural, formal)* a lot of letters.

To clarify or emphasize the indirect object, a prepositional phrase (**a** + *prepositional pronoun*) can be added, as in the following sentences.

Le presto mis cintas <u>a</u> <u>él</u>, pero no le presto nada <u>a</u> <u>ella</u>.

¿**Me** preguntas <u>a</u> <u>mí</u>?

I'm loaning <u>him</u> my cassettes, but I'm not lending <u>her</u> anything. (clarification)

Are you asking <u>me</u>? (emphasis)

8 **¿Quién habla?**   You overhear the following bits of conversation between a father and his son. You do not want to be rude and turn around to see who is speaking, but you are sure you can tell who is speaking just by what is being said. In pairs, take turns answering the question **¿Quién lo dice?** *(Who says it?).*

Modelos   **Lo dice el hijo.**

             Lo dice el padre.

1. Te recomiendo estudiar mucho.
2. Te pido manejar con cuidado *(drive carefully).*
3. Te digo la verdad.
4. Te prometo estudiar mucho.
5. Te presto el coche si recibes buenas notas.
6. Quiero salir con Chepe. ¿Me das unas pesetas?

9 **¡Qué consejos!**   Remember freshman orientation on your campus? Imagine you are listening to an orientation advisor. Would he or she say the following things? Check **sí** if he or she would make the following statements, check **no** if not.

	Sí	No
1. Les prometo ayudar.		
2. Les pido información sobre sus familias.		
3. Les pregunto cuáles son sus especialidades.		
4. Les doy las reglas *(rules)* de la universidad.		
5. Les digo que tenemos una universidad muy buena.		
6. Les recomiendo la cafetería.		
7. También les recomiendo el restaurante Taco Grande.		
8. Les explico que no deben *(should not, must not)* estudiar mucho.		
9. Les recomiendo clases fáciles.		
10. Les digo que pueden salir hasta muy tarde todas las noches.		
11. Les digo que no tienen que regresar a la residencia hasta las dos de la mañana.		
12. Finalmente, les recomiendo una clase de español.		

10 **Te toca a ti.**   Now you get the chance! Play the role of a mentor with your partner. Choose five of the statements from **actividad 9** and share your sage advice about your school with your partner. Look at the models for some ideas. Be creative!

Modelos   **Te prometo ayudar.**

             Te digo que puedes salir hasta muy tarde todas las noches pero no debes hacerlo.

11 **¿De veras?**   With a partner, play the roles of a freshman advisee and an orientation advisor. The advisee asks the orientation advisor five questions, based on **actividad 9,** to make sure that everything was heard correctly! The advisor responds. Then, reverse roles.

Modelo   **Estudiante 1:**   ¿Me recomiendas el restaurante Taco Grande?

             Estudiante 2:   No, no te recomiendo el Taco Grande. Te recomiendo el Pecos Grill.

12 **¿Quién ayuda más?** ¿Eres una de esas personas que tiene la suerte de tener el compañero de cuarto perfecto? ¿Qué hacen Uds. para ayudarse el uno al otro *(each other)?* Haz una lista de por lo menos cinco cosas que tú haces para tu compañero.

Modelo **Le arreglo la sala.**

Le contesto el teléfono.

Then make a list of at least five things that your roommate does for you. Does one person do more than the other or is it pretty evenly matched? Share your list with your partner. Are your lists similar?

If you have several roommates, how would you change the above model?*

¡ASÓMATE! 2
Unos lugares de una ciudad o de un pueblo

Unos lugares y unas cosas de una ciudad o de un pueblo

1. el almacén
2. el banco *bank*
3. el café
4. el centro *center*
5. el centro comercial
6. el cheque *check*
7. el cine *movie*

8. el correo
9. la cuenta *check*
10. la iglesia *church*
11. la librería *bookstore*
12. mandar una carta
13. el mercado
14. el museo *museum*

15. el parque
16. la película
17. la plaza
18. el restaurante
19. el supermercado
20. el teatro
21. la tienda

Otras palabras útiles

delante (de)	*in front (of)*
derecho	*straight ahead*
detrás de	*behind*
enfrente (de)	*in front (of)*
al lado de	*next to*
el mejor	*the best*
el peor	*the worst*

¿Dónde está el supermercado Fuentes? *Where's the Fuentes supermarket?*
— Está al lado de la librería. — *It's next to the bookstore.*
Ah sí. Enfrente del Banco Federal. *Oh yes. In front of the Federal Bank.*

The preposition **de** combines with the masculine definite article **el** to form the contraction **del.** The feminine article **la** does not contract.

---

*Les arreglo la sala. / Les contesto el teléfono.

13 **¡No puede ser!** Suena el teléfono. Lo contestas. Es tu mejor amiga que está casi histérica. ¿Por qué? ¡Porque en este momento tu actor favorito / actriz favorita camina por la calle principal de tu ciudad! Tu mejor amiga intenta explicarte lo que ocurre pero está tan emocionada que la información queda incompleta. Completa la información explicando dónde debe estar el Sr. Guapo o la Srta. Guapa.

Modelo **TU MEJOR AMIGA:** Quiere comprar frutas.

TÚ: Ah, debe estar en el mercado.

1. Quiere leer y necesita comprar un libro.
2. Quiere mandar una carta.
3. Tiene hambre y quiere comer algo *(something)*.
4. Quiere ver una exposición de arte.
5. Quiere ver una película.
6. Tiene sed y quiere tomar algo.

14 **¿Cuál es el mejor?** You have seen them before — the best pizza, the best video store, the top five restaurants. Now make your own list of bests. They can be the best in your town, the best that you have seen, or the best that you have heard of from your friends. After you have completed your list, compare it with a classmate's list. Do you match on any? What does your class rank as **El mejor de los mejores?** Finally, tell a partner where these places are located, or how to get there, using terms such as **delante de** and **al lado de.**

Modelo **ESTUDIANTE 1:** ¿Cuál es el mejor almacén?

ESTUDIANTE 2: El mejor es Macy's.

ESTUDIANTE 1: ¿Dónde está?

ESTUDIANTE 2: Está al lado del Banco Nacional.

1. almacén
2. banco
3. centro comercial
4. cine
5. librería
6. museo
7. teatro
8. tienda
9. restaurante
10. supermercado

15 **Y a la derecha...** You have a new neighbor. Your partner will play the role of your new neighbor. Describe the location of at least five places in your town and where they are in relation to other places. Your partner will draw what you describe, creating a map. How well did your partner understand you? Now switch roles.

16 **Andamos conociéndonos.** One of the pleasures of going to a university is getting to know new people. Besides getting to know your classmates, you are becoming familiar with the characters Rafi, Chema, and Adriana, three college students who are about to become involved in a mysterious and dangerous affair. Work with a partner to find out more about them. Fill in the information gaps in the **Etapa 1, actividad 16** chart in **capítulo 4** of your **Manual de actividades.**

¡Dime más!

¡ENTÉRATE!
La arquitectura hispana

Architects have an ongoing debate as to which comes first, form or function. As you look at the pictures on this page and the next page, try to decide what style influenced these buildings. What is your opinion regarding the form versus function debate?

¿Qué te parece?

Consider geography when answering the following questions. If necessary, refer to your maps in the front of this book.

1. What important issues must architects consider in your hometown and in other parts of the United States? What important issues must they consider in Mexico, D.F.; Puerto Rico; Costa Rica; Bolivia; and Guatemala?
2. Can you tell whether the buildings pictured are in a Spanish-speaking country or in the United States? How?

¡FÍJATE! 3
Los pronombres de los complementos directos e indirectos usados juntos

You have worked with two types of object pronouns, direct and indirect. Now note how they are used together in the same sentence.

La profesora nos devuelve <u>los</u>
<u>exámenes</u> a <u>nosotros.</u>

La profesora <u>nos</u> <u>los</u> devuelve.

Marta me pide <u>un favor</u> a <u>mí.</u>

Marta <u>me</u> <u>lo</u> pide.

1. You know that direct and indirect objects come after the verb. Where do you find the direct and indirect object pronouns?
2. Reading from left to right, which pronoun comes first? Which pronoun comes second?

Note the change that occurs when you use **le** or **les** along with a direct object pronoun that begins with **-l (lo, la, los, las): le** or **les** changes to **se.**

	les ➠ **se**	
La profesora les devuelve	➠	La profesora <u>se</u> <u>los</u> devuelve.
los <u>exámenes</u> **a** <u>ellos</u>.		

	le ➠ **se**	
Marta le pide **un** <u>favor</u> **a** <u>él</u>.	➠	Marta <u>se</u> <u>lo</u> pide.

The following grammar boxes review the direct and indirect object pronouns, along with their English equivalents.

Los pronombres de los complementos directos

me	*me*	**nos**	*us*
te	*you (familiar, singular)*	**os**	*you (familiar, plural)*
lo, la	*him, her, it, you (formal, singular)*	**los, las**	*them, you (formal, plural)*

Los pronombres de les complementos indirectos

me	*to / for me*	**nos**	*to / for us*
te	*to / for you (familiar, singular)*	**os**	*to / for you (familiar, plural)*
le (se)	*to / for him, her, it, you (formal, singular)*	**les (se)**	*to / for them, you (formal, plural)*

---

1 **Carlos, ¿me puedes...?**   Antonio loves to spend time with his big brother Carlos. Today they are studying together and Antonio keeps asking Carlos to lend him things. Give Carlos' answers, using both direct and indirect object pronouns. Carlos is very good natured and says yes to all but one request. You decide which request he denies.

Modelo   prestar / un lápiz

ESTUDIANTE 1 (ANTONIO):   ¿Me prestas un lápiz?

ESTUDIANTE 2 (CARLOS):   Sí, te lo presto.

1. prestar / tus cuadernos
2. prestar / tu bicicleta
3. prestar / diez dólares
4. prestar / tu disco compacto de Garth Brooks
5. prestar / tu calculadora

2 **Mi recomendación es...**   You have seen the newspaper columns or books that rate restaurants, hotels, movies, and the like. Well, now it is your turn. Check whether you would recommend the items in the following list to the following people. Then share your opinions with a classmate. Tell your partner your opinions in complete sentences, following the model.

Modelo **ESTUDIANTE 1:** ¿Recomiendas los libros de Michael Crichton a tus primas?

ESTUDIANTE 2: No, no se los recomiendo.

	Sí	No
1. los libros de Michael Crichton (a tus primas)		
2. la música de Jon Secada (a tu compañero o compañera de cuarto)		
3. el restaurante Taco Bell (a tus padres)		
4. el hotel Hilton (a tu amiga que no tiene dinero)		
5. la película *Drácula* (a tus primos de cinco años)		
6. el parque Central (a tu hermano)		
7. el museo de Arte Moderno (a tu profesor o profesora)		
8. la clase de español (a tu mejor amigo o amiga)		

3 **¿En qué puedo servirle?** You have just started an internship with the biggest advertising agency in your region. You are thrilled but you have come to realize that your work has little to do with your future career and more to do with organizing the big wigs of the company. You are helping one of the vice presidents get ready for an overseas trip. What follows are her requests. Tell your answers to a partner, using both direct and indirect object pronouns. By the way, will you address your boss with **tú** or **Ud.?**

1. ¿Me puedes traer un café?
2. ¿Me puedes comprar los boletos *(tickets)* para un viaje a Nueva York?
3. ¿Me puedes arreglar los apuntes y los papeles para la reunión de esta tarde?
4. ¿Me puedes buscar un libro de misterio para leer?
5. ¿Me puedes hacer el favor de mandarles esta información a nuestros clientes en Japón?
6. ¿Me puedes reservar una mesa en un restaurante elegante para esta noche?
7. ¿Me puedes comprar unas rosas para la recepcionista? Es su cumpleaños hoy.

¡FÍJATE! 4
El verbo ir

Another important verb is **ir.** Note the present tense forms below.

ir	*to go*	
yo	voy	nosotros, nosotras vamos
tú	vas	vosotros, vosotras vais
él, ella, Ud.	va	ellos, ellas, Uds. van

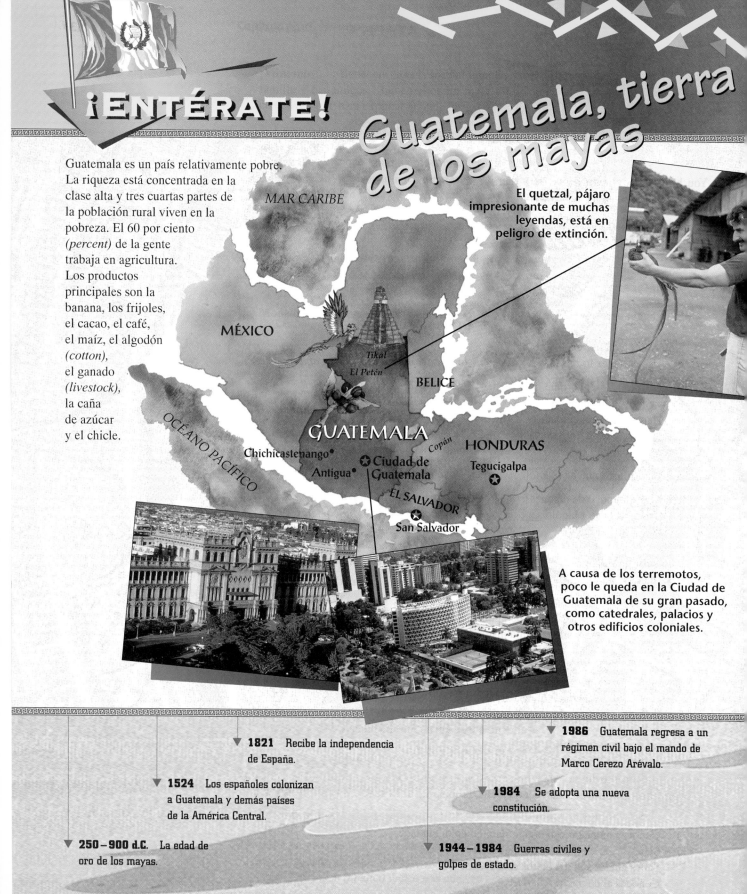

¡ENTÉRATE!

Guatemala, tierra de los mayas

Guatemala es un país relativamente pobre. La riqueza está concentrada en la clase alta y tres cuartas partes de la población rural viven en la pobreza. El 60 por ciento (*percent*) de la gente trabaja en agricultura. Los productos principales son la banana, los frijoles, el cacao, el café, el maíz, el algodón (*cotton*), el ganado (*livestock*), la caña de azúcar y el chicle.

MAR CARIBE

MÉXICO

Tikal
El Petén

BELICE

El quetzal, pájaro impresionante de muchas leyendas, está en peligro de extinción.

OCÉANO PACÍFICO

GUATEMALA

Copán

HONDURAS

Chichicastenango•

Antigua•

☆ Ciudad de Guatemala

Tegucigalpa ☆

EL SALVADOR

San Salvador

A causa de los terremotos, poco le queda en la Ciudad de Guatemala de su gran pasado, como catedrales, palacios y otros edificios coloniales.

1821 Recibe la independencia de España.

1524 Los españoles colonizan a Guatemala y demás países de la América Central.

250 – 900 d.C. La edad de oro de los mayas.

1986 Guatemala regresa a un régimen civil bajo el mando de Marco Cerezo Arévalo.

1984 Se adopta una nueva constitución.

1944 – 1984 Guerras civiles y golpes de estado.

Antigua es una ciudad
colonial encantadora.

En Chichicastenango, y en
otras ciudades y pueblos, hay
festivales donde se usan
máscaras ceremoniales.

Hay gente indígena
que todavía lleva ropa tradicional.
La ropa es de colores brillantes y
los diseños identifican al grupo o al
pueblo de la persona.

¿Qué te parece?

1. ¿Cuáles son unas semejanzas y diferencias entre
Guatemala y el resto de Centroamérica y México?

2. ¿Por qué tiene México más éxito económico que
Guatemala y otros países de Centroamérica como
Nicaragua, El Salvador y Honduras?

LA RED ¡Navega la Internet!

To discover more information on
the culture of this chapter, check
the Holt Web site and other
suggestions listed in your
Manual de actividades.

http://www.hrwcollege.com/

1992   Rigoberta Menchú gana
el Premio Nóbel de la Paz por
su trabajo en derechos civiles

1995   (25 de mayo) Una crisis
política causa caos en el país. El
presidente Serrano disuelve el
Congreso y la Corte Superior, y
suspende la constitución.
Después de unos días, Serrano
tiene que ir al exilio.

●ETAPA 3

¡Cuéntame!
¡Cuéntame!

Ya lo sabemos

In this episode Rafi and Adriana

♦ find something mysterious in Uncle Pedro's trunk
♦ discover some incredible information about Uncle Pedro and his profession

The title of this episode is **La carta.** Which do you think is true?*

1. Rafi receives an intriguing letter from his uncle.
2. Adriana writes Rafi a "Dear John" letter.
3. Rafi and Adriana find a letter in the trunk.

Preguntas personales

Answer the questions to prepare for reading and discussing this episode.

1. ¿Escribes muchas cartas? ¿A quiénes? ¿Recibes muchas cartas? ¿De quiénes?
2. Describe una carta importante que una persona puede escribir o recibir.
3. ¿Guardas las cartas que recibes? ¿Tus padres o tus abuelos tienen cartas viejas guardadas en sus casas?

Estrategias de lectura
More Practice with Skimming and Scanning

Continue to practice techniques for focusing on main ideas and important information. Remember, when you *skim* a passage you read quickly to get the gist of the passage. When you *scan* a passage you already know what you need to find out, so you concentrate on searching for that particular information.

Skim the first paragraph and the text of the letter, then respond to the following questions.

1. Who wrote the letter? To whom was it written?
2. Which of the following statements appears to describe best the relationship between the person writing the letter and the person to whom it was written?
   a. They do not know each other.
   b. They are merely colleagues.
   c. They are romantically involved.
   d. They dislike each other.

---

*You are correct if you chose number 3.

Now scan the same passage, looking for the following information:

1. Who finds the letter?
2. Where is the letter found?
3. When was it written and from where?

Rafi y el sacrificio final

Episodio 4: La carta

Esa noche, después de comer, Rafi y Adriana regresan a la guardilla y abren el baúl del tío Pedro. Lo miran todo —fotos, libros, papeles y... una carta. La abren y se encuentran con algo fascinante. También encuentran periódicos de muchos países: Colombia, Italia, México y Egipto.

¡Todos tienen artículos acerca del tío Pedro! Todos hablan de cómo Pedro Lara es un héroe por encontrar unos objetos de arte muy importantes, robados de unos museos nacionales y de unas tumbas arqueológicas. También hablan de cómo Pedro Lara siempre sigue la pista° de los criminales internacionales de arte.

°**la pista** route, path

¡Tío Pedro, un héroe internacional! ¡Rafi no lo puede creer! Rafi y Adriana se miran pero no se dicen nada. Devuelven todo a su lugar en el baúl y regresan a la oficina del señor Martín.

—Papá —le pregunta Rafi, —exactamente qué hace el tío Pedro?

—Es un crítico de arte. Escribe libros y consulta con los museos.

—¿Es todo?

—Sí, ¿por qué?

—No, nada —le contesta Rafi. Rafi y Adriana se miran. Luego, Rafi mira intensivamente las dos copias de *Cómo descifrar códigos*.

7 de junio de 1...
Mérida, México
Querido Pedro:

Cuando recibas esta carta, voy a estar muy lejos de ti. Tomo una decisión que tú no vas a entender. Te quiero mucho, pero prefiero perderte que continuar en este dilema. No pienses mal en mí. No me busques. Y sobre todo, no pienses mal en « Roma... el sacrificio final ». Si descifras ese código, vas a morir.

Adiós para siempre.

Te quiere,
Pilar

Comprensión

1. ¿Por qué escribe esta carta Pilar?
2. ¿Qué tipo de relación existe (o existió — pasado) entre Pedro y Pilar?
3. ¿Cuál es el trabajo verdadero del tío Pedro? ¿Cómo lo sabes? Según el padre, ¿cuál es su trabajo?
4. ¿Es importante la frase «Roma... sacrificio final»? Explica.
5. En tu opinión, ¿por qué guarda el tío Pedro sus cosas en la casa de los padres de Rafi?
6. En tu opinión, ¿por qué no le cuenta *(tell)* Rafi a su padre lo que encontraron (pasado) en el baúl?
7. En tu opinión, ¿qué van a hacer Rafi y Adriana con esa información nueva sobre el tío Pedro?

Expansión

(1) In small groups, discuss the following questions and be prepared to report any interesting findings to the class. ¿Hay personas misteriosas en tu familia? ¿Entre *(among)* tus amigos? ¿Hay personas con secretos del pasado? Explica.

(2) Imagine that this episode is a scene from a play and rehearse it with a partner. Be as dramatic and creative as you like! First, write your dialogue (maximum three-quarter page length) and think about any stage directions you may need, then rehearse. Your instructor will call on some of you to perform the scene in class.

(3) Rafi says that his uncle is his hero. With a partner, make a list of characteristics that describe Uncle Pedro. Make a second list of characteristics that you feel describe a hero. Compare the two lists. Are they similar?

A mirar o escuchar

(4) View the video or listen to the audio CD to find out what happens next to Rafi and his friends. Consult the pre- and post-listening/viewing comprehension activities in your **Manual de actividades.**

¡Sí, se puede!

1.   **El juego de la narración.** En dos equipos (o más), van a escribir una narración sobre «La historia de Rafi». Van a recibir la primera frase de la narración. Después, el equipo A escribe una oración apropiada para continuar la narración. El equipo B añade otra oración, y así hasta que no se pueda escribir más. Las metas *(goals)* pueden ser los usos correctos de:

Equipo A	Equipo B
un verbo regular	un verbo irregular
un complemento indirecto	un complemento directo
una forma de **ir**	un verbo regular
los complementos directos e indirectos juntos	una forma de **saber**

> **Modelo**   Primera oración: **La vida de Rafi es muy complicada ahora.**

2. **Hay que escoger.** Necesitas escoger *(choose)* diez lugares de la lista de vocabulario de **¡Asómate! 2.** Para cada lugar que escoges, escribe el nombre del lugar más conocido de tu pueblo o ciudad. También debes escribir dónde está el lugar en relación con otro lugar importante.

> **Modelo**   la agencia ➡ **Small World Travel**
> de viajes   **está a la derecha del cine Rialto.**

3.   **Las negociaciones.** Haz una lista de cinco hechos importantes sobre Guatemala. Después comparte tu lista con un compañero, y entre los dos, decidan cuáles son los cinco hechos más importantes para Uds. Después, compartan esta nueva lista con la lista de otra pareja y juntos decidan cuáles son los cinco hechos más importantes para Uds. cuatro. Finalmente, cada grupo de cuatro debe compartir su lista con el profesor o la profesora mientras él / ella prepara una lista para la clase.

4.   **El turismo.** Uds. son agentes de viajes y tienen que diseñar un cartel *(design a poster)* para uno de los siguientes países: Guatemala, México, España o los países del Caribe. En grupos de tres o cuatro estudiantes, deben decidir cómo será *(will be)* (fotos, dibujos, etc.) y deben escribir la información que debe tener. Al terminar, van a compartir sus ideas con los otros grupos. Nota: Antes de hacer esta actividad, pueden buscar información interesante en las secciones **¡No me digas!** de su **Manual de actividades** de los capítulos 1 hasta 4.

Para recordar

Having finished this chapter, you are now able to:

Etapa 1 ¡Sígueme!

- ❏ use stem-changing verbs appropriately
- ❏ replace indirect object nouns with pronouns
- ❏ talk about your home and / or university town

Etapa 2 ¡Dime más!

- ❏ discuss some architectural issues of form and function
- ❏ replace direct and indirect object nouns with pronouns
- ❏ use the verb **ir**
- ❏ talk about things that will happen, using the construction **ir** + **a** + *infinitive*
- ❏ state five facts that have impacted Guatemala

Etapa 3 ¡Cuéntame!

- ❏ share the contents of the letter Rafi and Adriana discover, as well as the newspaper articles about Uncle Pedro

 For additional practice of concepts from this and previous chapters, do the **¡Recuérdate!** *section in your* **Manual de actividades.**

VOCABULARIO ACTIVO

¿Qué tiene que hacer?

almorzar (ue)   *to have lunch*
cerrar (ie)   *to close*
comenzar (ie)   *to begin*
costar (ue)   *to cost*
dormir (ue)   *to sleep*
encontrar (ue)   *to find*
entender (ie)   *to understand*

mostrar (ue)   *to show*
pedir (i)   *to ask for*
pensar (ie)   *to think*
perder (ie)   *to lose; to waste*
preferir (ie)   *to prefer*
querer (ie)   *to want; to love*
recordar (ue)   *to remember*

repetir (i)   *to repeat*
seguir (i)   *to follow; to continue*
   (doing something)
servir (i)   *to serve*
volver (ue)   *to return*

Unos verbos

demostrar (ue)   *to demonstrate*
devolver (ue)   *to return (an*
   object)
empezar (ie)   *to begin*
encerrar (ie)   *to enclose*

ir   *to go*
jugar (ue)   *to play*
mandar   *to send*
mentir (ie)   *to lie*
morir (ue)   *to die*

perseguir (i)   *to chase*
recomendar (ie)   *to recommend*
saber   *to know*

Unos lugares y unas cosas de una ciudad o de un pueblo

el almacén   *department store*
el banco   *bank*
el café   *cafe*
el centro   *downtown*
el centro comercial   *mall; business / shopping district*
el cheque   *bank check*

el cine   *movie theater*
el correo   *post office*
la cuenta   *bill, account*
la iglesia   *church*
la librería   *bookstore*
mandar una carta   *to send a letter*
el mercado   *market*
el museo   *museum*

el parque   *park*
la película   *movie*
la plaza   *town square*
el restaurante   *restaurant*
el supermercado   *supermarket*
el teatro   *theater*
la tienda   *store, shop*

Otras palabras útiles

delante (de)   *in front (of)*
derecho   *straight ahead*
detrás de   *behind*

enfrente (de)   *in front (of)*
al lado de   *next to*

el mejor   *the best*
el peor   *the worst*

As you have already discovered, the Spanish-speaking world is quite diverse. Some words vary in meaning from one country to another. One such word is **tortilla.** In Mexico, a **tortilla,** made of either corn or flour, is one of the staples of the Mexican diet, while in Spain, a **tortilla** is similar to an omelet.

¿Qué te parece?

1. Other cultures have their equivalent of the **tortilla.** Can you name some of the cultures?
2. Are ethnic foods popular where you live? If so, which ones?
3. If there are ethnic restaurants where you live, do they serve authentic food, or has it been adapted for the American palate?

¡Buen provecho!

By the end of this chapter you will be able to:

ETAPA 1 *¡Sígueme!*
- discuss your food preferences
- talk and write about things you did and events that occurred in the past

ETAPA 2 *¡Dime más!*
- order your favorite foods in a restaurant
- list three interesting facts about Argentina

ETAPA 3 *¡Cuéntame!*
- find out what radical decision Rafi and Chema make

¡Sígueme!
¡Sígueme!

¡ASÓMATE! 1
Unas comidas

Las carnes y aves

1. el biftec
2. la hamburguesa
3. el jamón

4. el perro caliente
5. el pollo

El pescado y los mariscos

6. el atún

7. los camarones *(pl.)*

Las frutas

8. la banana
9. la manzana
10. el melón

11. la naranja
12. la pera
13. el tomate

Las verduras

14. el arroz
15. la cebolla
16. el chile
17. la ensalada
18. los frijoles *(pl.)*

19. la lechuga
20. el maíz
21. la papa / la patata
22. las papas fritas *(pl.)*

Los postres

23. el dulce
24. la galleta
25. el helado

26. el pastel
27. la torta

Las bebidas

28. el agua
29. el café
30. la cerveza
31. el jugo

32. la leche
33. el refresco (con hielo)
34. el té (helado / caliente)
35. el vino

Más comidas

36. el cereal
37. el huevo
38. el pan

39. el queso
40. la sopa
41. la tostada

Las comidas

el almuerzo	*lunch*
la cena	*dinner*
el desayuno	*breakfast*
la merienda	*snack*

1 **¿Con qué empieza?** Work with a partner. Choose any five letters of the alphabet and write them at the top of a sheet of paper. In three minutes, write as many new food words as you can that begin with those letters. Check your list against your partner's. For every word that you wrote that your partner did not, you receive a point.

Use your experience with cognates to decipher word meaning of those words not formally presented in **¡Asómate! 1.**

Comida	Calorías	Proteína	Grasa	Carbohidratos	Vitaminas
biftec	455	27	36	0	A, B
hamburguesa con queso	950	50	60	54	B
jugo de naranja	100	1	0	16	A, B, C
naranja	50	1	0	16	A, B, C
pan	150	6	2	38	B
papa	100	3	0	23	B, C
perro caliente	200	5	14	1	B, C
salmón	200	24	10	0	A, B
torta	455	4	13	76	A, B, C
lechuga	10	1	0	2	A, B, C

2 **¿Cuántas calorías tiene?** ¿Cuentas las calorías? Mira la gráfica y di qué comidas se describen.

Modelo   Esta comida tiene mucha ➠ **Es la lechuga.**
agua, es verde y tiene 10 calorías.

Esta comida...
1. tiene proteína, es carne y tiene 455 calorías.
2. tiene hierro *(iron),* es pescado y tiene 200 calorías.
3. tiene vitamina C y 100 calorías. Es una verdura.
4. tiene carbohidratos y 150 calorías.
5. tiene mucha grasa y proteínas.
6. tiene vitaminas, es anaranjada y tiene 50 calorías.

See the **También se dice...** *section at the end of the book for additional food vocabulary to use in* **actividad 3.**

3 **¿Cuáles son tus preferencias?** Llena la gráfica en **Etapa 1, actividad 3** en **capítulo 5** de tu **Manual de actividades.**

4 **¿Qué comes?** Llena las gráficas en **Etapa 1, actividad 4** en **capítulo 5** de tu **Manual de actividades** con comidas que tú crees son nutritivas y que pertenecen a una dieta balanceada. Compara tu gráfica con la de un compañero. ¿Están representados todos los grupos de comida? ¿Quién tiene las sugerencias más saludables *(healthy)?*

Refer to the **También se dice...** *section as needed.*

5 **¿Qué comes tú?**   Contesta estas preguntas con un compañero de clase.

1. ¿Comes bien o comes mal? ¿Por qué?
2. ¿Qué tipo de comida prefieres?
3. ¿Qué te gusta comer de merienda?
4. ¿Qué come el estudiante típico?
5. ¿Te preocupa tu nivel de colesterol?
6. ¿Qué comidas tienen vitaminas A y C?
7. ¿Qué comidas tienen minerales?
8. ¿Qué comidas tienen proteínas?
9. ¿Estás a dieta? Si contestas que sí, ¿por qué?
10. ¿Cómo compara la dieta americana a la dieta japonesa?
11. ¿Cómo compara la dieta americana a las dietas de otros países industriales?
12. ¿Cómo compara la dieta americana a las de los países pobres?

¡ENTÉRATE!
La palabra *comida*

La palabra comida significa varias cosas en español: *food, meal, lunch (the main meal of the day)*. Hay semejanzas con nuestras comidas y también hay unas diferencias. Por ejemplo, **el desayuno** en el mundo *(world)* hispano normalmente consiste en café y unos panes o panes dulces. Generalmente es una comida ligera *(light)*.

El almuerzo normalmente es la comida más grande y más fuerte del día. En lugares con una cultura más tradicional, el almuerzo empieza a eso de *(around)* las 2:00 de la tarde. Toda la familia regresa a casa para comer: los niños regresan de la escuela y el papá (y la mamá si trabaja fuera *[outside]* de la casa) comen juntos en casa. No tienen que regresar a trabajar o a la escuela hasta las 5:00 o 6:00 de la tarde. Entonces, hay un tiempo para descansar *(to rest)*. En los países donde hay mucha influencia de los Estados Unidos, ahora tienen un horario de almuerzo similar al nuestro.

La cena puede ser una comida más ligera. La gente en los países hispanohablantes cena más tarde que la mayoría de los norteamericanos. ¡Algunos no cenan hasta las 10:00 u 11:00 de la noche!

¿Qué te parece?

1. ¿Cómo es un desayuno típico en el mundo hispano? ¿un almuerzo? ¿una cena?
2. ¿A qué hora normalmente comen los hispanos las diferentes comidas?
3. Normalmente, ¿a qué horas comes el desayuno, almuerzo y cena?

¡FÍJATE! 1
El pretérito

Up to this point, you have been communicating in the present and future time. To talk about something you did or something that occurred in the past, you can use the **pretérito** (preterit). Below are the endings for regular verbs in the **pretérito.** What do you notice about the endings for **-er** and **-ir** verbs?

-ar: comprar			
yo	compré	nosotros, nosotras	compramos
tú	compraste	vosotros, vosotras	comprasteis
él, ella, Ud.	compró	ellos, ellas, Uds.	compraron

-er: comer			
yo	comí	nosotros, nosotras	comimos
tú	comiste	vosotros, vosotras	comisteis
él, ella, Ud.	comió	ellos, ellas, Uds.	comieron

-ir: vivir (-ir)			
yo	viví	nosotros, nosotras	vivimos
tú	viviste	vosotros, vosotras	vivisteis
él, ella, Ud.	vivió	ellos, ellas, Uds.	vivieron

Los verbos que terminan en -car, -zar, y -gar

Several verbs have small spelling changes in the preterit. Look at the charts below.

tocar (c ➧ qu)			
yo	toqué	nosotros, nosotras	tocamos
tú	tocaste	vosotros, vosotras	tocasteis
él, ella, Ud.	tocó	ellos, ellas, Uds.	tocaron

empezar (z ➧ c)			
yo	empecé	nosotros, nosotras	empezamos
tú	empezaste	vosotros, vosotras	empezasteis
él, ella, Ud.	empezó	ellos, ellas, Uds.	empezaron

jugar (g ➡ gu)			
yo	jugué	nosotros, nosotras	jugamos
tú	jugaste	vosotros, vosotras	jugasteis
él, ella, Ud.	jugó	ellos, ellas, Uds.	jugaron

Verbs like **leer** and **creer** change the **i** to **y** in the third-person singular and plural.

leer (i ➡ y)			
yo	leí	nosotros, nosotras	leímos
tú	leíste	vosotros, vosotras	leísteis
él, ella, Ud.	leyó	ellos, ellas, Uds.	leyeron

In verbs that end in **-car,** the **c** changes to **qu** in the **yo** form to preserve the sound of the hard **c** of the infinitive (since **c** before **e** or **i** has an **s** sound). In verbs that end in **-zar,** the **z** changes to **c** to avoid having a **z** before **e** (with a few exceptions, Spanish spelling rules do not allow **z** before **e** or **i**). In verbs that end in **-gar,** the **g** changes to **gu** to preserve the sound of the hard **g** (**g** before **e** or **i** sounds like the **j** sound in Spanish).

Otras palabras útiles

anoche	*last night*
anteayer	*day before yesterday*
ayer	*yesterday*
el año pasado	*last year*
el fin de semana	*weekend*
la semana pasada	*last week*

6 **Cuéntame.**   Your instructor will give you a list of verbs to write on small pieces of paper, one verb per small piece. Group them according to **-ar, -er,** and **-ir** verbs. Next, write on a sheet of paper six different subject pronouns and a number from 1 to 6 next to each pronoun as in the model below. Select an **-ar** verb, and have your partner roll a die. Your partner, who rolls the die, must give the correct **pretérito** form of the verb matching the number rolled with the corresponding pronoun. Verify the form by using the preceding verb charts as needed. Take turns. When it's your partner's turn, draw from the **-er** verbs, and then from the **-ir.** Keep practicing until you always get them correct.

Modelo

1. nosotros	3. ellos	5. tú
2. yo	4. ella	6. Ud.

7 **Sí lo tengo.**   Make a grid, like the one in the **modelo,** on a sheet of paper. With a partner, select one **-ar** verb. Write a different preterit form of the verb in each blank space on your grid. Write each preterit form with a different pronoun. Do not show your partner what you have written.

Take turns randomly selecting pronouns (maybe by using a die as in **actividad 6**) and say the corresponding verb forms. When you say a form of the verb that your partner has, your partner marks an X over the word. The first person to get three Xs either vertically, horizontally, or diagonally wins the round. After doing an **-ar** verb, repeat with an **-er** and an **-ir** verb.

Modelo

tú estudiaste	nosotros estudiamos	ellos estudiaron
yo estudié	Uds. estudiaron	vosotros estudiasteis
ella estudió	ellas estudiaron	él estudió

8 **Y la respuesta es...** Work with a partner to find out who did what today. Partner A uses the drawings and questions that follow; Partner B goes to **Etapa 1, actividad 8** in **capítulo 5** of the **Manual de actividades** for his or her questions and drawings.

José Miguel

Rosario

Rolando

Pepe

Ana

Partner A, find out the following information from Partner B.

1. ¿Quién perdió su mochila la semana pasada?
2. ¿Quién vivió en Buenos Aires el año pasado?
3. ¿Quién estudió cinco horas anoche?
4. ¿Quién tocó la trompeta en la banda el fin de semana pasado?
5. ¿Quién recomendó el restaurante Perredies?

9 **Una encuesta.** Entrevista a cinco estudiantes diferentes en tu clase y anota sus respuestas en la gráfica en **Etapa 1, actividad 9** en **capítulo 5** de tu **Manual de actividades.**

¡Dime más!
¡Dime más!

¡ASÓMATE! 2
Cómo preparar las comidas

Los condimentos y las especias

1. el aceite
2. el azúcar
3. la mantequilla
4. la mayonesa
5. la mermelada

6. la mostaza
7. la pimienta
8. la sal
9. la salsa de tomate
10. el vinagre

Unos términos de la cocina

al horno	*baked*	duro / dura	*hard-boiled*
a la parrilla	*grilled*	fresco / fresca	*fresh*
bien cocido,	*well-done,*	frito / frita	*fried*
bien hecho	*well-cooked*	helado / helada	*iced*
caliente	*hot*	hervido / hervida	*boiled*
	(temperature)	picante	*spicy*
cocido /cocida	*boiled; baked*	poco hecho	*rare*
crudo /cruda	*rare; raw*	término medio	*medium*

1 **¿Qué dice tu nombre en realidad?** Write your first and last names across the top of a sheet of paper. Now, with each of the letters, write either **especias, condimentos o términos de la cocina** that begin with each of the letters of your name.

2 **¿Cuál es la especia más cara?** Saffron is currently the most expensive spice on the market, but what is the most expensive spice in *¡Atrévete!?* Fill in the chart in your **Manual de actividades, capítulo 5, actividad 2** in **Etapa 2** to discover the most and least expensive *¡Atrévete!* food items.

3
¿**Cómo lo prefieres?** Pregúntale a un compañero lo que sigue. Las respuestas deben usar el objeto directo. Sigue el modelo.

Modelo   ¿Cómo quieres tu hamburguesa?   ➡   **La quiero término medio.**

1. ¿Cómo quieres tu biftec?
2. ¿Con qué condimento(s) lo quieres?

3. ¿Cómo quieres tu ensalada?
4. ¿Cómo prefieres el pescado?
5. ¿Cómo te gustan los huevos?
6. ¿Cómo prefieres la pizza?
7. ¿Cómo quieres tu refresco, con o sin hielo?
8. ¿Cómo te gusta tu té, helado o caliente?
9. ¿Cómo prefieres la sopa, con mucha o poca sal?
10. ¿Cómo quieres tu café?

Refer to **Etapa 1, ¡Asómate! 1** *or the* **También se dice...** *section at the end of the book for additional vocabulary as needed.*

¡ENTÉRATE!
El picante

La comida en los países hispanohablantes no es necesariamente picante. La mayoría *(ma-jority)* de las comidas tienen las salsas picantes al lado. Esto se debe a que hay personas que no pueden comer picante o a quienes no les gusta.

Hay una variedad muy grande de salsas picantes. Es imposible predecir el sabor o lo picante que sea *(how hot it is)* la salsa a menos que lleve un aviso que diga «picante» o «suave». Aunque lleven el aviso de picante o suave, esto tampoco asegura uniformidad ya que lo que es picante para el paladar de uno puede ser suave para el paladar de otro.

Las salsas se usan en formas diferentes. Algunos países las usan para sazonar la comida, otros para ponerlas en la mesa como aderezo *(seasoning)*. En España, así como en algunos países latinoamericanos, la salsa picante no se usa en la mesa.

¿Qué te parece?

1. Are there any dishes that are typical of the region where you live? If so, what are they? Have you ever had that same dish prepared by someone, or in a restaurant, outside of your region? Was it the same?
2. Are there misconceptions about certain regional dishes in the United States? If so, what are they?

¡FÍJATE! 2
Unos verbos irregulares en el préterito

In **¡Fíjate! 1** you learned the verbs that are regular in the **pretérito.** The following verbs are irregular in the **pretérito;** they follow a pattern of their own. Study the verb charts.

andar	*to walk*		
yo	anduve	nosotros, nosotras	anduvimos
tú	anduviste	vosotros, vosotras	anduvisteis
él, ella, Ud.	anduvo	ellos, ellas, Uds.	anduvieron

estar			
yo	estuve	nosotros, nosotras	estuvimos
tú	estuviste	vosotros, vosotras	estuvisteis
él, ella, Ud.	estuvo	ellos, ellas, Uds.	estuvieron

tener			
yo	tuve	nosotros, nosotras	tuvimos
tú	tuviste	vosotros, vosotras	tuvisteis
él, ella, Ud.	tuvo	ellos, ellas, Uds.	tuvieron

conducir	*to drive*		
yo	conduje	nosotros, nosotras	condujimos
tú	condujiste	vosotros, vosotras	condujisteis
él, ella, Ud.	condujo	ellos, ellas, Uds.	condujeron

decir			
yo	dije	nosotros, nosotras	dijimos
tú	dijiste	vosotros, vosotras	dijisteis
él, ella, Ud.	dijo	ellos, ellas, Uds.	dijeron

traer			
yo	traje	nosotros, nosotras	trajimos
tú	trajiste	vosotros, vosotras	trajisteis
él, ella, Ud.	trajo	ellos, ellas, Uds.	trajeron

ir			
yo	fui	nosotros, nosotras	fuimos
tú	fuiste	vosotros, vosotras	fuisteis
él, ella, Ud.	fue	ellos, ellas, Uds.	fueron

ser			
yo	fui	nosotros, nosotras	fuimos
tú	fuiste	vosotros, vosotras	fuisteis
él, ella, Ud.	fue	ellos, ellas, Uds.	fueron

Note that the third-person plural ending of **conducir, decir,** and **traer** is **-eron,** not **-ieron.** Also note that **ser** and **ir** have the same forms in the preterit.

dar			
yo	di	nosotros, nosotras	dimos
tú	diste	vosotros, vosotras	disteis
él, ella, Ud.	dio	ellos, ellas, Uds.	dieron

ver			
yo	vi	nosotros, nosotras	vimos
tú	viste	vosotros, vosotras	visteis
él, ella, Ud.	vio	ellos, ellas, Uds.	vieron

hacer			
yo	hice	nosotros, nosotras	hicimos
tú	hiciste	vosotros, vosotras	hicisteis
él, ella, Ud.	hizo	ellos, ellas, Uds.	hicieron

poder			
yo	pude	nosotros, nosotras	pudimos
tú	pudiste	vosotros, vosotras	pudisteis
él, ella, Ud.	pudo	ellos, ellas, Uds.	pudieron

poner			
yo	puse	nosotros, nosotras	pusimos
tú	pusiste	vosotros, vosotras	pusisteis
él, ella, Ud.	puso	ellos, ellas, Uds.	pusieron

querer			
yo	quise	nosotros, nosotras	quisimos
tú	quisiste	vosotros, vosotras	quisisteis
él, ella, Ud.	quiso	ellos, ellas, Uds.	quisieron

saber			
yo	supe	nosotros, nosotras	supimos
tú	supiste	vosotros, vosotras	supisteis
él, ella, Ud.	supo	ellos, ellas, Uds.	supieron

venir			
yo	vine	nosotros, nosotras	vinimos
tú	viniste	vosotros, vosotras	vinisteis
él, ella, Ud.	vino	ellos, ellas, Uds.	vinieron

Sometimes verbs change meaning in the preterit. For example, in the preterit, **querer** usually means *tried to,* **no querer** means *refused,* and **saber** means *found out.*

Unos verbos de cambios radicales

The next group of verbs also follows its own pattern. In these stem-changing verbs, the first letters in the notations next to the verbs represent the present-tense spelling changes; the last letter in the notation indicates a spelling change in the **él** and **ellos** forms of the **pretérito.**

dormir (o ➧ ue ➧ u)			
yo	dormí	nosotros, nosotras	dormimos
tú	dormiste	vosotros, vosotras	dormisteis
él, ella, Ud.	durmió	ellos, ellas, Uds.	durmieron

pedir (e ➧ i ➧ i)			
yo	pedí	nosotros, nosotras	pedimos
tú	pediste	vosotros, vosotras	pedisteis
él, ella, Ud.	pidió	ellos, ellas, Uds.	pidieron

preferir (e ➧ ie ➧ i)			
yo	preferí	nosotros, nosotras	preferimos
tú	preferiste	vosotros, vosotras	preferisteis
él, ella, Ud.	prefirió	ellos, ellas, Uds.	prefirieron

3 **¿Quién dijo qué?**   Form groups of at least six students and sit in a circle. **Estudiante 1** starts by saying his or her name and something that he or she did yesterday, last week, or last year. **Estudiante 2** gives his or her name, says something that he or she did, and then tells what the preceding person (**Estudiante 1**) did. **Estudiante 3** tells his or her name, says what he or she did, and then tells what classmates **Estudiante 2** and **Estudiante 1** did (in that order). Follow the model.

Modelo   ESTUDIANTE 1:   Soy Meche y fui al cine ayer.

ESTUDIANTE 2:   Soy Roberto e hice ejercicios. Meche fue al cine ayer.

ESTUDIANTE 3:   Soy Bárbara y tuve que llamar a mis padres.
Roberto hizo ejercicios. Meche fue al cine ayer.

4 **¿Cuántas veces hiciste estas actividades?**   ¿Cuántas veces hiciste estas cosas la semana pasada?

Modelo   La semana pasada, ¿cuántas   ➧   **Fui una vez (dos veces).**
veces fuiste al correo?

La semana pasada ¿cuántas veces... ?

1. fuiste al cine?
2. hiciste tu tarea?
3. dormiste ocho horas?
4. viste un partido en la televisión?
5. diste la respuesta incorrecta en la clase?
6. tuviste razón?
7. anduviste por el centro?
8. condujiste a la universidad?
9. jugaste un deporte?
10. no viniste a la clase de español?
11. comiste comida rápida?

5 **¿Me conoces bien?**   Pair up with someone in the class who knows you well. See if he or she can guess how many times you did each of the activities listed in **actividad 4.** Were the guesses close? Were you honest? Use the following model to discover each other's answers.

Modelos   ESTUDIANTE 1:   La semana pasada, ¿cuántas veces piensas que fui al cine?

ESTUDIANTE 2:   Pienso que fuiste una vez.

ESTUDIANTE 1:   Sí, tienes razón. Fui una vez.

(o)

ESTUDIANTE 1:   ¿Cuántas veces piensas que fui al cine?

ESTUDIANTE 2:   Pienso que no fuiste.

ESTUDIANTE 1:   No, no tienes razón. Fui una vez.

6 **Tus vacaciones favoritas.** Piensa en tus vacaciones más memorables. ¿Cuándo fueron? ¿El año pasado? ¿Hace cinco años *(five years ago)*? Entre tú y un compañero, háganse las siguientes preguntas basadas en esas vacaciones. Antes de hacer la última pregunta, trata de adivinar adónde fue tu compañero de vacaciones.

1. ¿Fuiste a la playa?
2. ¿Fuiste a un museo?
3. ¿Viste un partido de béisbol?
4. ¿Montaste en bicicleta?
5. ¿Fuiste de compras?
6. ¿Comiste mariscos?
7. ¿Tomaste el sol?
8. ¿Jugaste al golf?
9. ¿Nadaste?
10. ¿Anduviste por la playa?
11. ¿Jugaste al tenis?
12. ¿Fuiste a un parque?
13. ¿Qué más hiciste?
14. ¿Adónde fuiste?

7 **Chismes.**   El periódico de tu escuela te ha nombrado el editor de la columna de chismes. Escribe tus respuestas a las preguntas que siguen. Ahora, entrevista a tres compañeros y anota sus respuestas. ¿Están de acuerdo?

1. ¿Quién hizo un disco recientemente?
2. ¿Qué actor salió en una película que no tuvo éxito?
3. ¿Quién tuvo éxito en una película?
4. ¿Quién en nuestro gobierno *(government)* dijo algo tonto?
5. ¿Quién vino a la clase tarde?
6. ¿Cuál de tus amigos estuvo antipático recientemente?
7. ¿Quién no trajo sus libros a la clase?
8. ¿Quién dio una manzana al / a la profesor / a para recibir una nota mejor?

8 **¿Conoces bien a tu compañero?**   One of your classmates will leave the room while the rest of your class generates five questions to ask this classmate about things that he or she did either yesterday or over the weekend. After you generate the questions, hypothesize how your classmate will answer. Write those answers on a slip of paper and give them to your instructor. When your classmate returns, ask him or her your five questions. How well did your class answers match your classmate's? How well do you really know him or her?

¡ASÓMATE! 3
El restaurante

En el restaurante

1. el camarero / la camarera
2. el cliente / la clienta
3. el cocinero / la cocinera
4. la cuchara
5. la cucharita
6. el cuchillo
7. la especialidad de la casa
8. el mantel
9. el menú
10. el plato
11. la propina
12. la servilleta
13. la tarjeta de crédito
14. la taza
15. el tenedor
16. el vaso

Otras palabras útiles

barato / barata	*cheap*
¡Buen provecho!	*Enjoy your meal!*
caro / cara	*expensive*
debajo (de)	*underneath*
encima (de)	*on top (of)*
reservar una mesa	*to reserve a table*

9 **¿Qué pasó?**   Mira el dibujo en la página 167 y escribe por lo menos cinco frases acerca de lo que pasó en el restaurante Buen Gusto.

El Restaurante Buen Gusto

Sopas y cremas
DE CEBOLLA GRATINADA	N$12.00
CON UN HUEVO	15.00
DE PESCADO	15.00
SOPA DE POLLO Y VERDURAS	15.00
CONSOME DE POLLO	12.00
CHAMPIÑONES	15.00
CREMA CONDE	15.00

Ensaladas y diversos
MIXTA DE VERDURAS	18.00
DE JAMON, POLLO O ATUN	20.00
DE FRUTAS	15.00
ENSALADA "CESAR"	18.00
JAMON YORK A LA HAWAIANA	26.00
JAMON VIRGINIA A LA PARRILLA O FRIO	26.00
QUESO FUNDIDO	18.00

Pescados y mariscos
CAMARONES AL MOJO DE AJO	65.00
CAMARONES A LA FRANCESA	65.00
LANGOSTINOS AL MOJO DE AJO	
FILETE SOL	35.00
FILETE DE PESCADO AL MOJO DE AJO	38.00
CALAMARES EN SU TINTA	32.00

Carnes y aves
FILETE A LA PIMIENTA	50.00
FILETE MIGNON	50.00
FILETE RANCHERO	50.00
CARNE ASADA A LA TAMPIQUEÑA	50.00
CARNE SELECTA CON CHAMPIÑONES	50.00
CHULETA DE CERDO	36.00
SIRLOIN O T-BONE STEAK	40.00
PECHUGA DE POLLO PARMESANA	38.00
½ POLLO A LA ORIENTAL	38.00
BROCHETAS DE FILETE	50.00

Pastas
SPAGHETTI A LA ITALIANA O A LA BOLOGNESA	25.00
RAVIOLES NAPOLITANOS	25.00
CREPAS DE POLLO	25.00

Sándwiches calientes
DE QUESO DERRETIDO	N$15.00
DE POLLO JAMON Y QUESO	24.00
DEFILETE CON PAPAS FRITAS	30.00
DE JAMON	15.00
ESPECIAL MONTECRISTO	25.00
CLUB SANDWICH	25.00

Sándwiches fríos
DE TOCINO, TOMATE Y LECHUGA	15.00
DE ENSALADA DE POLLO	20.00
DE JAMON Y QUESO	18.00

Hamburguesas
ARISTOCRATA	20.00
DE QUESO	20.00
ESPECIAL DEL CHEF	22.00

Platillos mexicanos
TACOS DE POLLO CON AGUACATE	25.00
ENCHILADAS POBLANAS	24.00
ENCHILADAS SUIZAS	24.00
CHILAQUILES CON POLLO GRATINADO	24.00
PUNTAS DE FILETE A LA MEXICANA	45.00
PEPITOS DE FILETE CON GUACAMOLE	30.00

Helados y postres
TRES MARIAS	12.00
BANANA SPLIT	14.00
HELADO ESPECIAL	15.00
PASTEL VARIADO	12.00
FLAN DE LA CASA	12.00

Bebidas y refrescos
CAFE AMERICANO	5.00
VASO DE LECHE	5.00
CHOCOLATE EN TAZA	5.00
TE NEGRO	5.00
TE HELADO	6.00
REFRESCOS FRIOS	5.00
LIMONADA O NARANJADA	6.00
CERVEZAS	10.00
COPA DE VINO	10.00

10 **¿Qué vas a pedir?**   Hace semanas que vienes ahorrando *(saving)* y ahora tú y tu persona favorita pueden ir a comer a ese restaurante elegante del que todo el mundo habla. Tienes $160.00 para gastar. ¿Qué ordenas para ti y tu acompañante?

¡ENTÉRATE!
La comida hispana

La comida hispana es muy variada. Se puede dividir en grupos de acuerdo a la localidad geográfica. En España en la parte norte como en Galicia, el pescado y los mariscos se destacan *(stand out)* por ser de los más deliciosos del mundo. Están preparados en una forma muy simple e insuperable. En Asturias, la fabada *(bean stew)*, los quesos de la región y una botella de sidra son parte de la dieta. En el área de Aragón se especializan en chilindrones *(marinade sauces)* y el excelente jamón hecho en Teruel. Cataluña es la tierra de las cazuelas *(casseroles)* y de las salchichas *(pork sausage)* regionales de fama mundial como las alioli, hechas con ajo *(garlic)* y aceite de oliva. Valencia y las regiones adyacentes se especializan en los platos de arroz como la famosa paella. Andalucía es la tierra de la comida frita. Su pescado frito es delicioso, también lo es el gazpacho, una sopa fría de vegetales. La parte central de España es conocida por su carne asada *(roasted)*. Las carnes de cordero *(lamb)*, ternera *(veal)*, lechoncito *(suckling pig)*, cabrito *(young goat)* y otras carnes se preparan muy despacio en hornos de madera para darles mejor sabor y textura. También aquí se encuentran algunos de los jamones y quesos más finos de España. Y por supuesto *(of course)*, el aceite de oliva, el ajo, el azafrán, las aceitunas, los garbanzos, los mariscos y el vino son parte indispensable de la comida española a través de toda España.

Las islas del Caribe (Cuba, la República Dominicana y Puerto Rico) tienen en común la herencia de las culturas española y africana combinadas con la cultura nativa. Así que las comidas de estos países tienen mucha sazón *(seasoning)* como bija *(annatto)* o achiote, orégano, cebolla, ajo y muchas más. El arroz es indispensable en la dieta caribeña, también el sancocho (sopa espesa de carne y legumbres), los plátanos, los mariscos y los frijoles (habichuelas en Puerto Rico).

La comida centroamericana es un poco diferente. El arroz también es un producto importante en la dieta centroamericana. También son importantes el maíz, los frijoles, las tortillas, las enchiladas, los vegetales, el pollo, los tamales y las frutas.

La comida mexicana es una de las cocinas más ricas del mundo. Esta riqueza proviene de la diversidad geográfica, climática y cultural del país y también de la imaginación del pueblo mexicano. La cocina mexicana hay que definirla por sus técnicas, características e ingredientes exclusivos de México. Las maneras de utilizar maíz, chiles y cactus son exclusivas de la cocina mexicana; así también lo es el cocinar verduras, carnes, mariscos, huevos, salsas, sopas y aves. Desde Baja California hasta la península de Yucatán, se pueden encontrar los platos típicos mexicanos de cada región.

Los países de Sudamérica llevan una dieta muy similar a los países del Caribe. El arroz, los frijoles, el pollo, algunas carnes, las frutas, los mariscos y la comida con mucha sazón son características de muchos países. En el Paraguay y el Uruguay se toma mucha sopa, vegetales, pan de maíz con queso y carne de cerdo *(pork)*. En la Argentina el plato principal es la carne de res *(beef)*. Y los argentinos la comen diariamente.

Las empanadas o empanadillas (un «*turnover*» de carne de res, legumbres, queso, mariscos o pollo) son famosas en toda la América Latina, desde Cuba hasta la Argentina.

El café es la bebida principal de todos los latinoamericanos, aunque también se bebe té en algunos países.

¿Qué te parece?

1. ¿En cuántos grupos se puede dividir la comida hispana?
2. ¿Qué es típico de la comida de las diferentes partes de España?
3. ¿Qué es típico de la comida del Caribe?
4. ¿Cuáles son las comidas típicas de Centroamérica? ¿de México?
5. ¿En qué se diferencia la comida de Sudamérica?
6. ¿Cuál es la bebida preferida?

¡FÍJATE! 3
El presente progresivo

The present progressive tense emphasizes actions that are currently happening. The English present progressive is made up of *to be + present participle.* Look at the sentences below and formulate a rule for creating the **presente progresivo** in Spanish.

Sí, <u>estoy</u> **estudiando.**	*Yes, I'm studying.*
¿<u>Estás</u> **mirando** la televisión?	*Are you watching television?*
Le <u>está</u> **haciendo** la cama a ella.	*He's making the bed for her.*
<u>Está</u> **haciéndole** la cama.	
<u>Estamos</u> **perdiendo** el tiempo.	*We're wasting time.*
¿No <u>estáis</u> **viviendo** en California ahora?	*Aren't you (all) living in California now?*
Les <u>están</u> **escribiendo** una carta a sus padres.	*They're writing a letter to their parents.*
<u>Están</u> **escribiéndoles** una carta.	

1. What are the infinitives of the verb forms in bold?
2. How do you form the words in bold?
3. What verb appears directly before *every* boldface verb?
4. In the **presente progresivo,** do any words come between the two parts of the verb?

Several verbs do not form the present participles by taking the infinitive, dropping the **-ar, -er,** or **-ir,** and adding **-ando** or **-iendo.** Some of these irregular verbs are:

Both direct and indirect object pronouns may be attached to the present participle.

pedir (e ➡ i ➡ i)	**pi**diendo
repetir (e ➡ i ➡ i)	re**pi**tiendo
dormir (o ➡ ue ➡ u)	d**u**rmiendo
morir (o ➡ ue ➡ u)	m**u**riendo
ir	**y**endo
caer	ca**y**endo
leer	le**y**endo

Stem-changing **-ir** verbs that change their stem vowel **e ➡ i** or **o ➡ u** in the third-person of the preterit also have this change in the present progressive: **pedir ➡ pidiendo.** Note that when an **-er** or **-ir** verb stem ends in a vowel, the ending **-iendo** changes to **-yendo: caer ➡ cayendo.**

11 **¿Dónde estás, mi hijito?**   José está en su casa de visita de la universidad. Su madre lo llama cada cinco minutos preguntándole lo que está haciendo. Sigue el modelo como lo haría José, usando el presente progresivo.

Modelo   **ESTUDIANTE 1 (MAMÁ):**   José, ¿estás afuera?

   ESTUDIANTE 2 (JOSÉ):   Sí, mamá, estoy lavando mi coche.

1. José, ¿estás en la cocina?
2. José, ¿estás en tu dormitorio?
3. José, ¿estás en la sala?
4. José, ¿estás en el garaje?
5. José, ¿estás en la oficina?

12 **¿Qué están haciendo?**   Mira la foto en la página 167 y describe con diez frases lo que está pasando. Usa el presente progresivo.

13 **¿Eres poeta?**   Have you ever written poetry? **Rime Cinquain** is an excellent form to express yourself poetically. Follow the directions below to write your poem. Then read it to a classmate.

Line 1: one or two words that state your subject or theme
Line 2: two or three words that describe your subject or theme
Line 3: three or four action words describing your subject
Line 4: four or five words that express a personal attitude
Line 5: one or two words that summarize your topic or refer once again to the theme

Modelo

Mi universidad

clases interesantes

estudiando, aprendiendo, viviendo

A veces tengo miedo.

Mi futuro.

●ETAPA 3

¡Cuéntame! ¡Cuéntame!

Ya lo sabemos

En este episodio Rafi va a tomar una decisión muy importante. Vas a saber:

◆ lo que Adriana encontró en el margen del libro del tío Pedro
◆ cómo es posible para Rafi y Chema ir a México en estos momentos
◆ por qué Rafi decide definitivamente ir a Mérida

1. Escribe una lista de los personajes que conoces de la historia de Rafi. Subraya *(Underline)* los nombres de los personajes que mejor conoces. Compara tu lista con la de un compañero. Juntos escriban lo que saben de los personajes subrayados. ¿De quién saben más?

2. Resume *(Summarize)* lo que pasa en el cuento de Rafi. Escribe una o dos oraciones de resumen para los episodios 2, 3 y 4. Sigue el modelo.
   Modelo **Conocimos a Rafi, un estudiante de premedicina, y nos habló de su familia y de su mejor amigo Chema.**

Preguntas personales Las preguntas a continuación pueden ayudar a prepararte para comprender mejor la lectura.

1. ¿Qué son los jeroglíficos? ¿Cuáles son algunas civilizaciones que usaron jeroglíficos?

2. ¿Cuáles son las vacaciones que Uds. tienen durante el año académico? ¿Cómo pasas esas vacaciones generalmente? ¿Viajas? ¿De dónde sacas *(Where do you get)* el dinero para pagar esos viajes?

Estrategias de lectura
Anticipating Content

You can often anticipate the content of a story by paying attention to the title, to any available illustrations, and by quickly reading through the comprehension questions that may follow the passage. Take a look at the following.

◆ *Title:* The title, **La búsqueda comienza,** refers to what search? A search by whom?
◆ *Comprehension questions:* After reading the questions, do you get a general feeling for what happens in this episode? You know that the story seems to concentrate on what Rafi does after he leaves Adriana — what he did when he got back to the dorm. You also find out that the search will most likely take them to Mérida and that something happens that helps Rafi make up his mind.

Now it is your turn to employ the reading strategies you have been learning (identifying cognates, skimming, scanning, and anticipating content). Enjoy the episode!

Rafi y el sacrificio final

Episodio 5: La búsqueda comienza

Rafi y Adriana regresaron a su apartamento donde Adriana le mostró a Rafi lo que encontró. Primero le mostró las palabras «Roma... sacrificio final», «Pedro Lara» y un número de teléfono. Luego Adriana le mostró el libro de su tío donde había un mapa con un código de palabras y jeroglíficos, y debajo del mapa, las palabras «Roma... sacrificio final».

—Mira este mapa con un código debajo. ¿Qué puede significar? —Adriana le preguntó.

—No tengo idea, —contestó Rafi. —No tengo idea. Pero lo que sí sé es que el número de teléfono que está en mi libro es el número del tío Pedro.

Adriana y Rafi hablaron un poco más y luego Rafi regresó a la residencia estudiantil. Cuando llegó, tocó en la puerta de Chema.

—Entra. ¿Qué pasa? —Chema le preguntó casi dormido. Rafi entró y le habló por más de una hora acerca del tío, los libros, la carta de Mérida que encontraron en el baúl, los apuntes que Adriana encontró en los márgenes de los libros y las palabras «Roma... sacrificio final».

Rafi regresó a su cuarto y empezó a leer intensamente «Cómo descifrar misterios de códigos». En la copia del tío, encontró notas que su tío había escrito. También buscó en un libro de México que tenía en su cuarto. Leyó toda la noche. De repente, sonó° el teléfono.

¡Caray! —pensó Rafi. —Son las siete y media de la mañana. ¡Tengo una clase en treinta minutos!

Contestó el teléfono. Era Adriana. Le dijo que trabajó toda la noche con el código en su computadora. —Tienes que pasar por la librería hoy. Tengo información fascinante para ti.

—Bueno, paso por allá esta tarde. —Al colgar° el teléfono, éste sonó de nuevo.

—Rafi, no dormí en toda la noche. Tenemos que ayudar a tu tío. Tenemos que irnos a Mérida. —dijo Chema.

—Chema, ¿cuándo y con qué? No tengo dinero ni para terminar el semestre.

—Escucha, —dijo Chema, —te acuerdas que te dije que mi hermano trabaja para una línea aérea. Pues, lo llamé esta mañana y él siempre recibe boletos gratis°. Creo que nos puede dar dos boletos. Y mañana empiezan las vacaciones. Podemos ir entonces. Además, mis abuelos viven en Mérida y podemos quedarnos° con ellos.

—No sé, no sé. Voy a pensarlo. Ahora, tengo que ir a mi clase. Te llamo después. —Al terminar de hablar con Chema, llamó a su tío. Sonó tres veces el teléfono y el contestador dijo, —Su llamada es importante. Por favor deje un mensaje y le llamo cuando regrese de mi viaje... —En ese momento, Rafi decidió ir a Mérida.

rang

hang up

boletos... *free tickets*

stay

Comprensión

1. ¿Qué le mostró Adriana a Rafi?
2. ¿Qué hizo Rafi al volver a la residencia estudiantil?
3. ¿Qué hizo Rafi al regresar a su cuarto?
4. ¿Qué ocurrió a las siete y media de la mañana?
5. ¿Qué le dijo Chema a Rafi cuando lo llamó por teléfono?
6. ¿Por qué tienen que ir a Mérida?
7. Al principio, Rafi no está convencido de ir. ¿Cuándo y por qué decide ir por fin?

Expansión

(1) Al regresar a la residencia estudiantil, Rafi va inmediatamente a ver a Chema. Según el cuento, hablaron por más de una hora y hablaron de todo. Inventa una parte de la conversación y represéntala con un compañero. (2−3 minutos)

(2) En parejas, inventen y representen la conversación por teléfono entre Chema y su hermano cuando le llama para pedir los boletos de avión. (2−3 minutos)

(3) Antes de salir Rafi llama a sus padres para informarles de su viaje a Mérida. No están en casa. Escribe el mensaje que Rafi les deja en el contestador para que ellos no se preocupen *(so that they don't worry)*.

Modelo   **Hola, soy yo...**

A mirar o escuchar

(4) View the video or listen to the audio CD to find out what happens next to Rafi and Chema. Consult the pre- and post-listening activities in your **Manual de actividades.**

¡Sí, se puede!

1. **La lista.** Tus padres no están convencidos *(convinced)* de que tú trabajas lo suficiente ahora que estás en la universidad. ¡Creen que hay muchas distracciones! Para convencerles de que sí trabajas mucho, escribe una lista de las cinco cosas más importantes (según los padres) que hiciste ayer. Después escribe otra lista de cinco cosas que hiciste que **no** mencionaste a tus padres.

2. **De compras en el mercado.** Algunos estudiantes van a ser vendedores y los otros, clientes. Tu profesor o profesora te va a dar una lista de lo que tienes para vender o de lo que necesitas comprar. Los vendedores necesitan ganar cien dólares y los clientes sólo pueden gastar cien. Va a haber competencia entre los vendedores y ¡sí puedes regatear!

3. **¿Qué estoy haciendo?** Divídanse en grupos de cinco o seis estudiantes. Uno por uno, cada estudiante debe decir lo que tiene en la(s) mano(s) mientras sus compañeros adivinan lo que el / la estudiante está haciendo.

| Modelo | ESTUDIANTE 1: | Tengo un libro abierto en las manos. |
| | GRUPO: | Estás leyendo. |

4. **Tu mejor memoria.** Piensa en el mejor día de Navidad o día festivo que tú pasaste de niño. Escribe un párrafo en que hablas de las cosas más importantes que ocurrieron aquel día. Puedes hablar de: (1) las personas con quienes celebraste; (2) qué comieron y bebieron; (3) las cosas que hicieron; (4) los regalos que dieron y recibieron.

Para recordar

Al terminar este capítulo, tú puedes:

Etapa 1 ¡Sígueme!

☐ talk about the foods you like and dislike

☐ explain the differences in meaning for the word **comida**

☐ talk and write about things you did and events that occurred in the past

Etapa 2 ¡Dime más!

☐ discuss how you like your favorite foods prepared

☐ describe the meanings of **picante**

☐ use irregular verbs in the **pretérito**

☐ order a meal in a restaurant

☐ explain some of the variety of the cuisine in the Spanish-speaking world

☐ use the **presente progresivo**

☐ list three interesting facts about Argentina

Etapa 3 ¡Cuéntame!

☐ list what leads up to Rafi's and Chema's decision to travel to Mérida

*You can practice the concepts from this and earlier chapters by doing the ¡**Recuérdate!** sections in your* **Manual de actividades.**

VOCABULARIO ACTIVO

Verbos

andar   *to walk*

conducir   *to drive*

Las carnes y las aves

el ave   *poultry*
el biftec   *beefsteak*
la carne   *meat*

la hamburguesa   *hamburger*
el jamón   *ham*

el perro caliente   *hot dog*
el pollo   *chicken*

El pescado y los mariscos

el atún   *tuna*
los camarones *(pl.)*   *shrimp*

los mariscos *(pl.)*   *seafood*
el pescado   *fish*

Las frutas

la banana   *banana*
la fruta   *fruit*
la manzana   *apple*

el melón   *melon*
la naranja   *orange*
la pera   *pear*

el tomate   *tomato*

Las verduras

el arroz   *rice*
la cebolla   *onion*
el chile   *chili pepper*
la ensalada   *salad*

los frijoles *(pl.)*   *beans*
la lechuga   *lettuce*
el maíz   *corn*
la papa   *potato*

las papas fritas *(pl.)*   *french fries;
      potato chips*
la patata   *potato*
la verdura   *vegetable*

Los postres

el dulce   *candy; sweet*
la galleta   *cookie*
el helado   *ice cream*

el pastel   *pastry; pie*
el postre   *dessert*
la torta   *cake*

Las bebidas

el agua   *water*
la bebida   *beverage*
el café   *coffee*
la cerveza   *beer*

el jugo   *juice*
la leche   *milk*
el refresco *(con hielo)*   *soft drink
      (with ice)*

el té (helado / caliente)   *tea (iced /
      hot)*
el vino   *wine*

Más comidas

el cereal *cereal*
el huevo *egg*

el pan *bread*
el queso *cheese*

la sopa *soup*
la tostada *toast*

Las comidas

el almuerzo *lunch*
la cena *dinner*

la comida *dinner; meal; food*
el desayuno *breakfast*

la merienda *snack*

Los condimentos y las especias
(Condiments and Spices)

el aceite *oil*
el azúcar *sugar*
la mantequilla *butter*
la mayonesa *mayonnaise*

la mermelada *jam; marmalade*
la mostaza *mustard*
la pimienta *pepper*
la sal *salt*

la salsa de tomate *ketchup*
el vinagre *vinegar*

Unos términos de la cocina
(Cooking Terms)

al horno *baked*
a la parrilla *grilled*
bien cocido, bien hecho *well done, well cooked*
caliente *hot (temperature)*
cocido / cocida *boiled; baked*

crudo / cruda *rare; raw*
duro / dura *hard-boiled*
fresco / fresca *fresh*
frito / frita *fried*
helado / helada *iced*
hervido / hervida *boiled*

picante *spicy*
poco hecho *rare*
término medio *medium*

En el restaurante

el camarero / la camarera *waiter / waitress*
el cliente / la clienta *customer*
el cocinero / la cocinera *cook*
la cuchara *soup spoon; tablespoon*
la cucharita *teaspoon*

el cuchillo *knife*
la especialidad de la casa *specialty of the house*
el mantel *tablecloth*
el menú *menu*
el plato *plate, dish*
la propina *tip*

la servilleta *napkin*
la tarjeta de crédito *credit card*
la taza *cup*
el tenedor *fork*
el vaso *glass*

Otras palabras útiles

anoche *last night*
anteayer *day before yesterday*
el año pasado *last year*
ayer *yesterday*

barato / barata *cheap*
¡Buen provecho! *Enjoy your meal!*
caro / cara *expensive*
debajo (de) *underneath*

encima (de) *on top (of)*
el fin de semana *weekend*
reservar una mesa *to reserve a table*
la semana pasada *last week*

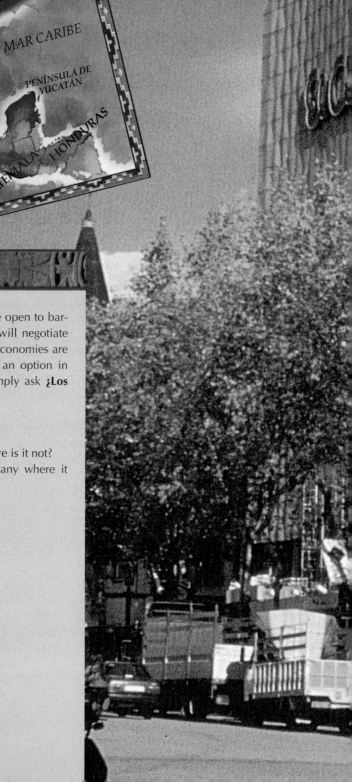

In Spanish-speaking countries, certain parts of the marketplace are open to bargaining or **el regateo.** Most open-air markets and street vendors will negotiate prices. However, not all segments of the Spanish-speaking world economies are open to or welcome negotiating. Interestingly, bargaining is not an option in most Hispanic countries when buying a car. When in doubt, simply ask **¿Los precios son fijos?**

¿Qué te parece?

1. Where in the U.S. marketplace is bargaining acceptable? Where is it not?
2. In what other cultures is bargaining acceptable? Are there any where it is not?
3. What are some bargaining techniques?

¡Qué está de moda?

By the end of this chapter you will be able to:

ETAPA 1 ¡Sígueme!
- explain what clothing you like and dislike
- describe your typical day

ETAPA 2 ¡Dime más!
- give orders and requests
- describe things in the past, telling how they used to be
- travel back in time to discover fascinating details regarding the Aztecs and the Mayans

ETAPA 3 ¡Cuéntame!
- learn what the old woman tells Rafi and Chema and where her information leads them next

■ETAPA 1

¡Sígueme!
¡Sígueme!

 *If this is the beginning of a new semester for you, review the vocabulary and grammar from chapters 1 through 5 so that you are familiar with what has preceded this chapter. Use the ¡Sí, se puede! sections of each chapter, as well as your **Manual de actividades**, to help you with the review. In addition, review what has happened to Rafi, Chema, and Adriana thus far in episodes 1 through 5 of **Rafi y el sacrificio final** so that you can pick up the storyline.*

¡ASÓMATE! 1
La ropa

La ropa

1. el abrigo
2. la blusa
3. el bolso
4. las botas *(pl.)*
5. los calcetines *(pl.)*
6. la camisa
7. la camiseta
8. la chaqueta
9. el cinturón
10. el conjunto
11. la corbata
12. la falda
13. la gorra

14. las medias *(pl.)*
15. los pantalones *(pl.)*
16. los pantalones cortos *(pl.)*
17. los (pantalones) vaqueros, los jeans *(pl.)*
18. el paraguas
19. las sandalias *(pl.)*
20. el sombrero
21. el suéter
22. el traje
23. el traje de baño
24. el vestido
25. el zapato
26. los zapatos de tenis *(pl.)*

Sígue a la pagina 184 por más palabras de vocabulario.

Unos adjetivos

ancho / ancha   *wide*
claro / clara   *light (colored)*
corto / corta   *short*
estampado / estampada   *print; with a design, pattern*
estrecho / estrecha   *narrow, tight*
formal   *formal*
informal   *casual*
largo / larga   *long*
liso / lisa   *solid-colored*
oscuro / oscura   *dark*

Un verbo

llevar   *to wear; to take; to carry*

---

1 **Vamos a viajar.** Do you like to travel? Where would you like to go if you had the time and the money? As a class, decide on a destination. Next, move your desks to form one large circle. Student 1 (**Estudiante 1**) says who he or she is and one item of clothing that he or she will take on the class trip. Student 2 (**Estudiante 2**) says who he or she is, what he or she will take, and repeats **Estudiante 1's** name and what he or she will take. Student 3 (**Estudiante 3**) will do the same, until you have gone around the entire circle. If you forget what someone has said, simply ask that person **¿Qué dijiste, por favor?** or **¿Me lo puedes repetir, por favor?** Follow the model.

Modelo **ESTUDIANTE 1:** Soy Jane y voy a llevar mis zapatos de tenis.

ESTUDIANTE 2: Soy Tom y voy a llevar una camiseta negra. Jane va a llevar sus zapatos de tenis.

ESTUDIANTE 3: Soy Jack y voy a llevar una chaqueta informal. Tom va a llevar una camiseta negra. Jane va a llevar sus zapatos de tenis.

 ¡Atrévete! *encourages pair and group work to provide you with many opportunities during the class period to practice Spanish. When working in pairs or groups, make every effort to speak only Spanish. Additionally, it is important to be supportive of your fellow classmates during pair / group activities, which includes making suggestions and helpful comments and corrections. Because you will be learning from each other, it is good to know the following expressions as ways of interacting:*

Estoy de acuerdo.   *I agree.*
Yo pienso que es...   *I think it's . . .*
¿No debe ser... ?   *Shouldn't it be. . . ?*

2 **¿Quién lleva qué?** Mira a tu alrededor y descríbele a tu compañero(a) lo que alguien en la clase lleva puesto, hablando del estilo *(style)* y el color. Por ejemplo: pantalones cortos o largos, de un solo color o con diseño. Describe por lo menos cinco cosas que la persona escogida lleva y deja que tu compañero(a) adivine a quién describes. Continúa con la descripción hasta que él / ella escoja a la persona correcta. Luego, cambia papeles con tu compañero(a), y que él / ella describa a alguien.

3 **Describe lo que ves.** Trae a la clase una revista de moda o un catálogo y descríbele a tu compañero lo que los modelos llevan puesto. Escoge a cuatro de los modelos y describe la ropa que más te gusta de dos de los modelos, y la que menos te gusta de otros dos. ¿Qué piensa tu compañero? ¿Están Uds. de acuerdo?

4 **¿Tienes una memoria fotográfica?** Mira alrededor de la clase por diez segundos. Cierra los ojos y en un minuto, describe con detalles «quién lleva puesto qué». Después es el turno de tu compañero.

Modelo **Mark lleva una camiseta estampada y unos pantalones negros. Brenda lleva unas botas negras, una falda y un suéter. Julie lleva zapatos de tenis, unos jeans y una chaqueta azul.**

5 **¿Cómo se visten?** Cierra los ojos. Tu compañero(a) te va a hacer cinco preguntas acerca de la ropa que llevan los estudiantes de la clase. Luego tú le haces preguntas a él / ella.

Modelos **¿Qué lleva Matt?**

(o)

¿Quién lleva una camisa negra estampada?

(o)

¿Lleva Sally unos zapatos o unas botas?

6 **De muchos colores.** En la gráfica en **Etapa 1, actividad 6** de tu **Manual de actividades**, llena los espacios en blanco de arriba con el nombre de cinco colores diferentes. Luego, en tres minutos, escribe debajo de cada color toda la ropa que veas en el salón de clase ese color.

1. ¿Qué colores son más populares en tu clase?
2. ¿Qué colores son menos populares en tu clase?

7 **Mi definición de «atractivo».** In a magazine or catalog, identify a model whom you find attractive. Give your partner a ten-page range where the model can be found. Your partner will ask you at least three questions to try to identify the model. Then switch roles.

Modelos **¿Lleva tu modelo favorito pantalones o falda?**

(o)

¿Lleva tu modelo favorito una corbata?

8 **¡Qué dichoso!** You work for a travel agency conducting tours to the following countries. Prepare information sheets for the travelers in your group and include a guide of what to wear. What should you and your fellow travelers take to the following destinations?

1. Argentina en enero
2. España en febrero
3. México en septiembre
4. Puerto Rico en diciembre

*Actividad 9 includes cognates such as **ejecutiva** and **reportar**. Look for other cognates throughout this and subsequent chapters.*

9 **¿Qué se pone?** Help the following people put together a wardrobe for their professional lives. List five things that you encourage them to buy and how many of each item.

1. Marisol va a trabajar para la IBM como ejecutiva.
2. Raúl va a trabajar durante el verano en el parque Yosemite como guardia forestal.
3. Concha, quien tiene su diploma en periodismo, va a reportar para la CNN.
4. Pilar tiene veinticinco años y va a vender *(sell)* ropa en Saks Fifth Avenue.
5. Felipe acaba de graduarse en negocios y tiene una posición con Arthur Andersen.

10 **¿Cuánto gastas** *(spend)* **en un año?** Llena la gráfica en **Etapa 1, actividad 10** de tu **Manual de actividades** con las cosas que has comprado y con las que necesitas comprar. Después, compáralas con las de un(a) compañero(a). Sigue el modelo.

*For additional vocabulary not found in the ¡Asómate! section, consult the **También se dice...** section in Appendix A.*

11 **Mi conjunto favorito.** Contesta las preguntas para describir tu conjunto favorito.

1. ¿Cuál es tu conjunto favorito?
2. ¿De qué color es?
3. ¿De qué tela *(fabric)* es?
4. ¿De qué estilo es?
5. ¿Te lo compraste? Si no, ¿quién te lo compró?
6. ¿Cuándo lo compraste o cuándo te lo compraron?
7. ¿Dónde lo compraste o dónde te lo compraron?
8. ¿Cuándo lo llevas?
9. ¿Por qué te gusta tanto *(so much)?*

¡ENTÉRATE!
La ropa

Si vas a cualquier país hispanohablante vas a ver a los estudiantes universitarios vestidos *(dressed)* más o menos igual que los de los Estados Unidos. Es decir los jeans, zapatos de tenis y camisetas forman el «uniforme» internacional de los estudiantes. También, la gente *(people)* de clase media y clase alta lleva la misma ropa que se ve internacionalmente en esa clase de personas.

Santiago, Chile

México, D.F.

Chanal, México

Colombia

Santa Cruz, Bolivia

Chinchero, Perú

Donde se nota la diferencia de ropa entre los países hispanohablantes es en lo que lleva la gente indígena. Por ejemplo, en México hay sarapes, ponchos y huaraches (sandalias); en Colombia hay rebozos (ponchos) y alpargatas *(espadrilles)*. En Bolivia las mujeres indígenas llevan sombreros distintos a los del Perú.

¿Qué te parece?

1. ¿Qué semejanzas hay entre la ropa de los Estados Unidos y la de los países hispanohablantes? ¿Diferencias?
2. ¿Qué semejanzas hay entre la ropa de la gente joven en los Estados Unidos? ¿Diferencias?
3. ¿Qué determina el uso y las preferencias de la ropa?

¡FÍJATE! 1
Los verbos reflexivos

Each drawing and caption on this page demonstrates that the direct object receives the action of the verb; the subject acts on the direct object noun or pronoun.

    The drawings and captions on the following page demonstrate reflexive verbs. A reflexive verb is used when the subject performs and receives the action of the verb. In order to use reflexive verbs, you need to know the reflexive pronouns. Look at the chart that follows; the reflexive pronouns are highlighted.

Los despiertan.

Alberto la acuesta.

Beatriz lava su coche.

Se despiertan.

Alberto **se** acuesta.

Beatriz **se** lava.

divertirse (e ➡ ie ➡ i)		*to have a good time*	
Siempre	**me**	**divierto**	en su casa.
Siempre	**te**	**diviertes**	en su casa.
Siempre	**se**	**divierte**	en su casa.
Siempre	**nos**	**divertimos**	en su casa.
Siempre	**os**	**divertís**	en su casa.
Siempre	**se**	**divierten**	en su casa.

Reflexive pronouns follow the same rules for position as other object pronouns. They precede a conjugated verb.

Siempre **te diviertes** en su casa.

Reflexive pronouns can either be attached to infinitives and present participles (**-ando, -iendo**) or precede the conjugated verb.

<u>Te</u> vas a divertir.   ¿<u>Te</u> estás divirtiendo?

   (o)   **(o)**

Vas a divertir<u>te</u>.   ¿Estás divirtiéndo<u>te</u>?

Unos verbos reflexivos

1. acordarse de (o ➡ ue)
2. acostarse (o ➡ ue)
3. afeitarse
4. bañarse
5. callarse
6. cepillarse
7. despertarse (e ➡ ie)
8. divertirse (e ➡ ie ➡ i)
9. dormirse (o ➡ ue ➡ u)
10. ducharse
11. irse
12. lavarse
13. levantarse

14. llamarse
15. maquillarse
16. olvidarse de
17. peinarse
18. ponerse (la ropa)
19. ponerse (nervioso)
20. quedarse
21. quitarse (la ropa)
22. reunirse
23. secarse
24. sentarse (e ➡ ie)
25. sentirse (e ➡ ie ➡ i)
26. vestirse (e ➡ i ➡ i)

*Be sure you understand the meaning of the preceding reflexive verbs. Consult the English definitions in the **Vocabulario activo** at the end of the chapter as needed.*

12 **Mímica.**   Juega a la mímica *(charades)* en grupos de cuatro. Escoge un verbo de la lista y actúalo para tu grupo. Todos deben seleccionar cuatro verbos diferentes.

13 **Y la respuesta es...**   Form groups of four to six. One person has a Nerf ball and calls out a reflexive verb infinitive and a pronoun. Then that person tosses the ball to a group member. The catcher has three seconds to give the correct form of the verb. If the catcher does not give the correct form, another member in the group has the opportunity to do so.

14 **Piccionario.**   Create groups of four (two teams of two people). Partner A from each team decides on the same reflexive verb. At the word **comienza,** both Partners A draw the verb on a sheet of scrap paper for his or her Partner B. The first Partner B to correctly say the verb gets a point for his or her team, then switch roles.

15 **¡Batalla!**   Work with a partner. Make a tic-tac-toe grid. In each of the nine spaces of the grid, write a different reflexive verb infinitive in Spanish. Do not show it to your partner. Next, take turns saying in English one of the infinitives. If your partner says one of the verbs you have written, mark it out with an *X*. The first person to mark off three verbs either horizontally, diagonally, or vertically wins the round.

16 **Los días de Lupe y Roberto.**   A continuación vas a encontrar descripciones fuera de orden de momentos en la vida diaria de Lupe y Roberto. Ordena las descripciones poniendo las actividades en orden cronológico.

El día de Lupe
1. Antes de irse de la casa, se acordó de la tarea que no hizo para su clase de historia.
2. Se duchó.
3. Se maquilló.
4. Llegó a la clase de historia y se quitó el abrigo.
5. Se vistió.
6. Se secó.

El día de Roberto
1. Se acostó tarde.
2. Se levantó rápidamente a las ocho.
3. Se despertó tarde.
4. No se durmió inmediatamente.
5. Se divirtió con sus amigos.
6. Se fue después de las clases para pasar el fin de semana con sus padres y ver a sus amigos.
7. Se fue a la clase de química.

17 **Mi día típico.** ¿Cómo es un día típico para ti? Escribe por lo menos *(at least)* cinco cosas que haces en un día típico y a qué hora haces estas cosas. Usa por lo menos cinco verbos reflexivos. Después, lee tu lista a un compañero de clase. ¿Cómo son similares sus listas? ¿Cómo son diferentes?

18 **¿Conoces bien a tus compañeros?** One classmate will leave the room and the rest will decide on five questions using reflexive verbs to ask the classmate, who is out in the hall. Then, as a class, predict how your classmate will answer. Call the classmate back into the room and ask the questions. How many of the answers did you predict correctly?

19 **¿Cuándo lo hace?** Isabel y Maruja son nuevas compañeras de cuarto. Isabel le pregunta a Maruja sobre sus hábitos. Contesta las preguntas siguientes como si fueras *(as if you were)* Maruja.

1. ¿A qué hora te despiertas?
2. ¿A qué hora te levantas?
3. ¿Prefieres ducharte o bañarte? ¿Cuándo?
4. ¿Te quedas en el cuarto para estudiar o te vas a la biblioteca?
5. ¿Qué haces para divertirte?
6. ¿A qué hora te acuestas?

Ahora, haz las mismas preguntas a un compañero de clase y reacciona a sus respuestas.

Modelo   **Estudiante 1:**   Me despierto a las siete.

               Estudiante 2:   Yo también me despierto a las siete.

(o)

                              Yo no. Me despierto a las siete y media.

20 **A conocerte más aún.** Aquí hay unas preguntas para dar más información a tu compañero sobre tus hábitos. Contesta las preguntas y luego escucha las respuestas de tu compañero.

1. ¿Qué te pones cuando sales con esa «persona especial»?
2. ¿Cuánto tiempo necesitas para dormirte?
3. ¿Prefieres a las mujeres que se maquillan mucho o poco?
4. Cuando te quitas la ropa, ¿dónde pones la ropa sucia?
5. ¿Cómo te diviertes?
6. ¿Siempre te acuerdas de hacer toda la tarea?
7. De vez en cuando, ¿qué te olvidas de hacer?
8. Si tienes tiempo, ¿con quién(es) te reúnes?
9. ¿Dónde te gusta sentarte en el cine, adelante o atrás?
10. Cuando estás durmiéndote, ¿te acuerdas de vez en cuando de cosas que no hiciste durante *(during)* el día?
11. ¿Cuándo te pones nervioso / nerviosa?
12. ¿Cuándo te sientes feliz?

¿Cuántas preguntas contestaron Uds. de manera similar? ¿De manera diferente?

¡ENTÉRATE!
Un día típico en la vida de…

Bob Vila

Carta de Bob Vila, el «Handyman»

¡Saludos estudiantes! Les escribo desde una altitud de treinta y siete mil pies y a una velocidad de más de 500 millas por hora. Resulta que ésta es una situación bastante típica para mí pues viajo en avión con mucha frecuencia.

Cuando tengo la dicha de quedarme en casa mi situación es mucho más acogedora *(welcoming, cozy)*. Vivo en una casa amplia y muy vieja en la ciudad de Cambridge, Massachusetts. Por costumbre me despierto temprano y generalmente me levanto entre las seis y las siete de la mañana, dependiendo de lo que hay que hacer ese día en particular. Nunca tengo un día verdaderamente típico y francamente así lo prefiero. Generalmente no desayuno más que una naranja y un café pues nunca tengo mucha hambre a esa hora. Aunque me encanta pasar un par de horas en el gimnasio, prefiero hacerlo por la tarde. Mantener una buena dieta es un asunto bien difícil porque no tengo rutina fija. Ayer comí un sándwich de langosta al mediodía. Hoy acabo de comerme una pechuguita de pollo *(chicken breast)* cortesía de American Airlines.

Tengo mi propia oficina en la casa. Las oficinas principales de mi negocio se encuentran en un pueblo en Cape Cod, donde vivo en el verano. Trato de terminar mis asuntos para las cuatro de la tarde, cuando mi hija de doce años regresa del colegio. Me gusta mucho salir al mercado con mi esposa y comprar todo para la cena. Nos gusta mucho cocinar juntos. Si no hay compromisos sociales tenemos que decidir si hay algo en la tele que valga la pena *(worthwhile)*. Muy a menudo nos gusta leer un buen libro y, a las once, nos acostamos.

Bob Vila

¿Qué te parece?

1. ¿Dónde está el señor Vila cuando nos escribe?
2. ¿Qué hace generalmente por la mañana?
3. ¿Qué le gusta hacer por la tarde?

Emelina Edwards

Un día típico en la vida de Emelina Edwards

Me levanto a las 6:00 de la mañana y me pongo la ropa de hacer ejercicios. Mientras corro, expreso gratitud por el nuevo día y busco motivación para terminar las dos millas mientras repito mi larga lista de afirmaciones. Es decir, soy saludable, fuerte, poderosa, agradecida, cariñosa y ¡esta carrera la puedo hacer! Entre mis compromisos con el programa de entrenamiento de pesas que se lleva a cabo en mi casa, preparo comidas saludables y nutritivas, medito, escribo y leo literatura motivacional de inspiración o de buena salud. Soy de la creencia de que cada día de mi vida debo alimentar tanto mi mente como mi cuerpo y espíritu.

¿Qué te parece?

1. ¿Cuántas millas corre la señora Edwards cada día?
2. ¿Qué tipos de comidas se prepara?
3. ¿Qué cree ella?

Rafael Romero Díaz

Un día típico en la vida de Rafael Romero Díaz

A las 7:30 de la mañana me levanto y me baño. Después, desayuno jugo de frutas y cereal. Salgo para el trabajo a las 8:30 de la mañana y sólo me toma veinte minutos en llegar ya que vivo bastante cerca del museo. Empezamos a trabajar a las 9:00. Primeramente leo el resumen de la prensa, las noticias culturales y artísticas de los tres diarios de Caracas. También consulto la Red internacional. Después de esto, contesto y firmo las cartas, faxes, memos y cualquier otra correspondencia que tenga pendiente. De costumbre hay una reunión con la gente de la oficina, mayormente con los gerentes, para discutir las decisiones que deben de tomarse en ese día. Entre las 10:00 y las 12:00 recibo a las personas que quieren reunirse conmigo. También contesto las llamadas telefónicas que tenga pendientes. Entre las 12:00 y la 1:00, voy a mi casa para almorzar. Generalmente, me como un sándwich con una ensalada y queso. Estoy de regreso a la oficina a las 2:00 de la tarde. Doy una ronda por las salas de exhibición y por los jardines para cerciorarme *(to make sure)* de que todo esté en orden y que no haya problemas. A las 3:00 me reúno con mi jefe. Ahí recibo instrucciones para preparar la agenda. También escribo cartas, memorandums y hago tiempo para tareas más intelectuales. Esto me lleva a las 6:00 ó 7:00 de la tarde y me voy para mi casa. Por lo general, camino 45 minutos por los alrededores. Si no tengo compromisos de relaciones públicas, ceno a eso de las 8:00 de la noche. Después, hablo con mi familia, leo un rato, veo la televisión, quizás una película o noticias. Me acuesto a la medianoche.

¿Qué te parece?

1. Después de leer la prensa, ¿qué hace el señor Díaz?
2. ¿Qué se come al mediodía?
3. ¿A qué hora se reúne con su jefe?
4. ¿A dónde se va a las 6:00 ó 7:00 de la tarde?

1 Ahora te toca a ti. Formen grupos de cuatro. Usen los siguientes verbos para indicar a los otros una acción. Cada uno debe tomar su turno para representar la acción que le tocó.

1. hablar en español	11. leer su libro de español
2. no hablar en inglés	12. comer los espaguetis
3. preparar unos huevos	13. no abrir los cuadernos
4. llevar su mochila	14. ponerse un sombrero
5. no cerrar los libros	15. ponerse el abrigo
6. levantarse	16. quitarse la chaqueta
7. bailar la salsa	17. no dormirse
8. cantar su canción favorita	18. despertarse
9. sentarse	19. divertirse
10. no beber agua	

2 Que no se olviden... Eduardo cannot help but overhear his loud neighbors. They are giving advice to their son and daughter who have been home for the weekend and are going back to college. What advice did they give them? Follow the model.

Modelo estudiar mucho ➠ **Estudien mucho.**

1. comer tres comidas balanceadas
2. hacer su tarea
3. dormir ocho horas cada noche
4. no olvidarse de tomar sus vitaminas
5. no acostarse tarde
6. acordarse de escribir a sus abuelos
7. no salir todas las noches
8. ponerse un abrigo si hace frío
9. llevar un paraguas si va a llover
10. ¡y divertirse!

3 ¿Cómo las contestaría tu profesor o profesora? How often have you heard the following questions asked in class? Maybe you have even asked some of them! Answer these questions as your instructor would answer them using **mandatos de Uds.** Work with a partner.

Modelo ESTUDIANTE 1: ¿Necesitamos hacer la tarea para mañana?

ESTUDIANTE 2: Sí, hagan la tarea para mañana.

(o)

Sí, háganla para mañana.

1. ¿Debemos llevar los libros a la clase?
2. ¿Necesitamos hablar en español todo el tiempo?
3. ¿Podemos salir temprano?
4. ¿Podemos llegar tarde?
5. ¿Tenemos que tomar un examen pasado mañana?
6. ¿Podemos usar nuestros apuntes durante el examen?
7. ¿Está bien si no venimos a la clase mañana?
8. ¿Podemos comer en la sala de clase?

4 **Los compañeros de cuarto imposibles.** Sad, but true. This year you have impossible roommates! Tell them five things they should or should not do around the dorm room or apartment. Share your list with a partner. Follow the model.

Modelo **Cierren la puerta del refrigerador.**

No dejen su ropa sucia en el suelo.

5 **El robot sirviente.** The year is 2020, and among your possessions you have a voice-activated robot housekeeper. Tell your robot five things you would like it to do. Follow the model.

Modelo **Jaime, saque la basura, por favor. Luego, vaya al mercado y compre pan, por favor.**

¡FÍJATE! 3
Un resumen de los pronombres de los complementos directos, indirectos y reflexivos

Los pronombres de los complementos directos	
me	nos
te	os
lo, la	los, las

Los pronombres de los complementos indirectos	
me	nos
te	os
le (se)	les (se)

Los pronombres reflexivos	
me	nos
te	os
se	se

Also, remember the following guidelines on position and sequence.

Position

◆ Object pronouns *must be attached* to affirmative commands.
Mándele la carta al señor Rodríguez.

◆ Object pronouns come *before* the verb *except* in affirmative commands.
Mi secretario le mandó la carta.

◆ Object pronouns can also be attached to the end of:
   a. infinitives
   El señor Rodríguez va a contestar<u>me</u> rápidamente.

   b. present participles (**-ando, -iendo**)
   Está leyéndo<u>la</u> ahora.

Sequence

◆ When a direct and indirect object pronoun are used together, the *indirect object precedes the direct object.*
   Sí, mánde<u>sela</u> ahora mismo.

¡FÍJATE! 4
El imperfecto

In chapter 5 you learned how to express certain ideas and notions that happened in the past with the preterit. Spanish has another past tense, **el imperfecto,** that expresses habitual past actions, descriptions, or conditions.

-ar: hablar		
yo habl**aba**	nosotros, nosotras	habl**ábamos**
tú habl**abas**	vosotros, vosotras	habl**abais**
él, ella, Ud. habl**aba**	ellos, ellas, Uds.	habl**aban**

-er: comer		
yo com**ía**	nosotros, nosotras	com**íamos**
tú com**ías**	vosotros, vosotras	com**íais**
él, ella, Ud. com**ía**	ellos, ellas, Uds.	com**ían**

-ir: vivir		
yo viv**ía**	nosotros, nosotras	viv**íamos**
tú viv**ías**	vosotros, vosotras	viv**íais**
él, ella, Ud. viv**ía**	ellos, ellas, Uds.	viv**ían**

There are only three irregular verbs in the **imperfecto: ir, ser,** and **ver.**

ir		
yo iba	nosotros, nosotras	íbamos
tú ibas	vosotros, vosotras	ibais
él, ella, Ud. iba	ellos, ellas, Uds.	iban

ser			
yo	era	nosotros, nosotras	éramos
tú	eras	vosotros, vosotras	erais
él, ella, Ud.	era	ellos, ellas, Uds.	eran

ver			
yo	veía	nosotros, nosotras	veíamos
tú	veías	vosotros, vosotras	veíais
él, ella, Ud.	veía	ellos, ellas, Uds.	veíamos

The **imperfecto** is used:

1. To provide background information, set the stage, or express a condition that existed

<u>Llovía</u> mucho.	*It was raining a lot.*
<u>Era</u> una noche oscura y nublada.	*It was a dark, cloudy night.*

2. To describe habitual or often repeated actions

<u>Comíamos</u> pescado los viernes.	*We ate (used to eat) fish on Fridays.*
<u>Íbamos</u> a las montañas para pasar las vacaciones cada año.	*We went (used to go) to the mountains for vacation every year.*
<u>Corrían</u> a las seis de la mañana.	*They ran (used to run) at 6:00 A.M.*

Some words or expressions that express habitual and repeated actions are:

a menudo	*often*
casi siempre	*almost always*
frecuentemente	*frequently*
generalmente	*generally*
muchas veces	*many times*
mucho	*a lot*
normalmente	*normally*
siempre	*always*
todos los días	*every day*

3. To express *was* or *were* _____ *ing*

¿<u>Dormías</u>?	*Were you sleeping?*
<u>Estudiaban</u> cuando llamé.	*They were studying when I called.*
Alberto <u>leía</u> mientras Alicia <u>escuchaba</u> música.	*Alberto was reading while Alicia was listening to music.*

4. To tell time

<u>Era</u> la una.	*It was 1:00.*
<u>Eran</u> las seis y media.	*It was 6:30.*

6 **¿Cierto o falso?** Lee las frases siguientes. Escribe una tacha (✓) en la columna «cierto» si la frase es correcta, o en la columna «falso» si la frase no es correcta.

Antes de venir a la universidad...

	Cierto	Falso
1. vivías en un apartamento.	✓	
2. tenías un animal.		✓
3. mirabas mucho la televisión.		
4. no te gustaba comer las verduras.		
5. eras un buen estudiante.		
6. tenías muchos amigos.		
7. estudiabas mucho.		
8. tenías mucho dinero para gastar.		
9. llevabas pantalones cortos.		
10. tocabas un instrumento.		
11. sacabas la basura.		
12. manejabas.		

Ahora compara tus respuestas con un compañero. Sigue el modelo.

Modelo   **Antes de venir a la universidad, vivía en un apartamento. No tenía un animal.**

7 **¿Con qué frecuencia hacías lo siguiente?** Busca la gráfica para **Etapa 2, actividad 7** en tu **Manual de actividades.** Escribe una tacha (✓) en la columna apropiada que mejor describa con qué frecuencia hacías las cosas siguientes en el pasado. Luego, compara tus respuestas con las de un compañero. ¿Qué hacían Uds. con más frecuencia? ¿Con menos frecuencia? ¿Tú y tu compañero tenían algunos hábitos similares?

*To do **actividad 8,** refer back to earlier chapters, especially chapter 3, for vocabulary related to the house, if necessary.*

8 **Mi primera casa.** Se dice que los estadounidenses se mudan *(move)* tres veces y media en su vida. ¿Y tú? ¿En cuántas casas has vivido *(have you lived)?* ¿Cómo era tu primera casa? Descríbele a un compañero tu primera casa. Dile cinco cosas.

Modelo   **Mi primera casa estaba en una ciudad pequeña. Tenía dos dormitorios. La cocina era amarilla. El comedor y la sala eran pequeños. Tenía solamente *(only)* un baño.**

9 **La vida en aquel entonces.** Mira el dibujo y con un compañero, hagan diez frases que contesten la pregunta, «¿cómo era la vida en los años cincuenta?» Usen verbos como **tener, estar, ser, haber, limpiar** y **arreglar.**

10 **Los días típicos.** ¿Qué hacías durante los veranos cuando eras niño o niña? ¿Cómo era un día típico para ti? Dile a un compañero cinco cosas que hacías. Contesta unas preguntas como éstas:

1. ¿A qué hora te levantabas?
2. ¿Te duchabas o te bañabas?
3. ¿Cómo te vestías?
4. ¿Dónde jugabas?
5. ¿Qué más hacías?

11 **Preguntas personales.** Cuando tenías dieciséis años, ¿qué hacías en las situaciones siguientes? Circula y pregunta a tres estudiantes y llena la gráfica en **Etapa 2, actividad 11** de tu **Manual de actividades** con tus resultados.

12 **A conocerme mejor.** Escribe una carta a tu mejor amigo o amiga. Incluye diez cosas de cuando eras niño o niña. Tu profesor o profesora va a leer las cartas a la clase para ver si Uds. pueden adivinar *(guess)* quién las escribió.

¡ENTÉRATE!

Los aztecas y los mayas

MAR CARIBE

El observatorio

MÉXICO

Chichén Itzá

•Tenochtitlán

Palenque

Tikal

GUATEMALA

Copán

HONDURAS

OCÉANO PACÍFICO

Chac Mool

El imperio maya

La civilización maya se desarrolló *(developed)* en el área que hoy se conoce como Yucatán, México y también en Guatemala y Honduras. La época maya comenzó alrededor *(around)* del siglo VII A.C. (antes de Cristo) y empezó a decaer *(to decline)* alrededor del año 1100. De todas las civilizaciones precolombinas, la cultura maya fue la más alta y superior. Los mayas eran expertos en las matemáticas y en la astronomía. Con su conocimiento de matemáticas y astronomía, los mayas desarrollaron un calendario muy preciso con 365 días.

También eran expertos en métodos de agricultura y en arquitectura. Esto se puede ver hoy en día en la ciudad maya de Palenque y la estructura de Chichén Itzá en el estado de Yucatán, México.

Unas mayas de hoy

Estatuas toltecas, Tula, México

Unos descendientes
de los aztecas

¿Qué te parece?

1. ¿Por qué se considera la cultura maya tan superior?

2. ¿Qué semejanzas hay entre los mayas y los aztecas?

3. ¿Por qué estaban tan avanzados los aztecas?

4. ¿Qué ciudad moderna está cerca de Tenochtitlán?

5. Probablemente, ¿qué problemas tenían los aztecas?

mperio azteca

…o Hernán Cortés (1485–1547) llegó a Tenochtitlán en 1519 describió
…al azteca como la octava *(eighth)* maravilla del mundo. Había tem-
…rámides, calles muy anchas, mercados y casas con arquitectura muy
…os aztecas eran una de las civilizaciones más avanzadas de la época
…mbina. Tenían una sociedad muy organizada. Había comerciantes,
…tes *(priests)*, militares y hasta una clase noble.

…nbién tenían un sistema de escritura y un calendario muy similar al
…con 365 días.

LA RED ¡Navega la Internet!

To discover more information on
the culture of this chapter, check
the Holt Web site and other
suggestions listed in your
Manual de actividades.

http://www.hrwcollege.com/

ETAPA 3

¡Cuéntame!
¡Cuéntame!

Ya lo sabemos

En el episodio «El viaje continúa», Rafi y Chema van a recibir otra clave *(key)* al misterio y eso les va a hacer pensar en varias teorías posibles. En este episodio:

◆ Rafi y Chema conocen a una camarera con información que puede ser valiosa.
◆ La información nueva les deja a Rafi y Chema con más preguntas de lo que deben hacer.

Preguntas personales

1. La clave tiene que ver con una foto que Rafi tiene en su cartera *(wallet)*. ¿Tú tienes fotos en tu cartera? ¿En tu cuarto? ¿De quiénes son? ¿Por qué tienes estas fotos?
2. Es una coincidencia que una camarera ve la foto de Rafi y recuerda que es la misma foto que vio la semana pasada. ¿Qué coincidencias importantes o interesantes puedes recordar de tu pasado? ¿Cómo afectaron o cambiaron tu vida o la vida de otra persona?

Estrategias de lectura
Prior Knowledge

You may have recognized that the **Ya lo sabemos** sections are designed to help you establish a link between your prior knowledge (what you have already learned or experienced) and the content of the episode. Cognitive psychologists tell us that it is much easier to learn something new or, in this case, to understand a reading passage if you can tap into and build upon prior knowledge. In the **Ya lo sabemos** section in this chapter you were directed toward thinking about photos you may have or carry in your wallet, as well as about coincidences that you or someone you may know have experienced. Perhaps they were even life-altering coincidences.

When you prepare to read, it is important to use all the tools you have (such as skimming, scanning, and anticipating content) to identify potential points of linkage between the passage and your own experience and knowledge. Then ask yourself questions to prepare you to relate better to that passage. In *¡Atrévete!,* this has been done for you in the **Ya lo sabemos** sections, so carefully ponder the questions provided.

Rafi y el sacrificio final

Episodio 6: El viaje continúa

Rafi no podía moverse. No podía hablar. No sabía qué hacer. Chema lo miraba sin saber qué decirle. —Mira, Rafi, tiene que ser una coincidencia, —dijo Chema finalmente.

—Sí, debe ser una coincidencia, —respondió Rafi, pero con poco entusiasmo. En ese momento llegó su comida.

Cuando terminaron, Lupe, la camarera, regresó para quitar los platos y dejar la cuenta. Lupe era una mujer baja, un poco gordita, con pelo largo y castaño. Tenía unos sesenta años, o quizás más. Rafi abrió su cartera para pagar cuando de repente° ella dijo, —¡Qué extraño! Ud. tiene la misma foto que otro cliente tenía.

suddenly

—¿Qué dijo? —Rafi y Chema gritaron a la misma vez.

—Sí, hace unos días un cliente abrió su cartera y tenía la misma foto. ¿Quiénes son?

—Es mi familia, —contestó Rafi. —Señora, dígame, por favor, ¿cómo era ese hombre?

—Pues, no me acuerdo muy bien. Tenía el pelo castaño, era alto y joven, de unos 30 ó 40 años. Y estaba con una mujer. Y me acuerdo de ella muy bien porque tenía un bolso muy elegante, fino y bonito con las iniciales PR.

Rafi y Chema no podían creer lo que oían. Había tantas teorías... una fue que Pedro Lara estaba aquí hace unos días en este mismo restaurante y estaba con una mujer, una mujer con las iniciales PR. ¿Podía ser la misteriosa Pilar de quien Pedro recibió la carta? Chema temía algo diferente y no quería que Rafi lo pensara. Quizás, pensó Chema, alguien había robado la cartera del tío y la usó.

Por fin Rafi pudo hablar y le preguntó a Lupe, —¿Ud. no se acuerda de lo que hablaban?

—Pues sí, señor, —les dijo con una sonrisa°, —Dijeron que tenían que ir o al Perú o a Chichén Itzá.

smile

Rafi y Chema salieron del restaurante. Cada uno pensaba en la misma cosa. Les quedaban sólo dos días de vacaciones y ya iban a empezar las clases de nuevo en la universidad. Lo que no sabían era lo que iban a hacer ahora.

Comprensión

1. ¿Quién es Lupe? ¿Cómo es ella?
2. ¿Cuándo vio Lupe la foto? ¿Qué dijo al verla?
3. ¿De quién es la foto?
4. En tu opinión, ¿quién fue el hombre que tenía la misma foto que Rafi? Explica.
5. ¿Con quién estaba el hombre con la foto?
6. Según Lupe, ¿de qué hablaron?

Expansión

(1) ¿Qué crees que Rafi y Chema van a hacer ahora? ¿Cuáles son las posibilidades? En grupos de tres estudiantes, discutan esas posibilidades. En la opinión de Uds., ¿cuál es la más probable?

(2) En grupos de tres, hagan los papeles de Rafi, Chema y Lupe y representen la escena en el restaurante. Sean creativos y añadan *(add)* la parte en que piden su comida.

(3) También en grupos de tres, inventen y representen la escena en el restaurante entre Lupe, el otro cliente con la misma foto que Rafi y la mujer con el bolso que tiene las iniciales PR.

(4) Rafi quiere escribir una carta electrónica a su padre para contarle lo que ocurrió en el restaurante. Ayúdale a escribir esa carta. Escribe la carta electrónica en tu **Manual de actividades (Etapa 3, Expansión,** en el **capítulo 6).**

A mirar o escuchar

(5) View the video or listen to the audio CD to find out what happens next to Rafi and Chema. Consult the pre- and post-listening activities in your **Manual de actividades.**

1. **Los anuncios comerciales.** En parejas, escriban un anuncio comercial de unos quince segundos para vender un producto. ¡No se olviden de los mandatos formales, los complementos directos e indirectos y los verbos reflexivos! Después, presenten el anuncio a sus compañeros.

2. **Otra vez poeta.** Mira las instrucciones en el capítulo 5, página 171 de cómo escribir un poema de tipo «cinquain». El tema esta vez es tu niñez. Usa el imperfecto de los verbos.

3. **El primer amor.** Casi siempre nos acordamos de nuestro primer amor. Imagínate que tu primer novio, o primera novia fuera una persona perfecta, ¡el novio, o la novia ideal! Escribe una descripción de cómo era él o ella. También debes hablar de las cosas que él o ella hacía que a ti te gustaban tanto.

4. **Si fueras millonario...** Imagínate que ya te graduaste y que tienes el trabajo de tus sueños. Te gusta vestirte bien y tienes el dinero para comprar la ropa que quieras. ¿Qué ropa compras? Describe dos o tres de tus compras, en detalle, a un compañero. Usa **ir a +** *infinitive.* Sigue el modelo.

Modelo   Primero, voy a comprar un traje. El traje va a ser gris y de lana de buena calidad. Voy a ir a Brooks Brothers para comprarlo. Luego, voy a comprar una cor-

bata de seda *(silk).* Va a ser gris estampada. También voy a comprar seis camisas blancas de manga *(sleeve)* larga.

 You can practice concepts from this and earlier chapters by doing the ***¡Recuérdate!*** *sections in your* ***Manual de actividades.***

Para recordar

Having finished this chapter, you are now able to:

Etapa 1 ¡Sígueme!

❏ explain what you and others are wearing

❏ go shopping for clothes, ask for, try on, and purchase what you need

❏ describe a typical day

Etapa 2 ¡Dime más!

❏ make requests and give instructions to people with whom you are not on a first-name basis

❏ review direct object, indirect object, and reflexive pronouns

❏ describe in the past, telling how things used to be

❏ relate at least three interesting facts about the Mayans and the Aztecs

Etapa 3 ¡Cuéntame!

❏ learn what a waitress tells Rafi and Chema and where her information could lead them next

VOCABULARIO ACTIVO

La ropa

el abrigo   *overcoat*
la blusa   *blouse*
el bolso   *purse*
las botas *(pl.)*   *boots*
los calcetines *(pl.)*   *socks*
la camisa   *shirt*
la camiseta   *T-shirt*
la chaqueta   *jacket*
el cinturón   *belt*
el conjunto   *outfit*

la corbata   *tie*
la falda   *skirt*
la gorra   *cap*
los jeans   *jeans*
las medias *(pl.)*   *stockings, hose*
los pantalones *(pl.)*   *pants*
    los pantalones cortos *(pl.)*   *shorts*
    los (pantalones) vaqueros *(pl.)*
        jeans
el paraguas   *umbrella*

las sandalias *(pl.)*   *sandals*
el sombrero   *hat*
el suéter   *sweater*
el traje   *suit*
el traje de baño   *swimsuit, bathing suit*
el vestido   *dress*
el zapato   *shoe*
los zapatos de tenis   *tennis shoes*

Unos adjetivos

ancho / ancha   *wide*
claro / clara   *light (colored)*
corto / corta   *short*
estampado / estampada   *print; with a pattern, design*

estrecho / estrecha   *narrow, tight*
formal   *formal*
informal   *casual*

largo / larga   *long*
liso / lisa   *solid-colored*
oscuro / oscura   *dark*

Un verbo

llevar   *to wear; to take; to carry*

Unos verbos reflexivos

acordarse de (o ➡ ue) *to remember*

acostarse (o ➡ ue) *to go to bed*

afeitarse *to shave*

bañarse *to bathe*

callarse *to get / keep quiet*

cepillarse *to brush (one's hair, teeth)*

despertarse (e ➡ ie) *to wake up, to awaken*

divertirse (e ➡ ie ➡ i) *to enjoy oneself, to have fun*

dormirse (o ➡ ue ➡ u) *to fall asleep*

ducharse *to shower*

irse *to go away, to leave*

lavarse *to wash oneself*

levantarse *to get up; to stand up*

llamarse *to be called*

maquillarse *to put on make up*

olvidarse de *to forget*

peinarse *to comb one's hair*

ponerse (la ropa) *to get (dressed)*

ponerse (nervioso) *to get (nervous)*

quedarse *to stay, to remain*

quitarse (la ropa) *to take off (one's clothes)*

reunirse *to get together, to meet*

secarse *to dry off*

sentarse (e ➡ ie) *to sit*

sentirse (e ➡ ie ➡ i) *to feel*

vestirse (e ➡ i ➡ i) *to get dressed*

Otras palabras útiles

casi siempre *almost always*

frecuentemente *frequently*

generalmente *generally*

muchas veces *many times*

normalmente *normally*

todos los días *every day*

¿Cómo puedes prolongar la vida? El secreto más grande para prolongar la vida es el poder escoger a tus padres y a tus abuelos. Pero, por supuesto, no tenemos control de quiénes serán nuestros padres. Sin embargo, sí tenemos control de seleccionar opciones que pueden prolongar y preservar la calidad de nuestro estilo de vida.

Las cuatro opciones que prolongan más la vida son: el ejercicio, la nutrición, la prevención de accidentes y el evitar el uso de productos que contienen el tabaco. Los accidentes son la causa principal de muertes durante la adolescencia y los años de los veinte. Como resultado, es muy importante tener precaución y observar reglas de seguridad.

En nuestra edad media y los años avanzados, el cáncer y las enfermedades del corazón son las causas principales de riesgo para nuestra salud. Para reducir el riesgo de estas enfermedades, es importante hacer ejercicios regularmente, seguir una dieta nutritiva y evitar el uso del tabaco. La combinación de todo esto puede ayudar al individuo a vivir una vida mucho más sana *(healthy)*.

¿Qué te parece?

1. ¿Vives una vida sana? ¿Qué haces (o no haces) para tener una vida más sana?
2. ¿Crees que tus padres viven una vida sana? Explica.
3. ¿Crees que es más fácil vivir una vida sana a ciertas edades? ¿Por qué?
4. ¿Qué tipo de ejercicios te gusta hacer? ¿Lo haces todos los días?
5. ¿Sigues una dieta nutritiva? Explica.

¿Cómo te sientes?

By the end of this chapter you will be able to:

ETAPA 1 ¡Sígueme!

- explain what ails you and understand when others tell you "where it hurts"
- tell your friends what to do and what not to do

ETAPA 2 ¡Dime más!

- distinguish between the "pretérito" and the "imperfecto" and use them correctly
- travel vicariously to Peru and explore the fascinating ancient world of the Incas

ETAPA 3 ¡Cuéntame!

- discover who lives or dies in a mysterious accident

¡Sígueme!

¡ASÓMATE! 1
El cuerpo humano

El cuerpo humano

1. la boca
2. el brazo
3. la cabeza
4. la cara
5. el corazón
6. el cuello
7. el cuerpo
8. el dedo
9. el dedo del pie
10. el diente
11. la espalda

12. el estómago
13. la garganta
14. la mano
15. la nariz
16. el ojo
17. la oreja
18. el pecho
19. el pelo
20. el pie
21. la pierna
22. la sangre

Unos verbos

doler (ue)	*to hurt*
estar enfermo / enferma	*to be sick*
estar sano / sana, saludable	*to be healthy*
ser alérgico / alérgica	*to be allergic*

Otras palabras útiles

el oído	*inner ear*
la salud	*health*

1 **Simón dice...**   ¿Jugabas al **Simón dice...** cuando eras niño / niña? ¿O quizás lo juegas ahora con algunos niños? Escucha a tu profesor o profesora para practicar el vocabulario nuevo.

2 **¿Es un monstruo o una obra de arte?** Con un compañero, muevan *(move)* sus sillas o escritorios para que **Estudiante 1** mire la pizarra y **Estudiante 2** no la mire. Su instructor va a dibujar un monstruo en la pizarra y **Estudiante 1** va a describir a **Estudiante 2** lo que se ve. **Estudiante 2** va a dibujar lo que **Estudiante 1** dice. Cuando terminen con el primer dibujo, cambien de posición.

Algunas expresiones útiles

El monstruo tiene...
Hay / No hay
A la derecha
A la izquierda

3 **Vamos a dibujar.** Su profesor les va a dar un papel largo y unos rotuladores *(markers)*. Una persona del grupo va a tumbarse *(lie down)* encima del papel. Otra persona va a calcar *(trace)* alrededor del compañero. Después de calcarla, cada persona en el grupo tiene que marcar *(label)* por lo menos *(at least)* tres partes del cuerpo.

4 **¿Cómo se escribe?** Escribe la primera y la última letra de una de sus palabras nuevas. Un compañero tiene que terminarla. Sigue el modelo. Luego, cambien de posición.

Modelo ESTUDIANTE 1: e _ _ _ _ _ a

ESTUDIANTE 2: e s p a l d a

5 **Doctor, ayúdeme por favor. Me duele(n)...** En grupos de cuatro o cinco sigan el modelo.

Modelo ESTUDIANTE 1: Doctor, ayúdeme por favor. Me duelen los ojos.

ESTUDIANTE 2: Doctor, ayúdeme también por favor. Me duele el brazo y me duelen los ojos.

ESTUDIANTE 3: Doctor, ayúdeme también. Me duele la garganta, me duele el brazo y me duelen los ojos.

¡FÍJATE! 1
Los mandatos informales

In chapter 6 you learned how to form and use **Ud.** and **Uds.** commands. Now you will learn how to make requests and give orders to friends and others with whom you use **tú:** friends, relatives, pets, and so on.

To form the *negative* **tú** commands:

1. Take the **yo** form of the present tense of the verb
2. Drop the **-o** ending
3. Add **-es** for **-ar** verbs, and add **-as** for **-er** and **-ir** verbs

-ar: hablar
no hablo
no hablø
no habl**es**

-er: comer
no como
no comø
no com**as**

-ir: pedir
no pido
no pidø
no pid**as**

To form the *affirmative* **tú** command:
Use the **él, ella, Ud.** form of the present tense of the verb.

Estudia.
Lee el cuento.
Escribe la respuesta.

Below are a few irregular affirmative **tú** commands.

decir	**di**	salir	**sal**
hacer	**haz**	ser	**sé**
ir	**ve**	tener	**ten**
poner	**pon**	venir	**ven**

Sé has a written accent to distinguish it from the reflexive pronoun **se**. Note the following examples of affirmative and negative **tú** commands.

<u>Compra</u> fruta.	<u>No compres</u> mucha carne.
<u>Sal</u> del cuarto.	<u>No salgas</u> con ellos esta noche.
<u>Prepara</u> la comida.	<u>No prepares</u> hígado *(liver)*.

Object and reflexive pronouns are used with **tú** commands as they are with **Ud.** and **Uds.** commands:

1. Object pronouns *are attached* to the end of *affirmative* commands. A written accent mark is placed over the stressed vowel when pronouns are attached.

    ¡<u>Dímelo</u>, por favor!
    Leván<u>tate</u>.

2. Object pronouns are placed *before negative* **tú** commands.

    ¡No <u>me lo</u> digas!
    No <u>te</u> levantes.

6 **¿Qué diría tu profesor?**   ¿Conoces bien a tu profesor de español? Entre los dos mandatos decide qué mandato diría *(would say)* tu profesor.

Modelo   Habla español. **(o)** No hables español.   ➧   **Habla español.**

1. Estudia. **(o)** No estudies.
2. Trae tus libros a todas las clases. **(o)** No traigas tus libros a todas las clases.
3. Lee con cuidado. **(o)** No leas con cuidado.
4. Ven tarde a la clase. **(o)** No vengas tarde a la clase.
5. Levántate sin razón durante la clase. **(o)** No te levantes sin razón durante la clase.
6. Sal temprano de la clase. **(o)** No salgas temprano de la clase.
7. Haz la tarea. **(o)** No hagas la tarea.
8. Ponte nervioso / nerviosa. **(o)** No te pongas nervioso / nerviosa.
9. Practica el español con un nativo. **(o)** No practiques el español con un nativo.
10. Diviértete en la clase. **(o)** No te diviertas en la clase.

7 **Hazlo, por favor.**   Con un compañero, di las formas afirmativas y negativas de los mandatos de **tú** de los siguientes verbos. Sigue los modelos.

Modelos   comer   ➧   **¡Come! ¡No comas!**

hablarme   ➧   **¡Háblame! ¡No me hables!**

1. estudiar
2. limpiarlo
3. tomarla
4. llevarlo
5. usarlas
6. pagar menos
7. ser
8. ponerlo aquí
9. salir temprano
10. venir ahora mismo
11. tener
12. hacerlo
13. decírmelo
14. dormirse
15. vestirse

8 **¡Déjame en paz!**   ¡Tu compañero de cuarto te vuelve loco! Usa los verbos siguientes para decirle lo que debe y no debe hacer. Sigue los modelos.

Modelos   poner tus libros en mi cama   ➧   **No pongas tus libros en mi cama.**

guardar tu comida en el refrigerador   ➧   **Guarda tu comida en el refrigerador.**

1. lavar los platos
2. limpiar el baño
3. sacar la basura
4. no comer en la sala
5. no beber de mi vaso
6. no ponerte mis pantalones
7. no hablar tanto por teléfono
8. tener más paciencia
9. no invitar siempre a tus amigos después de las once de la noche

Ahora dile lo que sí se debe hacer. Sigue los modelos.

Modelos poner tus libros en mi cama ➠ **No pongas tus libros en mi cama. Ponlos en tu cama.**

guardar tu comida en el refrigerador ➠ **Guarda tu comida en el refrigerador. No la dejes** (leave) **en la mesa.**

*Remember to use the **tú** commands with a friend and the **Ud.** commands with your boss or someone with whom you are not on a first-name basis. Refer to **capítulo 6** if you need to review how to form the **Ud.** commands.*

9 Por favor... ¿Cómo pides favores o cosas de tus amigos? ¿De tu jefe (boss)? Con un compañero, haz los mandatos siguientes.

Modelo llamarme mañana

A TU AMIGO / AMIGA: **Llámame mañana.**

A TU JEFE: **Llámeme mañana.**

1. decirme la verdad
2. tener paciencia conmigo
3. sentarse aquí
4. divertirse
5. no salir temprano
6. no vestirse formalmente
7. acordarse de la reunión
8. no ser tonto / tonta

¡ASÓMATE! 2
Unas enfermedades y unos tratamientos médicos

Unas enfermedades y unos tratamientos médicos

1. el antiácido
2. el antibiótico
3. la aspirina
4. el catarro / el resfriado
5. la curita
6. el doctor / la doctora
7. el dolor
8. el enfermero / la enfermera
9. el estornudo
10. el examen físico
11. la fiebre
12. la gripe
13. la herida
14. la inyección
15. el jarabe
16. la pastilla / la píldora
17. la receta
18. la sala de emergencia
19. la tos
20. la venda / el vendaje
21. cortar(se)
22. estornudar
23. lastimar(se)
24. quemar(se)
25. toser
26. la farmacia
27. el hospital

Unos verbos

darse cuenta de	*to realize*
enfermar(se)	*to get sick*
evitar	*to avoid*
mejorar(se)	*to get better, to improve*
ocurrir	*to occur*
romper(se)	*to break*
tratar de	*to try to*
vendar	*to bandage; to dress (a wound)*
tener dolor de cabeza	*to have a headache*
tener dolor de espalda	*to have a backache*
tener dolor de estómago	*to have a stomach ache*
tener dolor de garganta	*to have a sore throat*
tener alergia	*to be allergic*
tener catarro	*to have a cold*
tener gripe	*to have the flu*
tener una infección	*to have an infection*
tener un resfriado	*to have a cold*
tener tos	*to have a cough*
tener un virus	*to have a virus*

Otras palabras útiles

la enfermedad	*illness*
el tratamiento	*treatment*

10 **Orden alfabético.** Pongan las palabras siguientes en español y luego en orden alfabético.

Modelo   pills, sneeze, cough ➧   **pastillas, estornudo, tos** ➧
                                                        estornudo, pastillas, tos

1. pain, treatment, pharmacy
2. bandage, wound, infection
3. aspirin, antibiotic, cough
4. cough syrup, shot, infection
5. to get hurt, to get sick, to get better

11 **¿Adónde vas?** Con las siguientes enfermedades o condiciones, ¿adónde tienes que ir a buscar *(to look for)* tratamiento? Pon tachas (✓) en las columnas correctas.

	a la cama	a la farmacia	al doctor	al hospital	a la sala de emergencia
1. la tos		✓			
2. el cáncer					
3. la depresión					
4. un dolor de garganta					
5. una infección de la sangre					
6. una herida en la pierna					
7. un catarro					
8. una fiebre					

12 **¡Doctor, doctor!** Imagina que tú eres el doctor y que tienes pacientes con las enfermedades siguientes. ¿Qué recomiendas?

Modelo   Doctor, tengo dolor de cabeza. ➧   **Tome Ud. dos aspirinas.**

1. Doctor, comí demasiado anoche y me duele el estómago.
2. Doctor, tengo tos y me duele mucho la garganta.
3. Doctor, me corté el dedo con un cuchillo. ¿Qué hago?
4. Doctor, me duele la espalda. ¿Qué debo hacer?
5. Doctor, tomé mi temperatura y tengo fiebre. ¿Qué necesito hacer?
6. Doctor, creo que tengo una infección de la garganta. Me duele mucho cuando hablo.

13 **Para evitar lo inevitable.** ¿Cómo tratas de evitar las siguientes enfermedades y condiciones? Dile a un compañero tus respuestas.

Modelo   **ESTUDIANTE 1:**   ¿Cómo tratas de evitar un dolor de garganta?

                       ESTUDIANTE 2:   Trato de tomar mucho jugo de naranja para evitar un dolor de garganta.

1. ¿Cómo tratas de evitar un dolor de cabeza?
2. ¿Cómo tratas de evitar un dolor de estómago?
3. ¿Cómo tratas de evitar un dolor de espalda?
4. ¿Cómo tratas de evitar enfermarte?
5. ¿Cómo tratas de evitar cortarte?

Bueno, ahora vamos a decir que no tuviste mucho éxito *(success)* en evitar las enfermedades y condiciones. Entonces, ¿cómo tratas de curar esas enfermedades y condiciones?

Modelo   **ESTUDIANTE 1:**   ¿Cómo tratas de curar un dolor de garganta?

ESTUDIANTE 2:   Trato de curar un dolor de garganta con unas pastillas para la garganta.

¡ENTÉRATE!
La música hispana

Gloria Estefan

Jon Secada

Juan Luis Guerra

Lucero

Enrique Inglesias

Sábana Grande

La música hispana, como la música de los Estados Unidos, es muy variada. Hay muchos tipos de música como el mariachi (de México), el merengue y la salsa (del Caribe), el flamenco (de España) y el tango (de la Argentina).

La música expresa las emociones y los pensamientos *(thoughts)* de la gente. Como en los Estados Unidos, no hay un solo tipo de música para todos los hispanos; hay una gran variedad.

¿Qué te parece?

1. ¿Qué música prefieres? ¿Por qué?
2. ¿Qué tipo de música no te gusta? ¿Por qué?
3. ¿Quién es tu artista favorito(a)?
4. ¿Cuántos discos compactos tienes? ¿Cintas?

◆ETAPA 2

¡Dime más!
¡Dime más!

¡FÍJATE! 2
*El pretérito **versus** el imperfecto*

In the last two chapters you learned about two past tenses in Spanish, **el pretérito** and **el imperfecto,** which are not interchangeable. Their uses are contrasted below.

El pretérito is used:

1. To relate an event or occurrence that happened once (or infrequently) in the past

   Fuimos a México el año pasado.
   We went to Mexico last year.
   Comimos en el restaurante Coco Loco y no nos gustó.
   We ate at the Coco Loco restaurant and didn't like it.

2. To state the beginning or end of a past action
   Empezó a llover.
   It started to rain.
   ¿Terminaste la tarea?
   Did you finish the homework?

3. To relate a sequence of events, each completed and each one moving the narrative along toward its conclusion

   Se levantó, se duchó y salió sin comer.
   She got up, showered, and left without eating.
   El viernes pasado decidieron ir al cine.
   Last Friday they decided to go to the movies.
   Vieron una película cómica. Después fueron a un restaurante chino. Se divirtieron mucho.
   They saw a comedy. Afterwards they went to a Chinese restaurant. They had a good time.

4. To relate an action that took place within a specified or specific amount (segment) of time

   Manejaron por dos horas.
   They drove for two hours.
   Hablamos por cinco minutos.
   We talked for five minutes.
   Miraron la televisión un rato.
   They watched television awhile.
   Viví en Barcelona por dos años.
   I lived in Barcelona for two years.

224

El imperfecto is used:

1. To provide background information, set the stage, or express a condition that existed

La casa era vieja.	*The house was old.*
Había mucho polvo en los muebles.	*There was a lot of dust on the furniture.*
María no se sentía muy bien.	*María didn't feel very well.*
El gato dormía en la chimenea.	*The cat was sleeping on the hearth.*

2. To express habitual or often repeated actions

Vivía en Ohio.	*I used to live in Ohio.*
Creía en Santa Claus.	*He used to believe in Santa Claus.*
¿Sacabas la basura cuando eras niña?	*Did you used to take out the garbage when you were a child?*

3. To express was / were _____ing

¿Dormías?	*Were you sleeping?*
Estudiaban cuando llamé.	*They were studying when I called.*
Alberto leía mientras Alicia escuchaba música.	*Alberto was reading while Alicia was listening to music.*

4. To tell time in the past

Era la una.	*It was 1:00.*
Eran las seis y media.	*It was 6:30.*

The **pretérito** and the **imperfecto** can occur in the same sentence.

Estudiaba cuando sonó el teléfono.	*I was studying when the phone rang.*

In the preceding sentence, an action was going on (**estudiaba**) when it was interrupted by another action (**sonó el teléfono**).

1 **¿Y ayer?**   Descríbele a un compañero lo que pasó ayer. Dile por lo menos cinco frases.

Modelo   **Ayer hacía mal tiempo cuando me desperté. No quería levantarme, pero me levanté finalmente. Fui a mi clase de español. El profesor nos dio mucha tarea. Luego fui a la biblioteca. Estudiaba cuando llegó mi mejor amigo Jeff.**

2 **Los días del verano.**   ¿Qué hiciste el verano pasado? Descríbele a un compañero:

1. un día típico (¿pretérito o imperfecto?)
2. un día que no fue típico (¿pretérito o imperfecto?)

Di por lo menos cinco frases para un día típico y cinco para un día no típico.

3 **Luces, cámara, acción.**   ¿Te gustan las películas? ¿Vas al cine a menudo? Descríbele a un compañero una película que viste. Di por lo menos siete frases. ¡Acuérdate! Generalmente se usa el imperfecto para la descripción y el pretérito para la acción.

 *Do **actividad 3** again without telling your partner what movie you are describing. See if he or she can guess after you say seven sentences.*

4 **¿Cuándo te diste cuenta de que... ?**   Entrevista *(Interview)* a un compañero para saber la información siguiente.

1. ¿Qué hacías mientras estudiabas anoche?
2. El 31 de diciembre del año pasado, ¿qué hacías cuando llegó el año nuevo?
3. ¿Qué hiciste el día siguiente (el 1º de enero)?
4. ¿Cuándo te diste cuenta de que no había un Santa Claus?
5. ¿Cuándo te diste cuenta de que tenías que estudiar para recibir buenas notas?

¡ENTÉRATE!
El imperio incaico

El imperio de los incas fue uno de los imperios más altos de las civilizaciones precolombinas. Se encontraba en lo que es hoy el Perú, Bolivia, el norte de Chile y parte del Ecuador. Los incas tenían un cacique (líder) principal. Este cacique tenía un templo gigante en Cuzco, la capital del imperio incaico.

El sistema de gobierno *(government)* de los incas era muy democrático. El imperio se dividía en tres partes iguales. Una tercera parte pertenecía *(belonged)* a los indígenas y pasaba de mano en mano — de padre a hijo. Otra tercera parte era del Inca, o sea, del Gobierno. La otra tercera parte pertenecía a la Iglesia.

Los incas adoraban al hijo del sol. Según la leyenda *(legend)*, él se cayó del sol en algún lugar cerca del lago *(lake)* Titicaca. Con él vino su hermana y la leyenda dice que ellos son los padres de todos los incas. Estos indígenas practicaban sacrificios de animales y algunas veces humanos. También ofrecían objetos preciosos y joyas *(jewels)* al sol.

El sistema de comunicación de los incas era muy avanzado. Tenían casi 3.000 millas de caminos *(roads)* anchos. Hoy se pueden ver ejemplos de la magnífica arquitectura incaica en las ruinas de Machu Picchu y Cuzco. Los edificios del imperio incaico eran muy ricos. El último cacique famoso de los incas fue Atahualpa. Francisco Pizarro conquistó el Perú en el nombre de España en el año 1533.

¿Qué te parece?

1. ¿Dónde se encontraba el imperio de los incas?
2. ¿Cómo se llamaba la capital del imperio?
3. Explica el sistema de gobierno de los incas.
4. Explica la leyenda del hijo del sol.
5. ¿Cómo era el sistema de comunicación de los incas?
6. ¿Cómo se llaman las dos ciudades más famosas del imperio?
7. ¿Quién fue el último jefe de los incas?

¡ENTÉRATE!

El Perú

COLOMBIA

ECUADOR

PERÚ

BRASIL

Los Andes

★ Lima

OCÉANO PACÍFICO

Machu Picchu

Cuzco

BOLIVIA

Lago Titicaca

CHILE

Cuzco es la capital arqueológica de las Américas. Era el centro del imperio incaico.

Francisco Pizarro

Simón Bolívar

1400–1525 Aunque existiera poco tiempo, el imperio incaico dejó *(left)* una impresión grande.

12.000 a.C El récord más viejo de habitantes en el Perú se encuentra en Cueva Pikimachay, cerca de Ayacucho.

1533 Pizarro conquistó el Perú en gran parte a causa de *(because of)* una guerra civil entre los incas y éste pronto se convirtió en la colonia española más rica de Sudamérica.

1826 Terminó la guerra de la independencia que empezó en 1821 con la ayuda de dos hombres: José de San Martín y Simón Bolívar.

1911 Machu Picchu fue descubierto por el norteamericano Hiram Bingham el 24 de julio de 1911. Debía de ser un centro ceremonial importante.

1933 Iniciaron una constitución que le dio al Perú un presidente y una cámara legislativa para ser elegidos cada seis años.

El Perú comparte con Bolivia el lago Titicaca, que tiene la distinción de ser el lago navegable más alto del mundo.

Hay muchas teorías de las líneas de Nazca. ¿Cuál es tu teoría?

¿Qué te parece?

1. ¿Por qué llegó a ser (*became*) el Perú la colonia más rica de España? Menciona dos razones.

2. Todos los países hispanoamericanos tuvieron al principio problemas con sus democracias. ¿Por qué?

3. ¿Cuáles serían los desafíos (*challenges*) del lago Titicaca y el hecho de que pertenezca al Perú y Bolivia? ¿Hay algo similar en los Estados Unidos?

4. Si el Perú tiene tantos recursos naturales (*natural resources*), ¿por qué no tiene una economía más fuerte?

1995 Fujimori ganó de nuevo la presidencia. La ganó por primera vez en 1981.

1980 El grupo terrorista «Sendero Luminoso» empezó diez años de violencia contra el gobierno.

1998 Los recursos naturales son el cobre, la plata, el oro, el petróleo, la madera y otros. La pesca en el Perú es una de las industrias más grandes del mundo y sufrió en 1998 a causa de «El Niño».

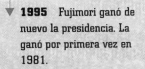

LA RED

¡Navega la Internet!

To discover more information on the culture of this chapter, check the Holt Web site and other suggestions listed in your **Manual de actividades.**

http://www.hrwcollege.com/

¡Cuéntame!
¡Cuéntame!

Ya lo sabemos

Considera el título de este episodio, «El accidente». Como leímos en la página 212 del capítulo 7, los accidentes son muy prevalentes durante la adolescencia y los años de los veinte. En este episodio, ¿a qué tipo de accidente se refiere? ¿El accidente de quién(es)?

En este episodio vas a averiguar *(find out)*

◆ quién tuvo el accidente
◆ los detalles del accidente
◆ el estado físico de la víctima

Preguntas personales

1. ¿Tuviste alguna vez un accidente? ¿Alguien de tu familia? ¿Un amigo? ¿Qué ocurrió? ¿Fue serio?
2. Si tienes información que puede causar problemas o hacerle daño *(to harm)* a un amigo, ¿se lo dices? ¿Por qué sí o no?

Estrategias de lectura
Predicting

You have been practicing many tools to make reading in Spanish easier and more enjoyable. You began by learning to use cognates to facilitate comprehension. You have also practiced skimming the text for the main idea and scanning for specific information. You have seen how titles, illustrations, and even comprehension questions can help you anticipate content. Finally, you have seen how important background knowledge is to comprehension.

The pre- and post-reading activities in the **¡Cuéntame!** sections of the *¡Atrévete!* program are designed to facilitate your comprehension. It is important that you recognize these tools and learn to incorporate them in your reading of other passages.

Now focus on this episode. Working with a partner, talk yourselves through these tools (use of cognates, skimming, scanning, background knowledge, and anticipating content), and based on your discussion, write a summary in Spanish of what you predict will happen in this episode.Then, read the passage independently and when finished, go back to the prediciton the two of you wrote. How accurate was your prediction?

Rafi y el sacrificio final

Episodio 7: El accidente

Adriana manejaba muy despacio. Ayer nevó mucho y la avenida estaba casi inmane-
jable. También manejaba despacio porque pensaba mucho en Rafi y en su vida tan
complicada. ¿Por qué no vino Rafi a verla ayer? ¿Qué sentía Rafi por ella? ¿Qué
sentía ella hacia él? Ella pensaba que estaba enamorada de él pero no estaba segura.

En estos momentos pensaba tanto en Rafi y su situación que no sabía que un
carro negro, grande, la seguía muy de cerca. Por fin se dio cuenta de que ocurría
algo raro. Trató de aumentar la velocidad. Estaba en una parte de la ciudad muy
desolada y necesitaba tener mucho cuidado. De repente el carro negro trató de
pasarla. Adriana miró con terror el coche que le chocaba° en el lado de su puerta.   *crashed*
Ella perdió el control y chocó contra un árbol.

Cuando Adriana se despertó, estaba en un cuarto de paredes blancas. La
observaban dos médicos. La preparaban para hacerle un electrocardiograma. Se dio
cuenta de que estaba en el hospital y sabía que no estaba muy bien de salud. Le dolía
mucho la cabeza, no podía mover las piernas y tenía la visión un poco obscura. Oía
cómo los médicos hablaban de una posible operación de la espalda. Adriana se
sentía muy sola y tenía mucho miedo.

Carmen Soledad supo del accidente de Adriana. Ayer le escribió a Rafi una
carta electrónica sobre algo que ella había oído decir de Adriana. Pero éste ya no
era el momento para eso. Tenía que comunicarse con él lo antes posible para decirle
lo del accidente.

Comprensión

1. ¿Por qué manejaba Adriana tan despacio?
2. ¿En qué pensaba Adriana mientras manejaba?
3. ¿Cómo ocurrió el accidente?
4. ¿Dónde estaba cuando se despertó?
5. ¿Qué problemas físicos tenía?
6. ¿Quién le va a decir a Rafi lo del accidente?

Expansión

1. En tu opinión ¿fue un verdadero accidente? Explica.

2. Con un compañero, hagan los papeles de Carmen y sus padres. Acaban de enterarse
del (*find out about*) accidente. Hablen de lo que ocurrió, de la condición física de
Adriana y de la necesidad de comunicarse con Rafi. Sean creativos.

231

③ En grupos de tres personas, hagan los papeles de Adriana, un doctor y un enfermero. Ellos examinan a Adriana y le hacen muchas preguntas sobre su estado físico.

④ Tú eres el doctor de Adriana. Tienes que describir el estado físico de ella en un informe oficial. Usando los detalles del episodio (y si quieres, inventando otros), escribe este informe de una página.

⑤ Imagina que Carmen Soledad decide mandarle a Rafi un fax para decirle lo del accidente. Escribe el fax que ella le manda.

A mirar o escuchar

⑥ View the video or listen to the audio CD for the next episode of **Rafi y el sacrificio final.** Consult your **Manual de actividades** for pre- and post-listening activities.

¡Sí, se puede!

1. **La gran búsqueda...** Tienes que circular por la clase en busca de los compañeros que hicieron las siguientes cosas.

   1. ¿Quién ganó un premio recientemente?
   2. ¿Quién conoció a una persona famosa?
   3. ¿Quién sufrió un accidente?
   4. ¿Quién tuvo una operación?
   5. ¿Quién viajó a un país hispano?
   6. ¿Quién perdió algo importante?

   Después, todos deben compartir su información con el instructor. Entonces les va a pedir a los estudiantes nombrados que digan sus historias.

2. **Un cuento de hadas...** Tu instructor va a formar cuatro o cinco grupos. A cada grupo, le va a dar unos papelitos en que están escritas algunas oraciones. Los grupos tienen que poner sus oraciones en orden. Cada grupo va a tener un cuento completo de hadas *(fairy tale)*. Al final, todos tienen que escuchar bien mientras un miembro de cada grupo lee su párrafo.

3. **Misión no imposible...** Eres investigador privado de la empresa Ojos Grandes. El caso nuevo tiene que ver con espiar a la gente que vive en los Apartamentos Vida Alegre porque los padres de un estudiante de primer año quieren saber si es un buen lugar para su

hijo. Entonces tienes que observar, durante veinticuatro horas, las actividades de uno de los apartamentos ¡Y claro que tienes gemelos *(binoculars)*! Haz una lista de las actividades que ves.

Modelo **Dos hombres viven en el apartamento que yo observé. Uno se levanta a las seis y se viste inmediatamente.**

4. **El reconocimiento médico...** En parejas, hagan una lista de lo que un doctor debe hacer en un examen médico.

Modelo **mirar la garganta**

5. **Amnesia...** Formen grupos de cinco o seis personas. En cada grupo su profesor va a darle a un estudiante la identidad de una persona famosa del pasado. El estudiante no puede saber su identidad pero el resto del grupo sí lo va a saber. El estudiante «famoso» tiene que hacerles preguntas a los estudiantes del grupo (claro, en el pasado) para averiguar quién es. Su profesor tiene identidades para todos.

Para recordar

Having completed this chapter, you are now able to:

Etapa 1 ¡Sígueme!

❏ explain to someone what ails you and understand when others tell you "where it hurts"

Etapa 2 ¡Dime más!

❏ tell your friends what to do and what not to do

❏ determine when to use the **pretérito** or the **imperfecto**

❏ sample the vast world of music throughout the Spanish-speaking world

❏ explore the fascinating ancient world of the Inca

❏ travel vicariously to Peru

Etapa 3 ¡Cuéntame!

❏ discover who lives or dies in a mysterious accident

 You can practice concepts from this chapter and earlier chapters by doing the **¡Recuérdate!** *sections in your* **Manual de actividades.**

VOCABULARIO ACTIVO

El cuerpo humano

la boca   *mouth*
el brazo   *arm*
la cabeza   *head*
la cara   *face*
el corazón   *heart*
el cuello   *neck*
el cuerpo   *body*
el dedo   *finger*

el dedo del pie   *toe*
el diente   *tooth*
la espalda   *back*
el estómago   *stomach*
la garganta   *throat*
la mano   *hand*
la nariz   *nose*
el ojo   *eye*

la oreja   *ear*
el pecho   *chest*
el pelo   *hair*
el pie   *foot*
la pierna   *leg*
la sangre   *blood*

Unas enfermedades y unos tratamientos médicos

el antiácido   *antacid*
el antibiótico   *antibiotic*
la aspirina   *aspirin*
el catarro   *cold*
la curita   *adhesive bandage*
el doctor / la doctora   *doctor*
el dolor   *pain*
el enfermero / la enfermera
          nurse
el estornudo   *sneeze*

el examen físico   *physical exam*
la farmacia   *pharmacy*
la fiebre   *fever*
la gripe   *flu*
la herida   *wound*
el hospital   *hospital*
la infección   *infection*
la inyección   *shot*
el jarabe   *cough syrup*
la pastilla   *pill*

la píldora   *pill*
la receta   *prescription*
el resfriado   *cold*
la sala de emergencia   *emergency
          room*
la tos   *cough*
la venda   *bandage*
el vendaje   *bandage*

Unos verbos

cortar(se)   *to cut (oneself)*
darse cuenta de   *to realize*
doler (ue)   *to hurt*
enfermar(se)   *to get sick*
estar...
   enfermo / enferma   *to be sick*
   saludable   *to be healthy*
   sano / sana   *to be healthy*
estornudar   *to sneeze*
evitar   *to avoid*
lastimar(se)   *to get hurt, to hurt
     oneself; to injure someone*

mejorar(se)   *to get better; to improve*
ocurrir   *to occur*
quemar(se)   *to burn (oneself)*
romper(se)   *to break*
ser alérgico / alérgica   *to be allergic*
tener...
   alergia   *to be allergic*
   catarro   *to have a cold*
   gripe   *to have the flu*
   una infección   *to have an infection*
   un resfriado   *to have a cold*

tos   *to have a cough*
un virus   *to have a virus*
tener dolor de...   *to have a . . .*
   cabeza   *headache*
   espalda   *backache*
   estómago   *stomach ache*
   garganta   *sore throat*
toser   *to cough*
tratar de   *to try to*
vendar   *to bandage, dress*

Otras palabras útiles

la enfermedad   *illness*
el oído   *inner ear*

la salud   *health*
el tratamiento   *treatment*

MAR CARIBE

◆ Caracas

VENEZUELA

◆ Bogotá
COLOMBIA

OCÉANO
PACÍFICO

◆ Quito

ECUADOR

BRASIL

PERÚ

¿Vas a viajar al extranjero *(abroad)*? Aquí tienes una lista de sugerencias:

1. Antes de hacer las maletas, averigua *(find out)* todo lo que puedas acerca del sitio que piensas visitar.
2. Estate seguro de que toda tu documentación esté al día.
3. Antes de salir, planea tu viaje con detalles.
4. Planea tus gastos usando un presupuesto *(budget)*.
5. Obtén un seguro de viajes *(travel insurance)*.
6. Evita actuar como turista. Ponte ropa conservadora y lleva tu cámara y mapa en una forma discreta.
7. Lleva tus cosas de valor en bolsillos ocultos o en un bolso que tenga correa *(strap)* que cruce el pecho.
8. Pon tu nombre, dirección y número de teléfono adentro y afuera de cada maleta.
9. Asegúrate de que sepas el límite de cada tarjeta de crédito que llevas. ¡En algunos países puedes ser arrestado por pasarte de tu límite!

Y ahora... ¡ya estás listo para tu viaje!

¿Qué te parece?

1. ¿Viajas mucho? ¿Adónde?
2. ¿Cuáles de las cosas de la lista haces normalmente?
3. ¿Por qué no tomaste las otras precauciones? ¿Las vas a tomar en el futuro?
4. ¿Tuviste problemas en uno de tus viajes? Explica. ¿Qué puedes hacer para evitar este problema en futuros viajes?

A viajar

By the end of this chapter you will be able to:

ETAPA 1 ¡Sígueme!

- plan an exciting journey
- share what you have done or completed in the past

ETAPA 2 ¡Dime más!

- ◆ describe how you feel in a variety of situations
- ◆ compare and contrast your holiday celebrations and other life events with those in the Spanish-speaking world
- ◆ explore Colombia and neighboring countries of northern South America

ETAPA 3 ¡Cuéntame!

- ● discover what Adriana learns about the codes before her accident

¡ASÓMATE! 1
El transporte

El transporte

1. el autobús
2. el avión
3. la bicicleta
4. el coche
5. el camión

6. el metro
7. la moto(cicleta)
8. el taxi
9. el tren

Unas cosas asociadas con el transporte

10. la autopista
11. el boleto
12. la calle
13. la cola
14. la estación de servicio
15. el estacionamiento
16. la multa

17. la parada
18. el peatón / los peatones
19. el permiso (de conducir)
20. el policía
21. el ruido
22. el semáforo
23. el tráfico

Unas partes de un vehículo

24. el aire acondicionado
25. el baúl
26. la calefacción
27. el limpiaparabrisas
28. la llanta

29. la llave
30. el motor
31. el parabrisas
32. la rueda
33. el tanque

Sígue a la pagina 240 por más palabras de vocabulario.

Unos verbos útiles

cambiar	*to change*
caminar, ir a pie	*to walk*
doblar	*to turn*
estacionarse	*to park*
funcionar	*to work; to function*
llenar	*to fill*
manejar	*to drive*
perder (e ➡ ie)	*to miss; to lose*
prestar	*to lend; to borrow*
revisar	*to check; to overhaul*
viajar	*to travel*
visitar	*to visit*
volar (o ➡ ue)	*to fly; to fly away*

If you cannot decipher the meaning of a vocabulary item by studying the drawing, consult the **Vocabulario activo** *at the end of the chapter.*

1 **¿Qué no pertenece?**   ¿Qué palabra no pertenece al grupo?

1. el taxi, el coche, la bicicleta, el camión
2. el coche, el semáforo, la moto, el metro
3. el boleto, el chofer, los peatones, el policía
4. la estación de servicio, la multa, el autobús, el camión

2 **¿Cómo viajas?**   Llena la gráfica en **Etapa 1, actividad 2** del **capítulo 8** de tu **Manual de actividades** con una tacha (✓) en la columna correcta para ti.

3 **¿Verdad o falso?**   Pon una tacha (✓) en la columna correcta. Luego, corrige las frases falsas. Finalmente, comparte tus respuestas con un(a) compañero(a).

	Verdad	Falso
1. Hay una parada de autobús cerca de donde tú vives.		
2. Se necesita cambiar el aceite de un coche cada 40,000 millas.		
3. Hay semáforos en la carretera.		
4. Se necesita la calefacción en el verano.		
5. Un coche no puede funcionar sin unos limpiaparabrisas.		

4 **¿Cómo llegas a tu destino?**   Pon una tacha (✓) en todos los medios de transporte que usas (o que se pueden usar) para llegar a los destinos. Usa la gráfica en **Etapa 1, actividad 4** del **capítulo 8** de tu **Manual de actividades.**

5 **Una encuesta.**   Circula por tu clase y busca a doce personas diferentes que puedan contestar «sí» a las situaciones en la gráfica en **Etapa 1, actividad 5** en **capítulo 8** de tu **Manual de actividades.**

6 **¿Qué tienen en común?** Trabajen en grupos de dos y miren la gráfica en **Etapa 1, actividad 6** en **capítulo 8** del **Manual de actividades.** En el círculo grande en el medio, escriban lo que los transportes tienen en común. Luego, en los círculos pequeños, escriban cosas distintas de cada transporte. Comparen su diagrama con el diagrama de otro grupo. ¿Son similares?

Use commands in your sentences in **actividad 7.** *What type of command is used in the* **modelo?**

7 **La estación de servicio.** Acabas de llegar a una gasolinera. Dile al asistente lo que necesitas.

Modelo Mis llantas necesitan aire. ➡ **Llene las llantas con aire, por favor.**

1. Necesito gasolina.
2. Mi parabrisas está sucio.
3. Mis limpiaparabrisas no funcionan.

4. Mi motor tiene un ruido extraño.
5. El baúl no abre.
6. El aceite está sucio.

¡FÍJATE! 1
El presente perfecto y el pluscuamperfecto

The present perfect (e.g., *has spoken*) and past perfect (e.g., *had spoken*) tenses are formed in English by using a form of the auxiliary, or helping verb *to have* plus the past participle. These tenses are formed in Spanish by using a form of the auxiliary verb **haber** plus the past participle of the verb. The past participle is formed by taking the infinitive, dropping the **-ar, -er,** or **-ir** endings, and adding **-ado** for **-ar** verbs and **-ido** for **-er** and **-ir** verbs.

-ar: hablar
habl*ar*
+**ado**
habl**ado**

-er: comer
com*er*
+**ido**
com**ido**

-ir: salir
sal*ir*
+**ido**
sal**ido**

If the stem of the past participle ends in **-a, -e,** or **-o,** the first vowel of the ending of the past participle requires a written accent.

caer   ➠   **caído**

leer   ➠   **leído**

oír   ➠   **oído**

A few common verbs form their past participles irregularly.

abrir	**abierto**	poner	**puesto**
decir	**dicho**	romper	**roto**
escribir	**escrito**	ver	**visto**
hacer	**hecho**	volver	**vuelto**
morir	**muerto**		

El presente perfecto

He	estudi**ado** mucho.	*I have studied a lot.*
Has	estudi**ado** mucho.	*You have studied a lot.*
Ha	estudi**ado** mucho.	*He / She has studied a lot.*
Hemos	estudi**ado** mucho.	*We have studied a lot.*
Habéis	estudi**ado** mucho.	*You (plural) have studied a lot.*
Han	estudi**ado** mucho.	*They have studied a lot.*

The present perfect, or **presente perfecto,** is used to express a completed action in the past.

¿**Han** limpiado el parabrisas?   *Have they cleaned the windshield?*

¿**Has** comprado un coche?   *Have you bought a car?*

El pluscuamperfecto

Había	estudi**ado**.	*I had studied.*
Habías	estudi**ado**.	*You had studied.*
Había	estudi**ado**.	*He / She had studied.*
Habíamos	estudi**ado**.	*We had studied.*
Habíais	estudi**ado**.	*You (plural) had studied.*
Habían	estudi**ado**.	*They had studied.*

The past perfect, or **pluscuamperfecto,** is used to talk about or describe actions that were completed prior to other actions.

¿**Habían** limpiado el parabrisas antes de salir?   *Had they cleaned the windshield before they left?*

¿**Habías** comprado un coche antes de graduarte?   *Had you bought a car before you graduated?*

To make sentences in the present or past perfect negative, add **no** before the auxiliary verb **haber.** Reflexive and object pronouns precede the auxiliary verb **haber.**

<u>No, no habían limpiado</u> el
  parabrisas antes de salir.

<u>No, no había comprado</u> un coche
  antes de graduarme.

<u>Sí, me lo había comprado</u> durante el
  segundo año de la universidad.

*<u>No, they had not cleaned</u> the windshield
  before they left.*

*<u>No, I had not bought</u> a car before I
  graduated.*

*I <u>had bought it (for) myself</u> during my
  sophomore year.*

8 **¿Cuántas veces has hecho lo siguiente?**   Llena la gráfica en **Etapa 1, actividad 8** del **capítulo 8** en tu **Manual de actividades.** Luego, circula y pregúntales a diez compañeros diferentes y escribe sus respuestas.

9 **Las experiencias de la vida.**   Llena la gráfica en **Etapa 1, actividad 9** del **capítulo 8** en tu **Manual de actividades,** siguiendo el modelo. Compara tus respuestas con las de un compañero. ¿Qué tienen en común?

10 **¿Qué te ha pasado?**   Tu amigo / amiga a se queja *(complains)* de todo. Sigue el modelo para saber lo que le pasa.

Modelo   ESTUDIANTE 1:   Me duele la pierna.

                ESTUDIANTE 2:   ¿Te has caído?

1. Me duele la cabeza.
2. Tengo dolor de estómago.
3. Tengo dolor de espalda.
4. Me duelen los pies.
5. Tengo sueño.
6. Me duele la mano derecha.
7. Me duelen los ojos.
8. Tengo dolor de garganta.
9. Estoy cansado / cansada.
10. Estoy nervioso / nerviosa porque tengo un examen mañana.

11 **Cinco preguntas.**   En grupos de cinco, escojan *(choose)* a una persona. Esa persona sale del salón por unos minutos mientras el resto del grupo escribe cinco preguntas que van a hacerle al compañero. Luego escriban cómo creen Uds. que su compañero va a contestarlas. Sigue el modelo. ¿Conocen bien a sus compañeros?

Modelo   **¿Has cambiado el aceite en tu coche?**

                ¿Has viajado a México?

¡ENTÉRATE!
Los días festivos

Semana Santa, Sevilla, España

El Día de San Fermín, Pamplona, España

El Cinco de Mayo,
México, D.F.

La Navidad (25 de diciembre), el Año Nuevo (1° de enero), el Día de la Raza y el descubrimiento de América (12 de octubre), son días festivos que se celebran en toda Latinoamérica. El Día de los Reyes Magos, o la Epifanía (6 de enero) también se celebra en casi todos los países hispanos.

Muchos países celebran el carnaval que ocurre mayormente la semana antes del Miércoles de Ceniza *(Ash Wednesday)*. Siendo la religión católica la que predomina en estos países, la Semana Santa, especialmente el Viernes Santo y el Día de Pascua Florida, también son días festivos en casi toda Latinoamérica.

Cada país independiente celebra su día de la independencia. También el día del trabajo (1° de mayo) se celebra en la mayoría de los países.

Otros días festivos son:

El Día de las Madres (los días varían de país en país, pero casi siempre es en el mes de mayo).

El Día de los Padres (la fecha varía, pero siempre es en junio).

El Día de Todos los Santos (1° de noviembre).

El Día de los Muertos (2 de noviembre).

¿Qué te parece?

1. ¿Qué día festivo ha sido tu preferido?
2. ¿Cómo ha celebrado tu familia los días festivos?
3. ¿En qué ciudad de los Estados Unidos celebran mucho el carnaval?

¡ASÓMATE! 2
El viaje

El viaje

1. el aeropuerto
2. la agencia de viajes
3. el boleto de ida y vuelta
4. la estación (de tren, de autobús)
5. la maleta
6. el pasaporte
7. los viajeros
8. el vuelo

El hotel

9. el botones
10. el cuarto doble
11. el cuarto individual
12. la propina
13. la recepción

Unos verbos útiles

14. arreglar / hacer la maleta
15. registrarse (en el hotel)
16. salir del hotel

Unos lugares

17. el lago
18. las montañas

19. el parque de atracciones
20. la playa

Otras palabras útiles

el barco	*boat*
el extranjero	*abroad*
el sello, el timbre	*postage stamp*
la tarjeta postal	*post card*
las vacaciones	*vacation*

12 **Asociación libre.** ¿Has oído el término psicológico «asociación libre?» Es cuando dices la primera cosa que piensas cuando oyes una palabra. Haz con un compañero «asociación libre» con las palabras siguientes.

Modelo   el aeropuerto   ⟹   **viajar**

1. el aeropuerto
2. registrarse en el hotel
3. el botones
4. las montañas

5. el extranjero
6. el pasaporte
7. la playa

13 **Categorías.**   Tienes tres minutos para escribir todas las palabras que pertenecen *(pertain)* a las tres categorías. Escribe las respuestas en la gráfica en **Etapa 1, actividad 13** en **capítulo 8** de tu **Manual de actividades.** Luego, compara tu lista con un compañero. Date un punto por cada respuesta que tienes que es diferente a la de tu compañero.

14 **Entrevista.**   Busca a nueve compañeros diferentes que hayan hecho las cosas indicadas y escribe sus nombres en los espacios de la gráfica en **Etapa 1, actividad 14** en **capítulo 8** de tu **Manual de actividades.**

15 **Mis mejores vacaciones.**   Piensa en tus mejores vacaciones y contesta las preguntas siguientes. Después, comparte tus respuestas con los otros miembros de la clase o con tus compañeros.

1. ¿Adónde fuiste?
2. ¿Cómo viajaste?
3. ¿Dónde te quedaste?
4. ¿Por cuánto tiempo estuviste allí?
5. ¿Qué hiciste durante aquellas vacaciones especiales?
6. ¿A quiénes mandaste unas tarjetas postales?

16 **¿Adónde van?**   Trabajas en una agencia de viajes y un señor quiere que planees sus vacaciones. Dice que tiene $2.000 para gastar.

1. Hazle por lo menos dos preguntas sobre sus preferencias.
2. Luego, descríbele lo que le has planeado con por lo menos cinco frases. Incluye el destino, cómo va a viajar, cuánto cuesta el boleto, qué puede hacer y ver allí y qué ropa necesita para hacer la maleta.
3. Escribe un itinerario que incluye los vuelos y las horas cuando puede / necesita registrarse y salir del hotel.

¡FÍJATE! 3
Otro uso del reflexivo y de se

The reflexive form is also used to mean *each other.* Notice how it is used below.

Ellos <u>se</u> miraron.	*They looked at <u>each</u> <u>other</u>.*
<u>Nos</u> escribimos el año pasado.	*We wrote <u>each</u> <u>other</u> last year.*

Se is commonly used in impersonal and passive constructions. English equivalents of such expresssions vary, as you see in the examples below.

<u>Se</u> <u>habla</u> inglés aquí.
{ *English <u>is</u> <u>spoken</u> here.*
<u>One speaks</u> English here.
People <u>speak</u> English here.

Se <u>alquila</u> este apartamento.   *This apartment <u>is</u> <u>for</u> <u>rent</u>.*
No <u>se</u> <u>estaciona</u> aquí.   *No <u>parking</u> here.*
<u>Se</u> <u>aceptan</u> Visa y Mastercard.   *Visa and Mastercard <u>are</u> <u>accepted</u>.*

¿Dónde <u>se</u> <u>encuentra</u> el cine Rex?   { *Where <u>is</u> the Rex Cinema?*
Where <u>does</u> <u>one</u> <u>find</u> the Rex Cinema?

5 ⟩ **¿Cómo las contestan?**   Contesta las preguntas siguientes y luego puedes compartir tus respuestas con un compañero de clase.

1. ¿Se hablan tú y tu mejor amigo todas las noches?
2. ¿Dónde se aceptan tarjetas de crédito en tu ciudad?
3. ¿Dónde se estaciona en tu universidad?
4. ¿Se escriben o se telefonean tú y tu familia?
5. ¿Se habla español en una tienda en tu ciudad?
6. ¿Dónde se encuentra comida china en tu ciudad?

¡ASÓMATE! 4
Ir de compras

Unas tiendas y unos negocios

1. el almacén
2. la carnicería
3. el centro comercial
4. la farmacia
5. la joyería
6. el mercado
7. la oficina
8. la panadería
9. la pastelería
10. la peluquería
11. el rascacielos
12. el supermercado
13. la tintorería
14. la zapatería

En la tienda

15. atender (e ➡ ie)
16. la caja
17. el cheque
18. el cheque de viajero
19. el cliente / la clienta
20. el dependiente / la dependienta
21. el descuento
22. en efectivo
23. la oferta

24. pagar
25. el precio
26. el probador
27. probarse (o ➡ ue)
28. no quedarle bien
29. el recibo
30. la talla / el tamaño
31. la tarjeta de crédito

Unos verbos útiles

aceptar	*to accept*
costar (o ➡ ue)	*to cost*
gastar	*to spend*
llevar	*to take; to carry; to wear*
pagar en efectivo, pagar al contado	*to pay cash*
usar	*to use*
valer	*to be worth*

Expresiones útiles

¿En qué puedo servirle?	*(How) can I help you?*
Estoy mirando nada más, gracias.	*I'm just looking, thank you.*
¿Qué número calza Ud.?	*What is your shoe size?; What size (shoe) do you wear?*
Qué talla lleva?	*What size do you wear?*

 If the meaning of any words are not clear, check the **Vocabulario activo** *at the end of the chapter.*

3 por $10

$100

$80

$50

6 **¿Cómo lo gastarías?** ¡Qué suerte! Tu tía te mandó $400 para que te compraras ropa nueva. Tu almacén favorito tiene una selección muy buena. Llena la gráfica en **Etapa 2, actividad 6** del **capítulo 8** en tu **Manual de actividades** con tus compras hasta los $400.

7 **Para contestar.** Contesta las preguntas siguientes.

1. ¿Prefieres pagar en efectivo o con una tarjeta de crédito?
2. ¿Prefieres ir a tiendas pequeñas o a los almaneces grandes?
3. ¿Qué tienda tiene las mejores gangas *(bargains)*?
4. ¿Qué ofertas hay en enero?
5. ¿Cuánto dinero gastaste el mes pasado en ropa?
6. ¿Cuánto dinero gastas al año en ropa?
7. ¿Siempre te pruebas la ropa antes de comprarla?
8. ¿En qué tienda no te atienden bien?
9. ¿Qué tienda o almacén tiene las mejores ofertas para las cosas deportivas?
10. Según tú *(In your opinion),* ¿un traje de Armani vale lo que cuesta?
11. Según tú, ¿un vestido de Donna Karan vale lo que cuesta?
12. Con una prenda que de verdad quieres mucho, ¿siempre esperas las liquidaciones con la posibilidad de no encontrar tu talla, o compras la prenda más cara cuando tienen tu talla para estar seguro / segura *(sure)*?

8 **Concièrge.** ¡Qué suerte tienes! Trabajas como el portero *(concierge)* en el mejor hotel de tu estado. ¿Cómo contestarías a las demandas siguientes de los clientes?

1. Mi hijo tiene dolor de estómago. ¿Dónde puedo comprar antiácido?
2. Necesito arreglar mi boleto de vuelta.
3. Quiero comprar un regalo para el día de las Madres.
4. ¿Adónde podemos ir para comprar esquís?
5. Mi chaqueta está sucia. ¿Adónde puedo ir para que me la limpien?
6. Necesito cortarme el pelo.
7. Quiero comprar unos dulces y unas galletas.

9 **Vamos de compras.** Tu instructor te ha pedido llevar una prenda de ropa a la clase para «donar» a la «tienda» de tu clase. Dile a tu instructor lo que la prenda vale / cuesta. Entonces tu instructor te va a dar «dinero» para gastar. ¿Qué decides comprar?

Algunas preguntas que vas a preguntar al dependiente son: **¿Cuánto cuesta?; ¿Cuánto vale?; ¿Qué tallas tiene?; ¿Aceptan tarjetas de crédito?; ¿Dónde están los probadores?; ¿Dónde están las cosas en oferta?; ¿Dónde está la caja?**

¡ASÓMATE! 5
Unos eventos importantes de la vida

Algunos eventos de la vida

la boda

la luna de miel

el aniversario (de boda)

la cita

el cumpleaños

el divorcio

la graduación

la muerte

el nacimiento

Unos verbos útiles

casarse (con)	*to marry; to get married (to)*
celebrar	*to celebrate*
discutir	*to argue; to discuss*
divorciarse	*to divorce*
enamorarse (de)	*to fall in love (with)*
engañar	*to deceive*
nacer	*to be born*
pelear	*to fight*
salir (con)	*to go out (with)*
tener una cita	*to have a date; to have an appointment*
estar casado / casada	*to be married*
estar comprometido / comprometida	*to be engaged*

Otras palabras útiles

el anillo	*ring*
la flor	*flower*
el regalo	*gift*
la tarjeta	*card*

10 **¿Qué les compro?**   Tu amigo Raúl te dice que han pasado muchas cosas recientemente a algunos amigos y miembros de su familia. Dale consejos a Raúl sobre lo que debe hacer en cada ocasión.

Modelo   **RAÚL:**   Mi hermana ha tenido un bebé. ➠

TÚ: **Para el nacimiento de tu sobrino, debes comprarle un regalo.**

RAÚL: El abuelo de mi amigo murió. ➠

TÚ: **Para la muerte de su abuelo, debes comprar una tarjeta y mandársela a tu amigo.**

Raúl dice:
1. Mi hermano José cumple diez años.
2. Mi prima Mariela ha terminado sus estudios en la universidad.
3. Mis abuelos van a celebrar 45 años de casados.
4. He peleado con mi novia.
5. Mi hermana Josefina se casa en una semana.

11 **Preguntas personales.**   Con un compañero, respondan a las preguntas siguientes. ¿Son similares sus respuestas y experiencias?

1. ¿Cómo era la vida de tus padres cuando naciste?
2. ¿Te has enamorado de alguien?
3. Describe la mejor cita que has tenido.
4. Describe la peor cita que has tenido.
5. ¿Piensas casarte algún día?
6. ¿Quieres tener una boda?
7. ¿Dónde quieres pasar la luna de miel?
8. ¿Conoces a alguien que se haya divorciado?

¡ENTÉRATE!
El Día de los Muertos

En varios países hispanohablantes se celebra el Día de los Muertos entre el 31 de octubre y el 2 de noviembre. Se barren y se limpian las tumbas. Se construyen altares en honor al recién *(recently)* muerto. Se le lleva la comida y la bebida favorita a la tumba. También se le llevan otras cosas que al muerto le gustaban. Estas cosas van a acompañar el alma *(soul)* del muerto en su viaje al otro mundo.

¿Qué te parece?

1. ¿Qué hace tu familia para recordar a los muertos?
2. ¿Cuáles son otros días en que recordamos a los muertos en los Estados Unidos ?

¡FÍJATE! 4
El comparativo y superlativo

El comparativo

Comparing two or more *unequal* things in Spanish follows the same pattern as in English.

El hotel Hilton es <u>más</u> caro <u>que</u> el Motel 6.	*The Hilton is <u>more</u> expensive <u>than</u> Motel 6.*
El Motel 6 es <u>menos</u> caro <u>que</u> el hotel Hilton.	*Motel 6 is <u>less</u> expensive <u>than</u> the Hilton.*
En esta ciudad hay <u>más</u> hoteles <u>que</u> moteles.	*In this city there are <u>more</u> hotels <u>than</u> motels.*
Los botones del Hotel Nacional trabajan <u>más</u> duro <u>que</u> los botones del Hotel Luz.	*The bell boys of the National Hotel work <u>harder than</u> the bell boys of the Luz Hotel.*
El Hilton de Bogotá tiene <u>más de</u> 200 habitaciones.	*The Hilton of Bogotá has <u>more than</u> 200 rooms.*

A formula for comparing unequal things is:

más / menos + *adjective / noun / adverb* + **que**	*more / less . . . than*

When comparing numbers, **que** becomes **de,** as in **más de 200 habitaciones.**

Comparing two or more *equal* things is to express that something is *as_____as* something else.

Marta es <u>tan</u> alta <u>como</u> Marco.	*Marta is <u>as</u> tall <u>as</u> Marco.*
Estas chaquetas son <u>tan</u> caras <u>como</u> ésas.	*These jackets are <u>as</u> expensive <u>as</u> those.*
No tengo <u>tantas</u> clases <u>como</u> tú.	*I don't have <u>as many</u> classes <u>as</u> you (do).*
No tenemos <u>tanta</u> tarea <u>como</u> el año pasado.	*We don't have <u>as much</u> homework <u>as</u> last year.*
Mi profesor de español habla <u>tan</u> rápido <u>como</u> mi profesor de inglés.	*My Spanish professor speaks <u>as</u> rapidly <u>as</u> my English professor.*

A formula for comparing equal things is:

tan + *adjective / adverb* + **como**	*as . . . as*
tanto(a / os / as) + *noun* + **como**	*as much / many . . . as*

El superlativo

To compare three or more things or people, use the superlative forms.

El español es <u>la</u> clase <u>más</u>
    interesante <u>de</u> la universidad.

Spanish is <u>the most</u> interesting class <u>at</u>
    the university.

¿Es el aeropuerto Hartsfield de
    Atlanta <u>el</u> aeropuerto <u>más</u>
    concurrido <u>de</u> los Estados
    Unidos?

Is Atlanta's Hartsfield Airport <u>the</u>
    <u>busiest</u> airport <u>in</u> the United States?

Sí, ¡y el aeropuerto de mi pueblo es
    <u>el</u> <u>menos</u> concurrido!

Yes, and my town's airport is <u>the</u> <u>least</u>
    busy!

The formula for expressing the superlative is:

el, la, los, las _____ + **más / menos** + *adjective* + **de**

The adjectives **bueno / buena** and **malo / mala** are irregular in the comparative and
the superlative.

	Comparative	*Superlative*
bueno / buena *good*	mejor *better*	el mejor / la mejor *best*
malo / mala *bad*	peor *worse*	el peor / la peor *worst*

Comparative

Mi clase de español es <u>mejor que</u>
    mis otras clases.

My Spanish class is <u>better than</u> my other
    classes.

Superlative

Mi clase de español es <u>la mejor de</u>
    mis clases.

My Spanish class is <u>the best (one)</u> of my
    classes.

12 **Adivina, adivina.** Trae un objeto personal a la clase y escribe de tres a cinco frases
sobre el objeto, usando las formas comparativas. No digas el nombre de tu objeto.
Lee las frases en grupos de cuatro o cinco estudiantes a ver si los compañeros pueden
adivinar *(guess)* lo que es.

Modelo   **un bolígrafo**

1. Es más grande que un anillo.
2. Es tan importante como un libro.
3. Es menos largo que mi zapato.
4. Seguramente Uds. lo usan tanto como yo.
5. Es tan útil como un lápiz.

13 **¡La vida es emocionante!** Haz una lista de cuatro o cinco estados emocionales
como **preocupado, triste, alegre** o **nervioso.** Después, pregunta a tus compañeros de
clase «quién es la persona más _____ de la televisión, el béisbol, la política,
etc.» Después comparte las respuestas.

14 **Los mejores regalos.**　En grupos de dos hagan listas en una hoja de papel de las siguientes cosas. Luego hagan una gráfica de clase que represente las respuestas.

1. los mejores regalos que han recibido
2. los mejores regalos que han dado
3. los regalos perfectos para tus mejores amigos
4. el regalo perfecto para su profesor y algunos compañeros de clase

¡FÍJATE! 5
Los adjetivos demostrativos

Spanish has three demonstrative adjectives: **este** *(this),* which refers to something near the speaker; **ese** *(that),* which refers to something farther away from the speaker; and **aquel** *(that over there),* which refers to something far away from both the speaker and listener in time or distance. Since **este, ese,** and **aquel** are adjectives, they must agree with the nouns they modify in gender and number.

Este libro es fascinante.	*This book is fascinating.*
Esta casa es muy bonita.	*This house is very pretty.*
Estos libros son fascinantes.	*These books are fascinating.*
Estas casas son muy bonitas.	*These houses are very pretty.*
Ese libro es fascinante.	*That book is fascinating.*
Esa casa es muy bonita.	*That house is very pretty.*
Esos libros son fascinantes.	*Those books are fascinating.*
Esas casas son muy bonitas.	*Those houses are very pretty.*
Aquel libro es fascinante.	*That book is fascinating*
Aquella casa es muy bonita.	*That house is very pretty.*
Aquellos libros son muy fascinantes.	*Those books are fascinating.*
Aquellas casas son muy bonitas.	*Those houses are very pretty.*

15 **¿Qué opinas?** Mira las ilustraciones y con un compañero de clase, haz dos frases de cada ilustración, expresando tu opinión y usando formas de **este, ese** y **aquel.**

Modelo   **Me gusta este Jaguar pero no me gusta ese Corvette.**

16 **Mi universidad.** ¿Qué hay en tu sala de clase? ¿Cómo es tu universidad? Con un compañero, habla de lo que te gusta o no te gusta usando formas de **este, ese** y **aquel.** Haz por lo menos cinco frases de cada uno.

Modelo   **Me gusta esa mochila azul. Nuestro profesor de español es más in-**
           teresante que aquel profesor de química.

Colombia y los países norteños de la América del Sur

MAR CARIBE

OCÉANO PACÍFICO

Caracas
VENEZUELA

Bogotá
COLOMBIA

Cali

Zipaquirá

Quito

ECUADOR

Los Andes

Santa Fe de Bogotá, con unos 3.982.941 habitantes, está a unos 2.600 metros de altura.

El Museo del Oro en Santa Fe de Bogotá.

Más de 90% de las esmeraldas del mundo son sacadas de las minas de Colombia.

Varias civilizaciones importantes como los Sinú, Muisca, Tolima, Nariño y San Agustín ocuparon la región que hoy en día es Colombia antes de la llegada de Cristóbal Colón. Hoy el Museo del Oro en Santa Fe de Bogotá tiene más de 30.000 objetos de oro de estas civilizaciones.

1819   Simón Bolívar y su ejército derrotaron a los españoles.

los 1500   Con la colonización española, Colombia fue parte de Nueva Granada, un territorio que hoy en día incluye Venezuela, Ecuador y Panamá también.

los 1970   Desde los setenta, el mercado de las drogas ha afectado la economía y la política de Colombia. Colombia controla el 80% del mercado mundial de la cocaína.

1948–1957   Hubo algunas guerras civiles entre los liberales y los conservadores.

Zipaquirá es famosa por sus minas de sal que preceden al período de los muiscas.

Las flores frescas y las bananas también proveen ganancias de exportación.

¿Qué te parece?

1. ¿Por qué ha tenido Colombia menos conflictos políticos que los países de Centroamérica?

2. ¿Por qué tiene Colombia una economía tan fuerte y vibrante?

3. ¿Por qué tiene Colombia tantos terremotos?

LA RED ¡Navega la Internet!

To discover more information on the culture of this chapter, check the Holt Web site and other suggestions listed in your **Manual de actividades.**

http://www.hrwcollege.com/

1995 Un temblor dejó a cientos sin hogar y docenas de muertos.

1994 Ernesto Samper conquistó la Presidencia de la República con una de las votaciones más altas de la historia reciente del país: 3.7 millones de votos.

1998 al presente: El café es el producto principal de exportación. Cuenta con un 30% de todas las ganancias de exportación.

ETAPA 3

¡Cuéntame!

Ya lo sabemos

Nosotros ya sabemos algunos detalles del accidente de Adriana. ¿Cómo ocurrió? Aunque *(even though)* Rafi no sabe nada del accidente todavía, tiene unas dudas muy grandes sobre Adriana. ¿Cuáles son esas dudas? Así, el misterio continúa.

En este episodio vas a averiguar:

◆ cómo se enteró Rafi del accidente de Adriana
◆ qué ocurrió en la reunión de Rafi y Adriana
◆ lo que Adriana ya ha descubierto

Preguntas personales

1. ¿Crees que Rafi ama a Adriana? En tu opinión, ¿qué va a hacer Rafi al enterarse del accidente? ¿Qué harías tú en la misma situación?
2. ¿Qué sabemos ya del «otro hombre» de Adriana? ¿Quién es? ¿Por qué pasaron la noche en cuestión juntos?

Estrategias de lectura
Guessing from Context

Before consulting a Spanish dictionary, always try to guess the meaning of an unfamiliar word from context. In other words, look closely at the words and sentences that surround it and use them to derive meaning. Also pay attention to the tone of the passage. Consider the following:

Le dije que tenía un código y que iba a tratar de <u>descifrarlo</u>.

If you don't already know the meaning of **descifrar,** you should be able to make a good guess by thinking about what you try to do with codes, that is, break them or decipher them.

Read the episode, employing this new strategy as needed. Afterward, you may be asked to share with your instructor the number of times you guessed from context and to verify those guesses.

Rafi y el sacrificio final

Episodio 8: Dudas

Rafi y Chema estaban en el avión. Rafi no había dormido en toda la noche. Cuando regresaron de Chichén Itzá, había un mensaje° para Rafi en el contestador del teléfono de los abuelos de Chema. Carmen lo había llamado para decirle que Adriana había tenido un accidente y que estaba grave. Rafi no sabía qué pensar. Primero, su tío y sus problemas e intrigas y ahora Adriana. Adriana había tenido un novio a la misma vez que salía con él. Casi no podía aguantar° el dolor° y los celos° que sentía en ese momento.

    Tomaron un taxi directamente del aeropuerto al hospital. Rafi y Chema entraron al Hospital General, donde estaba Adriana. Después de pedir el número de la habitación, llegaron a un pasillo° donde había un guardia de seguridad que estaba de pie afuera de la habitación de ella. En ese momento Rafi creía que iba a morir de ansiedad°.

    Después de identificarse, el guardia los escoltó adentro de la habitación. Allí estaba Adriana, más bella que nunca. Rafi no sabía qué hacer hasta que vio los brazos de Adriana extendidos hacia él. Ella lloraba°.

    Chema y el guardia decidieron conversar fuera de la habitación. Después de un abrazo° eterno que Rafi había pensado que nunca iba a llegar, Adriana le dijo, —Escúchame porque no hay mucho tiempo.

    Adriana empezó a contarle a Rafi un cuento interesantísimo. Resulta que aquella noche cuando se despidieron y Rafi regresó a la residencia a eso de las once, Adriana recibió una llamada. —Era mi vecino° Miguel. Dijo que había oído un ruido y quería saber si yo estaba bien. Le dije que sí y que nada más iba a estar trabajando hasta tarde. Le dije que tenía un código y que iba a tratar de descifrarlo. Miguel me recordó que era arqueólogo y me preguntó si podía ayudarme.

    —Entonces lo invité al apartamento. Él vino inmediatamente y trabajamos toda la noche. Los dibujos debajo del mapa resultaron ser escritura incaica. Indicaron dónde había una tumba con las reliquias de un sacrificio final cerca de Cuzco, Perú. El mapa mostraba el lugar donde se podía encontrar aquella tumba.

    —Miguel salió de mi apartamento a eso de las seis y media de la mañana y yo había estado pensando en algo toda la noche. No se lo había dicho a Miguel, pero tenía una idea sobre lo que significaba «Roma». Había empezado a buscar en la Red° cuando decidí llamarte para decirte lo que había descubierto. Cuando me dijiste que ibas a venir a visitarme aquella tarde, yo sabía que iba a tener más tiempo para investigar lo de «Roma». ¡Más tarde descubrí algo más de lo que esperaba!

(marginal glosses:)
- message
- bear / pain / jealousy
- hall
- **morir de ansiedad** to die of anxiety
- was crying
- hug
- neighbor
- the Internet

Comprensión

1. ¿Cómo se enteró Rafi del accidente?
2. ¿Por qué no sabía qué pensar Rafi?
3. ¿Cómo reaccionó al saber del accidente?
4. Al llegar al hospital, ¿pudo ver a Adriana inmediatamente?
5. Por fin, ¿cómo recibió Adriana a Rafi?
6. ¿Qué información le da Adriana a Rafi sobre lo siguiente?
   a. Miguel
   b. sus propios sentimientos
   c. la pista de las reliquias cerca de Cuzco

Expansión

(1) ¿Cuáles son las decisiones que Rafi tiene que tomar ahora? En tu opinión, ¿qué va a hacer después de salir del hospital? ¿Va a continuar la búsqueda?

(2) Basado en lo que ya saben del misterio, hablen de los posibles significados para «Roma, sacrificio final.»

(3) En parejas, dramaticen la escena entre Adriana y Rafi desde el momento que Rafi entra en la habitación de ella en el hospital.

(4) En parejas, inventen y realicen la escena entre Chema y el guardia en el pasillo mientras esperaban a Rafi.

(5) Eres reportero / reportera y tienes que escribir un breve artículo para el periódico sobre el accidente de Adriana. No te olvides de contestar las preguntas ¿qué?, ¿quién?, ¿dónde? y ¿cuándo?

(6) En el vuelo de vuelta a los Estados Unidos, Rafi y Chema hablan del tío Pedro, de cómo empezó la búsqueda, de Adriana y de lo que hicieron en México. Ayúdalos a organizar esta información. Escribe un resumen de una página de lo que dicen.

A mirar o escuchar

(7) View the video or listen to the audio CD to find out what happens next to Rafi. Consult your **Manual de actividades** for pre- and post-listening activities.

¡Sí, se puede!

1. **Tic-tac-toe.** Haz una cuadrícula de tic-tac-toe en una hoja de papel. Llena cada cuadro con una palabra en español usando la lista del vocabulario nuevo de este capítulo. Puedes usar el orden que quieras. Asegúrate de que las palabras estén deletreadas correctamente.

   Ahora escoge una palabra de la lista y dísela a tu compañero en inglés. Si tu compañero ha escrito la misma palabra en español en su cuadrícula, pueden entonces tacharla. Ahora tu compañero va a seleccionar una palabra en inglés para decírtela. Y así se continúa. El primero / La primera en tener tres palabras seguidas, —ya sea, horizontal, diagonal o vertical— es el primero / la primera ganador.

2. **¿Se conocen bien?** En parejas, escribe (¡en secreto!) tres semejanzas y tres diferencias entre tú y tu compañero. Después comparen sus listas y reaccionen. Estén preparados para compartir sus diferencias y semejanzas con los otros miembros de la clase.

3. **El coche no funciona bien.** Necesitas llevar tu coche a un mecánico. En parejas, hagan los papeles del conductor y del mecánico. Necesitan descubrir el problema con el coche, hablar de posibles soluciones y de cuánto tiempo se necesita para repararlo.

4. **El transporte.** Con un compañero, hablen de por lo menos tres formas de transporte que han usado y compárenlas, pensando en los puntos positivos y negativos de cada uno.

5. **Querido mío...** Escribe una carta de amor a una persona verdadera o ficticia. Puedes usar estos términos de cariño si quieres:

mi alma	*my love (literally, my soul)*
mi amor	*my love*
cariño *(adj.; n.)*	*affection; honey; dear*
mi cielo	*my heaven / love*
mi corazón	*my heart / love*

Querido / Querida _____:

Besos,

_____

Para recordar

Having completed this chapter, you are now able to:

Etapa 1 ¡Sígueme!

❒ talk about different means of transportation

❒ use the present and past perfect tenses to express what has and had happened in the past

❒ compare your holiday celebrations and those of the Spanish-speaking world

❒ plan a trip

Etapa 2 ¡Dime más!

❒ use past participles as adjectives

❒ use **se** to express *each other* and *one*

❒ buy and sell things

❒ describe **el día de los muertos**

❒ use the comparative and superlative to compare and contrast items and express ideas

❒ identify items using the demonstrative adjectives **este, ese,** and **aquel**

❒ explore Colombia and some neighboring countries of northern South America

Etapa 3 ¡Cuéntame!

❒ share what Adriana learned about the codes before her accident.

 *You can practice concepts from this and earlier chapters by doing the* **¡Recuérdate!** *section in your* **Manual de actividades.**

VOCABULARIO ACTIVO

El transporte

el autobús *bus*	el coche *car*	la moto(cicleta) *motorcycle*
el avión *airplane*	el camión *truck*	el taxi *taxi*
el barco *boat*	el metro *subway*	el tren *train*
la bicicleta *bicycle*		

Unas cosas asociadas con el transporte

la autopista *freeway*	el estacionamiento *parking*	el permiso (de conducir) *driver's*
el boleto *ticket*	la multa *traffic ticket, fine*	*license*
la calle *street*	la parada *bus stop*	el policía *policeman*
la cola *line (of people)*	el peatón / los peatones *pedestrian /*	el ruido *noise*
la estación de servicio *gas*	*pedestrians*	el semáforo *traffic light*
station		el tráfico *traffic*

Unas partes de un vehículo

el aire acondicionado *air*	el limpiaparabrisas *windshield*	el motor *motor; engine*
conditioning	*wiper*	el parabrisas *windshield*
el baúl *trunk*	la llanta *tire*	la rueda *wheel*
la calefacción *heater*	la llave *key*	el tanque *gas tank*

Unos verbos útiles

aceptar *to accept*	estacionarse *to park*	prestar *to lend; to borrow*
arreglar la maleta *to pack a*	estar... *to be . . .*	probarse (o ➠ ue) *to try on*
suitcase	casado(a) *married*	(no) quedarle bien *to (not) fit*
cambiar *to change*	comprometido(a) *engaged*	registrarse (en el hotel) *to check in*
caminar *to walk*	funcionar *to work; to function*	revisar *to check; to overhaul*
casarse (con) *to marry; to get*	gastar *to spend*	salir (con) *to go out (with)*
married (to)	hacer la maleta *to pack a suitcase*	salir del hotel *to leave the hotel; to*
celebrar *to celebrate*	ir a pie *to walk*	*check out*
costar (o ➠ ue) *to cost*	llenar *to fill*	tener una cita *to have a date; to*
discutir *to argue; to discuss*	llevar *to take; to carry; to wear*	*have an appointment*
divorciarse *to divorce*	manejar *to drive*	valer *to be worth*
doblar *to turn*	nacer *to be born*	viajar *to travel*
enamorarse de *to fall in love with*	pelear *to fight*	visitar *to visit*
engañar *to deceive*	perder (e ➠ ie) *to miss; to lose*	volar (o ➠ ue) *to fly; to fly away*

El viaje

el aeropuerto *airport*	la estación (de tren, de autobús)	el pasaporte *passport*
la agencia de viajes *travel*	*(train, bus) station*	los viajeros *travelers*
agency	la maleta *suitcase*	el vuelo *flight*
el boleto de ida y vuelta *round-*		
trip ticket		

El hotel

el botones   *bellman*
el cuarto doble   *double room*
el cuarto individual   *single room*
la propina   *tip*
la recepción   *front desk*

Unos lugares

el lago   *lake*
las montañas   *mountains*
el parque de atracciones   *theme park*
la playa   *beach*

Cómo te sientes

estar animado / animada   *to be excited*
estar avergonzado / avergonzada   *to be ashamed, embarrassed*
estar celoso / celosa   *to be jealous*
estar deprimido / deprimida   *to be depressed*
estar desilusionado / desilusionada   *to be disappointed, disillusioned*
estar despistado / despistada   *to be absent-minded, flaky*
estar emocionado / emocionada   *to be moved, touched; upset*
estar enamorado / enamorada   *to be in love*
estar entusiasmado / entusiasmada   *to be enthusiastic*
estar harto / harta   *to be fed up, tired*
estar molesto / molesta   *to be bothered, upset*
estar ocupado / ocupada   *to be busy; occupied*
estar orgulloso / orgullosa   *to be proud*
estar perdido / perdida   *to be lost; wasted*

Unas tiendas y unos negocios

el almacén   *department store*
la carnicería   *butcher shop*
el centro comercial   *mall; business district*
la farmacia   *pharmacy*
la joyería   *jewelry store*
el mercado   *market*
la oficina   *office*
la panadería   *bakery, bread shop*
la pastelería   *pastry shop*
la peluquería   *beauty salon; barber shop*
el rascacielos   *skyscraper*
el supermercado   *supermarket*
la tintorería   *dry cleaners*
la zapatería   *shoe store*

En la tienda

atender (e ⟹ ie)   *to assist; to wait on*
la caja   *cash register*
el cheque   *bank check*
el cheque de viajero   *traveler's check*
el cliente / la clienta   *client*
el dependiente / la dependiente   *salesclerk*
el descuento   *discount*
en efectivo   *cash*
la oferta   *offer, sale*
pagar   *to pay*
el precio   *price*
el probador   *fitting room*
el recibo   *receipt*
la talla   *size*
el tamaño   *size*
la tarjeta de credito   *credit card*

Algunos eventos de la vida

el aniversario (de boda)   *wedding anniversary*
la boda   *wedding*
la cita   *date; meeting*
el cumpleaños   *birthday*
el divorcio   *divorce*
la graduación   *graduation*
la luna de miel   *honeymoon*
la muerte   *death*
el nacimiento   *birth*

Otras palabras útiles

el anillo   *ring*
el extranjero   *abroad*
el regalo   *gift*
el sello   *postage stamp*
la tarjeta   *card*
la tarjeta postal   *post card*
el timbre   *postage stamp*
las vacaciones   *vacation*

NICARAGUA

MAR CARIBE

COSTA RICA

San José

PANAMÁ

OCÉANO PACÍFICO

¿Qué peligros del medio ambiente existen hoy en día? Hay más de 5.000 especies de animales que están en peligro de extinción. El 70% de los habitantes de las ciudades respiran aire contaminado. Otro 10% respiran aire que probablemente está contaminado. Las selvas tropicales cubren menos del 10% de la superficie del mundo; sin embargo, contienen más del 50% de todas las especies de plantas y animales existentes. Se cree que hay millones de especies que aún no hemos descubierto. Hoy en día queda menos de la mitad de la selva tropical original. Los campesinos y rancheros queman (burn) la tierra para limpiarla y cultivarla, y venden la madera de los árboles que cortan. En un año cortan un área del tamaño de Bélgica. Cada minuto que pasa, destrozan (destroy) cien acres de selva tropical. A este paso, dentro de 40 años, las selvas tropicales habrán desaparecido, y con ellas todos los productos y medicinas que nos suministran (supply).

¿Qué te parece?

1. ¿Puedes nombrar algunos animales que están en peligro de extinción? ¿Por qué crees que están en peligro?
2. ¿Qué factores contribuyen a la contaminación del aire?
3. ¿Por qué es tan importante proteger las selvas?
4. ¿Qué podemos hacer como nación, estado e individuos para mejorar el medio ambiente?

El mundo actual

By the end of this chapter you will be able to:

ETAPA 1 ¡Sígueme!

- give your opinion on environmental issues
- express what is important or necessary for you or others to do

ETAPA 2 ¡Dime más!

- ◆ comment on social issues, government, and current affairs
- ◆ travel to the environmentally conscious Costa Rica

ETAPA 3 ¡Cuéntame!

- ● discover who caused Adriana's accident and what has to be done to save the treasures of Peru

¡ASÓMATE! 1
Los animales

Unos animales

1. el caballo
2. el cerdo
3. el conejo
4. el elefante
5. la gallina
6. el gato
7. la hormiga
8. el insecto
9. el león
10. la mosca

11. el mosquito
12. el oso
13. el pájaro
14. el perro
15. el pez (*pl.* los peces)
16. la rata
17. el ratón
18. la serpiente
19. el toro
20. la vaca

Otras palabras útiles

un animal doméstico	*a domesticated animal, pet*
un animal en peligro de extinción	*an endangered species*
un animal salvaje	*a wild animal*
el árbol	*tree*
el bosque	*forest*
la cueva	*cave*
la finca	*farm*
la granja	*farm*
el hoyo	*hole*
el lago	*lake*
la montaña	*mountain*
el océano	*ocean*
el rancho	*farm*
el río	*river*
la selva	*jungle*
peligroso / peligrosa	*dangerous*

Unos verbos

cuidar   *to take care of*
preocuparse por   *to worry about; to concern oneself with*

*For additional names of animals, see the **También se dice...** section, in Appendix A, at the end of the book.*

1 **Los que me gustan.**   ¿Te gustan los animales? ¿Cuáles son tus animales favoritos? ¿Cuáles son los que menos te gustan? Llena la gráfica con tus respuestas.

Los animales que me gustan	Los animales que no me gustan
1.	1.
2.	2.
3.	3.

Ahora compara tu gráfica con el de un compañero. ¿Son idénticos? Expliquen por qué les gustan o no les gustan. Reporten sus respuestas a la clase. En tu clase, ¿qué animal es el más popular? ¿El menos popular?

2 **¿Me ayudas?**   Con un compañero, hagan una lista de los animales que (1) más nos ayudan y que (2) menos nos ayudan. Usen la gráfica en **Etapa 1, actividad 2** en **capítulo 9** de tu **Manual de actividades.** Luego, expliquen a la clase por qué los escogieron.

3 **¿Qué opinas?**   Es tiempo para hacer una encuesta de tus compañeros. Pregúntales a tus compañeros las preguntas de la gráfica en **Etapa 1, actividad 3** en **capítulo 9** de tu **Manual de actividades.** Escribe el nombre de un estudiante diferente en cada cuadrado.

4 **¿Quién... ?**   En grupos pequeños, lean la lista a continuación. Después, háblenles a sus compañeros sobre los asuntos de la lista que a Uds. o a alguien conocido les han ocurrido. Cuando una persona dice algo, apúntenlo, porque después van a compartir lo que descubrieron con la clase. Sigan el modelo.

Modelo   **tener miedo de las serpientes**

COMPAÑERO: Tengo miedo de las serpientes.

ESCRIBES: *(Nombre del compañero / de la compañera)* tiene miedo de las serpientes.

COMPAÑERO: Mi amigo / amiga *(nombre del compañero / de la compañera)* vio un oso el año pasado.

ESCRIBES: El amigo / la amiga de *(nombre del compañero / de la compañera)* vio un oso el año pasado.

1. tener miedo de las serpientes
2. ver un oso el año pasado
3. gustarle los gatos / los perros
4. tener un tipo de animal
5. preocuparse por los animales en peligro de extinción
6. haber montado a caballo
7. haber tenido hormigas en la casa
8. haber tenido pájaros / peces de niño

9. gustarle cuidar animales
10. odiar los insectos, incluyendo moscas
    y mosquitos
11. ver un conejo cerca de la casa
12. ordeñar *(to milk)* una vaca

¡FÍJATE! 1
Los adverbios

Many Spanish adverbs end in the suffix **-mente,** which is equivalent to the English suffix *-ly.* Such Spanish adverbs are formed by adding **-mente** to the feminine form of an adjective. If the adjective ends in a consonant or in **-e,** simply add **-mente.** If the adjective has a written accent, it is retained when **-mente** is added.

Adjetivo masculino		*Adjetivo femenino*		*Adverbio*
lento	➡	lenta	➡	lenta**mente**
fácil	➡	fácil	➡	fácil**mente**
suave	➡	suave	➡	suave**mente**

5 **Practicándolo.**   Cambia los adjetivos siguientes en adverbios.

Modelo   normal   ➡   **normalmente**

1. general
2. triste
3. feliz

4. nervioso
5. formal
6. claro

6 **Para conocerte.**   Describe cómo haces lo siguiente cambiando los adjetivos siguientes en adverbios. Sigue el modelo.

alegre • cómodo • difícil • divino • fácil • frecuente • rápido • tranquilo • único

Modelo   ¿Cómo bailas?   ➡   **Bailo divinamente.**

1. ¿Cómo estudias?
2. ¿Cómo cocinas?
3. ¿Cómo cantas?
4. ¿Cómo manejas?

5. ¿Cómo hablas?
6. ¿Cómo duermes?
7. ¿Cómo limpias la casa?

¡ENTÉRATE!

Los animales en peligro de extinción

Por todo el mundo, hay muchos animales que están en peligro de extinción. Esto ocurre por varias razones. Primero, los animales y los humanos compiten por los mismos recursos naturales. Por ejemplo, los búhos necesitan árboles para hacer sus nidos *(nests)* y bosques para cazar *(hunt)* su comida. El hombre compite por los mismos árboles y tierras para construir sus casas.

También, hay animales como los cocodrilos que tienen una piel que vale mucho dinero en el mercado internacional. La demanda es tan alta que el hombre ha matado animales en exceso.

¿Qué te parece?

1. ¿Por qué hay animales en peligro de extinción? (dos razones)
2. ¿Es importante proteger y preocuparse por los animales en peligro de extinción? ¿Por qué?
3. ¿Hay animales en tu estado que están en peligro de extinción? Si los hay, ¿cuáles son? ¿Por qué están en peligro?

el águila calva

el manatí

la ballena azul

la pantera

el oso pardo

el elefante

el búho

el cocodrilo

la tortuga

¡ENTÉRATE!
Los animales en los deportes y espectáculos

Como en los Estados Unidos, hay deportes y espectáculos en los países hispanohablantes que utilizan animales. Por ejemplo, hay carreras *(races)* de caballos y perros.

También, hay un espectáculo que el mundo asocia más con los hispanohablantes, la corrida de toros. La corrida de toros se originó en España, pero los españoles la llevaron al Nuevo Mundo, a sus colonias. Todavía, hay corridas de toros en algunos países hispanohablantes.

En la ciudad de Pamplona, España, se celebra la famosa fiesta de San Fermín en la semana del 7 de julio. La tradición es que los toros corren por las calles de la ciudad hasta llegar a la plaza de toros. Jóvenes vestidos de blanco con pañuelo y cinturón rojo demuestran su valentía al correr enfrente de los toros.

¿Qué te parece?

1. ¿Cuáles son algunos deportes o espectáculos que utilizan animales?
2. Donde tú vives, ¿hay carreras de caballos o perros?
3. ¿Cuál es la carrera de caballos más famosa en los Estados Unidos?
4. ¿Cómo crees que se originó la corrida de toros?
5. ¿Qué opinas de los jóvenes que corren enfrente de los toros durante la celebración de San Fermín? ¿Son valientes o tontos?
6. ¿Te gustan los deportes con animales? ¿Por qué sí o por qué no?

Una corrida de toros, Madrid, España

Una carrera de caballos en
Hialeah, Florida

La fiesta de San Fermín,
Pamplona, España

Una carrera de perros en Miami, Florida

¡ASÓMATE! 2
El medio ambiente

El medio ambiente

1. el aluminio
2. la botella
3. la caja (de cartón)
4. la contaminación
5. el derrame de petróleo
6. el huracán
7. el incendio
8. la inundación
9. la lata
10. el papel
11. el periódico
12. el plástico
13. el terremoto
14. la tormenta
15. el tornado
16. el vidrio
17. botar
18. reciclar
19. sembrar (e ➡ ie)

Unos verbos

contaminar	*to pollute*
evitar	*to avoid*
hacer daño	*to (do) damage*
matar	*to kill*
proteger	*to protect*
reforestar	*to reforest*
rehusar	*to refuse*

Otras palabras útiles

el aire	*air*
la basura	*garbage*
el calentamiento de la tierra	*global warming*
la calidad	*quality*
la capa de ozono	*ozone layer*
el cielo	*sky; heaven*
el desastre	*disaster*
la destrucción	*destruction*
la ecología	*ecology*
la lluvia ácida	*acid rain*
la naturaleza	*nature*
el planeta	*planet*
puro / pura	*pure*
el recurso	*resource*
la selva tropical	*(tropical) rain forest; jungle*
la Tierra	*Earth*
la tierra	*land; soil*
la tragedia	*tragedy*
el vertedero	*dump*
vivo / viva	*alive, living*

Sígue a la página 282 para más dibujos.

7 **¡Qué desastre!** La siguiente es una lista de desastres naturales que mataron a un sinnúmero de personas. Adivina qué tipo de tragedia ocurrió en cada uno.

¿Cuándo?	¿Dónde?	Muertos	Desastre
1. agosto de 1931	el río Huang He, China	3.700.000	**una inundación**
2. el 24 de enero de 1556	Shaanxi, China	830.000	
3. el 18 de marzo de 1925	Missouri, Illinois, Indiana	689	
4. el 25–27 de marzo de 1913	Ohio, Indiana	732	
5. el 13 de noviembre de 1970	Bangladesh	300.000	
6. agosto–septiembre de 1900	Galveston, Texas	6.000	

Ahora, comparte tus adivinanzas con un compañero. ¿Están de acuerdo? Ahora, comparen sus respuestas con las del **Manual de actividades,** en **capítulo 9, Etapa 1, actividad 7.** Escribe una oración para cada tragedia.

8 **Hay que reciclar.** ¿Qué hacen tu familia, tu pueblo y tu universidad para proteger el medio ambiente? Reporta quién hace qué para mantener nuestro universo. El modelo te dará algunas ideas.

Modelo   **Yo voy a la universidad en bicicleta para evitar la contaminación del aire. Mi familia y yo reciclamos el plástico. Mi pueblo ofrece programas de prevención contra incendios. Mi universidad dio un seminario sobre el calentamiento de la Tierra y la destrucción de la capa de ozono.**

9 **El reportero.** En preparación para un artículo para el periódico de tu universidad, escribe tres oraciones sobre lo que se puede hacer para proteger el medio ambiente y tres cosas que se deben hacer en el futuro. Puedes usar la lista a continuación como guía. Después, en grupos pequeños, comparen sus oraciones y juntos escriban un artículo con recomendaciones para proteger el medio ambiente.

Modelo   **Para evitar la destrucción de los bosques, no se deben cortar árboles. En el futuro, se deben sembrar dos árboles por cada uno que se corte.**

sembrar muchos árboles y plantas

reciclar el plástico y el vidrio

rehusar el uso de productos del petróleo

andar en bicicleta

usar carros eléctricos

proteger los animales en vías de extinción

apoyar las instituciones de conservación de los recursos naturales

volver a usar las cajas de cartón

proteger la selva tropical

reforestar los bosques

usar el carro lo menos posible

usar la energía solar

no prender *(to turn on)* a menudo el aire acondicionado

educar a los campesinos a no quemar la tierra para evitar la erosión

¡ENTÉRATE!
El medio ambiente

Como en el resto del mundo, hay países hispanos que le dan más importancia a los asuntos del medio ambiente que otros. Costa Rica, por ejemplo, inició un programa de establecimiento y desarrollo de parques nacionales y reservas en 1970. Al principio hubo muchos problemas. Había poco personal, poco apoyo público y poca legislación. Algunas áreas estaban en peligro de perder sus recursos naturales. Pero gracias al interés de algunos costarricenses y extranjeros, al apoyo internacional y al enorme esfuerzo del pequeño Departamento de Parques Nacionales, el sistema de parques creció. En la actualidad, hay muchos parques nacionales que abarcan aproximadamente unas 525.000 hectáreas y constituyen un 10% del territorio nacional. Los parques han beneficiado la ciencia, la educación, el turismo y la economía. Entre los más conocidos están los parques nacionales de Manuel Antonio, Corcovado, Isla de Coco, Braulio Carrillo y Tortuguero. En los parques de Costa Rica hay cataratas *(waterfalls),* cavernas, volcanes activos, aguas termales, monumentos históricos y arqueológicos y un sinfín de plantas y animales, además de playas hermosas y mucho sol.

¿Qué te parece?

1. ¿Qué ha hecho Costa Rica para proteger el medio ambiente?
2. ¿Cómo se ha beneficiado Costa Rica con su sistema de parques?
3. ¿Qué porcentaje del territorio nacional está protegido?
4. ¿Qué haces tú personalmente para proteger el medio ambiente?
5. ¿Qué haces que daña el medio ambiente?
6. Según tú, ¿qué debemos hacer para proteger el medio ambiente?
7. ¿Te gustaría visitar alguno de los parques de Costa Rica? ¿Por qué sí o por qué no?

¡FÍJATE! 2
El subjuntivo, parte 1

In addition to *tenses,* such as the present, past, and future tense, there are two *moods:* the indicative and the subjunctive. Up to this point you have studied the *indicative* mood, which is the mood or mode of reporting what happened, is happening, or will happen. The *subjunctive* mood is one that expresses doubt, insecurity, influence, opinion, feelings, hope, wishes, or desires.

To form the subjunctive, take the **yo** form of the present tense, drop the **-o,** and add the endings below. There is one set of endings for **-ar** verbs and another set for **-er** and **-ir** verbs.

estudiar			
Es necesario que	yo	**estudie**	más.
Es necesario que	tú	**estudies**	más.
Es necesario que	él, ella, Ud.	**estudie**	más.
Es necesario que	nosotros, nosotras	**estudiemos**	más.
Es necesario que	vosotros, vosotras	**estudiéis**	más.
Es necesario que	ellos, ellas, Uds.	**estudien**	más.

comer

Es necesario que	yo	**coma**	menos grasa.
Es necesario que	tú	**comas**	menos grasa.
Es necesario que	él, ella, Ud.	**coma**	menos grasa.
Es necesario que	nosotros, nosotras	**comamos**	menos grasa.
Es necesario que	vosotros, vosotras	**comáis**	menos grasa.
Es necesario que	ellos, ellas, Uds.	**coman**	menos grasa.

vivir

Es necesario que	yo	**viva**	en un lugar económico.
Es necesario que	tú	**vivas**	en un lugar económico.
Es necesario que	él, ella, Ud.	**viva**	en un lugar económico.
Es necesario que	nosotros, nosotras	**vivamos**	en un lugar económico.
Es necesario que	vosotros, vosotras	**viváis**	en un lugar económico.
Es necesario que	ellos, ellas, Uds.	**vivan**	en un lugar económico.

venir

Es necesario que	yo	**venga**	temprano.
Es necesario que	tú	**vengas**	temprano.
Es necesario que	él, ella, Ud.	**venga**	temprano.
Es necesario que	nosotros, nosotras	**vengamos**	temprano.
Es necesario que	vosotros, vosotras	**vengáis**	temprano.
Es necesario que	ellos, ellas, Uds.	**vengan**	temprano.

Some Irregular Forms

Verbs ending in **-car, -gar,** and **-zar** have a spelling change in all present subjunctive forms, in order to maintain the sound of the infinitive.

Verbs ending in **-car** change **c** to **qu: yo busco** ⟶ **que busque**

Verbs ending in **-gar** change **g** to **gu: yo pago** ⟶ **que pague**

Verbs ending in **-zar** change **z** to **c: yo empiezo** ⟶ **que empiece**

buscar

yo	busque	nosotros, nosotras	busquemos
tú	busques	vosotros, vosotras	busquéis
él, ella, Ud.	busque	ellos, ellas, Uds.	busquen

pagar			
yo	pague	nosotros, nosotras	paguemos
tú	pagues	vosotros, vosotras	paguéis
él, ella, Ud.	pague	ellos, ellas, Uds.	paguen

empezar			
yo	empiece	nosotros, nosotras	empecemos
tú	empieces	vosotros, vosotras	empecéis
él, ella, Ud.	empiece	ellos, ellas, Uds.	empiecen

Dar has a written accent on the first- and third-person singular forms (**dé**) to distinguish it from the preposition **de.** All forms of **estar,** except the **nosotros** form, have a written accent in the present subjunctive. The verbs **ir, saber,** and **ser** have irregular subjunctive stems.

dar			
yo	dé	nosotros, nosotras	demos
tú	des	vosotros, vosotras	deis
él, ella, Ud.	dé	ellos, ellas, Uds.	den

estar			
yo	esté	nosotros, nosotras	estemos
tú	estés	vosotros, vosotras	estéis
él, ella, Ud.	esté	ellos, ellas, Uds.	estén

saber			
yo	sepa	nosotros, nosotras	sepamos
tú	sepas	vosotros, vosotras	sepáis
él, ella, Ud.	sepa	ellos, ellas, Uds.	sepan

ser			
yo	sea	nosotros, nosotras	seamos
tú	seas	vosotros, vosotras	seáis
él, ella, Ud.	sea	ellos, ellas, Uds.	sean

ir			
yo	vaya	nosotros, nosotras	vayamos
tú	vayas	vosotros, vosotras	vayáis
él, ella, Ud.	vaya	ellos, ellas, Uds.	vayan

Stem-Changing Verbs

In the present subjunctive, stem-changing **-ar** and **-er** verbs make the same vowel change that they do in the present indicative: **e ➡ ie** and **o ➡ ue.** The pattern is different with stem-changing **-ir** verbs. In addition to their usual changes of **e ➡ ie, e ➡ i,** and **o ➡ ue,** in the **nosotros** and **vosotros** forms the stem vowels change **e ➡ i** and **o ➡ u.**

pensar (e ➡ ie)			
yo	piense	nosotros, nosotras	pensemos
tú	pienses	vosotros, vosotras	penséis
él, ella, Ud.	piense	ellos, ellas, Uds.	piensen

poder (o ➡ ue)			
yo	pueda	nosotros, nosotras	podamos
tú	puedas	vosotros, vosotras	podáis
él, ella, Ud.	pueda	ellos, ellas, Uds.	puedan

sentir (e ➡ ie, i)			
yo	sienta	nosotros, nosotras	sintamos
tú	sientas	vosotros, vosotras	sintáis
él, ella, Ud.	sienta	ellos, ellas, Uds.	sientan

dormir (o ➡ ue, u)			
yo	duerma	nosotros, nosotras	durmamos
tú	duermas	vosotros, vosotras	durmáis
él, ella, Ud.	duerma	ellos, ellas, Uds.	duerman

pedir (e ➡ i, i)			
yo	pida	nosotros, nosotras	pidamos
tú	pidas	vosotros, vosotras	pidáis
él, ella, Ud.	pida	ellos, ellas, Uds.	pidan

Using the Subjunctive

One of the uses of the subjunctive is with fixed expressions. The following expressions are always followed by the subjunctive.

Es bueno / malo / mejor que...	*It's good / bad / better that . . .*
Es dudoso que...	*It's doubtful that . . .*
Es increíble que...	*It's incredible that . . .*
Es importante que...	*It's important that . . .*
Es imposible que...	*It's impossible that . . .*
Es improbable que...	*It's unlikely that . . .*
Es (una) lástima que...	*It's a pity that . . .*
Es necesario que...	*It's necessary that . . .*
Es posible que...	*It's possible that . . .*
Es preferible que...	*It's preferable that . . .*
Es probable que...	*It's likely that . . .*
Es raro que...	*It's rare (that) . . .*
Ojalá (que)...	*Let's hope that . . . / Hopefully . . .*

The expression **Ojalá (que)** *comes from an Arabic expression meaning* May it be Allah's will. *The conjunction* **que** *is optional in this expression.*

Es necesario que <u>protejamos</u> los animales en peligro de extinción.	*It's necessary that <u>we protect</u> the endangered animals.*
Es una lástima que algunas personas <u>no quieran</u> reciclar el plástico, el vidrio, el aluminio y el papel.	*It's a shame that some people <u>don't want</u> to recycle plastic, glass, aluminum, and paper.*
Ojalá (que) <u>haya</u> menos destrucción del medio ambiente en el futuro.	*Let's hope that <u>there is</u> less destruction of the environment in the future.*

To review:

1. What is the difference between the subjunctive and the indicative moods?
2. What other verb forms look like the subjunctive?
3. Where does the subjunctive verb come in relation to the word **que?**

10 **Para practicar.**   Termina las frases siguientes. Haz una frase para cada persona.

Modelo   Es preferible que ella / nosotros / tú (reciclar el vidrio)   ➭

    Es preferible que ella recicle el vidrio.

    Es preferible que nosotros reciclemos el vidrio.

    Es preferible que tú recicles el vidrio.

1. Es necesario que yo / ellos / Uds. / nosotros (cuidar el perro)
2. Es dudoso que tú / Marta y yo / ella (manejar con cuidado)
3. Es bueno que ellos / él / nosotros (revisar las llantas)
4. Es posible que nosotros / yo / tú / Uds. (no tener un examen la semana próxima)

When a classmate asks you a question in **actividad 11,** *use the subjunctive and answer the question in a complete sentence.*

11 **¿Para quién es necesario que...?**   Levántate y encuentra a un compañero que tenga que... Usa el subjuntivo en tus preguntas.

Modelo   ESTUDIANTE 1:   ¿Es necesario que estudies esta noche?

ESTUDIANTE 2:   Sí, es necesario que estudie esta noche porque mañana tengo un examen.

ESTUDIANTE 1:   ¿Es necesario que busques un apartamento nuevo?

ESTUDIANTE 3:   No, no es necesario que busque un apartamento nuevo porque me gusta vivir en la residencia / me gusta el apartamento que tengo ahora.

1. estudiar esta noche
2. comer menos
3. arreglar su cuarto
4. gastar menos dinero
5. buscar un apartamento nuevo
6. dormir más

7. sacar mejores notas
8. perder cinco kilos
9. comprar un coche nuevo
10. reciclar más
11. ir al correo
12. limpiar su coche

12 **Es importante que...**   Llena la gráfica en **Etapa 1, actividad 12** en **capítulo 9** de tu **Manual de actividades** con tus mejores consejos *(advice).* Luego, comparte tu información con un compañero de clase y entonces con toda la clase.

13 **Desde tu punto de vista...**   Tú y tu mejor amigo están hablando por teléfono de otros amigos que conocen. Mira los dibujos en tu **Manual de actividades, Etapa 2, actividad 13,** en **capítulo 9.** Sigue el modelo para compartir lo que sabes de ellos usando el subjuntivo.

14 **Mis deberes.**   Haz una lista de cinco cosas que debes hacer este fin de semana o que a lo mejor van a pasar. Sigue el modelo.

Modelo   **Es necesario que estudie más este fin de semana. También es impor-tante que vaya al supermercado. Después de ir al supermercado, es necesario que limpie la cocina. Es probable que salga con mis amigos el sábado. Finalmente, es posible que mis padres vengan a visitarme.**

15 **Las resoluciones.**   ¿Has hecho resoluciones para el año nuevo? Escribe cinco re-soluciones o tus comentarios sobre ellas. Sigue el modelo.

Modelo   **Es necesario que no coma tanto chocolate pero es dudoso que yo pueda evitarlo. ¡Me fascina el chocolate! Es importante que haga más ejercicios. Es una lástima que no me guste hacer ejercicios.**

3 **Dime la razón.**   Termina las frases siguientes.

1. Tengo que ir a la tintorería para...
2. Tengo que ir a la biblioteca para...
3. Voy a ir al gimnasio para...
4. Mis padres fueron a la playa para...
5. Mi hermano fue a la estación de servicio para...

4 **¿Cuánto será...?**   Trabajas en la oficina de contabilidad *(accounting)* de una compañía internacional. El presidente de la compañía tiene que ir a las ciudades mencionadas por dos días cada una y tienes que preparar su adelanto *(advance)* de dinero. Tienes que estimar cuánto va a gastar él por las mencionadas cosas. Escribe tus estimaciones en la gráfica en **Etapa 2, actividad 4** en **capítulo 9** de tu **Manual de actividades.**

5 **Combinaciones.**   En parejas, combinen elementos de la columna a con elementos de la columna b en **Etapa 2, actividad 5** en **capítulo 9** de tu **Manual de actividades,** y agreguen **para** o **por,** según sea necesario. Escriban diez oraciones completas. Puede ser una oración larga o dos cortas. Hay varias combinaciones posibles.

6 **Mi hermana Eleonor.**   Completa el siguiente párrafo con **por** o **para,** de acuerdo al contenido.

Eleonor, mi hermana, estuvo en mi casa el verano pasado (1) _____ un mes. Vino (2) _____ mi cumpleaños. Llegó (3) _____ tren con tres maletas y una enorme caja misteriosa. El día de mi cumpleaños me dijo que yo tenía que estar lista (4) _____ las cinco de la tarde. Efectivamente, a las cinco en punto estaba sentada en la sala cuando vi (5) _____ la ventana a un grupo de amigos. Venían con un trío de guitarras. ¡Era una serenata (6) _____ mí! ¡Qué emoción tan grande! La serenata comenzó y Eleonor bajó (7) _____ la escalera *(staircase)* con la inmensa caja. —Es (8) _____ ti— me dijo. La abrí, y ¡qué sorpresa! Era una hamaca de yute *(jute hammock)* de Yucatán, México, donde Eleonor había estado (9) _____ una semana unos días antes. — ¡Una hamaca (10) _____ el patio! — exclamé, —(11) _____ leer y dormir al sol. ¡Qué delicia! — Y enseguida pregunté: — Pero, Eleonor, ¿cómo trajiste esta hamaca desde México? ¿La trajiste (12) _____ avión o la mandaste (13) _____ correo?

Eleonor se rió y me contestó: — (14) _____ ti, querida hermana, soy capaz de hacer muchas cosas. En México me monté en un autobús que iba (15) _____ la frontera *(border)*. Pasé (16) _____ muchos pueblos interesantes. En la frontera alquilé *(rented)* un carro y me vine (17) _____ San Diego. (18) _____ ser un viaje tan largo, no estuvo mal. Puse mucha música para mantenerme despierta. Fue bien divertido. ¡Feliz cumpleaños!

¡FÍJATE! 4
Las preposiciones y los pronombres preposicionales

Besides the prepositions **por** and **para,** there are a variety of useful prepositions and prepositional phrases, many of which you have already been using throughout *¡Atrévete!* Study the following list to review the ones you already know and to acquaint yourself with those that are new to you.

Las preposiciones			
a	*to; at*	después de	*after*
a la derecha de	*to the right of*	detrás de	*behind*
a la izquierda de	*to the left of*	en	*in*
acerca de	*about*	encima de	*on top of*
afuera de	*outside of*	enfrente de	*across from; facing*
al lado de	*next to*	entre	*among; between*
antes de	*before (time / space)*	hasta	*until*
cerca de	*near*	lejos de	*far from*
con	*with*	para	*for; in order to*
de	*of; from*	por	*for; through; by; because of*
debajo de	*under*	sin	*without*
delante de	*in front of*	sobre	*over; about*

Note the pronouns used after prepositions in the following box.

Los pronombres preposicionales			
mí	*me*	**nosotros, nosotras**	*us*
ti	*you*	**vosotros, vosotras**	*you*
él	*him*	**ellos**	*them*
ella	*her*	**ellas**	*them*
usted	*you*	**ustedes**	*you*

Para <u>mí</u>, es muy aburrido tomar el sol.	*For <u>me</u>, it's really boring to sunbathe.*
¿Quién vive enfrente <u>de ti</u>?	*Who lives across <u>from you</u>?*
Se fueron <u>sin nosotros</u>.	*They left <u>without us</u>.*

Note that **con** has two special forms:

1. **conmigo**	*with me*
2. **contigo**	*with you*

¿Vienes <u>conmigo</u>?	*Are you coming <u>with</u> <u>me</u>?*
Sí, voy <u>contigo</u>.	*Yes, I'm going <u>with</u> <u>you</u>.*

7 **Descríbemelo.**   Mira el dibujo con los animales. Haz frases con un compañero con las siguientes preposiciones.

Modelo   **El pájaro está encima de la vaca.**

1. al lado de	6. delante de
2. a la derecha de	7. detrás de
3. a la izquierda de	8. encima de
4. cerca de	9. lejos de
5. debajo de	

8 **En mi clase de español...**   Con un compañero, haz diez oraciones con preposiciones que describan tu clase de español.

Modelos   **Ryan se sienta al lado de George.**

Los libros de mi profesor están encima de su escritorio.

Las ventanas están lejos de nosotros.

9 **La universidad.**   En parejas, túrnense para decir dónde están los siguientes edificios en su universidad.

Modelo   **La biblioteca está detrás del centro estudiantil.**

1. la biblioteca	6. la cafetería
2. el gimnasio	7. mi dormitorio
3. el centro estudiantil	8. el registro *(registration)*
4. la librería	9. el centro de salud
5. la capilla *(chapel)*	10. la cancha de fútbol

¡ASÓMATE! 3
La política

La política

1. el alcalde / la alcaldesa
2. el candidato / la candidata
3. el congreso
4. el dictador / la dictadora
5. el diputado / la diputada
6. el discurso
7. la guerra
8. la huelga
9. la monarquía
10. el presidente / la presidenta
11. el rey / la reina

Unos verbos

apoyar	*to support*
combatir	*to fight, to combat*
elegir	*to elect*
estar en huelga	*to be on strike*
llevar a cabo	*to carry out*
luchar	*to fight, to combat*
meterse en política	*to get involved in politics*
resolver (o ➡ ue)	*to resolve*
votar	*to vote*

Las cuestiones políticas

el bienestar	*well-being; welfare*
el crimen	*crime*
la defensa	*defense*
el desempleo	*unemployment*
la deuda (externa)	*(foreign) debt*
el impuesto	*tax*
la inflación	*inflation*

Otras palabras útiles

la campaña	*campaign*
la democracia	*democracy*
la dictadura	*dictatorship*
la elección	*election*
la encuesta	*survey; poll*
el estado	*state*
el gobernador / la gobernadora	*governor*
el gobierno	*government*
la ley	*law*
el partido político	*political party*
la presidencia	*presidency*
la provincia	*province*
la región	*region*
el senado	*senate*
el senador / la senadora	*senator*

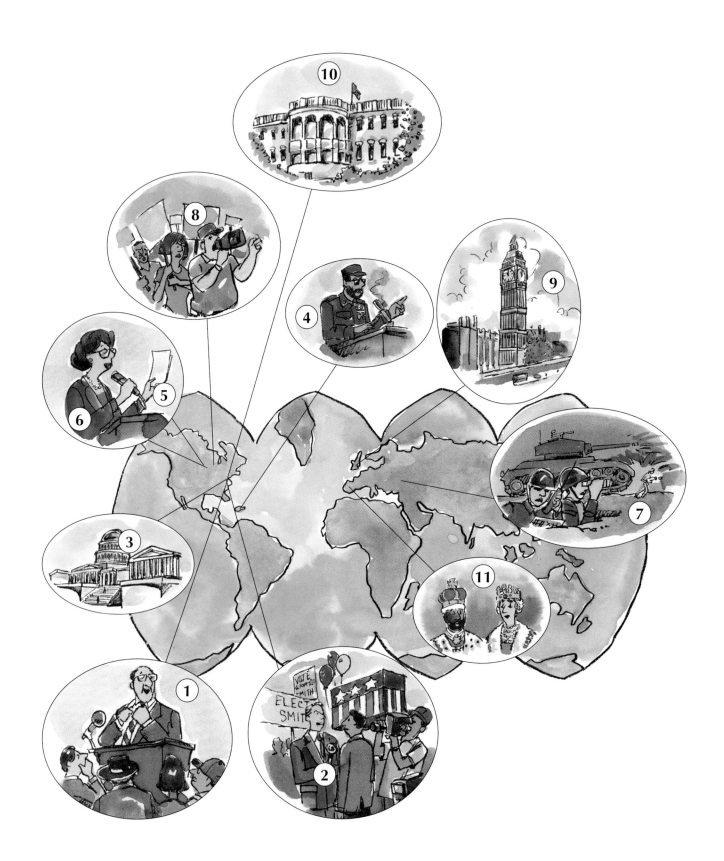

10 **Batalla.** Mira la gráfica en **Etapa 2, actividad 10,** en **capítulo 9** de tu **Manual de actividades.** Llena cada cuadrado con un lugar o una persona. Luego, compara tus respuestas con las de un compañero. Dense un punto por cada pareo *(match)*.

11 **Asociación.** Haz una lista con las palabras nuevas de **¡Asómate! 3** que asocias con los lugares siguientes en la gráfica en **Etapa 2, actividad 11** del **capítulo 9** de tu **Manual de actividades.**

12 **Pareos.** Primero, combina palabras de la **columna a** con las expresiones de la **columna b.** Luego, en parejas, conviertan *(turn)* los pareos *(matches)* en oraciones completas. Después, en grupos pequeños, comparen sus oraciones.

| Modelo | Este gobierno (reducir) el crimen considerablemente. ➡ | **Este gobierno ha reducido el crimen considerablemente.** |

Columna a

1. (combatir)
2. (elegir)
3. (ser) el gobernador
4. (votar) por Doña Jimena para
5. el presidente (apoyar)
6. la reina (apoyar) la nueva ley
7. el rey (llevar) a cabo una reforma
8. el gobierno (ir) a aumentar
9. la encuesta (decir) que la gente
10. los trabajadores (estar)

Columna b

a. alcaldesa de la municipalidad de San Pedro
b. sobre el bienestar social
c. la droga, el desempleo y la inflación
d. quiere resolver el conflicto
e. un candidato a la presidencia
f. de la monarquía
g. en huelga
h. de la provincia de Puntarenas
i. los impuestos el mes que viene
j. la decisión del congreso

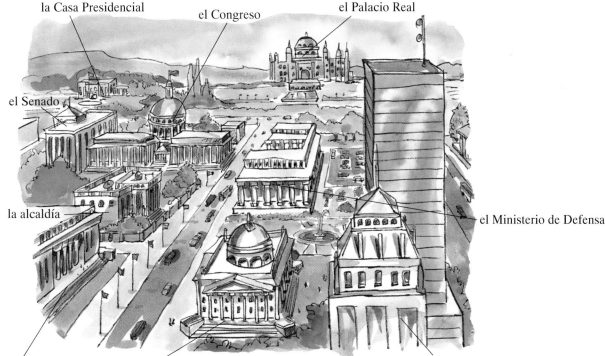

la Casa Presidencial

el Congreso

el Palacio Real

el Senado

la alcaldía

el Ministerio de Defensa

el Banco Central

la Dirección General de Correos (y Telégrafos)

el Ministerio de Bienestar Social

13 **¿Dónde están?**　En parejas, expliquen dónde están los siguientes edificios en el mapa.

Modelo　La alcaldía está enfrente de...

1. la Casa Presidencial
2. el Ministerio de Bienestar Social
3. el Ministerio de Defensa
4. el Senado
5. el Congreso

6. el Palacio Real
7. la alcaldía
8. la Dirección General de Correos
9. el Banco Central

14 **El futuro político**　Escribe una composición de por lo menos cinco frases que describa lo que debe pasar en el futuro en tu ciudad, estado, país o en el mundo. También incluye tus comentarios. Sigue el modelo.

Modelo　**Es necesario que los partidos políticos no se combatan tanto. También es importante que el presidente resuelva los problemas económicos como la inflación. Es dudoso que podamos bajar la deuda nacional porque todos quieren dinero para sus programas.**

Juan Perón

¡ENTÉRATE!
Los hispanos en la política

Rigoberta Menchú

Federico Peña

Fidel Castro

Violeta Barrio de Chamorro

La historia política de América Latina es la lucha dramática del ser humano contra fuerzas destructivas como la colonización, el imperialismo, la esclavitud y el genocidio —en siglos anteriores— y en épocas más recientes, la pobreza, la corrupción, el nepotismo, la división rígida de clases y el militarismo. Muchos países hispanohablantes han sufrido bajo severas dictaduras o democracias débiles e ineficientes.

No obstante, en décadas recientes, España ha surgido de sus dificultades como un país moderno y avanzado, con un rey progresista y amante de la democracia. América Latina, a su vez, ha experimentado en la segunda mitad del siglo XX un momento de paz y esperanza. En la actualidad, el único país que continúa teniendo un dictador es Cuba con Fidel Castro. La guerra que azotó a Centroamérica en la década de los ochenta acabó, y aunque las dislocaciones aún se sienten y la recuperación es lenta en algunos países del istmo, el estándar de vida en Centroamérica ha aumentado, así como el comercio y el deseo de fortalecer las instituciones democráticas. Oscar Arias Sánchez, presidente de Costa Rica en esa época, fue honrado con el Premio Nóbel de la Paz por sus esfuerzos por poner fin a la guerra en Centroamérica. Más recientemente, Rigoberta Menchú obtuvo el Premio Nóbel de la Paz debido a su lucha por los derechos humanos de los indígenas en Guatemala. Panamá abolió *(abolished)* el ejército y en Chile, el pueblo repudió *(rejected)* la dictadura del General Pinochet. Hoy día, Chile goza de una de las mejores situaciones económicas de la América hispana.

Más, el símbolo principal de la nueva era latinoamericana es el fortalecimiento *(strengthening)* de antiguos tratados comerciales y la creación de tratados nuevos: TLC (NAFTA; México), el Mercado Común Centroamericano, Mercosur y el Pacto Andino (América del Sur). A estos núcleos comerciales se unen un sinfín de *(a number of)* instituciones dedicadas a luchar por el desarrollo económico de América Latina, tales como la Asociación Latinoamericana de Integración y la Corporación Andina de Fomento. Este gran apetito por el libre comercio que abarca desde México hasta la Patagonia, ha despertado un gran interés en los Estados Unidos, Canadá y Europa. Hay una carrera *(race)* para ver quién logra penetrar y establecerse primero en la vida comercial de los países hispano-hablantes. Esta situación representa una gran oportunidad para las personas bilingües que hablan español e inglés.

También en los Estados Unidos los hispanos han progresado y cada vez participan más en la política. Federico Peña y Linda Chávez-Thompson son ejemplos de hispanos en los Estados Unidos que han contribuido a nuestro sistema político.

¿Qué te parece?

1. ¿Cuál es la situación en España ahora?
2. ¿Qué cambios han experimentado muchos de los países de Latinoamérica en los últimos quince o veinte años?
3. ¿Quiénes son los latinoamericanos que han ganado el Premio Nóbel de la Paz? En qué lo ganaron?
4. ¿Cuáles son los beneficios de los tratados comerciales?
5. ¿Hay algunos hispanos que participan en tu gobierno local? ¿En qué capacidad?

Costa Rica: Amor por la paz y la ecología

NICARAGUA

Este parque es uno de los más populares debido a la actividad del imponente volcán Poás.

Sarchí

Alajuela

⊗ San José · PuertoLimón

COSTA RICA

MAR CARIBE

Se hacen a carretas en Sarchí. La carreta es artesanía tradicional y representa la Costa Rica agrícola.

OCÉANO PACÍFICO

PANAMÁ

1502 Colón llegó al área conocida hoy como Puerto Limón, en su cuarto y último viaje. Durante mucho tiempo, el país permaneció aislado e ignorado por los españoles, debido a la gran distancia entre Costa Rica y la capital del Reino de Guatemala, al que Costa Rica pertenecía.

1838 Costa Rica se independizó de la República Federal de Centro América y, en 1848, se convirtió en la República de Costa Rica.

1821 El 15 de septiembre, en la Ciudad de Guatemala, se firmó el Acta de Independencia de España que resultó en la soberanía de los países del istmo.

1970 Creación del sistema nacional de parques.

1948 Costa Rica ha gozado de una fuerte tradición democrática desde sus inicios, interrumpida por muy pocos golpes de estado (tres en 150 años). Pero en 1948 hubo una crisis que resultó en la guerra civil de 1948. José Figueres fue el líder de un movimiento revolucionario que ganó la guerra.

Costa Rica exporta el café y la banana.

El Museo del Jade es el museo más famoso de Costa Rica y tiene la colección de jade más grande del mundo.

¿Qué te parece?

1. ¿Cómo afectó la geografía al desarrollo político de Costa Rica?

2. ¿Puedes nombrar dos conflictos importantes que contribuyeron a la formación del estado moderno en Costa Rica?

3. De todos los acontecimientos históricos de Costa Rica, ¿cuál te parece el más significativo y de más repercusiones para la época en que vivimos?

1987 Oscar Arias Sánchez, presidente de Costa Rica desde 1986 a 1990, ganó el Premio Nóbel de la Paz por sus esfuerzos para conseguir la paz en Centroamérica.

1998 En las elecciones de 1998, Costa Rica mostró la importancia de la mujer en el país. En Costa Rica hay dos vicepresidentes y dos mujeres fueron elegidas.

1994 José María Figueres, hijo de José Figueres, llega a ser el presidente más joven del país con 39 años. Se le considera un presidente «verde» por su apoyo al medio ambiente.

LA RED ¡Navega la Internet!

To discover more information on the culture of this chapter, check the Holt Web site and other suggestions listed in your **Manual de actividades.**

http://www.hrwcollege.com/

ETAPA 3

Ya lo sabemos

Rafi y Adriana se han reunido y Rafi pudo aclarar las dudas que tenía sobre ella. ¿Qué información nueva le dio Adriana a Rafi? ¿Qué preguntas o dudas tenemos nosotros todavía? En este episodio vas a averiguar

- ◆ por qué Adriana está preocupada y nerviosa
- ◆ cómo reaccionan los padres al oír la historia de Rafi y Chema
- ◆ cuál fue la civilización moche

Preguntas personales

En este episodio Rafi y Chema vuelven a la casa de los padres de Rafi después de salir del hospital.

1. ¿Por qué Rafi y Chema creen que es necesario ir a la casa de los padres? ¿Qué harías tú en la misma situación?
2. ¿Crees que van a explicar todo lo que saben a los padres? ¿Por qué? ¿Tú les cuentas todas las cosas importantes a tus padres? ¿Cuáles son algunas de las cosas que no les cuentas a tus padres?
3. ¿Cuál será *(will probably be)* la reacción de los padres al oírlo todo? ¿Van a tener consejos para Rafi y Chema sobre lo que deben hacer ahora? ¿Les pides consejos a tus padres?

Estrategias de lectura
More Practice with Guessing from Context

In chapter 8, you worked with guessing the meaning of unfamiliar words from context. You were reminded to look closely at the words, phrases, and sentences that surround unfamiliar words as well as to consider the tone of the passage. Guess the meaning of the words or phrases in boldface that follow and be prepared to explain your reasoning. Turn to chapter 8, **Estrategias de lectura,** for review.

1. Le dijo [a Adriana] que un **testigo** había visto el coche que chocó con ella y llevaba **placas** que leían «ROMA».
2. La policía **había averiguado** que el coche **pertenecía** a un Miguel Covarrubias.
3. Se despidió de ella y **colgó** el teléfono. **Al voltearse,** su familia lo miraba intensamente.

Now read the episode, employing this strategy as needed. You will be asked to share with your instructor the number of times you guessed from context and to verify those guesses.

Rafi y el sacrificio final

Episodio 9: El peligro continúa

Rafi salió del cuarto de Adriana; Chema estaba esperándolo. Rafi le contó lo que Adriana le había dicho. Los dos se pusieron a pensar en lo que tenían que hacer. Decidieron ir a la casa de los padres de Rafi.

Cuando llegaron, los padres de Rafi lo esperaban. No habían estado en la casa más de dos minutos cuando el teléfono sonó. Era Adriana y parecía muy nerviosa. Dijo que no sabía que había policías fuera de su cuarto y que uno de ellos entró para hablar con ella. Le dijo que un testigo había visto el coche que chocó con ella y llevaba placas que leían «ROMA». La policía había averiguado que el coche pertenecía a un Miguel Covarrubias.

Rafi le dijo que no debía preocuparse y que iba a ir al otro día a visitarla. Se despidió de ella y colgó el teléfono. Al voltearse, su familia lo miraba intensamente.

Rafi y Chema pasaron la próxima hora explicándolo todo a sus padres. La madre de Rafi no dijo nada; sólo miraba al espacio. El padre dijo, —Es necesario que Uds. se comuniquen inmediatamente con las autoridades del Perú para advertirles° de lo que saben y de lo que tienen miedo.— El padre subió a la guardilla y regresó con un librito negro. Allí adentro encontró un número de teléfono y se fue a llamar inmediatamente.

warn them

—¿Aló? Es importante que hable con el director del museo. Hablamos desde los Estados Unidos y tengo información sobre un crimen de una magnitud internacional —dijo el padre. Al mismo tiempo, Rafi y Chema buscaban en la Red la dirección de los científicos que habían hecho el descubrimiento de la civilización moche. Hacía una semana que Rafi, buscando en la Red, había encontrado una información acerca de una civilización que floreció en el norte de la costa del Perú entre los años 100 y 800 después de Cristo. De la civilización moche, que así se llama, se habían descubierto las tumbas de Sipán. Estas tumbas que fueron descubiertas en 1987, después de haber sido infiltradas por ladrones, todavía contenían un inmenso tesoro en arte: máscaras de oro, un cetro° de oro, vestidura de guerra en oro, incluyendo el yelmo° con cresta y muchos artefactos de alfarería que demostraban que esta tumba había pertenecido a un gran jefe moche.

scepter

helmet

Nadie sabía si era demasiado tarde o no. Tampoco sabían si Pedro Lara era héroe o criminal. Sólo sabían que tenían que advertir a las autoridades peruanas de que algo terrible iba a pasar, a menos que ya hubiese pasado.

—Las autoridades peruanas no pueden hacer nada en estos momentos, —continuó don Manuel después de colgar el teléfono. —El director del museo ha estado frustrado con todos los problemas internos del país que impiden a las autoridades darle prioridad a los robos de arte.

Comprensión

1. ¿Por qué estaba nerviosa y preocupada Adriana cuando ella llamó a Rafi?
2. ¿Cómo reaccionaron los padres al oír la historia que les contaron Rafi y Chema?
3. ¿Cuál fue el consejo del padre?
4. ¿A quién llamó don Manuel?
5. Mientras el padre hablaba por teléfono, ¿que hicieron Rafi y Chema? ¿Qué encontraron?

Expansión

(1) ¿Quién puede ser Miguel Covarrubias?

(2) Debatan entre todos: ¿Es Pedro Lara héroe o criminal?

(3) ¿Por qué no podían hacer nada en esos momentos las autoridades peruanas? Explica tu respuesta con ejemplos concretos de la situación sociopolítica del país.

(4) Busca en la Red información sobre la civilización moche y fotos de algunos de los tesoros. ¿Es verdad lo que se escribió en el episodio? ¿Encontraste más información interesante?

(5) En parejas, inventen y representen la conversación por teléfono entre don Manuel y el director del museo.

(6) Rafi no puede dejar de pensar en su tío Pedro — ¿estará envuelto en la Red de ladrones o no? Para aclarar un poco su mente decide organizar las pistas que tiene sobre su tío y la vida de él. Ayúdale a escribir esta lista de pistas. Para algunas de las ideas, piensa en el debate que tuvieron en clase (**Expansión 2**).

Pistas — héroe   Pistas — criminal

A mirar o escuchar

(7) View the video or listen to the audio CD to find out what happens next to Rafi and Chema. Consult the pre- and post-listening activities in your **Manual de actividades**.

¡Sí, se puede!

1. LA RED Exploración. Explora algunos sitios en la Red que tienen que ver con Costa Rica. Después, haz una lista de unos cinco a diez puntos que Costa Rica y los Estados Unidos tienen en común. Compara tu lista con las de los otros estudiantes de la clase. ¿En qué aspectos son similares los dos países?

2. Mi querido animalito. ¿Cuál es tu animal doméstico preferido? Escribe un correo electrónico a un amigo contándole sobre un animal que compraste recientemente. Explica por qué lo escogiste, dónde lo compraste y cómo te sientes desde que lo compraste. Al terminar, intercambia tu nota con un compañero. Primero, corrijan los errores juntos. Segundo, contesten las cartas. Las cartas modelo les pueden dar algunas ideas.

Querida Dialá:

Te cuento que la semana pasada compré una lora *(parrot)* en el nuevo centro comercial La Plaza. Quería un animalito casero, un compañero, y las loras son fáciles de cuidar. La lora es verde, pero también tiene plumas *(feathers)* azules, rojas y amarillas. Es preciosa y muy simpática. Ya habla y dice cosas divertidas como «¡Hola!», «Lorita, dame la patita», «¡Maríaaa, tengo hambre!», «¡Ay, ay, un perro! ¡qué miedo!» Estoy muy contento con mi linda lorita.

Bueno, es todo por hoy. Otro día te escribo más.

Cuando puedas, escríbeme.

Saludos,

Carlos Manuel

Querido Carlos Manuel:

Te felicito por tu nueva lorita. ¿Tienes fotos? Mándame una. No me dijiste cómo se llamaba. Yo fui al cine a ver *Amistad.* Tienes que verla. Es una película hermosa. Oye, te llamo la semana entrante para contarte otras cosas porque ahora tengo que estudiar.

Un abrazo,

Dialá

3. **¿Sabes que compró?** En grupos de cuatro, cuéntenles a sus compañeros sobre el animal que compró la persona con la que intercambiaron el correo electrónico.

Modelo **¿Saben qué compró Carlos Manuel? Una lora. Su lora es verde y de otros colores también. Habla mucho, por ejemplo, dice...**

4. **Así pienso yo.** Completa estas frases con tus propias opiniones.

1. Es increíble que Costa Rica...
2. Para proteger el medio ambiente es necesario que...
3. Es una lástima que algunos animales...
4. Es importante que los humanos...
5. Es improbable que yo...
6. Es bueno que los profesores...
7. Es raro que los estudiantes...

5. **¡Atención!** Diseña un cartel *(poster)* de propaganda para el público norteamericano basado en uno de los siguientes temas. Usa el subjuntivo cuando sea apropiado.

1. un animal en peligro de extinción
2. un problema con el medio ambiente
3. el turismo en Costa Rica

6. **Dibújamelo.** Descríbele tu cuarto o apartamento a un compañero y usa por lo menos cinco preposiciones. Tu compañero va a dibujar lo que tu dices. ¿Lo explicaste bien?

7. **Es importante que...** En parejas, escojan una situación para desarrollar y escriban un diálogo en el que una persona le da consejos a otra. Luego, intercambien su diálogo con el de otra pareja y corrijan los errores. Finalmente, en turnos, presenten su diálogo a la clase.

SITUACIÓN A: La doctora Montoya es especialista en nutrición. Ana Cecilia es una joven universitaria de dieciocho años que va a hacerle una consulta a la doctora sobre cómo mejorar el cutis *(complexion).*

SITUACIÓN B: Eugenio quiere comprar un carro usado y le pide a su amigo Rodolfo, que trabaja en una agencia de carros, que le ayude.

SITÚACIÓN C: El sargento López está enamorado de la linda Carolina, pero es tan tímido que nunca la ha invitado a salir. Su amiga Carmen trata de ayudarlo.

SITUACIÓN D: Armando, se mata estudiando para el examen de matemáticas. Un día antes del examen, se da cuenta de que no tenía un examen de matemáticas, ¡sino de español! Va a su consejero para ver qué le aconseja que haga.

8. **¡A conocer la prensa!** Tu instructor va a seleccionar a unos cuatro o cinco estudiantes para representar a unos periodistas muy conocidos de los Estados Unidos. Los otros estudiantes van a hacerles preguntas sobre algunas situaciones políticas actuales. Tu instructor va a ser el moderador.

Para recordar

Al terminar este capítulo, tú podrás:

Etapa 1 ¡Sígueme!

❏ hablar de los animales que más te gustan y los que menos te gustan y sobre los animales en peligro de extinción

❏ formar y usar adverbios terminados en **-mente**

❏ decir cosas que son importantes o necesarias que tú hagas

❏ discutir unos asuntos que tratan del medio ambiente

❏ comparar los asuntos del medio ambiente en los países hispanohablantes con los nuestros

Etapa 2 ¡Dime más!

❏ saber cómo usar **por** y **para**

❏ hablar y escribir con preposiciones

❏ hacer comentarios de tu gobierno local y nacional

❏ aprender sobre los hispanos en el mundo político

❏ explorar Costa Rica

Etapa 3 ¡Cuéntame!

❏ descubrir quién chocó con Adriana y qué hacen para proteger los tesoros del Perú.

 You can practice concepts from this and earlier chapters by doing the **¡Recuérdate!** *section in your* **Manual de actividades.**

VOCABULARIO ACTIVO

Unos animales

el caballo *horse*
el cerdo *pig*
el conejo *rabbit*
el elefante *elephant*
la gallina *chicken, hen*
el gato *cat*
la hormiga *ant*

el insecto *insect*
el león *lion*
la mosca *fly*
el mosquito *mosquito*
el oso *bear*
el pájaro *bird*
el perro *dog*

el pez (*pl.*, los peces) *fish*
la rata *rat*
el ratón *mouse*
la serpiente *snake*
el toro *bull*
la vaca *cow*

El medio ambiente

el aluminio *aluminum*
la botella *bottle*
la caja (de cartón) *(cardboard) box*
la contaminación *pollution*
el derrame de petróleo *oil spill*

el huracán *hurricane*
el incendio *fire*
la inundación *flood*
la lata *can*
el papel *paper*
el periódico *newspaper*

el plástico *plastic*
el terremoto *earthquake*
la tormenta *storm*
el tornado *tornado*
el vidrio *glass*

Unos verbos

apoyar *to support*
botar *to throw away*
combatir *to fight, to combat*
contaminar *to pollute*
cuidar *to take care of*
elegir *to elect*
estar en huelga *to be on strike*
evitar *to avoid*

hacer daño *to (do) damage*
llevar a cabo *to carry out*
luchar *to fight, to combat*
matar *to kill*
meterse en política *to get involved in politics*
preocuparse por *to worry about; to concern oneself with*

proteger *to protect*
reciclar *to recycle*
reforestar *to reforest*
rehusar *to refuse*
resolver (o ➡ ue) *to resolve*
sembrar (e ➡ ie) *to plant*
volver *to return*
votar *to vote*

Las preposiciones

a *to; at*
a la derecha de *to the right of*
a la izquierda de *to the left of*
acerca de *about*
afuera de *outside of*
al lado de *next to*
antes de *before (time / space)*
cerca de *near*

con *with*
de *of; from*
debajo de *under*
delante de *in front of*
después de *after*
detrás de *behind*
en *in*
encima de *on top of*

enfrente de *across from; facing*
entre *among; between*
hasta *until*
lejos de *far from*
para *for; in order to*
por *for; through; by; because of*
sin *without*
sobre *over; about*

La política

el alcalde / la alcaldesa *mayor*
el candidato / la candidata *candidate*
el congreso *congress*
el dictador / la dictadora *dictator*

el diputado / la diputada *representative*
el discurso *speech*
la guerra *war*
la huelga *strike*

la monarquía *monarchy*
el presidente / la presidenta *president*
el rey / la reina *king / queen*

Las cuestiones políticas

el bienestar *well-being; welfare*
el crimen *crime*
la defensa *defense*

el desempleo *unemployment*
la deuda (externa) *(foreign) debt*
el impuesto *tax*

la inflación *inflation*

Otras palabras útiles

el aire *air*
un animal doméstico *a domesticated animal, pet*
un animal en peligro de extinción *an endangered species*
un animal salvaje *a wild animal*
el árbol *tree*
la basura *garbage*
el bosque *forest*
el calentamiento de la tierra *global warming*
la calidad *quality*
la campaña *campaign*
la capa de ozono *ozone layer*
el cielo *sky; heaven*
la cueva *cave*
la democracia *democracy*
el desastre *disaster*
la destrucción *destruction*

la dictadura *dictatorship*
la ecología *ecology*
la elección *election*
la encuesta *survey; poll*
el estado *state*
la finca *farm*
el gobernador / la gobernadora *governor*
el gobierno *government*
la granja *farm*
el hoyo *hole*
el lago *lake*
la ley *law*
la lluvia ácida *acid rain*
la montaña *mountain*
la naturaleza *nature*
el océano *ocean*
el partido político *political party*
peligroso / peligrosa *dangerous*

el planeta *planet*
la presidencia *presidency*
la provincia *province*
puro / pura *pure*
el rancho *farm*
el recurso *resource*
la región *region*
el río *river*
la selva *jungle*
la selva tropical *(tropical) rain forest; jungle*
el senado *senate*
el senador / la senadora *senator*
la Tierra *Earth*
la tierra *land; soil*
la tragedia *tragedy*
el vertedero *dump*
vivo / viva *alive, living*

En los últimos años, los hispanohablantes han llegado a ser más y más importantes en el mundo de negocios en los Estados Unidos. En años anteriores, los hispanos se habían limitado sólo a negocios que pertenecían *(belonged)* a la familia, como restaurantes o negocios pequeños. Hoy en día los hispanos se destacan *(distinguish themselves)* más y más en el mundo de negocios y algunos de ellos de manera impresionante. Por ejemplo, Joseph A. Unanue, el propietario de Goya Foods, es el hispano más rico de los Estados Unidos con un capital neto de $340 millones de dólares. Otros hispanos que han tenido mucho éxito en los negocios son Roberto Goizueta, ex-Presidente de la Junta de Coca-Cola, y Linda y Robert Alvarado, propietarios de Alvarado Construction de Denver, Colorado, y propietarios parciales del equipo de béisbol de los Colorado Rockies.

¿Qué te parece?

1. ¿Por qué tienen recientemente en los Estados Unidos más importancia los negocios de los hispanohablantes?
2. ¿Por qué se oye más hoy en día de los negocios internacionales y los países hispanohablantes?

Tu vida profesional

By the end of this chapter you will be able to:

ETAPA 1 ¡Sígueme!

- compare and contrast a variety of professions
- learn about Hispanic women in the world of business
- express wishes, wants, fears, and desires
- use the language of technology

ETAPA 2 ¡Dime más!

- express doubts
- discuss future and conditional plans

ETAPA 3 ¡Cuéntame!

- discover whether Rafi is able to solve the mystery

¡Sígueme!

¡ASÓMATE! 1
Las profesiones

Unas profesiones

1. el abogado / la abogada
2. el actor / la actriz
3. el artista / la artista
4. el autor / la autora
5. el bombero
6. el cantante / la cantante
7. el cocinero / la cocinera
8. el consejero / la consejera
9. el contador / la contadora
10. el dentista / la dentista
11. el granjero / la granjera
12. el hombre / la mujer de negocios
13. el médico / la médica
14. el músico / la música
15. el obrero / la obrera
16. el peluquero / la peluquera
17. el policía / la mujer policía
18. el secretario / la secretaria

Otras palabras útiles

el empleado / la empleada	*employee*
el gerente / la gerente	*manager*
el jefe / la jefa	*boss*
el propietario / la propietaria	*owner*

1

2

3

4

5

6

7

8

9

10

11

12

13

14

15

16

17

18

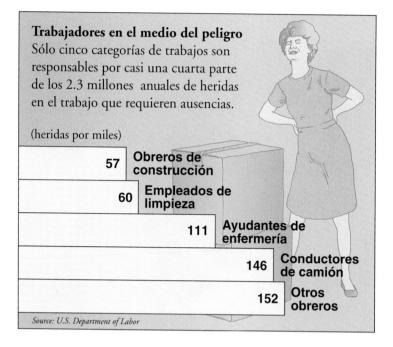

Trabajadores en el medio del peligro
Sólo cinco categorías de trabajos son responsables por casi una cuarta parte de los 2.3 millones anuales de heridas en el trabajo que requieren ausencias.

(heridas por miles)

57	**Obreros de construcción**
60	**Empleados de limpieza**
111	**Ayudantes de enfermería**
146	**Conductores de camión**
152	**Otros obreros**

Source: U.S. Department of Labor

1 | **Pirámide.** Escribe diez o quince profesiones en papelitos. En grupos de cuatro, formen dos parejas (equipos) por grupo. Estudiante A del Equipo 1 escoge un papelito y lo muestra a Estudiante A del Equipo 2. Los Estudiantes A van a decir palabras para que su compañero diga la profesión. Sigue el modelo.

Modelo   (The word selected is **chofer.**)

　　　　　　　Equipo 1:   Estudiante A dice **coche.**

　　　　　　　Equipo 1:   Estudiante B adivina **mecánico.**

　　　　　　　Equipo 2:   Estudiante A dice **taxi.**

　　　　　　　Equipo 2:   Estudiante B adivina correctamente **chofer.**

Hay más profesiones en la sección **También se dice...** *al final del libro.*

2 | **¿Qué se necesita... ?**   Todos los trabajos no son iguales. Escribe tres trabajos que necesitan las características en la gráfica en **Etapa 1, actividad 2** del **capítulo 10** en tu **Manual de actividades.** Sigue el modelo.

3 **Consejero, ¿qué puedo hacer?**   Eres consejero de profesión y tienes unos clientes que vienen a tu oficina con las siguientes cualidades. Diles tres profesiones que pueden seguir. Llena la gráfica en **Etapa 1, actividad 3** del **capítulo 10** en tu **Manual de actividades.** Sigue el modelo.

Diana   Milagros   Carlos   Raúl

Jimena

4 **Al conocerlos.**   Un domingo, tú y tu compañero de cuarto están hablando de las otras personas que viven en su barrio. Como todo el mundo trabaja, tienen muy poco tiempo para visitar y conocerse. Conoces a unos, tu compañero a otros. Tu compañero te explica cómo se ven las personas y tú le dices qué hacen como trabajo. Luego explicas cómo se ven otros y tu compañero te dice lo que hacen. Uno de Uds. necesita mirar el dibujo en esta página y el otro necesita mirar el dibujo en **Etapa 1, actividad 4** del **capítulo 10** en tu **Manual de actividades.**

Modelo   ESTUDIANTE 1:   ¿Qué hace la mujer alta con lentes y pelo rubio?

ESTUDIANTE 2:   Se llama Diana y es médica.

¡ENTÉRATE!
El mundo profesional y la mujer

La revolución femenina ha llegado al mundo hispano. Empezó un poco más tarde en la mayoría de los países hispanohablantes que en los Estados Unidos. Sin embargo, las mujeres están llegando al mismo nivel *(level)* de los hombres en términos de oportunidades y salarios. También hay mujeres que se han destacado de manera impresionante. Por ejemplo, Amalita Fortabat (n. 1921) ha acumulado una fortuna que incluye siete fábricas *(factories)* de cemento, dos estaciones de radio y el periódico más viejo de Argentina, *La Prensa.* Shauna Doyle de Brun es la jefa ejecutiva de Texel, una compañía de textiles y una de las 100 compañías más grandes en México.

Donde las mujeres trabajan
Estadísticas en el mundo de la más grande a la más pequeña de las mujeres trabajando fuera de la casa.

23.9% **Colombia**

45.2% **Estados Unidos**

49.2% **Hungría**

Source: The World Competitiveness Report

¿Qué te parece?

1. ¿Tienen las mujeres las mismas oportunidades profesionales que los hombres en los Estados Unidos? ¿Por qué?
2. ¿Ganan las mujeres lo mismo que los hombres por el mismo trabajo? ¿Por qué?
3. ¿Hay un techo de vidrio *(glass ceiling)* para las mujeres? Da unos ejemplos.

¡FÍJATE! 1
El subjuntivo, parte 2

Let's review what you learned about the subjunctive mood in chapter 9.

1. Does the subjunctive exist in English?
2. How do you form the subjunctive in Spanish?
3. What are some of the expressions in Spanish that require the subjunctive?

Besides the expressions you learned in chapter 9 that take the subjunctive, there are additional situations that require the use of the subjunctive. Look at the following examples expressing *doubt, hope, desire,* and *want.*

Dudo que Marco <u>pueda</u> ir.	*I <u>doubt</u> (that) Marco <u>can</u> go.*
Esperamos que Uds. <u>vengan</u> temprano.	*We <u>hope</u> (that) you <u>come</u> early.*
Mi mamá **quiere que** yo <u>sea</u> doctor.	*My mom <u>wants</u> me <u>to be</u> a doctor.*
Sus padres **desean que** ella <u>estudie</u> medicina.	*Her parents <u>want</u> her <u>to study</u> medicine.*

Most subjunctive constructions contain both a main clause and a dependent clause introduced by **que.** If the main clause contains a verb in the indicative that expresses doubt, insecurity, hope, and so on, then the dependent clause contains a verb in the subjunctive. However, if the subject of the main clause and the dependent clause is the same, the infinitive is used instead of the subjunctive. Compare the following drawings.

Nosotros queremos **ir** al teatro.   Nosotros queremos que **tú vayas** al teatro.

The sentences that follow express a person or group of people wishing, wanting, hoping, desiring, or doubting something about or for himself, herself, or themselves, which is expressed as an infinitive. In other words, there is no change of subject and the subjunctive is *not* used.

<u>Dudo ir.</u>	*<u>I doubt I can go.</u>*
<u>Esperamos venir</u> temprano.	*<u>We hope to come</u> early.*
Mi mamá <u>quiere viajar</u> a las montañas.	*My mom <u>wants to travel</u> to the mountains.*
Sus padres <u>desean comprar</u> un coche nuevo.	*Her parents <u>want to buy</u> a new car.*

Although **creer** and **pensar** take the indicative, **no creer** and **no pensar,** as well as **creer** and **pensar** in interrogative sentences, take the subjunctive because they express doubt. Compare the affirmative and negative uses of **creer** and **pensar** in the pairs of sentences below.

Creo que <u>hay</u> un buen restaurante aquí.	*I think (that) <u>there is</u> a good restaurant here.*
No creo que <u>haya</u> un buen restaurante aquí.	*I don't think (that) <u>there is</u> a good restaurant here.*
Piensan que Alan <u>está</u> aquí hoy.	*They think (that) Alan <u>is</u> here today.*
No piensan que Alan <u>esté</u> aquí hoy.	*They don't think (that) Alan <u>is</u> here today.*
Creo que <u>es</u> un buen mecánico.	*I think (that) he <u>is</u> a good mechanic.*
¿Crees que <u>sea</u> un buen mecánico?	*Do you think (that) he <u>is</u> a good mechanic?*

5 | **Complétala.**   Completa las frases siguientes según tu mamá o tu abuela.

1. Quiero que Uds... (comer más verduras)
2. No quiero que tú... (escuchar esa música)
3. No me gusta que nosotros... (tener que gastar tanto en la comida)
4. Espero que los vecinos... (limpiar su patio)
5. Dudo que... (haber tiempo para terminar todo)
6. Tu papá y yo deseamos que tú... (ser feliz)

6 | **En tus sueños.**   ¡Soñaste *(you dreamed)* que tenías el primer robot personal! Repite a un compañero cinco cosas que le dijiste al robot.

Modelo   **Robot, quiero que tú limpies mi cuarto.**

7 | **Lo siento, pero lo dudo.**   Tu instructor te va a decir las frases siguientes. Reacciona siguiendo el modelo.

Modelo   **INSTRUCTOR:**   Yo salgo con Tom Cruise / Sharon Stone.

   ESTUDIANTE: Yo dudo que Ud. salga con Tom Cruise / Sharon Stone.

1. Tengo dieciocho años.
2. Escribo cinco libros cada año.
3. Leo dos libros cada noche.
4. Soy un amigo de Celine Dion.
5. Miro la televisión cuatro horas cada día.
6. Vivo en una casa de veinte dormitorios.
7. Manejo un Mercedes y un Porsche.

8 | **¿Lo crees o no lo crees?**   Con un compañero, reacciona a las frases siguientes según el modelo.

Modelo   **ESTUDIANTE 1:**   Mis padres saben cuánto estudio.

   ESTUDIANTE 2:   No creo que mis padres sepan cuánto estudio.
   (o)
   Creo que mis padres saben cuánto estudio.

1. Los médicos ganan poco dinero.
2. La cantante Whitney Houston canta muy bien.
3. La universidad recicla lo suficiente.
4. Las enfermeras tienen que trabajar mucho.
5. La contaminación del aire es un problema grande.
6. Las mujeres no son suficientemente fuertes para ser bomberos o policías.
7. Nunca vamos a tener una presidenta en este país.
8. En general, los atletas profesionales y los actores no son muy inteligentes.

9 | **El futuro.**   ¿Cómo ves el futuro? ¿Eres optimista o pesimista? Escribe tres frases usando el subjuntivo para hacer comentarios sobre el futuro.

Modelo   **Espero que mis padres estén en buena salud. Dudo que limpiemos el medio ambiente. Deseo que mi novio y yo nos casemos.**

¡ASÓMATE! 2
La tecnología

La tecnología

1. el archivo
2. el computador / la computadora
3. el computador portátil / la computadora portátil
4. el disco no removible
5. el disquete
6. el fax
7. la impresora

8. el localizador, el bíper (MEXICO), el buscapersonas (SPAIN)
9. las máquinas / los equipos
10. la página en la Internet
11. la pantalla
12. el procesador de texto
13. el programa de computación / el software
14. el teléfono celular

Unos verbos

borrar	*to erase*
enviar por fax / faxear / mandar	*to fax*
guardar / salvar	*to save*
imprimir	*to print*
mandar, enviar	*to send*
navegar la Internet	*to surf the Net*

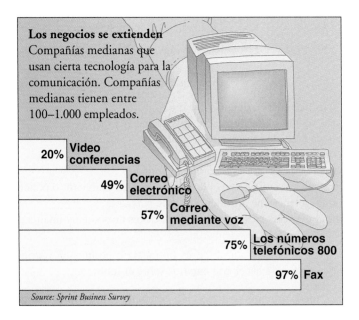

Los negocios se extienden
Compañías medianas que usan cierta tecnología para la comunicación. Compañías medianas tienen entre 100–1.000 empleados.

20% Video conferencias
49% Correo electrónico
57% Correo mediante voz
75% Los números telefónicos 800
97% Fax

Source: Sprint Business Survey

Otras palabras útiles

la carta de correo electrónico   *E-mail letter*
el contestador (automático; *Spain)*   *answering machine*
la contestadora   *answering machine*
el correo electrónico   *E-mail*
el correo mediante voz   *voice mail*
el demodulador / la demoduladora,   *modem*
  el módem *(Spain)*

la memoria   *memory*
la realidad virtual   *virtual reality*
la Red   *Internet, World Wide Web*

10 **Preguntas personales.**   Contesta las preguntas siguientes.

1. ¿Sabes utilizar bien una computadora? ¿Qué (no) puedes hacer?
2. ¿Va a ser importante la computadora en tu trabajo? ¿Por qué?
3. ¿Tienes un teléfono celular? Si no, ¿quieres uno? ¿Por qué?
4. ¿Quién necesita un localizador personal? ¿Por qué?
5. Según tú, ¿cuál es el aparato tecnológico más necesario? ¿menos necesario?
6. ¿ Qué aparatos tecnológicos tienes y usas tú? ¿Cuáles quieres usar (pero no tienes)? ¿Cuáles prefieres no usar? Explica.

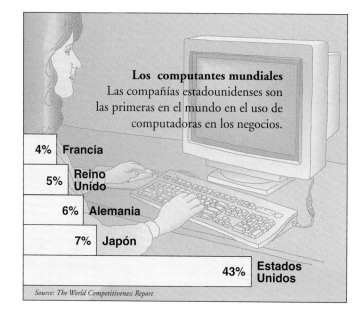

Los computantes mundiales
Las compañías estadounidenses son las primeras en el mundo en el uso de computadoras en los negocios.

4% **Francia**

5% **Reino Unido**

6% **Alemania**

7% **Japón**

43% **Estados Unidos**

Source: The World Competitiveness Report

¡ENTÉRATE!
El mundo tecnológico

El mundo tecnológico se ha popularizado tanto en el mundo hispano como en los Estados Unidos. Por ejemplo, igual que en los Estados Unidos, es común ver a personas con sus teléfonos celulares caminando por las calles. Enviar un fax es normal en el mundo de negocios. La computadora personal ha llegado a ser una parte importante en la vida de personas profesionales. Y sin decir, la Red ha conectado a todo el mundo de una manera inesperada.

También es interesante observar cómo el idioma español se enfrenta *(copes)* a la gran cantidad de nuevas palabras en inglés que vienen al idioma a causa de esta revolución tecnológica. Hay muchas palabras que varios países en Latinoamérica y España han deci-

dido no traducir. Pues, las palabras como CD-ROM, fax, módem e Internet se quedan igual en español. ¡Simplemente las pronuncias con un acento español!

¿Qué te parece?

1. ¿Cómo ha cambiado tu vida la tecnología? ¿La vida de tu familia?
2. ¿En qué aspectos es beneficioso el uso de la tecnología ? ¿En qué aspectos es negativo?
3. ¿Qué opinas de la idea siguiente? «Adoptar palabras en un idioma sin traducirlas contamina el idioma.»

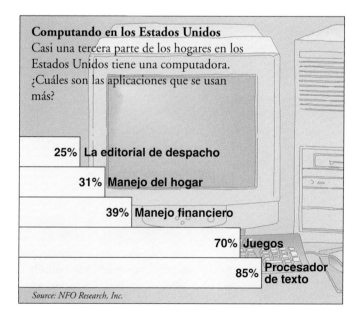

Computando en los Estados Unidos
Casi una tercera parte de los hogares en los Estados Unidos tiene una computadora. ¿Cuáles son las aplicaciones que se usan más?

- **25%** La editorial de despacho
- **31%** Manejo del hogar
- **39%** Manejo financiero
- **70%** Juegos
- **85%** Procesador de texto

Source: NFO Research, Inc.

¡Dime más!
¡Dime más!

¡FÍJATE! 2
El futuro y el condicional

El futuro

In English, the future tense is formed with *will* plus the main verb, for example, *we will save*. In Spanish, the future tense of regular verbs is formed with a set of endings attached to the infinitive, for example, **guardaremos.**

Infinitive +	-é	-emos
	-ás	-éis
	-á	-án

The same set of endings is used for **-ar, -er,** and **-ir** verbs.

-ar: guardar			
yo	guardar**é**	nosotros, nosotras	guardar**emos**
tú	guardar**ás**	vosotros, vosotras	guardar**éis**
él, ella, Ud.	guardar**á**	ellos, ellas, Uds.	guardar**án**

-er: perder			
yo	perder**é**	nosotros, nosotras	perder**emos**
tú	perder**ás**	vosotros, vosotras	perder**éis**
él, ella, Ud.	perder**á**	ellos, ellas, Uds.	perder**án**

-ir: imprimir			
yo	imprimir**é**	nosotros, nosotras	imprimir**emos**
tú	imprimir**ás**	vosotros, vosotras	imprimir**éis**
él, ella, Ud.	imprimir**á**	ellos, ellas, Uds.	imprimir**án**

¿Me <u>mandarás</u> una fax con la información hoy?	*Will you fax me the information today?*
Si no, <u>imprimiré</u> lo que tengo en la computadora.	*If not, I'll print what I have in the computer.*

A few common verbs do not use the infinitive as the stem. They are:

decir	**dir-**	saber	**sabr-**
haber	**habr-**	salir	**saldr-**
hacer	**har-**	tener	**tendr-**
poder	**podr-**	valer	**valdr-**
poner	**pondr-**	venir	**vendr-**
querer	**querr-**		

¿<u>Sabrás</u> encontrar ese periódico en la Red?	*Will you know how to find this newspaper on the Net?*
¿<u>Saldrá</u> tu padre sin su teléfono celular?	*Will your father leave without his cell phone?*

El condicional

In English, the conditional is formed with *would* plus the main verb, for example, *we would go*. In Spanish, the conditional of regular verbs is formed with a set of endings attached to the infinitives, for example, **iríamos.**

	-ía	**-íamos**
Infinitive +	**-ías**	**-íais**
	-ía	**-ían**

As with the future tense, the same set of endings is used for **-ar, -er,** and **-ir,** verbs.

-ar: guardar			
yo	guardar**ía**	nosotros, nosotras	guardar**íamos**
tú	guardar**ías**	vosotros, vosotras	guardar**íais**
él, ella, Ud.	guardar**ía**	ellos, ellas, Uds.	guardar**ían**

-er: perder			
yo	perder**ía**	nosotros, nosotras	perder**íamos**
tú	perder**ías**	vosotros, vosotras	perder**íais**
él, ella, Ud.	perder**ía**	ellos, ellas, Uds.	perder**ían**

-ir: imprimir			
yo	imprimir**ía**	nosotros, nosotras	imprimir**íamos**
tú	imprimir**ías**	vosotros, vosotras	imprimir**íais**
él, ella, Ud.	imprimir**ía**	ellos, ellas, Uds.	imprimir**ían**

Mi compañero me dijo que <u>imprimiría</u> la carta que escribimos.

My partner told me <u>he would print</u> the letter we wrote.

Con cinco mil dólares, yo <u>compraría</u> una nueva computadora.

With $5,000 <u>I would buy</u> a new computer.

El profesor me explicó que no <u>tendría</u> tiempo hoy para leer su correo electrónico.

The teacher explained to me that <u>he would</u> not <u>have time</u> today to read his E-mail.

Entonces, ¿tú <u>podrías</u> decirle que no puedo asistir a la clase hoy?

So, <u>could you</u> tell him that I can't come to class today?

The eleven verbs that are irregular in the future are also irregular in the conditional.

The conditional is often used to explain what someone would do in certain circumstances or under certain conditions. It is also sometimes used to soften a request or criticism.

Con un poco más de tiempo <u>limpiaría</u> toda la casa para ti.

With a little bit more time, <u>I would clean</u> the whole house for you.

<u>Me gustaría</u> que estudiaras un poco más.

<u>I would like</u> it if you studied a little more.

1 ¿**Qué harás?**   ¿Te gusta hacer planes? ¿Cuándo harás las cosas siguientes? ¿Cómo será tu horario la semana que viene? Contesta las preguntas siguientes con un compañero y comparen sus respuestas.

1. ¿Cuándo estudiarás español?
2. ¿Cuándo escribirás una carta por correo electrónico?
3. ¿Cuándo irás al supermercado?
4. ¿Cuándo limpiarás tu cuarto / apartamento / casa?
5. ¿Cuándo te comprarás una computadora nueva?
6. ¿Cuándo navegarás la Internet?
7. ¿Cuándo tendrás el dinero para ir a un país hispanohablante?

2 **Si tuvieras...**   Siempre tenemos deseos, ¿verdad?   Pues, si tuvieras *(you had)* el tiempo o el dinero, ¿qué harías en las siguientes circunstancias?

Modelo   **ESTUDIANTE 1:**   Si tuvieras el tiempo, ¿qué película verías?

ESTUDIANTE 2:   Si tuviera el tiempo, vería *El Titánico* otra vez.

1. Si tuvieras el dinero, ¿adónde irías para las vacaciones?
2. Si tuvieras el dinero, ¿cómo sería tu casa?
3. Si tuvieras el tiempo, ¿qué harías este fin de semana?
4. Si tuvieras el tiempo, ¿qué libro leerías?
5. Si tuvieras el tiempo, ¿qué deporte aprenderías?
6. Si tuvieras el dinero, ¿qué comprarías?

¡FÍJATE! 3
Las expresiones afirmativas y negativas

You have seen and used a number of the affirmative and negative expressions, which are shown in the following box, throughout this book. Study the list and learn the ones that are new to you. Many of the negative expressions are frequently contrasted with their affirmative indefinite counterparts, such as **nunca** and **siempre** or **ninguno** and **alguno.**

Afirmativas		Negativas	
a veces	*sometimes*	jamás	*never*
algo	*something*	nada	*nothing*
alguien	*someone*	nadie	*no one, nobody*
algún, alguno(a / os / as)	*some*	ningún, ninguno / ninguna	*none, no*
cada	*each*		
siempre	*always*	nunca	*never*
también	*also, too*	tampoco	*neither, not either*
y... o	*either . . . or*	ni... ni	*neither . . . nor*

Look at the sentences below, paying special attention to the position of the negative words.

¿Quién llamó?	*Who called?*
1. <u>No</u> llamó <u>nadie</u>.	<u>No one</u> *called.*
2. <u>Nadie</u> llamó.	<u>No one</u> *called.*

¿Siempre vas al cine los martes?	*Do you always go to the movies on Tuesdays?*
1. <u>No, no</u> voy <u>nunca</u>.	*No, I <u>never</u> go.*
2. <u>No, nunca</u> voy.	*No, I <u>never</u> go.*

Negative expressions can either precede or follow the verb. When a negative expression follows the verb, **no** must precede the verb, as shown in the first sentences of the above examples.

 Unlike English, Spanish can have two or more negatives in the same sentence. A double negative expression is actually quite common.

Alguno and **ninguno** agree in number and gender with the noun they describe; they become **algún** and **ningún** before masculine singular nouns. Forms of **ninguno / ninguna** are not used in the plural.

MARÍA:	¿Tienes **algunas** clases fáciles este semestre?
JUAN:	No, no tengo **ninguna**. ¡Y **ningún** profesor es simpático tampoco!
MARÍA:	¿No hay **algún** cambio que puedas hacer?
JUAN:	No, no hay **ninguno**.

(o)

No, no hay **ningún** otro curso que pueda tomar.

3 **La alta vida.** ¿Qué tipo de vida tienes? Trabaja con un compañero y contesta las preguntas siguientes, usando las expresiones negativas ¡si las necesitas!

| **Modelo** | **ESTUDIANTE 1:** | ¿Has recibido algún regalo de tu novio hoy? |
| | **ESTUDIANTE 2:** | No, no he recibido ninguno. |

1. ¿Has comprado algo en Tiffany's?
2. ¿Has ido a Japón alguna vez?
3. ¿Has ido a China?
4. ¿Tienes un Mercedes o un Lexus?
5. ¿Siempre vas a la Riviera para pasar el verano?
6. ¿Has ido de safari en Kenya?
7. ¿Navegarás el río Amazonas pronto?

4 **No tienes razón.** Tu compañero de cuarto piensa en una manera poca realista. Dile que debe ser más realista, usando expresiones negativas. Sigue el modelo.

Modelo   Tengo que buscar una profesión sin estrés.   ➠   **No hay ninguna profesión sin estrés.**

1. Voy a casarme con la persona perfecta e ideal.
2. Siempre estudio veinte horas para un examen.
3. Alguien me quiere regalar $100.000.000 de dólares.
4. También quiere regalarme un viaje por todo el mundo.
5. IBM y Macintosh me ofrecen trabajo después de graduarme.

 *The conjunction **y** becomes **e** before words beginning with an [i] sound. Similarly, **o** changes to **u** before words beginning with an [o] sound. Examples: **padres e hijos; joven e inteligente; siete u ocho; casa u hoteles.***

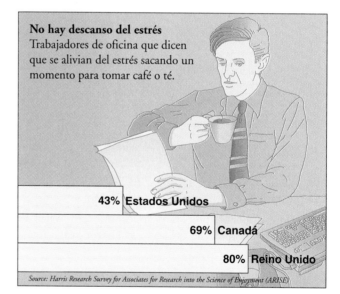

No hay descanso del estrés
Trabajadores de oficina que dicen que se alivian del estrés sacando un momento para tomar café o té.

43% Estados Unidos

69% Canadá

80% Reino Unido

Source: Harris Research Survey for Associates for Research into the Science of Enjoyment (ARISE)

¡FÍJATE! 4
El subjuntivo, parte 3

Up to this point, you have learned two different scenarios for using the subjunctive.

1. In impersonal expressions such as **Es necesario que...** and **Es importante que...**
2. After verbs of *hope, want, desire,* and *doubt*

A third use of the subjunctive is when there is doubt that something exists. This may simply mean that the person, place, or things referred to do not exist yet for the speaker. Compare the following pairs of sentences, which contrast the indicative and subjunctive.

Vivo en un apartamento que <u>tiene</u> piscina.	*I live in an apartment that has a swimming pool.*
Buscan un apartamento que <u>tenga</u> piscina.	*They are looking for an apartment that has a swimming pool.*
Tengo un novio que <u>sabe</u> cocinar.	*I have a boyfriend who knows how to cook.*
Busco un novio que <u>sepa</u> cocina.	*I'm looking for a boyfriend who knows how to cook.*
Conozco a una secretaria que <u>entiende</u> muy bien la computadora.	*I know a secretary who understands the computer very well.*
¿Conoces a una secretaria que <u>entienda</u> muy bien la computadora?	*Do you know a secretary who understands the computer very well?*
Tengo una mamá que me <u>puede</u> comprender.	*I have a mom who can understand me.*
Mamá, no hay nadie que me <u>pueda</u> comprender.	*Mom, there is no one who can understand me.*

The paired sentences above illustrate adjective clauses beginning with **que**. In the first sentence of each pair, the verb in the adjective clause is in the *indicative* because the speaker describes something that exists. In the second sentence of each pair, the adjective clause is in the *subjunctive* because the speaker is not sure that something exists.

5 ¿**Qué buscas?** Llena la gráfica en **Etapa 2, actividad 5** del **capítulo 10** en tu **Manual de actividades** con tus deseos.

6 ¿**Conoces a alguien que... ?** Levántate, circula por tu clase y busca a alguien que pueda contestar afirmativamente las preguntas que están en **Etapa 2, actividad 6** del **capítulo 10** en tu **Manual de actividades.**

7 **La realidad y tus deseos.** Describe en dos o tres frases una de las cosas o personas siguientes. Luego, describe lo que prefieres o quieres en dos o tres frases. Sigue el modelo.

Modelo tu coche ➠ **Mi coche es viejo y no funcionan ni la calefacción ni el aire acondicionado. No tengo una llanta de repuesto *(spare tire)* y el color, después de muchos años, está muy feo.**

Busco un coche que tenga calefacción y aire acondicionado. También quiero uno que tenga una llanta de repuesto y que sea rojo. Me gusta el color rojo.

1. tu habitación / apartamento / casa
2. tu coche
3. tu clase de _____
4. tu hermano / hermana
5. tu compañero de cuarto

¿Qué es un hispano? Esto es difícil de definir porque el mundo hispano es tan variado como el mundo norteamericano. El hispano tiene muchas caras. La verdad es que los hispanos vienen de muchas culturas diferentes y hablan muchas lenguas. Hasta con el mismo español existen muchas variedades en pronunciación y vocabulario. Por ejemplo, para decir «autobús» se dice «guagua» en Puerto Rico y «camión» en México. Sin embargo, «guagua» en algunos países es un bebé y «camión» en Puerto Rico es un «*truck*». Aunque estas diferencias existen, no es difícil entender y el hacerse entender porque la comunicación siempre ocurre dentro de un contexto.

Para muchos de los hispanos es importante conservar su identidad nacional. Por ejemplo, la escritora puertorriqueña Esmeralda Santiago habla de la lucha personal de haber nacido en Puerto Rico y de haber sido traída a los Estados Unidos en la adolescencia. Hoy en día cuando le preguntan si es hispana, ella prefiere decir que es puertorriqueña. Y así hay muchos casos.

Como en los Estados Unidos, sí hay diferencias pero hay cosas que unen a toda la raza humana: la necesidad básica de comida, casa y ropa. De todas clases sociales y culturales, la gente es trabajadora y lucha por el mejoramiento del estado de vida y por mantener la autoestima.

¿Qué te parece?

1. ¿Cuál es la nacionalidad de tus padres? ¿De tus abuelos?

2. ¿Cuál es tu identidad?

3. ¿Te importa que la gente sepa de dónde eres? ¿Por qué?

4. ¿Has conocido a alguien que haya tenido una lucha con su identidad? Explica.

LA RED ¡Navega la Internet!

To discover more information on the culture of this chapter, check the Holt Web site and other suggestions listed in your **Manual de actividades.**

http://www.hrwcollege.com/

●ETAPA 3

¡Cuéntame!
¡Cuéntame!

Ya lo sabemos

¿Puedes resumir lo que sabes del tío Pedro y el sacrificio final? ¿De la relación entre Rafi y Adriana? ¿Cuáles son las preguntas que nos quedan por contestar? Pues, en este último episodio vamos a recibir más información del Perú y de México sobre:

◆ los artefactos robados
◆ la doble vida de Pedro Lara
◆ Pilar
◆ los verdaderos «asuntos de amor»

Preguntas personales

1. ¿Qué es la telecomunicación?
2. ¿Cuáles son los usos de la telecomunicación? ¿Hay usos internacionales?
3. ¿Qué es una teleconferencia? ¿Cuáles son los beneficios de esta tecnología? ¿Los puntos negativos?
4. ¿Tienes experiencia personal con la telecomunicación? Explica.

Estrategias de lectura
Asking Yourself Questions

In *¡Atrévete!*, you have learned ways to get meaning from words and phrases by identifying cognates and guessing meaning from context. You have also practiced identifying the main ideas through skimming and focusing on specific information through scanning. The next step involves learning to ask yourself "check" questions as you read, which help you summarize and organize information.

To illustrate this strategy, read the first sentence of the first paragraph of Episode 10. Why was it a night filled with calls, faxes, and E-mail messages? By answering that question, you have read and summarized the first two paragraphs. Now read the third paragraph. It is about Roberto Ávila. Who is he? What new and important information does he provide?

Continue to read the episode, writing down specific questions that you could ask yourself that would help you summarize and organize the ideas from the story. When finished, share these questions with your classmates.

Rafi y el sacrificio final

Episodio 10: Y mañana... ¿qué?

Era una noche llena de llamadas, faxes y mensajes por correo electrónico. El señor Martín tenía un amigo en la universidad que era profesor de telecomunicaciones y él podría establecer una telecomunicación entre el Perú y los Estados Unidos.

A las ocho de la mañana Rafi, el señor Martín y Chema estaban en la oficina de telecomunicaciones de la universidad. Allí hablaban en vivo con el director de los museos nacionales del Perú, un científico y el jefe de la policía internacional.

Roberto Ávila, el científico, había estado estudiando los tesoros de la civilización moche desde que se empezaron las excavaciones de las tumbas. Rafi, el señor Martín y Chema lo escucharon contar unas historias increíbles de sus experiencias. Acababa de regresar de Sipán donde personalmente había supervisado la excavación de unas tumbas. Según él, ninguno de los artefactos había desaparecido.

El señor Reimundo Huertas era el director de los museos nacionales. No sólo había oído hablar de Pedro Lara, sino que también lo conocía muy bien desde hacía mucho tiempo. Hace muchos años empezaron a aparecer en el mercado del arte algunos artefactos robados de oro y plata de una belleza y un valor increíble. Eran de una época precolombina, más o menos del año 300 después de Cristo. Huertas había llamado a Pedro Lara quien había venido siguiendo la pista de unos ladrones. Gracias a Lara, las autoridades arrestaron a algunos de ellos. Hace dos semanas Pedro dijo que iba a venir en seguida pero que primero tenía que ir a México para arreglar otro asunto. —No sé —continuó diciendo el señor Huertas con una sonrisa picaresca,° —pero esta vez me parece que eran asuntos de amor.

El señor Huertas terminó diciendo que no había oído nada de Pedro Lara desde hacía dos semanas. El policía reportó que por el momento nada había desaparecido. Y así acabó la teleconferencia.

Rafi no podía creer lo que oía. ¡Artefactos precolombinos... oro... plata... un valor inestimable... y la doble vida de su tío Pedro! Y... ¿dónde estaba él en este momento? ¿Estaba bien o estaba en peligro°?

Regresaron a la casa de los padres de Rafi. Carmen estaba allí; la señora Martín había ido a recogerla a la cárcel mientras el señor Martín, Rafi y Chema se ocupaban con lo del tío. Apenas habían empezado a contarles a Carmen y a su mamá lo que les había pasado cuando sonó el teléfono. El señor Martín lo contestó. Se le fue el color de la cara.

—¿Dónde estás? —preguntó el señor Martín con una voz casi inaudible. Volviéndose a todos. —Es Pedro. Todavía está en México.

Rafi tomó la extensión y escuchó con asombro° la conversación. Pedro había ido a México en busca de Pilar. Rafi pensó en lo que les había dicho el señor Huertas, «asuntos de amor». Pero resultó que no eran asuntos de amor. Pedro estaba siguiendo la pista de unos ladrones y Pilar era una de ellos.

Pedro se había dado cuenta de las andanzas° de Pilar hacía muchísimo tiempo. La había visto un día en el parque hablando con un hombre que él había estado investigando y se dio cuenta inmediatamente que era uno de sus cómplices. Pilar, sin querer, lo había ayudado con su investigación. Pero ahora ella sabía que Pedro la seguía y no fue al Perú por miedo a que Pedro la incriminara. Ahora se daba cuenta Rafi de por qué el tío andaba por Mérida.

mischievous smile

danger

surprise

whereabouts

331

Comprensión

1. ¿Qué tuvieron que hacer para arreglar la teleconferencia?
2. ¿Quiénes hablaron? ¿Quiénes son estos hombres?
3. ¿Qué dijo Roberto Ávila sobre los tesoros? ¿Qué dijo el señor Huertas del tío Pedro? ¿Sabía dónde estaba Pedro?
4. ¿Dónde ha estado Carmen? ¿Por qué?
5. ¿Era Pilar la novia de Pedro? Explica.

Expansión

(1) ¿Por qué fue mejor una teleconferencia que una simple llamada telefónica?

(2) ¿Cómo era la doble vida de Pedro Lara? ¿Por qué no compartió la otra vida con su familia?

(3) En grupos pequeños, hablen de sus escenas o episodios favoritos de la historia **Rafi y el sacrificio final.** Entre todos, elijan una y preséntenla a sus compañeros de clase.

(4) En grupos de cinco, hagan los papeles de Chema, Rafi, Carmen y los señores Martín. Hablen de la manifestación de Carmen, la teleconferencia y la llamada del tío Pedro.

(5) Después de mirar el video o escuchar el CD que aclara aún más este misterio, escribe un nuevo fin para el **Episodio 10,** haciendo los cambios que tú crees que sean necesarios e interesantes.

A mirar o escuchar

(6) View the video or listen to the audio CD to find out what happens to Rafi. Consult your **Manual de actividades** for pre- and post-listening activities.

¡Sí, se puede!

1. **Viaje de aventura.** Eres profesor / profesora de historia, inglés o español en una escuela secundaria y estás planeando un viaje escolar de un día para tus estudiantes. Describe adónde piensas llevar a los estudiantes, cómo van a llegar, y qué van a hacer allí. Tienes grandes esperanzas *(hopes)* para este viajecito y tienes los siguientes pensamientos *(thoughts)*. Después comparte tus planes y estos pensamientos con tus compañeros de clase.

1. Espero que nosotros...
2. Deseo que algunos de los estudiantes...
3. Tengo miedo de que dos o tres de ellos...
4. Estoy seguro que ningún estudiante...
5. Necesito a alguien que...

2. **¡Símbolos! ¡Símbolos!** ¿Cuáles son las profesiones que más te interesan? En grupos, decidan cuáles son las dos profesiones más interesantes para Uds. y es-

cojan un símbolo que represente a cada una. Después, dibujen el símbolo con palabras apropiadas.

Modelo

3. **Anuncios personales.** Estás desesperado(a) con tantas citas aburridas y decides poner un anuncio personal en el periódico de la universidad para ver si así puedes encontrar a la persona ideal. Para el anuncio, tienes que completar la siguiente información de manera interesante (¡y honesta!).

Modelo **Yo soy... Busco una persona...**

4. **El psicólogo.** Cada estudiante debe inventar un problema por el cual necesita consejo. Después, en parejas, cada uno(a) debe compartir su problema, describiendo la situación con bastante detalle, mientras el / la otro(a) estudiante reacciona y ofrece consejos.

Modelo **ESTUDIANTE 1:** Tengo un gran problema. Mis padres no quieren que...

 ESTUDIANTE 2: Es lástima que Ud. tenga ese problema pero es bueno que hable Ud. conmigo. Le aconsejo que...

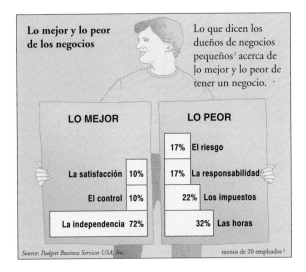

Lo mejor y lo peor de los negocios

Lo que dicen los dueños de negocios pequeños[1] acerca de lo mejor y lo peor de tener un negocio.

LO MEJOR		LO PEOR	
		17%	El riesgo
La satisfacción	10%	17%	La responsabilidad
El control	10%	22%	Los impuestos
La independencia	72%	32%	Las horas

Source: Padgett Business Services USA, Inc. menos de 20 empleados [1]

Para recordar

Al terminar este capítulo, tú puedes:

Etapa 1 ¡Sígueme!

❏ comparar y contrastar una variedad de profesiones

❏ aprender de las mujeres hispanas en el mundo de trabajo

❏ expresar deseos y temores

❏ usar el idioma de la tecnología

Etapa 2 ¡Dime más!

❏ hablar de tus planes futuros y condicionales

❏ usar expresiones afirmativas y negativas

❏ expresar dudas

❏ discutir sobre la identidad hispana

Etapa 3 ¡Cuéntame!

❏ descubrir si Rafi puede resolver el misterio

VOCABULARIO ACTIVO

Unas profesiones

el abogado / la abogada
    lawyer
el actor / la actriz   *actor / actress*
el artista / la artista   *artist*
el autor / la autora   *author*
el bombero   *firefighter*
el cantante / la cantante   *singer*
el cocinero / la cocinera   *cook*

el consejero/ la consejera   *counselor*
el contador / la contadora
    accountant
el dentista / la dentista   *dentist*
el granjero / la granjera   *farmer*
el hombre / la mujer de negocios
    businessman / businesswoman
el médico / la médica   *doctor*

el músico / la música   *musician*
el obrero / la obrera   *manual laborer,*
    worker
el peluquero / la peluquera   *hair*
    stylist; barber
el policía / la mujer policía   *police*
    officer
el secretario / la secretaria   *secretary*

La tecnología

el archivo   *file*
el bíper (MEXICO)   *personal*
    pager
el buscapersonas (SPAIN)
    personal pager
el computador / la computadora
    computer
el computador portátil / la
    computadora portátil
    laptop computer

el disco no removible   *hard drive*
el disquete   *diskette*
los equipos   *hardware*
el fax   *fax*
la impresora   *printer*
el localizador   *personal pager*
las máquinas   *hardware*
el módem (SPAIN)   *modem*
la página en la Internet   *home page*
la pantalla   *screen*

el procesador de texto   *word*
    processor
el programa de computación
    software
el software   *software*
el teléfono celular   *cell phone*

Unos verbos útiles

borrar   *to erase*
enviar   *to fax*
enviar por fax   *to fax*

faxear   *to fax*
guardar   *to save*
imprimir   *to print*

mandar   *to send, to fax*
navegar la Internet   *to surf the Net*
salvar   *to save*

Las expresiones afirmativas y negativas

algo   *something*
alguien   *someone*
algún, alguno(a / os / as)   *some*
cada   *each*

jamás   *never*
nada   *nothing*
ni.... ni   *neither . . . nor*
ningún   *none, no*

ninguno(a)   *none, no*
tampoco   *neither, not either*
y... o   *either . . . or*

Otras palabras útiles

la carta de correo electrónico
    E-mail letter
el contestador (automático;
    SPAIN)   *answering
    machine*
la contestadora   *answering
    machine*

el correo electrónico   *E-mail*
el correo mediante voz   *voice mail*
el demodulador / la demoduladora
    modem
el empleado / la empleada   *employee*
el gerente / la gerente   *manager*
el jefe / la jefa   *boss*

la memoria   *memory*
el propietario / la propietaria   *owner*
la realidad virtual   *virtual reality*
la Red   *Internet, World Wide Web*

También se dice...

Capítulo 1

Otros saludos y otras despedidas

El gusto es mío.	*Pleased to meet you; The pleasure is mine.*
Hasta entonces.	*Until then.*
¿Qué hubo?	*How's it going?; What's happening?; What's new?*
¿Qué pasa?	*How's it going?; What's happening?; What's new?*
¿Qué pasó?	*How's it going?; What's happening?; What's new?*
Nos vemos.	*See you.*

Más familia

el cuñado / la cuñada	*brother-in-law / sister-in-law*
el hermanastro / la hermanastra	*stepbrother / stepsister*
el hijastro / la hijastra	*stepson / stepdaughter*
el hijo único / la hija única	*only child*
la madrastra	*stepmother*
mami (LATIN AMERICA)	*Mommy, Mom*
el medio hermano / la media hermana	*half brother / half sister*
los medios hermanos	*half brothers and sisters*
el nieto / la nieta	*grandson / granddaughter*
los nietos	*grandchildren*
la nuera	*daughter-in-law*
el padrastro	*stepfather*
el pariente	*relative*
los sobrinos	*nieces and nephews*
el suegro / la suegra	*father-in-law / mother-in-law*
los suegros	*in-laws*
el yerno	*son-in-law*

Más nacionalidades

argentino / argentina	*Argentinean*
boliviano / boliviana	*Bolivian*
chileno / chilena	*Chilean*
colombiano / colombiana	*Colombian*
costarricense	*Costa Rican*
dominicano / dominicana	*Dominican*
ecuatoriano / ecuatoriana	*Ecuadorian*
guatemalteco / guatemalteca	*Guatemalan*
hondureño / hondureña	*Honduran*
nicaragüense	*Nicaraguan*

panameño / panameña	Panamanian
paraguayo / paraguaya	Paraguayan
peruano / peruana	Peruvian
uruguayo / uruguaya	Uruguayan
venezolano / venezolana	Venezuelan

Capítulo 2

Más materias y especialidades

la agronomía	agriculture
el cálculo	calculus
las ciencias políticas	political science
las comunicaciones	communications
la contabilidad	accounting
la economía	economics
la educación física	physical education
la enfermería	nursing
la filosofía	philosophy
la física	physics
la geografía	geography
la geología	geology
la ingeniería	engineering
el mercadeo	marketing
la química	chemistry
la religión	religion
los servicios sociales	social work
la sociología	sociology

Más adjetivos

alegre	cheerful, happy
frustrado / frustrada	frustrated
histérico / histérica	crazy

Más deportes y pasatiempos

| cazar | to hunt |
| conversar con amigos | to talk with friends |

esquiar	to ski
hablar por teléfono	to talk on the phone
hacer alpinismo	to go hiking
hacer el footing	to jog
hacer gimnasia	to exercise
ir al centro comercial	to go to the mall; to go downtown
ir a fiestas	to go to parties
ir a un partido de...	to go to a . . . (game)
jugar al ajedrez	to play chess
jugar al boliche	to bowl
jugar al ráquetbol	to play racquetball
jugar al voleibol	to play volleyball
jugar juegos electrónicos	to play video games
levantar pesas	to lift weights
mirar videos	to watch videos
montar a caballo	to go horseback riding
pasear	to go out for a ride; to take a walk
pasear en barco (de vela)	to sail
pescar	to fish
practicar el boxeo	to box
practicar el ciclismo	to cycle
practicar la lucha libre	to wrestle
practicar las artes marciales	to do martial arts
tirar un platillo volador	to throw a Frisbee

Palabras útiles con los deportes y los pasatiempos

el aficionado / la aficionada	fan
el bate	bat
el campo	field
los libros de...	
acción	action books
aventura	adventure books
cuentos cortos	short stories books
ficción (ciencia-ficción)	fiction (science fiction) books
horror	horror books
misterio	mystery books
romance	romance books
espías	spy books
el palo de golf	golf club
la pista	track
pista y campo	track and field
la raqueta	racket

Capítulo 3

La casa

el balcón	balcony
el despacho	office
el pasillo	hall

el patio	*patio; yard*
el porche	*porch*
la recámara *(MEXICO)*	*bedroom*
el salón	*salon; lounge; living room*
el sótano	*basement*
la terraza	*terrace, porch*
el vestíbulo	*entrance hall*

Más cosas y aparatos en la casa

la almohada	*pillow*
el aparato eléctrico	*electric appliance*
la chimenea	*fireplace*
la cómoda	*chest of drawers*
las cortinas	*curtains*
el espejo	*mirror*
el fregadero	*kitchen sink*
los gabinetes	*cabinets*
el horno	*oven*
la lavadora	*washing machine*
el librero *(MEXICO)*	*bookcase*
la mesita	*nightstand*
la nevera *(LATIN AMERICA)*	*refrigerator*
las persianas	*window blinds*
la sábana	*sheet*
la secadora	*dryer*
el televisor	*television set*

Más quehaceres

barrer	*to sweep*
cortar el césped	*to cut the grass*
fregar los platos *(LATIN AMERICA)*	*to do the dishes*
planchar la ropa	*to iron*
regar las plantas	*to water the plants*

El tiempo

el arco iris	*rainbow*
Está despejado.	*It's clear.*
Hace fresco.	*It's cool.*
Hay neblina.	*It's foggy.*
el pronóstico	*weather report*

Capítulo 4

Más lugares de una ciudad o de un pueblo

la alberca *(MEXICO, SPAIN)*	*swimming pool*
el aseo *(SPAIN)*	*public restroom*

el consultorio	doctor's office
la cuadra	block
la frutería	fruit store
la gasolinera	service station
la heladería	ice cream shop
la mezquita	mosque
la papelería	stationery store
la pescadería	fish shop
los servicios	public restroom
la sinagoga	synagogue
el templo	temple
la tienda de juguetes	toy store
la tienda de ropa	clothing store
el zócalo (MEXICO)	plaza

Capítulo 5

Más comidas, condimentos y especias

la aceituna	olive
el aguacate	avocado
el ajo	garlic
la alcaparra	caper
las almejas	clams
el apio	celery
la avena	oatmeal
el banano	banana; banana tree
la batida	milkshake
el bombón	sweets; candy
la calabaza	squash; pumpkin
los calamares	squid
el caldo	broth
el cangrejo	crab
el caramelo	sweets; candy
la carne de cerdo	pork
la carne de cordero	lamb
la carne de res	beef
la carne molida (picada; SPAIN)	ground beef
la cereza	cherry
el champán	champagne
los champiñones	mushrooms
el chillo (PUERTO RICO)	red snapper
la chuleta	chop
la ciruela	plum
la col	cabbage
la coliflor	cauliflower
la dona	donut
el durazno	peach
los espárragos	asparagus
las espinacas	spinach

los fideos	*noodles*
el flan	*caramel custard*
la fresa	*strawberry*
las gambas	*shrimps*
los guisantes	*peas*
las habichuelas	*green beans; beans*
la harina	*flour*
los hongos	*mushrooms*
el huachinango *(MEXICO)*	*red snapper*
la jalea *(SPAIN, PUERTO RICO)*	*jelly; marmalade*
las judías verdes	*green beans*
la langosta	*lobster*
el lenguado	*flounder*
la mantequilla	*butter*
la margarina	*margarine*
los mejillones	*mussels*
el melocotón	*peach*
la miel	*honey*
la ostra	*oyster*
el pan dulce	*sweet roll*
el panqueque	*pancake*
la papaya	*papaya*
el pavo	*turkey*
el pepino	*cucumber*
el pimiento	*sweet pepper*
la piña	*pineapple*
el plátano	*plantain*
el repollo	*cabbage*
la salchicha	*sausage*
la salsa	*sauce*
la sandía	*watermelon*
la sardina	*sardine*
la ternera	*veal*
el tocino	*bacon*
la toronja	*grapefruit*
la zanahoria	*carrot*
el zumo *(SPAIN)*	*juice*

La nutrición

el calcio	*calcium*
la caloría	*calorie*
el carbohidrato	*carbohydrate*
el colesterol	*cholesterol*
la comida rápida	*fast food*
descafeinado / descafeinada	*caffeine free, decaffeinated*
la dieta	*diet*
el fósforo	*phosphorous*
la grasa	*fat*
el hierro	*iron*
el mineral	*mineral*

las proteínas   *proteins*
la vitamina   *vitamin*

Más terminos de la cocina

el aderezo   *seasoning, dressing*
agregar   *to add*
asar   *to roast; to broil*
aumentar libras   *to gain weight*
el batidor   *beater*
batir   *to beat*
la cacerola   *sauce pan*
el caldero   *kettle, pot*
calentar   *to heat*
la copa   *goblet, wine glass*
derretir   *to melt*
engordar   *to gain weight, to get fat*
espesarse   *to thicken*
freír   *to fry*
el fuego (lento, mediano, alto)   *(low, medium, high) heat*
hervir   *to boil*
el ingrediente   *ingredient*
el kilogramo   *kilogram (or 2.2 lbs.)*
mezclar   *to mix*
el nivel   *level*
la olla   *pot*
el pedazo   *piece*
el platillo   *saucer*
el plato hondo   *bowl*
la receta   *recipe*
revolver   *to stir*
la sartén   *frying pan*
servir   *to serve*
subir de peso   *to gain weight, to get fat*
unir   *to combine*
verter   *to pour*

Capítulo 6

Más prendas y ropa

los aretes   *earrings*
la bata (de baño)   *bathrobe*
la bufanda   *scarf*
la capa de agua (PUERTO RICO)   *raincoat*
la cartera   *wallet, purse*
el collar   *necklace*
la correa   *belt*
el guante   *glove*
el impermeable   *raincoat*
los pendientes   *earrings*

el peine	*comb*
la peinilla	*comb*
el pijama	*pajamas*
la prenda	*piece of clothing*
las prendas	*clothing*
la pulsera	*bracelet*
la ropa interior	*underwear*
la sombrilla	*umbrella*
las zapatillas de tenis	*sneakers; tennis shoes*

Más tipos y estilos de tela

con lunares	*polka dotted*
de algodón	*(made of) cotton*
de buena / mala calidad	*good / poor quality*
a / de cuadros	*checked*
de cuero	*(made of) leather*
de goma	*(made of) rubber*
de lana	*(made of) wool*
de lino	*(made of) linen*
de manga corta / larga	*short / long sleeved*
de oro	*(made of) gold*
de plata	*(made of) silver*
de puntitos	*polka dotted*
a / de rayas	*striped*
de seda	*(made of) silk*

Para comprar la ropa

el escaparate	*store window*
la ganga	*bargain*
la liquidación	*clearance sale*
el mostrador	*counter*
la rebaja	*sale, discount*
el tacón alto / bajo	*high / low heel*
la venta	*clearance sale*
la vitrina	*store window*

Capítulo 7

El cuerpo humano

el cabello	*hair*
la cadera	*hip*
la ceja	*eyebrow*
la cintura	*waist*
el codo	*elbow*
la costilla	*rib*
la frente	*forehead*
el hombro	*shoulder*
el hueso	*bone*

el labio	lip
la lengua	tongue
la muñeca	wrist
el músculo	muscle
el muslo	thigh
las nalgas	buttock
los nervios	nerves
la pestaña	eyelash
la piel	skin
las pompas (MEXICO)	buttock
el pulmón	lung
la rodilla	knee
el talón	heel
el tobillo	ankle
la uña	fingernail
las venas	veins

Enfermedades y otras cosas

el alcoholismo	alcoholism
el ataque del corazón	heart attack
el cáncer	cancer
contagiarse de	to catch
la depresión	depression
desmayarse	to faint
la diabetes	diabetes
doblarse	to sprain
el dolor de cabeza	headache
hinchar	to swell
la hipertensión	high blood pressure
el infarto	heart attack
el mareo	dizziness
la narcomanía	drug addiction
las náuseas	nausea
la presión alta / baja	high / low blood pressure
la quemadura	burn
el sarampión	measles
el SIDA	AIDS
torcerse	to sprain
la varicela	chicken pox
vomitar	to vomit

La atención médica

el antihistamínico	antihistamine
la camilla	stretcher
la cura	cure
la dosis	dosage
enyesar	to put in a cast
fracturar(se)	to fracture; to break
las gotas para los ojos	eyedrops
hacer gárgaras	to gargle

las muletas	*crutches*
operar	*to operate*
el paciente	*patient*
la penicilina	*penicillin*
el pulso	*pulse*
la quemadura	*burn*
la radiografía	*X ray*
recetar	*to prescribe*
respirar	*to breathe*
el resultado	*result*
sacar la sangre	*to draw blood*
la silla de ruedas	*wheelchair*
el síntoma	*symptom*
el termómetro	*thermometer*
tomarle la presión	*to take someone's blood pressure*
tomarle el pulso	*to take someone's pulse*
tomarle la temperatura	*to check someone's temperature*
la vacuna	*vaccination*

Capítulo 8

El transporte

el aparcamiento	*parking lot*
el billete	*ticket*
el camión *(MEXICO)*	*bus*
la camioneta	*pickup; van; station wagon*
el carnet *(SPAIN)*	*driver's license*
la carretera	*highway*
enviar	*to send, to dispatch*
la goma *(LATIN AMERICA)*	*tire*
la guagua *(CUBA, PUERTO RICO)*	*bus*
el guía *(PUERTO RICO)*	*steering wheel*
el tiquete / la tiqueta	*ticket*
el volante	*steering wheel*

Más palabras útiles con el viaje

la dirección	*address*
la estampilla	*(postage) stamp*
el paquete	*package*
el sobre	*envelope*

Las emociones

amar	*to love*
el amor	*love*
el cariño	*affection*
los celos	*jealousy*
con coraje	*mad, angry*

despreciar	*to scorn*
el desprecio	*scorn*
enfadado / enfadada	*mad, angry*
enojado / enojada	*mad, angry*
la esperanza	*hope*
estar celoso / celosa	*to be jealous*
odiar	*to hate*
el odio	*hatred*

Las relaciones de amor y cariño

el abrazo	*hug*
el amante	*lover*
el beso	*kiss*
la madrina	*bridesmaid / matron*
el matrimonio	*married couple; marriage*
el noviazgo	*engagement; courtship*
el padrino	*best man*
el recién casado / la recién casada	*newlywed*
la relación	*relationship*
el romance	*romance*

Más eventos de la vida

el bautizo	*baptism*
el compromiso	*engagement*
cumplir... años	*to have a birthday; to be . . . years old*
dar a luz	*to give birth*
el embarazo	*pregnancy*
el entierro	*burial, funeral*
estar de luto	*to be in mourning*
la nota necrológica	*obituary*
el noviazgo	*engagement, courtship*
la primera comunión	*First Communion*
el velorio	*wake, vigil*

Capítulo 9

Otros animales

la abeja	*bee*
la ardilla	*squirrel*
la cabra	*goat*
el cangrejo	*crab*
el ciervo	*deer*
el cochino	*pig*
la culebra	*snake*
el dinosaurio	*dinosaur*
la foca	*seal*
el gallo	*rooster*
el gorila	*gorilla*

la iguana	*iguana*
la jirafa	*giraffe*
el lobo	*wolf*
el loro	*parrot*
la mariposa	*butterfly*
el marrano	*pig*
el mono	*monkey*
el nido	*nest*
la oveja	*sheep*
la paloma	*pigeon; dove*
el pato	*duck*
el pingüino	*penguin*
el puerco	*pig*
el pulpo	*octopus*
el puma	*puma*
la rana	*frog*
el rinoceronte	*rhinoceros*
el saltamontes	*grasshopper*
el tiburón	*shark*
el tigre	*tiger*
la tortuga	*turtle*
el venado	*deer*
el zorro	*fox*

El medio ambiente

el agua subterránea	*ground water*
el aerosol	*aerosol*
la Antártida	*Antarctica*
el Ártico	*the Arctic*
la atmósfera	*atmosphere*
atrapar	*to trap*
el aumento	*increase*
el bióxido de carbono	*carbon dioxide*
el carbón	*coal*
el clorofluorocarbono	*chlorofluorocarbon*
el combustible fósil	*fossil fuel*
corroer	*to corrode*
la cosecha	*crop; harvest*
desarrollar	*to evolve, to develop*
la descomposición	*decomposition*
descongelarse	*to melt*
el desperdicio de patio	*yard waste*
destruir	*to destroy*
el ecosistema	*ecosystem*
el efecto de invernadero	*greenhouse effect*
la energía	*energy*
hundirse	*to sink*
la industria	*industry*
insoportable	*unbearable, unsustainable*
el medio ambiente	*environment*

el oxígeno	oxygen
el país	country
el pesticida	pesticide
el petróleo	petroleum
la piedra	rock, stone
la piel	skin
la planta eléctrica	power plant
el plomo	lead
el polvo	dust
el rayo de sol	sun ray
el rayo ultravioleta	ultraviolet ray
el riesgo	risk

El gobierno

el ciudadano / la ciudadana	citizen
el juez / la jueza	judge

Las cuestiones políticas

el aborto	abortion
la pena capital	death penalty

Capítulo 10

Más profesiones

el administrador / la administradora	administrator
el agente	agent
el agente comprador	purchasing agent
el amo / la ama de casa	homemaker
el azafato / la azafata	flight attendant
el cajero / la cajera	cashier
el director / la directora	director, principal
el diseñador / la diseñadora de publicidad	advertising designer
el economista	economist
el escritor / la escritora	author, writer
el gerente comprador	purchasing manager
el gerente de desarrollo y tecnología	manager of development and technology
el gerente financiero	financial manager
el ingeniero / la ingeniera	engineer
el ingeniero / la ingeniera de sistema de ventas	system engineer / sales
el ingeniero químico / la ingeniera química	chemical engineer
el jefe / la jefa de personal	director of personnel
el maestro / la maestra	teacher
el mecánico / la mecánica	mechanic
el periodista	journalist
el piloto	pilot
el político / la mujer político	politician
el programador / la programadora de computadoras	computer programmer
el psicólogo / la psicóloga	psychologist

el psiquiatra	*psychiatrist*
el reportero / la reportera	*reporter*
el supervisor / la supervisora de computadoras	*PC-desktop computer supervisor*
el supervisor técnico / la supervisora técnica	*technical supervisor*
el veterinario / la veterinaria	*veterinarian*

Las carreras y profesiones

la asesoría, consejería de profesión	*career counselor, guidance counselor*
el bancario	*banking*
las ciencias acuáticas	*aquatic science*
las ciencias políticas	*political science*
el comercio	*business*
la enfermería	*nursing*
la gerencia de hotel	*hotel management*
el guardián de zoológico	*zookeeper*
la ingeniería	*engineering*
la justicia criminal	*criminal justice*
el mercadeo	*marketing*
la moda	*fashion*
los negocios	*business*
la psicología	*psychology*
la publicidad	*advertising*
las ventas	*sales*
las ventas en el mercadeo de televisión	*telemarketing sales*

El mundo de negocios

las acciones	*stocks*
el accionista	*share holder*
el ambiente de vestir casual	*casual dress environment*
la asesoría de empleados	*employee counseling*
la compañía	*company*
la contribución sobre ingresos	*income tax*
el desarrollo	*development*
la editorial de despacho	*desktop publishing*
financiar	*to finance*
el impuesto sobre la renta	*income tax*
la inversión	*investment*
el medio ambiente de mercadeo	*working environment*
el mercado de divisas	*foreign exchange market*
la mercancía	*merchandise*
el procesamiento (la elaboración) de datos	*data processing*
el proyecto	*project*
publicar	*to publish*
el salario básico	*base salary*
el seguro de salud	*health insurance*
la solicitud	*application*
la tecnología	*technology*
el trabajo de tiempo completo	*full-time job*
el trabajo permanente	*full-time job*
el trabajo de medio tiempo	*part-time job*

Regular Verbs

Basic Forms

Infinitive	hablar	comer	vivir
	to speak	*to eat*	*to live*
Present Participle	hablando	comiendo	viviendo
	speaking	*eating*	*living*
Past Participle	hablado	comido	vivido
	spoken	*eaten*	*lived*

Simple Tenses

Present Indicative	hablo	como	vivo
I speak, am speaking, do speak	hablas	comes	vives
I eat, am eating, do eat	habla	come	vive
I live, am living, do live	hablamos	comemos	vivimos
	habláis	coméis	vivís
	hablan	comen	viven

Imperfect Indicative	hablaba	comía	vivía
I was speaking, used to speak, spoke	hablabas	comías	vivías
I was eating, used to eat, ate	hablaba	comía	vivía
I was living, used to live, lived	hablábamos	comíamos	vivíamos
	hablabais	comíais	vivíais
	hablaban	comían	vivían

Preterit	hablé	comí	viví
I spoke, did speak	hablaste	comiste	viviste
I ate, did eat	habló	comió	vivió
I lived, did live	hablamos	comimos	vivimos
	hablasteis	comisteis	vivisteis
	hablaron	comieron	vivieron

Future	hablaré	comeré	viviré
I will speak, shall speak	hablarás	comerás	vivirás
I will eat, shall eat	hablará	comerá	vivirá
I will live, shall live	hablaremos	comeremos	viviremos
	hablaréis	comeréis	viviréis
	hablarán	comerán	vivirán

Conditional	hablaría	comería	viviría
I would speak	hablarías	comerías	vivirías
I would eat	hablaría	comería	viviría

I would live	hablaríamos	comeríamos	viviríamos
	hablaríais	comeríais	viviríais
	hablarían	comerían	vivirían

Present Subjunctive

[that] I speak	hable	coma	viva
[that] I eat	hables	comas	vivas
[that] I live	hable	coma	viva
	hablemos	comamos	vivamos
	habléis	comáis	viváis
	hablen	coman	vivan

Imperfect Subjunctive

[that] I speak, [that] I might speak	hablara	comiera	viviera
[that] I eat, [that] I might eat	hablaras	comieras	vivieras
[that] I live, [that] I might live	hablara	comiera	viviera
	habláramos	comiéramos	viviéramos
	hablarais	comierais	vivierais
	hablaran	comieran	vivieran

Commands

		—	—	—
Speak				
Eat	*(Informal)*	habla	come	vive
Live		(no hables)	(no comas)	(no vivas)
	(Formal)	hable	coma	viva
		hablen	coman	vivan

Compound Tenses

Present Perfect Indicative
I have spoken, eaten, lived

he	hemos			
has	habéis	hablado	comido	vivido
ha	han			

Past Perfect Indicative
I had spoken, eaten, lived

había	habíamos			
habías	habíais	hablado	comido	vivido
había	habían			

Present Progressive
I am speaking, eating, living

estoy	estamos			
estás	estáis	hablando	comiendo	viviendo
está	están			

Past Progressive
I was speaking, eating, living

estaba	estábamos			
estabas	estabais	hablando	comiendo	viviendo
estaba	estaban			

Stem-Changing Verbs

	e ➠ ie		o ➠ ue	
	pensar	**perder**	**contar**	**volver**
Present Indicative	pienso	pierdo	cuento	vuelvo
	piensas	pierdes	cuentas	vuelves
	piensa	pierde	cuenta	vuelve
	pensamos	perdemos	contamos	volvemos
	pensáis	perdéis	contáis	volvéis
	piensan	pierden	cuentan	vuelven
Present Subjunctive	piense	pierda	cuente	vuelva
	pienses	pierdas	cuentes	vuelvas
	piense	pierda	cuente	vuelva
	pensemos	perdamos	contemos	volvamos
	penséis	perdáis	contéis	volváis
	piensen	pierdan	cuenten	vuelvan

	e ➠ ie, i	e ➠ i, i	o ➠ ue, u
	sentir	**pedir**	**dormir**
Present Indicative	siento	pido	duermo
	sientes	pides	duermes
	siente	pide	duerme
	sentimos	pedimos	dormimos
	sentís	pedís	dormís
	sienten	piden	duermen
Present Subjunctive	sienta	pida	duerma
	sientas	pidas	duermas
	sienta	pida	duerma
	sintamos	pidamos	durmamos
	sintáis	pidáis	durmáis
	sientan	pidan	duerman
Preterit	sentí	pedí	dormí
	sentiste	pedistee	dormiste
	sintió	pidió	durmió
	sentimos	pedimos	dormimos
	sentisteis	pedisteis	dormisteis
	sintieron	pidieron	durmieron
Present Participle	sintiendo	pidiendo	durmiendo

(NOTE: The verb **jugar** changes **u ➠ ue.**)

Irregular Verbs

Infinitive	Participles	Present Indicative	Imperfect	Preterit
abrir *(to open)*	abriendo abierto	abro abres abre abrimos abrís abren	abría abrías abría abríamos abríais abrían	abrí abriste abrió abrimos abristeis abrieron
andar *(to walk)*	andando andado	ando andas anda andamos andáis andan	andaba andabas andaba andábamos andabais andaban	anduve anduviste anduvo anduvimos anduvisteis anduvieron
caer *(to fall)*	cayendo caído	caigo caes cae caemos caéis caen	caía caías caía caíamos caíais caían	caí caíste cayó caímos caísteis cayeron
conocer *(to know)* **-cer** verbs c ➠ zc before **a, o**	conociendo conocido	conozco conoces conoce conocemos conocéis conocen	conocía conocías conocía conocíamos conocíais conocían	conocí conociste conoció conocimos conocisteis conocieron
construir *(to build)* **-uir** verbs: i ➠ y y inserted before **a, e, o**	construyendo construido	construyo construyes construye construimos construís construyen	construía construías construía construíamos construíais construían	construí construiste construyó construimos construisteis construyeron
continuar *(to continue)*	continuando continuado	continúo continúas continúa continuamos continuáis continúan	continuaba continuabas continuaba continuábamos continuabais continuaban	continué continuaste continuó continuamos continuasteis continuaron

Future	Conditional	Present Subjunctive	Formal and Informal Commmands
abriré	abriría	abra	—
abrirás	abrirías	abras	abre (no abras)
abrirá	abriría	abra	abra
abriremos	abriríamos	abramos	—
abriréis	abriríais	abráis	—
abrirán	abrirían	abran	abran
andaré	andaría	ande	—
andarás	andarías	andes	anda (no andes)
andará	andaría	ande	ande
andaremos	andaríamos	andemos	—
andaréis	andaríais	andéis	—
andarán	andarían	anden	anden
caeré	caería	caiga	—
caerás	caerías	caigas	cae (no caigas)
caerá	caería	caiga	caiga
caeremos	caeríamos	caigamos	—
caeréis	caeríais	caigáis	—
caerán	caerían	caigan	caigan
conoceré	conocería	conozca	—
conocerás	conocerías	conozcas	conoce (no conozcas)
conocerá	conocería	conozca	conozca
conoceremos	conoceríamos	conozcamos	—
conoceréis	conoceríais	conozcáis	—
conocerán	conocerían	conozcan	conozcan
construiré	construiría	construya	—
construirás	construirías	construyas	construye (no construyas)
construirá	construiría	construya	construya
construiremos	construiríamos	construyamos	—
construiréis	construiríais	construyáis	—
construirán	construirían	construyan	construyan
continuaré	continuaría	continúe	—
continuarás	continuarías	continúes	continúa (no continúes)
continuará	continuaría	continúe	continúe
continuaremos	continuaríamos	continuemos	—
continuaréis	continuaríais	continuéis	—
continuarán	continuarían	continúen	continúen

Appendix D *Irregular Verbs*

Infinitive	Participles	Present Indicative	Imperfect	Preterit
dar	dando	doy	daba	di
(to give)	dado	das	dabas	diste
		da	daba	dio
		damos	dábamos	dimos
		dais	dabais	disteis
		dan	daban	dieron
decir	diciendo	digo	decía	dije
(to say, to tell)	dicho	dices	decías	dijiste
		dice	decía	dijo
		decimos	decíamos	dijimos
		decís	decíais	dijisteis
		dicen	decían	dijeron
empezar (e ⟹ ie)	empezando	empiezo	empezaba	empecé
(to begin)	empezado	empiezas	empezabas	empezaste
-zar verbs:		empieza	empezaba	empezó
z ⟹ c		empezamos	empezábamos	empezamos
before **e**		empezáis	empezabais	empezasteis
		empiezan	empezaban	empezaron
escoger	escogiendo	escojo	escogía	escogí
(to choose)	escogido	escoges	escogías	escogiste
-ger verbs		escoge	escogía	escogió
g ⟹ j		escogemos	escogíamos	escogimos
before **a, o**		escogéis	escogíais	escogisteis
		escogen	escogían	escogieron
esquiar	esquiando	esquío	esquiaba	esquié
(to ski)	esquiado	esquías	esquiabas	esquiaste
		esquía	esquiaba	esquió
		esquiamos	esquiábamos	esquiamos
		esquiáis	esquiabais	esquiasteis
		esquían	esquiaban	esquiaron
estar	estando	estoy	estaba	estuve
(to be)	estado	estás	estabas	estuviste
		está	estaba	estuvo
		estamos	estábamos	estuvimos
		estáis	estabais	estuvisteis
		están	estaban	estuvieron
haber	habiendo	he	había	hube
(to have)	habido	has	habías	hubiste
		ha [hay]	había	hubo
		hemos	habíamos	hubimos
		habéis	habíais	hubisteis
		han	habían	hubieron

Future	Conditional	Present Subjunctive	Formal and Informal Commmands
daré	daría	dé	—
darás	darías	des	da (no des)
dará	daría	dé	dé
daremos	daríamos	demos	—
daréis	daríais	deis	—
darán	darían	den	den
diré	diría	diga	—
dirás	dirías	digas	di (no digas)
dirá	diría	diga	diga
diremos	diríamos	digamos	—
diréis	diríais	digáis	—
dirán	dirían	digan	digan
empezaré	empezaría	empiece	—
empezarás	empezarías	empieces	empieza (no empieces)
empezará	empezaría	empiece	empiece
empezaremos	empezaríamos	empecemos	—
empezaréis	empezaríais	empecéis	—
empezarán	empezarían	empiecen	empiecen
escogeré	escogería	escoja	—
escogerás	escogerías	escojas	escoge (no escojas)
escogerá	escogería	escoja	escoja
escogeremos	escogeríamos	escojamos	—
escogeréis	escogeríais	escojáis	—
escogerán	escogerían	escojan	escojan
esquiaré	esquiaría	esquíe	—
esquiarás	esquiarías	esquíes	esquía (no esquíes)
esquiará	esquiaría	esquíe	esquíe
esquiaremos	esquiaríamos	esquiemos	—
esquiaréis	esquiaríais	esquiéis	—
esquiarán	esquiarían	esquíen	esquíen
estaré	estaría	esté	—
estarás	estarías	estés	está (no estés)
estará	estaría	esté	esté
estaremos	estaríamos	estemos	—
estaréis	estaríais	estéis	—
estarán	estarían	estén	estén
habré	habría	haya	—
habrás	habrías	hayas	—
habrá	habría	haya	—
habremos	habríamos	hayamos	—
habréis	habríais	hayáis	—
habrán	habrían	hayan	—

Infinitive	Participles	Present Indicative	Imperfect	Preterit
hacer	haciendo	hago	hacía	hice
(to do; to make)	hecho	haces	hacías	hiciste
		hace	hacía	hizo
		hacemos	hacíamos	hicimos
		hacéis	hacíais	hicisteis
		hacen	hacían	hicieron
ir	yendo	voy	iba	fui
(to go)	ido	vas	ibas	fuiste
		va	iba	fue
		vamos	íbamos	fuimos
		vais	ibais	fuisteis
		van	iban	fueron
leer	leyendo	leo	leía	leí
(to read)	leído	lees	leías	leíste
i ➠ y:		lee	leía	leyó
stressed **i ➠ í**		leemos	leíamos	leímos
		leéis	leíais	leísteis
		leen	leían	leyeron
oír	oyendo	oigo	oía	oí
(to hear)	oído	oyes	oías	oíste
i ➠ y		oye	oía	oyó
		oímos	oíamos	oímos
		oís	oíais	oísteis
		oyen	oían	oyeron
pagar	pagando	pago	pagaba	pagué
(to pay)	pagado	pagas	pagabas	pagaste
-gar verbs:		paga	pagaba	pagó
g ➠ gu		pagamos	pagábamos	pagamos
before **e**		pagáis	pagabais	pagasteis
		pagan	pagaban	pagaron
poder	pudiendo	puedo	podía	pude
(to be able, can)	podido	puedes	podías	pudiste
		puede	podía	pudo
		podemos	podíamos	pudimos
		podéis	podíais	pudisteis
		pueden	podían	pudieron
poner	poniendo	pongo	ponía	puse
(to place, to put)	puesto	pones	ponías	pusiste
		pone	ponía	puso
		ponemos	poníamos	pusimos
		ponéis	poníais	pusisteis
		ponen	ponían	pusieron

Future	Conditional	Present Subjunctive	Formal and Informal Commmands
haré	haría	haga	—
harás	harías	hagas	haz (no hagas)
hará	haría	haga	haga
haremos	haríamos	hagamos	—
haréis	haríais	hagáis	—
harán	harían	hagan	hagan
iré	iría	vaya	—
irás	irías	vayas	ve (no vayas)
irá	iría	vaya	vaya
iremos	iríamos	vayamos	—
iréis	iríais	vayáis	—
irán	irían	vayan	vayan
leeré	leería	lea	—
leerás	leerías	leas	lee (no leas)
leerá	leería	lea	lea
leeremos	leeríamos	leamos	—
leeréis	leeríais	leáis	—
leerán	leerían	lean	lean
oiré	oiría	oiga	—
oirás	oirías	oigas	oye (no oigas)
oirá	oiría	oiga	oiga
oiremos	oiríamos	oigamos	—
oiréis	oiríais	oigáis	—
oirán	oirían	oigan	oigan
pagaré	pagaría	pague	—
pagarás	pagarías	pagues	paga (no pagues)
pagará	pagaría	pague	pague
pagaremos	pagaríamos	paguemos	—
pagaréis	pagaríais	paguéis	—
pagarán	pagarían	paguen	paguen
podré	podría	pueda	—
podrás	podrías	puedas	—
podrá	podría	pueda	—
podremos	podríamos	podamos	—
podréis	podríais	podáis	—
podrán	podrían	puedan	—
pondré	pondría	ponga	—
pondrás	pondrías	pongas	pon (no pongas)
pondrá	pondría	ponga	ponga
pondremos	pondríamos	pongamos	—
pondréis	pondríais	pongáis	—
pondrán	pondrían	pongan	pongan

Infinitive	Participles	Present Indicative	Imperfect	Preterit
querer	queriendo	quiero	quería	quise
(to want, to wish)	querido	quieres	querías	quisiste
		quiere	quería	quiso
		queremos	queríamos	quisimos
		queréis	queríais	quisisteis
		quieren	querían	quisieron
romper	rompiendo	rompo	rompía	rompí
(to break)	roto	rompes	rompías	rompiste
		rompe	rompía	rompió
		rompemos	rompíamos	rompimos
		rompéis	rompíais	rompisteis
		rompen	rompían	rompieron
saber	sabiendo	sé	sabía	supe
(to know)	sabido	sabes	sabías	supiste
		sabe	sabía	supo
		sabemos	sabíamos	supimos
		sabéis	sabíais	supisteis
		saben	sabían	supieron
salir	saliendo	salgo	salía	salí
(to leave)	salido	sales	salías	saliste
		sale	salía	salió
		salimos	salíamos	salimos
		salís	salíais	salisteis
		salen	salían	salieron
seguir (e ➡ i, í)	siguiendo	sigo	seguía	seguí
(to follow)	seguido	sigues	seguías	seguiste
gu ➡ g		sigue	seguía	siguió
before **a, o**		seguimos	seguíamos	seguimos
		seguís	seguíais	seguisteis
		siguen	seguían	siguieron
ser	siendo	soy	era	fui
(to be)	sido	eres	eras	fuiste
		es	era	fue
		somos	éramos	fuimos
		sois	erais	fuisteis
		son	eran	fueron
tener	teniendo	tengo	tenía	tuve
(to have)	tenido	tienes	tenías	tuviste
		tiene	tenía	tuvo
		tenemos	teníamos	tuvimos
		tenéis	teníais	tuvisteis
		tienen	tenían	tuvieron

Future	Conditional	Present Subjunctive	Formal and Informal Commmands
querré	querría	quiera	—
querrás	querrías	quieras	quiere (no quieras)
querrá	querría	quiera	quiera
querremos	querríamos	queramos	—
querréis	querríais	queráis	—
querrán	querrían	quieran	quieran
romperé	rompería	rompa	—
romperás	romperías	rompas	rompe (no rompas)
romperá	rompería	rompa	rompa
romperemos	romperíamos	rompamos	—
romperéis	romperíais	rompáis	—
romperán	romperían	rompan	rompan
sabré	sabría	sepa	—
sabrás	sabrías	sepas	sabe (no sepas)
sabrá	sabría	sepa	sepa
sabremos	sabríamos	sepamos	—
sabréis	sabríais	sepáis	—
sabrán	sabrían	sepan	sepan
saldré	saldría	salga	—
saldrás	saldrías	salgas	sal (no salgas)
saldrá	saldría	salga	salga
saldremos	saldríamos	salgamos	—
saldréis	saldríais	salgáis	—
saldrán	saldrían	salgan	salgan
seguiré	seguiría	siga	—
seguirás	seguirías	sigas	sigue (no sigas)
seguirá	seguiría	siga	siga
seguiremos	seguiríamos	sigamos	—
seguiréis	seguiríais	sigáis	—
seguirán	seguirían	sigan	sigan
seré	sería	sea	—
serás	serías	seas	sé (no seas)
será	sería	sea	sea
seremos	seríamos	seamos	—
seréis	seríais	seáis	—
serán	serían	sean	sean
tendré	tendría	tenga	—
tendrás	tendrías	tengas	ten (no tengas)
tendrá	tendría	tenga	tenga
tendremos	tendríamos	tengamos	—
tendréis	tendríais	tengáis	—
tendrán	tendrían	tengan	tengan

Infinitive	Participles	Present Indicative	Imperfect	Preterit
tocar	tocando	toco	tocaba	toqué
(to play)	tocado	tocas	tocabas	tocaste
-car verbs:		toca	tocaba	tocó
c ⟹ qu		tocamos	tocábamos	tocamos
before **e**		tocáis	tocabais	tocasteis
		tocan	tocaban	tocaron
traducir	traduciendo	traduzco	traducía	traduje
(to translate)	traducido	traduces	traducías	tradujiste
-cir verbs		traduce	traducía	tradujo
c ⟹ zc		traducimos	traducíamos	tradujimos
before **a, o**		traducís	traducíais	tradujisteis
		traducen	traducían	tradujeron
traer	trayendo	traigo	traía	traje
(to bring)	traído	traes	traías	trajiste
		trae	traía	trajo
		traemos	traíamos	trajimos
		traéis	traíais	trajisteis
		traen	traían	trajeron
valer	valiendo	valgo	valía	valí
(to be worth)	valido	vales	valías	valiste
		vale	valía	valió
		valemos	valíamos	valimos
		valéis	valíais	valisteis
		valen	valían	valieron
venir	viniendo	vengo	venía	vine
(to come)	venido	vienes	venías	viniste
		viene	venía	vino
		venimos	veníamos	vinimos
		venís	veníais	vinisteis
		vienen	venían	vinieron
ver	viendo	veo	veía	vi
(to see)	visto	ves	veías	viste
		ve	veía	vio
		vemos	veíamos	vimos
		veis	veíais	visteis
		ven	veían	vieron
volver (o ⟹ ue)	volviendo	vuelvo	volvía	volví
(to return)	vuelto	vuelves	volvías	volviste
		vuelve	volvía	volvió
		volvemos	volvíamos	volvimos
		volvéis	volvíais	volvisteis
		vuelven	volvían	volvieron

Future	Conditional	Present Subjunctive	Formal and Informal Commmands
tocaré	tocaría	toque	—
tocarás	tocarías	toques	toca (no toques)
tocará	tocaría	toque	toque
tocaremos	tocaríamos	toquemos	—
tocaréis	tocaríais	toquéis	—
tocarán	tocarían	toquen	toquen
traduciré	traduciría	traduzca	—
traducirás	traducirías	traduzcas	traduce (no traduzcas)
traducirá	traduciría	traduzca	traduzca
traduciremos	traduciríamos	traduzcamos	—
traduciréis	traduciríais	traduzcáis	—
traducirán	traducirían	traduzcan	traduzcan
traeré	traería	traiga	—
traerás	traerías	traigas	trae (no traigas)
traerá	traería	traiga	traiga
traeremos	traeríamos	traigamos	—
traeréis	traeríais	traigáis	—
traerán	traerían	traigan	traigan
valdré	valdría	valga	—
valdrás	valdrías	valgas	vale (no valgas)
valdrá	valdría	valga	valga
valdremos	valdríamos	valgamos	—
valdréis	valdríais	valgáis	—
valdrán	valdrían	valgan	valgan
vendré	vendría	venga	—
vendrás	vendrías	vengas	ven (no vengas)
vendrá	vendría	venga	venga
vendremos	vendríamos	vengamos	—
vendréis	vendríais	vengáis	—
vendrán	vendrían	vengan	vengan
veré	vería	vea	—
verás	verías	veas	ve (no veas)
verá	vería	vea	vea
veremos	veríamos	veamos	—
veréis	veríais	veáis	—
verán	verían	vean	vean
volveré	volvería	vuelva	—
volverás	volverías	vuelvas	vuelve (no vuelvas)
volverá	volvería	vuelva	vuelva
volveremos	volveríamos	volvamos	—
volveréis	volveríais	volváis	—
volverán	volverían	vuelvan	vuelvan

This end vocabulary includes the active vocabulary words presented in the **¡Asómate!** and **¡Fíjate!** sections of the chapters with the exception of definite and indefinite articles, pronouns, most numbers, and names of countries. The chapter number where a word or expression is first introduced is provided for all active vocabulary. The Spanish–English Vocabulary also includes recognition vocabulary found in headings, grammar terminology, and captions.

A

a   *to, at* **9**
a causa de   *because of*
a la derecha   *to the right* **3**
a la izquierda   *to the left* **3**
a la parrilla   *grilled* **5**
a la... / a las...   *at . . .* (time) **2**
a menudo   *often* **2**
¿A qué hora?   *At what time?* **2**
a veces   *sometimes, from time to time* **2**
el abogado / la abogada   *lawyer* **10**
el abrigo   *overcoat* **6**
abril   *April* **2**
abrir   *to open;* Abra(n) el libro en la página... *Open your book to page . . .* **P**
el abuelo / la abuela   *grandfather / grandmother* **1**; los abuelos   *grandparents* **1**
aburrido / aburrida   *boring* **1**; *bored (with estar)* **2**
acabar de   *to have just* **3**
el aceite   *oil* **5**
acentuar   *to accent, to stress*
aceptar   *to accept* **8**
acerca de   *about* **9**
acordarse de (ue)   *to remember* **6**
acostarse (ue)   *to go to bed* **6**
el actor / la actriz   *actor / actress* **10**
actual   *current*
Adiós.   *Good-bye.* **P**
el adjetivo   *adjective;* el adjetivo demostrativo   *demonstrative adjective;* el adjetivo posesivo   *possessive adjective*
¿Adónde?   *To where?* **2**
el adverbio   *adverb*
el aeropuerto   *airport* **8**
afeitarse   *to shave* **6**
afuera de   *outside of* **9**
la agencia de viajes   *travel agency* **8**
agosto   *August* **2**
el agua   *water* **5**
el águila calva   *bald eagle*
el aire   *air* **9**; el aire acondicionado   *air conditioning* **8**
el alcalde / la alcaldesa   *mayor* **9**
la alcoba   *bedroom* **3**
alemán / alemana   *German* **1**
alérgico / alérgica   *allergic* **7**
el alfabeto   *alphabet*
la alfombra   *rug, carpet* **3**
algo   *something* **10**

alguien   *someone* **10**
algún   *some* **10**
alguno(a / os / as)   *some* **10**
el almacén   *department store* **4**
almorzar (ue)   *to have lunch* **4**
el almuerzo   *lunch* **5**
alrededor de   *around*
alto / alta   *tall* **1**
la altura   *altitude*
el aluminio   *aluminum* **9**
amarillo / amarilla   *yellow* **3**
el amigo / la amiga   *friend* **1**
anaranjado / anaranjada   *orange* **3**
ancho / ancha   *wide* **6**
el anillo   *ring* **8**
animado / animada   *excited* **8**
el animal   *animal;* el animal doméstico *domesticated animal, pet* **9**; el animal en peligro de extinción   *endangered species* **9**; el animal salvaje   *wild animal* **9**
el aniversario (de boda)   *wedding anniversary* **8**
el año   *year;* el año pasado   *last year* **5**
anoche   *last night* **5**
anteayer   *day before yesterday* **5**
antedatar   *to antedate, to backdate*
antes (de)   *before* **3**
el antiácido   *antacid* **7**
el antibiótico   *antibiotic* **7**
antipático / antipática   *unpleasant* **1**
el aparato   *appliance*
el apartamento   *apartment* **2**
el apellido   *last name*
el apodo   *nickname*
apoyar   *to support* **9**
los apuntes (pl.)   *notes* **2**
el árbol   *tree* **3**
el archivo   *file* **10**
el armario   *closet* **3**
la arquitectura   *architecture* **2**
arreglar   *to straighten up* **3**; arreglar la maleta   *to pack a suitcase* **8**
el arroz   *rice* **5**
el arte   *art* **2**
la artesanía   *craft*
el artículo   *article;* el artículo definido   *definite article;* el artículo indefinido   *indefinite article*
el artista   *artist* **10**

Así, así.   *So, so.* **P**
¡Asómate!   *Take a look!, Check it out!*
la aspirina   *aspirin* **7**
atender (ie)   *to assist, to wait on* **8**
¡Atrévete!   *Try it!, Take a chance!, Go for it!*
el atún   *tuna* **5**
aumentar   *to increase, to augment*
el auto   *car* **3**
el autobús   *bus* **8**
la autopista   *freeway* **8**
el autor / la autora   *author* **10**
el ave   *poultry* **5**
avergonzado / avergonzada   *ashamed* **8**
el avión   *airplane* **8**
ayer   *yesterday* **2**
ayudar   *to help* **3**
el azúcar   *sugar* **5**
azul   *blue* **3**

B

el bailador / la bailadora   *dancer*
bailar   *to dance* **2**
bajo / baja   *short* **1**
la ballena azul   *blue whale*
la banana   *banana* **5**
bañarse   *to bathe* **6**
el banco   *bank* **4**
la bañera   *bathtub* **3**
el baño   *bathroom* **3**
barato / barata   *cheap* **5**
el barco   *boat* **8**
la basura   *garbage* **9**
el baúl   *trunk, chest* **3**
la bebida   *beverage* **5**
beige   *beige* **3**
la biblioteca   *library* **2**
la bicicleta   *bicycle* **8**
Bien.   *Fine.* **P**; Bastante bien.   *Just fine.* **P**
el bienestar   *welfare, well-being* **9**
el biftec   *beefsteak* **5**
la biología   *biology* **2**
el bíper (México)   *personal pager* **10**
blanco / blanca   *white* **3**
la blusa   *blouse* **6**
la boca   *mouth* **7**
la boda   *wedding* **8**
el boleto   *ticket* **8**; el boleto de ida y vuelta   *round-trip ticket* **8**
el bolígrafo   *pen* **2**
el bolso / la bolsa   *purse* **6**

el bombero   *firefighter* **10**
bonito / bonita   *pretty* **1**
el borrador   *eraser* **2**
borrar   *to erase* **10**
el bosque   *forest* **9**
botar   *to throw away* **9**
las botas   *boots* **6**
la botella   *bottle* **9**
el botones   *bellman* **8**
el brazo   *arm* **7**
bueno / buena   *good* **1;** Buen provecho!
    Enjoy your meal! **5;** Buenas noches.
    Good evening. **P;** Buenas tardes.
    Good afternoon. **P;** Buenos días.
    Good morning. **P**
el búho   *owl*
el buscapersonas (SPAIN)   *personal pager* **10**

C
el caballo   *horse* **9**
la cabeza   *head* **7**
cada   *each* **10**
caer   *to fall* **3**
café   *brown* **3**
el café   *cafe* **4;** *coffee* **5**
la cafetería   *cafeteria* **2**
la caja   *box; cash register* **8**
el calcetín   *sock* **6**
la calculadora   *calculator* **2**
la calefacción   *(car) heater* **8**
el calentamiento de la tierra   *global warm-*
    ing **9**
la calidad   *quality* **9**
caliente   *hot (temperature)* **5**
callarse   *to get / keep quiet* **6**
la calle   *street* **8**
la cama   *bed* **3**
el camarero / la camarera   *waiter, waitress* **5**
el camarón   *shrimp* **5**
cambiar   *to change* **8**
caminar   *to walk* **2**
el camión   *truck* **8**
la camisa   *shirt* **6**
la camiseta   *T-shirt* **6**
la campaña   *campaign* **9**
canadiense   *Canadian* **1**

la cancha de tenis   *tennis court* **2**
el candidato / la candidata   *candidate* **9**
cansado / cansada   *tired* **2**
el cantante / la cantante   *singer* **10**
la capa de ozono   *ozone layer* **9**
la cara   *face* **7**
la carne   *meat* **5**
la carnicería   *butcher shop* **8**
caro / cara   *expensive* **5**
la carrera   *race*
la carreta   *cart*
la carretera   *highway* **8**
el carro   *car* **3**
la carta   *letter* **2;** *menu* **5**
casado / casada   *married* **8**
casarse (con)   *to marry, to get married (to)* **8**
casi siempre   *almost always* **6**
el catarro   *cold* **7**
la cebolla   *onion* **5**
celebrar   *to celebrate* **8**
celoso / celosa   *jealous* **8**
la cena   *dinner* **5**
el centro   *downtown* **4;** el centro comercial
    mall; business / shopping district **4;** el
    centro estudiantil   *student union* **2**
cepillarse   *to brush (one's hair, teeth)* **6**
cerca (de)   *close, near* **2**
el cerdo   *pig* **9**
el cereal   *cereal* **5**
cerrar (ie)   *to close* **4;** cierre(n)...
    close . . . **P**
la cerveza   *beer* **5**
Chao.   *Bye.* **P**
la chaqueta   *jacket* **6**
el cheque   *bank check* **4;** el cheque de via-
    jero   *traveler's check* **8**
el chico / la chica   *boy / girl* **1**
el chile   *chili pepper* **5**
el cielo   *sky; heaven* **9**
cien   *one hundred;* cien mil   *one hundred*
    thousand; cien millones   *one hundred*
    million
la ciencia   *science* **2**
el científico / la científica   *scientist*
el cine   *movie theater* **4**
la cinta   *cassette tape* **2**

el cinturón   *belt* **6**
la cita   *date, meeting* **8**
la ciudad   *town, city*
claro / clara   *light* **6**
el cliente   *customer* **5**
el coche   *car* **3**
cocido / cocida   *boiled, baked;* bien cocido
    well-done, well-cooked (cooking term) **5**
la cocina   *kitchen* **3**
cocinar   *to cook* **3**
el cocinero / la cocinera   *cook* **5**
el cocodrilo   *crocodile*
el cognado   *cognate*
la cola   *line* **8**
combatir   *to fight, to combat* **9**
el comedor   *dining room* **3**
comenzar (ie)   *to begin* **4**
comer   *to eat* **2**
cómico / cómica   *funny, comical* **1**
la comida   *dinner; meal; food* **5**
¿Cómo?   *What?, How?* **P;** ¿Cómo estás? /
    ¿Cómo está?   *How are you? (familiar /*
    formal) **P;** ¿Cómo se dice... en español?
    How do you say . . . in Spanish? **P;**
    ¿Cómo se escribe… en español?   *How*
    do you write . . . in Spanish? **P;**
    ¿Cómo se llama usted?   *What is your*
    name? (formal) **P;** ¿Cómo te llamas?
    What is your name? (familiar) **P**
el compañero / la compañera   *companion,*
    colleague, mate; el compañero / la com-
    pañera de clase   *classmate* **2;** el com-
    pañero / la compañera de cuarto   *room-*
    mate **2**
el comparativo   *comparative*
compartir   *to share*
la composición   *composition* **2**
comprar   *to buy* **2**
comprender   *to understand;* (No) com-
    prendo.   *I (don't) understand.* **P**
la comprensión   *comprehension*
comprometido / comprometida   *engaged* **8**
el computador / la computadora   *compu-*
    ter **2;** el computador / la computadora
    portátil   *laptop computer* **10**
con   *with* **2**

el condicional   *conditional*
los condimentos   *condiments 5*
el conejo   *rabbit 9*
el congreso   *congress 9*
el conjunto   *outfit 6*
conocer   *to know 3*
conocido / conocida   *famous*
el consejero / la consejera   *counselor 10*
al contado   *cash 8*
el contador / la contadora   *accountant 10*
la contaminación   *pollution 9*
contaminar   *to pollute 9*
contento / contenta   *content, happy 2*
el contestador (automático; SPAIN)   *answering machine 10*
la contestadora   *answering machine 10*
contestar   *to answer 2;* Conteste(n)... *Answer . . . P*
el corazón   *heart 7*
la corbata   *tie 6*
el correo   *post office 4;* el correo electrónico *E-mail 10;* el correo mediante voz *voice mail 10*
correr   *to run 2*
cortar(se)   *to cut (oneself) 7*
corto / corta   *short 6*
la cosa   *thing 3*
costar (ue)   *to cost 4*
creer   *to believe 2*
el crimen   *crime 9*
crudo / cruda   *rare; raw 5*
el cuaderno   *notebook 2*
el cuadro   *picture 3*
¿Cuál(es)?   *Which? 2*
¿Cuándo?   *When? 2*
¿Cuánto(a / os / as)?   *How much?, How many? 2*
el cuarto   *room 2;* el cuarto doble *double room 8;* el cuarto individual *single room 8*
cubano / cubana   *Cuban 1*
la cuchara   *soup spoon, tablespoon 5*
la cucharilla   *teaspoon*
la cucharita   *teaspoon 5*
el cuchillo   *knife 5*
el cuello   *neck 7*
la cuenta   *bill, account 4*
¡Cuéntame!   *Tell me!*
el cuerpo   *body 7;* el cuerpo humano *human body 7*
la cueva   *cave 9*
cuidar   *to take care of 9*
el cumpleaños   *birthday 8*
la curita   *adhesive bandage 7*
el curso   *course 2*

D

dar   *to give 3*
darse cuenta de   *to realize 7*
de   *of, from 9;* ¿De dónde... ? *From where . . . ? P;* de la mañana *in the morning 2;* de la noche *in the evening 2;* de la tarde *in the afternoon 2;* De nada. *You're welcome. P*
debajo (de)   *underneath 5*
debido a   *due to*
débil   *weak 1*
decir (i)   *to say 3*
el dedo   *finger 7;* el dedo del pie *toe 7*
la defensa   *defense 9*
delante de   *in front of 4*
delgado / delgada   *thin 1*
demasiado   *too much 2*
la democracia   *democracy 9*
el demodulador / la demoduladora   *modem 10*
demostrar (ue)   *to demonstrate 4*
el dentista   *dentist 10*
el dependiente / la dependiente   *salesclerk 8*
el deporte   *sport*
deprimido / deprimida   *depressed 8*
derecho   *straight ahead 4*
el derecho   *law 2*
el derrame de petróleo   *oil spill 9*
el desastre   *disaster 9*
el desayuno   *breakfast 5*
el descendiente   *descendant*
el descuento   *discount 8*
desear   *to want, to desire 3*
el desempleo   *unemployment 9*
desilusionado / desilusionada   *disappointed 8*
las despedidas *(pl.)*   *farewells*
el despertador   *alarm clock 2*
despertarse (ie)   *to wake up, to awaken 6*
despistado / despistada   *absentminded, flaky 8*
después (de)   *after 3*
la destrucción   *destruction 9*
detrás de   *behind 4*
la deuda (externa)   *(foreign) debt 9*
devolver (ue)   *to return an object 4*
el día   *day;* el día festivo *holiday;* todos los días *every day 6*
diciembre   *December 2*
el dictador / la dictadora   *dictator 9*
la dictadura   *dictatorship 9*
el diente   *tooth 7*
difícil   *difficult 2*
¡Dime más!   *Tell me more!*
el dinero   *money 2*
el diputado / la diputada   *representative (congressional) 9*
el disco compacto   *compact disk 2;* el disco no removible *hard drive 10*
el discurso   *speech 9*
discutir   *to argue; to discuss 8*
el disquete   *diskette 10*
divertirse (ie, i)   *to enjoy oneself, to have fun 6*
divorciarse   *to divorce 8*
el divorcio   *divorce 8*
doblar   *to turn 8*
el doctor / la doctora   *doctor 7*

doler (ue)   *to hurt 7*
el dolor   *pain 7*
domingo   *Sunday 2*
¿Dónde?   *Where? 2*
dormir (ue, u)   *to sleep 4;* dormirse (ue, u) *to fall asleep 6*
el dormitorio   *bedroom 3*
la ducha   *shower 3*
ducharse   *to shower 6*
dulce   *sweet*
el dulce   *candy, sweet 5*
duro   *hard-boiled (cooking term) 5*

E

la ecología   *ecology 9*
el edificio   *building 2*
la educación   *education 2*
efectivo: en efectivo   *in cash 8*
la elección   *election 9*
el elefante   *elephant 9*
elegir (i, i)   *to elect 9*
emocionado / emocionada   *excited 8*
empezar (ie)   *to begin 4*
el empleado / la empleada   *employee 10*
en   *in 9*
enamorado / enamorada   *in love 8*
enamorarse   *to fall in love 8*
Encantado. / Encantada.   *Nice to meet you. P*
encantador / encantadora   *enchanting*
encantar   *to love, to delight 2*
el encanto   *enchantment*
encerrar (ie)   *to enclose 4*
encima (de)   *on top (of) 5*
encontrar (ue)   *to find 4;* se encuentra *one finds, you find 3*
la encuesta   *survey, poll 9*
enero   *January 2*
enfermarse   *to get sick 7*
la enfermedad   *illness 7*
el enfermero / la enfermera   *nurse 7*
enfermo / enferma   *ill, sick 2*
enfrente de   *in front of 4*
engañar   *to deceive 8*
enojado / enojada   *angry 2*
la ensalada   *salad 5*
enseñar   *to teach; to show 2*
entender (ie)   *to understand 4*
¡Entérate!   *Take note!, Become aware!*
entrar   *to enter, to go in 2*
entre   *between 2*
entusiasmado / entusiasmada   *enthusiastic 8*
el equipo   *team 2*
los equipos   *(computer) hardware 10*
Es la... / Son las...   *It's . . . (time) 2*
la escalera   *stair 3*
escribir   *to write 2;* Escriba(n). *Write. P*
el escritorio   *desk 2*
escuchar (música)   *to listen to (music) 2;* escuche(n) *listen P*
la espalda   *back 7*
español / española   *Spanish 1*

la especialidad *major;* la especialidad de la casa *specialty of the house* **5**

las especias *spices* **5**

el espectáculo *show*

esperar *to wait for; to hope* **2**

el esposo / la esposa *husband / wife* **1**

la estación *season;* la estación (de tren, de autobús) *(train, bus) station* **8;** la estación de servicio *gas station* **8**

el estacionamiento *parking* **8**

estacionarse *to park* **8**

el estadio *stadium* **2**

el estado *state* **9**

estadounidense *American* **1**

estampado / estampada *print* **6**

el estante de libros *bookcase* **3**

estar *to be* **2;** estar de moda *to be in fashion*

el estereo *stereo* **2**

el estereotipo *stereotype*

el estómago *stomach* **7**

estornudar *to sneeze* **7**

el estornudo *sneeze* **7**

las estrategias de lectura *reading strategies*

estrecho / estrecha *narrow, tight* **6**

el estudiante *student* **2**

estudiar *to study* **2**

la estufa *stove* **3**

evitar *to avoid* **7**

el examen *exam* **2;** el examen físico *physical exam* **7**

la expansión *expansion*

exportar *to export*

la expresión *expression*

el extranjero *abroad* **8**

F

fácil *easy* **2**

la falda *skirt* **6**

la familia *family* **1**

la farmacia *pharmacy* **7**

fascinar *to fascinate* **2**

el fax *fax* **10**

faxear *to fax* **10**

febrero *February* **2**

feliz *happy* **2**

el femenino / la femenina *feminine*

feo / fea *ugly* **1**

la fiebre *fever* **7**

¡Fíjate! *Look!, Imagine that!*

el fin de semana *weekend* **5**

la finca *farm*

la flor *flower* **3**

formal *formal* **6**

francés / francesa *French* **1**

la frazada *blanket* **3**

frecuentemente *frequently* **6**

fresco / fresca *fresh* **5**

los frijoles *(pl.) beans* **5**

frito / frita *fried* **5**

la fruta *fruit* **5**

fuerte *strong* **1**

funcionar *to work* **8**

el futuro *future*

G

la galleta *cookie* **5**

la gallina *chicken, hen* **9**

la ganancia *profit*

el garaje *garage* **3**

la garganta *throat* **7**

gastar *to spend* **8**

el gato / la gata *cat* **9**

generalmente *generally* **6**

la gente *people*

el gerente / la gerente *manager* **10**

el gimnasio *gymnasium* **2**

el gobernador / la gobernadora *governor* **9**

el gobierno *government* **9**

gordo / gorda *fat* **1**

la gorra *cap* **6**

gracias *thank you* **P**

la graduación *graduation* **8**

grande *big, large* **1**

la granja *farm*

el granjero / la granjera *farmer* **10**

la gripe *flu* **7**

gris *gray* **3**

guapo / guapa *pretty, handsome* **1**

guardar *to put away* **3;** *to save* **10**

la guardilla *attic* **3**

la guerra *war* **9**

gustar *to like* **2**

H

el habitante *inhabitant*

hablar *to speak* **2**

hacer *to do; to make* **3;** Hace buen tiempo. *It's nice weather.* **3;** Hace calor. *It's hot.* **3;** Hace frío. *It's cold.* **3;** Hace mal tiempo. *It's bad weather.* **3;** Hace sol. *It's sunny.* **3;** Hace viento. *It's windy.* **3;** hacer daño *to (do) damage* **9;** hacer ejercicios (aeróbicos) *to exercise (do aerobics)* **2;** hacer falta *to need; to be lacking* **2;** hacer la cama *to make the bed* **3;** hacer la maleta *to pack a suitcase* **8**

la hamburguesa *hamburger* **5**

harto / harta *fed up* **8**

hasta *until* **2;** Hasta luego. *See you later.* **P;** Hasta mañana. *See you tomorrow.* **P;** Hasta pronto. *See you soon.* **P**

hay *there is / there are* **2**

hecho *done, cooked;* bien hecho *well done (cooking term)* **5**

helado / helada *iced*

el helado *ice cream* **5**

la herida *wound* **7**

el hermano / la hermana *brother / sister* **1;** los hermanos *brothers and sisters, siblings* **1**

hervido / hervida *boiled* **5**

el hielo *ice* **5**

el hijo / la hija *son / daughter* **1;** los hijos *sons and daughters* **1**

hispano / hispana *Hispanic*

el hogar *home*

¡Hola! *Hi!, Hello!* **P**

el hombre *man* **1;** el hombre de negocios *businessman* **10**

el horario (de clases) *schedule* **2**

la hormiga *ant* **9**

al horno *baked* **5**

el hospital *hospital* **7**

hoy *today* **2**

el hoyo *hole* **9**

la huelga *strike* **9**

el huevo *egg* **5**

húmedo / húmeda *humid* **3**

el huracán *hurricane* **9**

I

la identidad *identity*

el idioma *language* **2;** los idiomas *(foreign) languages* **2**

la iglesia *church* **4**

Igualmente. *The same to you., You too.* **P**

el imperfecto *imperfect*

imponente *imposing*

importar *to matter; to be important* **2**

la impresora *printer* **10**

imprimir *to print* **10**

el impuesto *tax* **9**

el incendio *fire* **9**

la infección *infection* **7**

la inflación *inflation* **9**

informal *casual; informal* **6**

la informática *computer science* **2**

inglés / inglesa *English* **1**

el inodoro *toilet* **3**

el insecto *insect* **9**

inteligente *intelligent* **1**

interesante *interesting* **1**

la inundación *flood* **9**

el invierno *winter* **2**

la inyección *shot* **7**

ir *to go* **4;** ir a pie *to walk* **8;** ir de compras *to go shopping* **2;** irse *to go away, to leave* **6;** Vaya(n) a la pizarra. *Go to the board.* **P**

la isla *island*

J

jamás *never* **10**

el jamón *ham* **5**

japonés / japonesa *Japanese* **1**

el jarabe *cough syrup* **7**

el jardín *garden* **3**

los jeans *jeans* **6**

el jefe / la jefa *boss* **10**

joven *young* **1;** el joven *young man / young woman* **1** la joyería *jewelry store* **8**

jueves *Thursday* **2**

jugar (ue) *to play* **4;** jugar al básquetbol *to play basketball* **2;** jugar al béisbol *to play baseball* **2;** jugar al fútbol *to play soccer* **2;** jugar al fútbol americano *to play football* **2;** jugar al golf *to play golf* **2;** jugar al tenis *to play tennis* **2**

el jugo *juice* **5**

julio *July* **2**

junio *June* **2**

L

el laboratorio *laboratory* **2**

al lado de *next to* **4**

el lago *lake* **8**

la lámpara *lamp* **3**

el lápiz *pencil* **2**

largo / larga *long* **6**

lastimarse *to get hurt, to hurt oneself* **7**

la lata *can* **9**

el lavabo *sink* **3**

el lavaplatos *dishwasher* **3**

lavar *to wash* **3**

lavar los platos *to wash the dishes* **3**

lavarse *to wash oneself* **6**

la leche *milk* **5**

la lechuga *lettuce* **5**

leer *to read* **2;** lea(n) *read*

lejos (de) *far, far away* **2**

el león *lion* **9**

levantarse *to get up, to stand up* **6**

la ley *law* **9**

la leyenda *legend*

la librería *bookstore* **2**

el libro *book* **2**

el limpiaparabrisas *windshield wiper* **8**

limpiar *to clean* **3**

limpio / limpia *clean* **3**

liso / lisa *solid-colored* **6**

la literatura *literature* **2**

llamarse *to be called* **6;** Me llamo... *My name is . . .* **P**

la llanta *tire* **8**

la llave *key* **8**

llegar *to arrive* **2**

llenar *to fill* **8**

llevar *to wear; to take, carry* **6;** llevar a cabo *to carry out* **9**

llover (ue) *to rain* **3;** Llueve. *It's raining.* **3**

la lluvia *rain* **3;** la lluvia ácida *acid rain* **9**

el localizador *personal pager* **10**

luchar *to fight, to combat* **9**

el lugar *place*

la luna de miel *honeymoon* **8**

lunes *Monday* **2**

M

la madre *mother* **1**

el maíz *corn* **5**

mal / malo *bad* **1**

la maleta *suitcase* **8**

la mamá *mom*

el manatí *manatee* **9**

mandar *to send* **4;** mandar por fax *to fax* **10**

el mandato *command*

manejar *to drive* **8**

la mano *hand* **7**

el mantel *tablecloth* **5**

la mantequilla *butter* **5**

la manzana *apple* **5**

mañana *tomorrow* **2**

el mapa *map* **2**

maquillarse *to put on makeup* **6**

las máquinas (*pl.*) *(computer) hardware* **10**

los mariscos (*pl.*) *seafood* **5**

marrón *brown* **3**

martes *Tuesday* **2**

marzo *March* **2**

más *more* **2;** más o menos *so-so* **P**

la máscara *mask*

el masculino / la masculina *masculine*

matar *to kill* **9**

las matemáticas (*pl.*) *mathematics* **2**

las materias (*pl.*) *courses*

mayo *May* **2**

la mayonesa *mayonnaise* **5**

las medias (*pl.*) *stockings, hose* **6**

la medicina *medicine* **2**

el médico / la médica *doctor* **10**

el mejor *the best* **4**

mejorarse *to get better* **7**

el melón *melon* **5**

la memoria *memory* **10**

menos *less* **2**

mentir (ie, i) *to lie* **4**

el menú *menu* **5**

el mercado *market* **4**

la merienda *snack* **5**

la mermelada *jam, marmalade* **5**

el mes *month*

la mesa *table* **2**

el metro *subway* **8**

mexicano / mexicana *Mexican* **1**

el microondas *microwave* **3**

miércoles *Wednesday* **2**

mil *one thousand*

millón *one million*

mirar la televisión *to watch television* **2**

la mochila *bookbag, knapsack* **2**

el módem (SPAIN) *modem*

molesto / molesta *bothered, upset* **8**

molestar *to bother* **2**

la monarquía *monarchy* **9**

la montaña *mountain* **8**

montar en bicicleta *to ride a bike* **2**

morado / morada *purple* **3**

morir (ue, u) *to die* **4**

la mosca *fly* **9**

el mosquito *mosquito* **9**

la mostaza *mustard* **5**

mostrar (ue) *to show* **4**

la moto(cicleta) *motorcycle* **8**

el motor *motor, engine* **8**

el muchacho / la muchacha *boy / girl* **1**

muchas veces *many times* **6**

mucho *a lot* **2;** Mucho gusto. *How do you do?, Nice to meet you.* **P**

los muebles (*pl.*) *furniture* **3**

la muerte *death* **8**

la mujer *woman* **1;** la mujer de negocios *businesswoman* **10;** la mujer policía *police officer* **10**

la multa *ticket, fine* **8**

el museo *museum* **4**

la música *music* **2**

el músico / la música *musician* **10**

muy *very* **1;** Muy bien. *Very well.* **P**

N

nacer *to be born* **8**

el nacimiento *birth* **8**

la nacionalidad *nationality*

nada *nothing* **10**

nadar *to swim* **2**

nadie *no one* **2**

la naranja *orange* **5**

la nariz *nose* **7**

la naturaleza *nature* **9**

navegar la Internet *to surf the Net* **10**

necesitar *to need* **2**

los negocios (*pl.*) *business* **2**

negro / negra *black* **3**

nervioso / nerviosa *upset, nervous* **2**

nevar (ie) *to snow* **3;** Nieva. *It's snowing.* **3**

ni... ni *neither . . . nor* **10**

la nieve *snow* **3**

nigeriano / nigeriana *Nigerian* **1**

ningún *none* **10**

ninguno / ninguna *none* **10**

el niño / la niña *little boy / little girl* **1**

no *no* **P**

¡No me digas! *You don't say!*

el nombre *name, first name*

normalmente *normally* **6**

norteamericano / norteamericana *American* **1**

norteño / norteña *northern*

noviembre *November* **2**

el novio / la novia *boyfriend / girlfriend* **1**

la nube *cloud* **3**

nublado / nublada *cloudy* **3**

el número *number*

nunca *never* **2**

O

el obrero / la obrera *manual laborer* **10**

el océano *ocean* **9**

octubre *October* **2**

ocupado / ocupada *busy* **8**

ocurrir *to occur* **7**

la oferta *offer, sale* **8**

la oficina *office* **3**

el oído   *inner ear 7*
oír   *to hear 3*
el ojo   *eye 7*
olvidarse de   *to forget 6*
la oreja   *ear 7*
orgulloso / orgullosa   *proud 8*
originar   *to originate*
oscuro / oscura   *dark 6*
el oso   *bear 9*
el otoño   *autumn 2*

P
el paciente   *patient 1*
el padre   *father 1;* los padres   *parents 1*
pagar   *to pay 8*
la página en la Internet   *home page 10*
el pájaro   *bird 9*
la palabra   *word*
el palacio   *palace*
el pan   *bread 5*
la panadería   *bread shop 8*
la pantalla   *screen 10*
los pantalones *(pl.)*   *pants 6;* los pantalones
     cortos   *shorts 6;* los pantalones vaque-
     ros   *jeans 6*
la pantera   *panther 9*
el papá   *dad 1*
la papa   *potato 5;* las papas fritas *(pl.)*
     french fries, potato chips 5
el papel   *paper 2*
para   *for, in order to 9;* para explorar   *for
     exploring, in order to explore;* para
     recordar   *for remembering*
el parabrisas   *windshield 8*
la parada   *bus stop 8*
el paraguas   *umbrella 6*
la pared   *wall 2*
el parque   *park 4;* el parque de atracciones
     theme park 8
el participio pasado   *past participle*
el partido político   *political party 9*
pasado / pasada   *past*
el pasaporte   *passport 8*
pasar la aspiradora   *to vacuum 3*
el pasatiempo   *pastime*
el pastel   *pastry, pie 5*
la pastelería   *pastry shop 8*
la pastilla   *pills 7*
la patata   *potato 5*
patinar   *to skate 2*
el pecho   *chest 7*
pedir (i, i)   *to ask for 4*
peinarse   *to comb one's hair 6*
pelear   *to fight 8*
la película   *movie 4*
el peligro   *danger*
peligroso / peligrosa   *dangerous 9*
el pelo   *hair 7*
la pelota   *ball 2*
la peluquería   *beauty salon / barber
     shop 8*

el peluquero / la peluquera   *hair stylist;
     barber 10*
pensar (ie)   *to think 4*
el peor   *the worst 4*
pequeño / pequeña   *small 1*
la pera   *pear 5*
perder (ie)   *to lose; to waste 4; to miss 8*
perdido / perdida   *lost 8*
perezoso / perezosa   *lazy 1*
el periódico   *newspaper 9*
el periodismo   *journalism 2*
el permiso (de conducir)   *driver's license 8*
pero   *but 2*
el perro   *dog 9;* el perro caliente   *hot dog 5*
perseguir (i, i)   *to chase 4*
el pescado   *fish 5*
el pez (los peces)   *fish 9*
picante   *spicy 5*
el pie   *foot 7*
la pierna   *leg 7*
la píldora   *pill 7*
la pimienta   *pepper 5*
la piscina   *swimming pool 2*
el piso   *floor 3*
la pizarra   *chalkboard 2*
el planeta   *planet 9*
la planta   *plant 3;* la planta baja   *ground
     floor 3*
el plástico   *plastic 9*
el plato   *plate, dish 5*
la playa   *beach 8*
la plaza   *town square 4*
el plural   *plural*
el pluscuamperfecto   *past perfect*
la población   *population*
pobre   *poor 1*
(un) poco   *a little 1*
poco hecho   *rare (cooking term) 5*
poder (ue)   *to be able to 3*
el policía / la mujer policía   *police officer 10*
la policía   *police force*
la política   *politics*
el pollo   *chicken 5*
poner   *to put, to place 3;* poner la mesa   *to
     set the table 3;* ponerse (la ropa)   *to get
     dressed 6;* ponerse nervioso / nerviosa
     to get nervous 6
por   *for, through, by, because of 9;* por favor
     please P; ¿Por qué?   *Why? 2*
porque   *because 2*
el postre   *dessert 5*
el precio   *price 8*
preferir (ie, i)   *to prefer 4*
la pregunta   *question*
preocupado / preocupada   *worried 2*
preocuparse de (por)   *to worry about, con-
     cern oneself with 9*
preparar   *to prepare; to get ready 2;*
     preparar una comida   *to cook 3*
la preposición   *preposition*
la presentación   *introduction*

presentar   *to introduce;* Quiero presentarte
     a...   *I would like to introduce you
     to . . . P*
el presente   *present;* el presente del indica-
     tivo   *present indicative;* el presente
     progresivo   *present progressive*
el presidente   *president 9*
prestar   *to lend; to borrow 8*
el pretérito   *preterit*
la primavera   *spring 2*
el primo / la prima   *cousin (m. / f.) 1*
el probador   *fitting room 8*
probarse (ue)   *to try on 8*
el procesador de texto   *word processor 10*
el profesor / la profesora   *professor 2*
el programa de computación   *software 10*
prometer   *to promise 3*
el pronombre   *pronoun;* el pronombre de los
     complementos directos   *direct-object
     pronoun;* el pronombre de los comple-
     mentos indirectos   *indirect-object pro-
     noun;* el pronombre personal   *personal
     pronoun*
el propietario / la propietaria   *owner 10*
la propina   *tip 5*
proteger   *to protect 9*
proveer   *to provide*
la provincia   *province 9*
la psicología   *psychology 2*
el pueblo   *village*
la puerta   *door 2*
puertorriqueño / puertorriqueña   *Puerto
     Rican 1*
puro / pura   *pure 9*

Q
¿qué?   *what? 2;* ¿Qué es esto?   *What is
     this? P;* ¿Qué hay?   *What's new?,
     What's up? P;* ¿Qué hora es?   *What
     time is it? 2;* ¿Qué significa?   *What
     does it mean? P;* ¿Qué tal?   *How's it
     going? P;* ¿Qué te parece?   *What do
     you think?;* Que tenga(s) un buen día.
     Have a nice day. P; ¿Qué tiempo hace?
     What's the weather like? 3
quedarse   *to stay, to remain 6;* (no)
     quedar(le) bien   *to (not) fit 8*
los quehaceres *(pl.)*   *chores, tasks*
quemar(se)   *to burn (oneself) 7*
querer (ie)   *to want; to love 3*
el queso   *cheese 5*
¿Quién(es)?   *Who(m)? P*
quitarse (la ropa)   *to take off (one's clothes) 6*

R
la radio   *radio 2*
el rancho   *farm 9*
el rascacielos   *skyscraper 8*
la rata   *rat 9*
el ratón   *mouse*
la realidad virtual   *virtual reality 10*

la recepción   *front desk* **8**
la receta   *prescription* **7**
recibir   *to receive* **2**
el recibo   *receipt* **8**
reciclar   *to recycle* **9**
recomendar (ie)   *to recommend* **4**
recordar (ue)   *to remember* **4**
el recurso   *resource* **9**
la Red   *Internet, World Wide Web* **10**
reforestar   *to reforest* **9**
el refresco   *soft drink* **5**
el refrigerador   *refrigerator* **3**
el regalo   *gift* **8**
la región   *region* **9**
registrarse   *to check in* **8**
regresar   *to return* **2**
Regular.   *OK.* **P**
rehusar   *to refuse* **9**
la reina   *queen*
el reloj   *clock, watch* **2**
el repaso   *review*
repetir (i, i)   *to repeat* **4**; Repita(n).
　　Repeat. **P**
reservar (una mesa)   *to reserve (a table)* **5**
el resfriado   *cold* **7**
la residencia estudiantil   *dormitory* **2**
resolver (ue)   *to resolve* **9**
responsable   *responsible* **1**
la respuesta   *answer*
el restaurante   *restaurant* **4**
el resumen   *summary*
reunirse   *to get together, to meet* **6**
revisar   *to check* **8**
el rey   *king*
rico / rica   *rich* **1**
el río   *river* **9**
rojo / roja   *red* **3**
romper(se)   *to break* **7**
rosado / rosada   *pink* **3**
la rueda   *wheel* **8**
el ruido   *noise* **8**

S

sábado   *Saturday* **2**
saber   *to know* **4**; Lo sé.   *I know.* **P**; No (lo)
　　sé.   *I don't know.* **P**
sacar   *to extract;* sacar la basura   *to take
　　out the garbage* **3**
sacudir   *to dust* **3**
la sal   *salt* **5**
la sala   *living room* **3**; la sala de clase
　　classroom **2**; la sala de emergencia
　　emergency room **7**
salir   *to leave* **3**; salir (con)   *to go out
　　(with)* **8**
la salsa de tomate   *tomato ketchup* **5**
la salud   *health* **7**
saludable   *healthy* **7**
los saludos *(pl.)*   *greetings*
salvar   *to save* **10**
las sandalias *(pl.)*   *sandals* **6**

la sangre   *blood* **7**
sano / sana   *healthy* **7**
secarse   *to dry off* **6**
seco / seca   *dry* **3**
el secretario / la secretaria   *secretary* **10**
seguir (i, i)   *to follow* **4**
el sello   *stamp* **8**
la selva   *jungle* **9**; la selva tropical   *(tropi-
　　cal) rain forest* **9**
el semáforo   *traffic light* **8**
la semana   *week;* la semana pasada   *last
　　week* **5**
sembrar (ie)   *to plant* **9**
el semestre   *semester* **2**
el senado   *senate* **9**
el senador / la senadora   *senator* **9**
el señor (Sr.)   *man, gentleman* **1**
la señora (Sra.)   *woman, lady* **1**
la señorita (Srta.)   *young woman, Miss* **1**
sentarse (ie)   *to sit* **6**
sentirse (ie, i)   *to feel* **6**
septiembre   *September* **2**
ser   *to be* **P**; Soy...   *I'm . . .* **P**
la serpiente   *snake* **9**
la servilleta   *napkin* **5**
servir (i, i)   *to serve* **4**
sí   *yes;* ¡Sí, se puede!   *Yes, you can!*
siempre   *always* **2**
¡Sígueme!   *Follow me!*
la silla   *chair* **2**
el sillón   *armchair* **3**
simpático / simpática   *nice* **1**
sin   *without* **9**
el singular   *singular*
sobre   *over, about* **9**
el software   *software* **10**
el sol   *sun* **3**
el sombrero   *hat* **6**
la sopa   *soup* **5**
el subjuntivo   *subjunctive*
sucio / sucia   *dirty* **3**
el suelo   *floor* **3**
el suéter   *sweater* **6**
el superlativo   *superlative*
el supermercado   *supermarket* **4**

T

la talla   *size* **8**
el tamaño   *size* **8**
también   *too, also* **2**
tampoco   *neither* **10**
el tanque   *gas tank* **8**
la tarea   *homework* **2**
la tarjeta   *card* **8**; la tarjeta de crédito
　　credit card **5**; la tarjeta postal   *post
　　card* **8**
el taxi   *taxi* **8**
la taza   *cup* **5**
el té   *tea* **5**
el teatro   *theater* **4**
el techo   *roof* **3**

tejano / tejana   *Texan*
el teléfono celular   *cell phone* **10**
la televisión   *television* **3**
la temperatura   *temperature* **3**
el tenedor   *fork* **5**
tener   *to have* **1**; tener alergia   *to be aller-
　　gic* **7**; tener... años   *to be . . . years
　　old* **3**; tener calor   *to be hot* **3**; tener
　　catarro   *to have a cold* **7**; tener una cita
　　to have a date **8**; tener cuidado   *to be
　　careful* **3**; tener dolor de cabeza   *to
　　have a headache* **7**; tener dolor de es-
　　palda   *to have a backache* **7**; tener do-
　　lor de estómago   *to have a stomach
　　ache* **7**; tener dolor de garganta   *to
　　have a sore throat* **7**; tener éxito   *to be
　　successful* **3**; tener frío   *to be cold* **3**;
　　tener ganas de...   *to feel like . . .* **3**;
　　tener gripe   *to have the flu* **7**; tener ham-
　　bre   *to be hungry* **3**; tener una infección
　　to have an infection **7**; tener miedo   *to
　　be afraid* **3**; tener prisa   *to be in a
　　hurry* **3**; tener que + *(inf.)*   *to have to
　　+ (inf.)* **3**; tener razón   *to be right* **3**;
　　tener un resfriado   *to have a cold* **7**;
　　tener sed   *to be thirsty* **3**; tener sueño
　　to be sleepy **3**; tener suerte   *to be
　　lucky* **3**; tener un virus   *to have a virus* **7**
la teoría   *theory*
terminar   *to finish, to end* **2**
término medio   *medium (cooking term)* **5**
el terremoto   *earthquake* **9**
la tienda   *store* **2**
la Tierra   *Earth* **9**
la tierra   *land, soil* **9**
el timbre   *stamp* **8**
la tintorería   *dry cleaners* **8**
el tío / la tía   *uncle / aunt* **1**; los tíos   *aunts
　　and uncles* **1**
típico / típica   *typical*
la tiza   *chalk* **2**
el tocador   *dresser* **3**
tocar un instrumento   *to play an instrument* **2**
todavía   *still*
tomar   *to take* **2**
el tomate   *tomato* **5**
tonto / tonta   *silly, dumb* **1**
la tormenta   *storm* **9**
el tornado   *tornado* **9**
el toro   *bull* **9**
la torta   *cake* **5**
la tortuga   *tortoise*
la tos   *cough* **7**
toser   *to cough* **7**
la tostada   *toast* **5**
trabajador / trabajadora   *hardworking* **1**
trabajar   *to work* **2**
traer   *to bring* **3**
el tráfico   *traffic* **8**
la tragedia   *tragedy* **9**
el traje   *suit* **6**; el traje de baño   *swimsuit* **6**

el tratamiento *treatment 7*
tratar de *to try 7*
el tren *train 8*
triste *sad 2*

U

único / única *unique; only*
la universidad *university*
usar *to use 2*
útil *useful*

V

la vaca *cow 9*
las vacaciones *(pl.)* *vacation 8*
valer *to be worth 8*
el vaso *glass 5*
la venda *bandage 7*
el vendaje *bandage 7*
vendar *to bandage; to dress (a wound) 7*

venir *to come 3*
ver *to see 3*
el verano *summer 2*
el verbo *verb;* el verbo de cambio radical
    stem-changing verb; el verbo reflexivo
    reflexive verb
verde *green 3*
la verdura *vegetable 5*
el vertedero *dump 9*
el vestido *dress 6*
vestirse (i, i) *to get dressed 6*
viajar *to travel 8*
el viajero / la viajera *traveler 8*
el vidrio *glass 9*
viejo / vieja *old 1*
viernes *Friday 2*
el vinagre *vinegar 5*
el vino *wine 5*
visitar *to visit 8*

vivir *to live 2*
vivo / viva *alive, living 9*
el vocabulario *vocabulary;* el vocabulario
    activo *active vocabulary*
volar (ue) *to fly 8*
el volcán *volcano*
volver (ue) *to return 4*
votar *to vote 9*
el vuelo *flight 8*

Y

y *and 2;* ¿Y tú? / ¿Y usted? *And you? (fa-
    miliar / formal) P*
Ya lo sabemos. *We already know it.*

Z

la zapatería *shoe store 8*
el zapato *shoe 6;* la zapatilla de tenis, el za-
    pato de tenis *tennis shoe 6*

This end vocabulary includes the active vocabulary words presented in the **¡Asómate!** and **¡Fíjate!** sections of the chapters with the exception of definite and indefinite articles, pronouns, most numbers, and names of countries. Active vocabulary items include the chapter number where a word or expression is first introduced. The English–Spanish Vocabulary also includes recognition vocabulary found in headings, grammar terminology, and captions.

A

a little   *(un) poco* **1**
a lot   *mucho* **2**
about   *acerca de, sobre* **9**
abroad   *el extranjero* **8**
absentminded   *despistado /despistada*
accent   *acentuar*
accept   *aceptar* **8**
account   *la cuenta* **4**
accountant   *el contador / la contadora* **10**
actor / actress   *el actor / la actriz* **10**
adhesive bandage   *la curita* **7**
adjective   *el adjetivo;* demonstrative adjective   *el adjetivo demostrativo;* possessive adjective   *el adjetivo posesivo*
adverb   *el adverbio*
after   *después (de)* **3**
afternoon   *tarde;* in the afternoon   *de la tarde* **2**
air   *el aire* **9;** air conditioning   *el aire acondicionado* **8**
airplane   *el avión* **8**
airport   *el aeropuerto* **8**
alarm clock   *el despertador* **2**
alive   *vivo / viva* **9**
allergic   *alérgico / alérgica* **7**
alphabet   *el alfabeto*
also   *también* **2**
altitude   *la altura*
aluminum   *el aluminio* **9**
always   *siempre* **2;** almost always   *casi siempre* **6**
American   *norteamericano / norteamericana, estadounidense* **1**
and   *y;* And you? (familiar / formal)   *¿Y tú? / ¿Y usted?* **P**
angry   *enojado / enojada* **2**
animal   *el animal*
answer   *la respuesta; contestar;* Answer . . .   *Conteste(n)...* **2**
answering machine   *el contestador (automático; SPAIN)* **9;** *la contestadora* **10**
ant   *la hormiga* **9**
antacid   *el antiácido* **7**
antedate   *antedatar*
antibiotic   *el antibiótico* **7**
apartment   *el apartamento* **2**
apple   *la manzana* **5**
appliance   *el aparato*
April   *abril* **2**

architecture   *la arquitectura* **2**
argue   *discutir* **8**
arm   *el brazo* **7**
armchair   *el sillón* **3**
around   *alrededor de*
arrive   *llegar* **2**
art   *el arte* **2**
article   *el artículo;* definite article   *el artículo definido;* indefinite article   *el artículo indefinido*
artist   *el artista* **10**
ashamed   *avergonzado / avergonzada* **8**
ask for   *pedir (i, i)* **4**
aspirin   *la aspirina* **7**
assist   *atender (ie)* **8**
at   *a* **9;** at . . . (time)   *a la... / a las...* **2;** At what time?   *¿A qué hora?* **2**
attic   *la guardilla* **3**
augment   *aumentar*
August   *agosto* **2**
aunt   *la tía* **1**
author   *el autor / la autora* **10**
autumn   *el otoño* **2**
avoid   *evitar* **7**
awaken   *despertarse (ie)* **6**

B

back   *la espalda* **7**
bad   *mal / malo* **1**
baked   *al horno, cocido / cocida* **5**
bald eagle   *el águila calva*
ball   *la pelota* **2**
banana   *la banana* **5**
bandage   *la venda, el vendaje* **7;** *vendar* **7**
bank   *el banco* **4;** bank check   *el cheque* **4**
barber   *el peluquero / la peluquera* **10;** barber shop   *la peluquería* **8**
bathe   *bañarse* **6**
bathroom   *el baño* **3**
bathtub   *la bañera* **3**
be   *estar* **2;** *ser* **P;** be able to   *poder (ue)* **3;** be afraid   *tener miedo* **3;** be allergic   *tener alergia* **7;** be born   *nacer* **8;** be called   *llamarse* **6;** be careful   *tener cuidado* **3;** be cold   *tener frío* **3;** be hot   *tener calor* **3;** be hungry   *tener hambre* **3;** be in fashion   *estar de moda;* be in a hurry   *tener prisa* **3;** be lucky   *tener suerte* **3;** be right   *tener razón* **3;** be

sleepy   *tener sueño* **3;** be successful   *tener éxito* **3;** be thirsty   *tener sed* **3;** be worth   *valer* **8;** be . . . years old   *tener... años* **3**
beach   *la playa* **8**
beans   *los frijoles* **5**
bear   *el oso*
beauty salon   *la peluquería* **8**
because   *porque* **2;** because of   *a causa de, por* **9**
bed   *la cama* **3**
bedroom   *la alcoba, el dormitorio* **3**
beefsteak   *el biftec* **5**
beer   *la cerveza* **5**
before   *antes (de)* **3**
begin   *comenzar (ie), empezar (ie)* **4**
behind   *detrás de* **4**
beige   *beige* **3**
believe   *creer* **2**
bellman   *el botones* **8**
belt   *el cinturón* **6**
best; the best   *el mejor* **4**
between   *entre* **2**
beverage   *la bebida* **5**
bicycle   *la bicicleta* **8**
big   *grande* **1**
bike ride   *montar en bicicleta* **2**
bill   *la cuenta* **4**
biology   *la biología* **2**
bird   *el pájaro* **9**
birth   *el nacimiento* **8**
birthday   *el cumpleaños* **8**
black   *negro / negra* **3**
blanket   *la frazada* **3**
blood   *la sangre*
blouse   *la blusa* **6**
blue   *azul* **3**
boat   *el barco* **8**
body   *el cuerpo* **7;** human body   *el cuerpo humano* **7**
boiled (cooking term)   *hervido / hervida, cocido / cocida* **5**
book   *el libro* **2;** bookbag   *la mochila* **2;** bookcase   *el estante de libros* **3**
bookstore   *la librería* **2**
boots   *las botas* **6**
bored   *aburrido / aburrida* (with *estar*) **2**
boring   *aburrido / aburrida* (with *ser*) **2**
borrow   *prestar* **8**
boss   *el jefe / la jefa* **10**

bother *molestar 2;* bothered *molesto / molesta 8*

bottle *la botella 9*

box *la caja*

boy *el chico, el muchacho 1;* little boy *el niño / la niña 1*

boyfriend *el novio 1*

bread *el pan 5;* bread shop *la panadería 8*

break *romper(se) 7*

breakfast *el desayuno 5*

bring *traer 3*

brother *el hermano 1;* brothers and sisters *los hermanos 1*

brown *café, marrón 3*

brush (one's hair, teeth) *cepillarse 6*

building *el edificio 2*

bull *el toro 9*

burn (oneself) *quemar(se) 7*

bus *el autobús;* bus station *la estación del autobús 8;* bus stop *la parada 8*

business *los negocios 2;* businessman *el hombre de negocios 10;* businesswoman *la mujer de negocios 10*

busy *ocupado / ocupada 8*

but *pero 2*

butcher shop *la carnicería 8*

butter *la mantequilla 5*

buy *comprar 2*

by *por 9*

Bye. *Chao. Adios. P*

C

cafe *el café 4*

cafeteria *la cafetería 2*

cake *la torta*

calculator *la calculadora 2*

campaign *la campaña 9*

can *la lata 9*

Canadian *canadiense 1*

candidate *el candidato / la candidata 9*

candy *el dulce 5*

cap *la gorra 6*

car *el auto, el carro, el coche 3;* car heater *la calefacción 8*

card *la tarjeta 8*

carpet *la alfombra 3*

carry *llevar 6;* carry out *llevar a cabo 9*

cart *la carreta*

cash *al contado, en efectivo 8;* cash register *la caja 8*

cassette tape *la cinta 2*

casual *informal 6*

cat *el gato 9*

cave *la cueva 9*

celebrate *celebrar 8*

cell phone *el teléfono celular 10*

cereal *el cereal 5*

chair *la silla*

chalk *la tiza*

chalkboard *la pizarra 2*

change *cambiar 8*

chase *perseguir (i, i) 4*

cheap *barato / barata 5*

check *revisar 8;* check in *registrarse 8*

cheese *el queso 5*

chest *el pecho 7; el baúl 3*

chicken *el pollo 5; la gallina 9*

chili pepper *el chile 5*

chores *los quehaceres (pl.)*

church *la iglesia 4*

city *la ciudad*

classmate *el compañero / la compañera de clase 2*

classroom *la sala de clase 2*

clean *limpiar; limpio / limpia 3*

clock *el reloj 2*

close *cerrar (ie) 4;* Close . . . *Cierre(n)... P*

close to *cerca (de) 2*

closet *el armario 3*

cloud *la nube 3*

cloudy *nublado 3*

coffee *el café 5*

cognate *el cognado*

cold *el catarro, el resfriado 7*

colleague *el compañero / la compañera 2*

comb one's hair *peinarse 6*

combat *combatir, luchar 9*

come *venir 3*

commercial mall *el centro comercial 4*

comical *cómico / cómica 1*

command *el mandato*

compact disk *el disco compacto 2*

companion *el compañero / la compañera 2*

comparative *el comparativo*

composition *la composición 2*

comprehension *la comprensión*

computer *la computadora 2;* computer hardware *los equipos, las máquinas 10;* computer science *la informática 2*

concern oneself with *preocuparse de, preocuparse por 9*

condiments *los condimentos 5*

conditional *el condicional*

congress *el congreso 9*

content *contento / contenta 2*

cook *cocinar; preparar una comida 3; el cocinero / la cocinera 5*

cooked (cooking term) *hecho 5*

cookie *la galleta 5*

corn *el maíz 5*

cost *costar (ue) 4*

cough *la tos; toser 7;* cough syrup *el jarabe 7*

counselor *el consejero / la consejera 10*

course *el curso 2*

courses *las materias (pl.)*

cousin *el primo / la prima 1*

cow *la vaca 9*

craft *la artesanía*

credit card *la tarjeta de crédito 5*

crime *el crimen 9*

crocodile *el cocodrilo*

Cuban *cubano / cubana 1*

cup *la taza 5*

current *actual*

customer *el cliente 5*

cut (oneself) *cortar(se) 7*

D

dad *el papá 1*

damage (to do) *hacer daño 9*

dance *bailar 2*

dancer *el bailador / la bailadora*

danger *el peligro*

dangerous *peligroso / peligrosa 9*

dark *oscuro / oscura 6*

date *la cita 8*

daughter   *la hija 1*
day   *el día;* day before yesterday
    anteayer 5; every day   *todos los días 6*
death   *la muerte 8*
debt   *la deuda;* foreign debt   *la deuda externa 9*
deceive   *engañar 8*
December   *diciembre 2*
defense   *la defensa 9*
delight   *encantar 2*
democracy   *la democracia 9*
demonstrate   *demostrar (ue) 4*
dentist   *el dentista 10*
department store   *el almacén 4*
depressed   *deprimido / deprimida 8*
descendant   *el descendiente*
desire   *desear 3*
desk   *el escritorio 2*
dessert   *el postre 5*
destruction   *la destrucción 9*
dictator   *el dictador / la dictadora 9*
dictatorship   *la dictadura 9*
die   *morir (ue, u) 4*
difficult   *difícil 2*
dining room   *el comedor 3*
dinner   *la cena 5; la comida 5*
direct object pronoun   *el pronombre de los complementos directos*
dirty   *sucio / sucia*
disappointed   *desilusionado / desilusionada 8*
disaster   *el desastre 9*
discount   *el descuento 8*
discuss   *discutir 8*
dish   *el plato 5*
dishwasher   *el lavaplatos 3*
diskette   *el disquete 10*
divorce   *el divorcio; divorciarse 8*
do   *hacer 3;* do exercises (aerobics)   *hacer ejercicios (aeróbicos) 2*
doctor   *el doctor / la doctora 7; el médico / la médica 10*
dog   *el perro 9*
domesticated animal   *el animal doméstico 9*
door   *la puerta 2*
dormitory   *la residencia estudiantil 2*
downtown   *el centro 4*
dress (a wound)   *vendar;* (article of clothing) *el vestido 6;* get dressed   *vestirse (i,i) 6*
dresser   *el tocador 3*
drive   *manejar 8*
driver's license   *el permiso (de conducir) 8*
dry   *seco / seca 3;* dry cleaners   *la tintorería 8;* dry off   *secarse 6*
due to   *debido a*
dumb   *tonto / tonta 1*
dump   *el vertedero 9*
dust   *sacudir 3*

E

E-mail   *el correo electrónico 10*
each   *cada 10*

ear   *la oreja 7;* inner ear   *el oído 7*
Earth   *la Tierra 9*
earthquake   *el terremoto 9*
easy   *fácil 2*
eat   *comer 2*
ecology   *la ecología 9*
education   *la pedagogía 2*
egg   *el huevo 5*
either . . . or   *y... o 10*
elect   *elegir (i, i) 9*
election   *la elección 9*
elephant   *el elefante 9*
emergency room   *la sala de emergencia 7*
employee   *el empleado / la empleada 10*
enchanting   *encantador / encantadora*
enchantment   *el encanto*
enclose   *encerrar (ie) 4*
end   *terminar 2*
endangered species   *el animal en peligro de extinción 9*
engaged   *comprometido / comprometida 8*
engine   *el motor 8*
English   *inglés / inglesa 1*
enjoy oneself   *divertirse (ie, i) 6;* Enjoy your meal!   *¡Buen provecho! 5*
enter   *entrar 2*
enthusiastic   *entusiasmado / entusiasmada 8*
erase   *borrar 10*
eraser   *el borrador 2*
evening   *noche;* in the evening   *de la noche 2*
exam   *el examen 2*
excited   *animado / animada, emocionado / emocionada 8*
expansion   *la expansión*
expensive   *caro / cara 5*
export   *exportar*
expression   *la expresión*
extract   *sacar*
eye   *el ojo 7*

F

face   *la cara 7*
fall   *caer 3;* fall asleep   *dormirse (ue, u) 6;* fall in love with   *enamorarse de 8*
family   *la familia 1*
famous   *conocido / conocida*
far (away)   *lejos (de) 2*
farewells   *las despedidas*
farm   *la finca; la granja; el rancho 9*
farmer   *el granjero / la granjera 10*
fascinate   *fascinar 2*
fat   *gordo / gorda 1*
father   *el padre 1*
fax   *el fax; mandar por fax; faxear 10*
February   *febrero 2*
fed up   *harto / harta 8*
feel   *sentirse (ie, i);* feel like . . .   *tener ganas de...*
feminine   *femenino / femenina*
fever   *la fiebre 7*

fight   *pelear 8; combatir, luchar 9*
file   *el archivo 10*
fill   *llenar 8*
find   *encontrar (ue) 4;* one finds, you find   *se encuentra 3*
fine   *bien P; la multa 8;* just fine   *bastante bien P*
finger   *el dedo 7*
finish   *terminar 2*
fire   *el incendio 9*
firefighter   *el bombero 10*
first name   *el nombre*
fish   *el pescado 5; el pez (los peces) 9*
fit   *quedar(le) bien 8*
fitting room   *el probador 8*
flaky   *despistado / despistada 8*
flight   *el vuelo 8*
flood   *la inundación 9*
floor   *el piso; el suelo 3*
flower   *la flor 3*
flu   *la gripe 7*
fly   *volar (ue) 8; la mosca 9*
follow   *seguir (i, i);* Follow me!   *¡Sígueme!*
food   *la comida 5*
foot   *el pie 7*
for   *para; por 9*
forest   *el bosque 9*
forget   *olvidarse de 6*
fork   *el tenedor 5*
formal   *formal 6*
freeway   *la autopista 8*
French   *francés / francesa 1;* french fries   *las papas fritas (pl.) 5*
frequently   *frecuentemente 6*
fresh   *fresco / fresca 5*
Friday   *viernes 2*
fried   *frito / frita 5*
friend   *el amigo / la amiga 1*
from   *de 9;* from time to time   *a veces 2;* From where . . . ?   *¿De dónde... ? P*
front desk   *la recepción 8*
fruit   *la fruta 5*
funny   *cómico / cómica 1*
furniture   *los muebles 3*
future   *el futuro*

G

garage   *el garaje 3*
garbage   *la basura 9*
garden   *el jardín 3*
gas station   *la gasolinera, la estación de servicio 8*
gas tank   *el tanque 8*
generally   *generalmente 6*
gentleman   *el señor (Sr.) 1*
German   *alemán / alemana 1*
get: get better   *mejorarse 7;* get dressed   *ponerse (la ropa); vestirse (i, i) 6;* get hurt   *lastimarse 7;* get married (to)   *casarse (con) 8;* get nervous   *ponerse nervioso / nerviosa 6;* get quiet

callarse 6; get ready *prepararse 2;*
get sick *enfermarse 7;* get together
reunirse 6; get up *levantarse 6*
gift *el regalo 8*
girl *la chica, la muchacha 1;* little girl *la niña 1*
girlfriend *la novia 1*
give *dar 3*
glass *el vaso 5; el vidrio 9*
global warming *el calentamiento de la tierra 9*
go *ir 4;* Go to the board. *Vaya(n) a la pizarra. P;* go away *irse 6;* go in *entrar 2;* go out (with) *salir (con) 8;* go shopping *ir de compras 2;* go to bed *acostarse (ue) 6*
good *bueno / buena 1;* Good afternoon. *Buenas tardes. P;* Good-bye. *Adiós. P;* Good evening.; Good night. *Buenas noches. P;* Good morning. *Buenos días. P*
government *el gobierno 9*
governor *el gobernador / la gobernadora 9*
graduation *la graduación 8*
grandfather / grandmother *el abuelo / la abuela 1;* grandparents *los abuelos 1*
gray *gris 3*
green *verde 3*
greetings *los saludos*
grilled *a la parrilla 5*
ground floor *la planta baja 3*
gymnasium *el gimnasio 2*

H

hair *el pelo 7;* hair stylist *el peluquero / la peluquera 10*
ham *el jamón 5*
hamburger *la hamburguesa 5*
hand *la mano 7*
handsome *guapo / guapa 1*
happy *feliz, contento / contenta 2*
hard drive *el disco no removible 10*
hard-boiled (egg) *(el huevo) duro 5*
hard-working *trabajador / trabajadora 1*
hat *el sombrero 6*
have *tener 1;* have a backache *tener dolor de espalda 7;* have a cold *tener catarro; tener un resfriado 7;* have a date *tener una cita 8;* have fun *divertirse (ie, i) 6;* have a headache *tener dolor de cabeza 7;* have an infection *tener una infección 7;* have just (done something) *acabar de + (inf.) 3;* have lunch *almorzar (ue) 4;* Have a nice day. *Que tenga(s) un buen día. P;* have a sore throat *tener dolor de garganta 7;* have a stomachache *tener dolor de estómago 7;* have to (do something) *tener que + (inf.) 3;* have a virus *tener un virus 7*
head *la cabeza 7*
health *la salud 7*

healthy *saludable, sano / sana 7*
hear *oír 3*
heart *el corazón 7*
heaven *el cielo 9*
Hello! *¡Hola! P*
hen *la gallina 9*
help *ayudar 3*
Hi! *¡Hola! P*
highway *la carretera 8*
Hispanic *hispano / hispana*
hole *el hoyo 9*
holiday *el día festivo*
home *el hogar;* home page *la página en la Internet 10*
homework *la tarea 2*
honeymoon *la luna de miel 8*
hope *esperar 2*
horse *el caballo 9*
hose *las medias (pl.) 6*
hospital *el hospital 7*
hot (temperature) *caliente 5;* hot dog *el perro caliente 5*
How? *¿Cómo? P;* How are you? (familiar / formal) *¿Cómo estás? / ¿Cómo está? P;* How do you do? *Mucho gusto. P;* How do you say . . . in Spanish? *¿Cómo se dice... en español? P;* How do you write . . . in Spanish? *¿Cómo se escribe... en español? P;* How's it going? *¿Qué tal? P;* How many? *¿Cuánto(a / os / as)? 2;* How much? *¿Cuánto(a / os / as)? 2*
humid *húmedo / húmeda 3*
hurricane *el huracán 9*
hurt *doler (ue) 7;* to hurt oneself *lastimarse 7*
husband *el esposo 1*

I

ice *el hielo 5;* ice cream *el helado 5;* ice skate *patinar 2*
iced *helado / helada*
identity *la identidad*
ill *enfermo / enferma 2*
illness *la enfermedad 7*
imperfect *el imperfecto*
important *importante;* to be important *importar 2*
imposing *imponente*
in *en 9;* in front of *delante de; enfrente de 4;* in love *enamorado / enamorada 8;* in order to *para 9*
increase *aumentar*
indicative present *el presente del indicativo*
indirect object pronoun *el pronombre de los complementos indirectos*
infection *la infección 7*
inflation *la inflación 9*
informal *informal 6*
inhabitant *el habitante*
insect *el insecto 9*

intelligent *inteligente 1*
interesting *interesante 1*
Internet *la Red, la Internet 10*
introduce *presentar;* I would like to introduce you to . . . *Quiero presentarte a... P*
introduction *la presentación*
island *la isla*
It's . . . (time) *Es la... / Son las... 2*
It's bad weather. *Hace mal tiempo. 3*
It's cold. *Hace frío. 3*
It's hot. *Hace calor. 3*
It's nice weather. *Hace buen tiempo. 3*
It's sunny. *Hace sol. 3*
It's windy. *Hace viento. 3*

J

jacket *la chaqueta 6*
jam *la mermelada 5*
January *enero 2*
Japanese *japonés / japonesa 1*
jealous *celoso / celosa 8*
jeans *los jeans; los pantalones vaqueros 6*
jewelry store *la joyería 8*
July *julio 2*
journalism *el periodismo 2*
juice *el jugo 5*
June *junio 2*
jungle *la selva*

K

keep quiet *callarse 6*
key *la llave 8*
kill *matar 9*
king *el rey 10*
kitchen *la cocina 3*
knapsack *la mochila 2*
knife *el cuchillo 5*
know *conocer 3; saber 4;* I know. *Lo sé. P;* I don't know. *No (lo) sé. P*

L

laboratory *el laboratorio 2*
lacking: to be lacking *hacer falta 2*
lady *la señora 1*
lake *el lago 8*
lamp *la lámpara 3*
land *la tierra*
language *el idioma 2,* (foreign) languages *los idiomas 2*
laptop computer *el computador / la computadora portátil 10*
large *grande 1*
last *último / última*
law *el derecho 2; la ley 9*
lawyer *el abogado / la abogada 10*
lazy *perezoso / perezosa 1*
leave *salir 3; irse 6*
left: to the left *a la izquierda 3*
leg *la pierna 7*
legend *la leyenda*

lend *prestar 8*
less *menos 2*
letter *la carta 2*
lettuce *la lechuga 5*
library *la biblioteca 2*
lie *mentir (ie, i) 4*
light *claro / clara 6*
like *gustar 2*
line *la cola 8*
lion *el león 9*
listen to (music) *escuchar (música) 2;* Listen. *Escuche(n). P*
literature *la literatura 2*
live *vivir 2*
living *vivo / viva 9;* living room *la sala 3*
long *largo / larga 6*
lose *perder (ie) 4*
lost *perdido / perdida 8*
love *encantar 2; querer (ie) 3*
lunch *el almuerzo 5*

M

major *la especialidad*
make *hacer;* make the bed *hacer la cama 3*
man *el hombre 1; el señor 1*
manager *el gerente / la gerente 10*
manatee *el manatí*
manual laborer *el obrero / la obrera 10*
many times *muchas veces 6*
map *el mapa 2*
March *marzo 2*
market *el mercado 4*
marmalade *la mermelada 5*
married *casado / casada 8*
marry *casarse (con) 8*
masculine *el masculino / la masculina*
mask *la máscara*
mate *el compañero / la compañera 2*
mathematics *las matemáticas (pl.) 2*
matter *importar 2*
May *mayo 2*
mayonnaise *la mayonesa 5*
mayor *el alcalde / la alcaldesa 9*
meal *la comida 5*
meat *la carne 5*
medicine *la medicina 2*
medium (cooking term) *término medio 5*
meet *reunirse 6*
meeting *la cita 8*
melon *el melón 5*
memory *la memoria 10*
menu *el menú; la carta 5*
Mexican *mexicano / mexicana 1*
microwave *el microondas 3*
milk *la leche 5*
miss *perder (ie) 8*
Miss *señorita (Srta.) 1*
modem *el módem (SPAIN) 10; el demodulador / la demoduladora 10*
mom *la mamá 1*

monarchy *la monarquía 9*
Monday *lunes 2*
money *el dinero 2*
month *el mes*
more *más 2*
morning *la mañana;* in the morning *de la mañana 2*
mosquito *el mosquito 9*
mother *la madre 1*
motor *el motor 8*
motorcycle *la moto(cicleta) 8*
mountain *la montaña 8*
mouse *el ratón 9*
mouth *la boca 7*
movie *la película 4;* movie theater *el cine 4*
museum *el museo 4*
music *la música 2*
musician *el músico / la música 10*
mustard *la mostaza 5*

N

name *el nombre;* last name *el apellido 1;* My name is . . . *Me llamo... P*
napkin *la servilleta 5*
narrow *estrecho / estrecha 6*
nationality *la nacionalidad*
nature *la naturaleza 9*
near *cerca (de) 2*
neck *el cuello 7*
need *necesitar 2; hacer falta 2*
neither *tampoco 10;* neither . . . nor *ni... ni 10*
nervous *nervioso / nerviosa 2*
never *jamás 10; nunca 2*
newspaper *el periódico 9*
next to *al lado de 4*
nice *simpático / simpática 1;* Nice to meet you. *Encantado. / Encantada., Mucho gusto. P*
nickname *el apodo*
Nigerian *nigeriano / nigeriana 1*
night *la noche;* last night *anoche 5*
no *no P;* no one *nadie 2*
noise *el ruido 8*
none *ningún, ninguno / niguna 10*
normally *normalmente 6*
northern *norteño / norteña*
nose *la nariz 7*
notebook *el cuaderno 2*
notes *los apuntes (pl.) 2*
nothing *nada 10*
November *noviembre 2*
number *el número*
nurse *el enfermero / la enfermera 7*

O

occur *ocurrir 7*
ocean *el océano 9*
October *octubre 2*
of *de 9*

offer *la oferta 8*
office *la oficina 3*
often *a menudo 2*
oil *el aceite 5;* oil spill *el derrame de petróleo 9*
OK. *Regular. P*
old *viejo / vieja 1*
on top (of) *encima (de) 5*
one: one hundred *cien;* one hundred thousand *cien mil;* one hundred million *cien millones;* one million *millón;* one thousand *mil*
onion *la cebolla 5*
only *único / única*
open *abrir;* Open your book to page . . . *Abra(n) el libro en la página... P*
orange *anaranjado / anaranjada 3; la naranja 5*
originate *originar*
outfit *el conjunto 6*
outside of *afuera de 9*
over *sobre 9*
overcoat *el abrigo 6*
owl *el búho*
owner *el propietario / la propietaria 10*
ozone layer *la capa de ozono 9*

P

pack *arreglar la maleta; hacer la maleta 8*
pain *el dolor 7*
palace *el palacio*
panther *la pantera*
pants *los pantalones 6*
paper *el papel 2*
parents *los padres 1*
park *el parque 4;* (a car) *estacionarse 8;* theme park *el parque de atracciones 8*
parking *el estacionamiento 8*
passport *el pasaporte 8*
past *pasado / pasada;* past participle *el participio pasado;* past perfect *el pluscuamperfecto*
pastime *el pasatiempo*
pastry *el pastel 5;* pastry shop *la pastelería 8*
patient *el paciente 1*
pay *pagar 8*
pear *la pera 5*
pen *el bolígrafo 2*
pencil *el lápiz 2*
people *la gente*
pepper *la pimienta 5*
personal pager *el bíper, (MEXICO), el localizador 10, el buscapersonas (SPAIN) 10*
personal pronoun *el pronombre personal*
pet *el animal doméstico 9*
pharmacy *la farmacia 7*
physical exam *el examen físico 7*
picture *el cuadro 3*
pie *el pastel 5*
pig *el cerdo 9*
pill *la pastilla; la píldora 7*

pink *rosado / rosada* **3**
place *el lugar; poner* **3**
planet *el planeta* **9**
plant *la planta* **3**; *sembrar (ie)* **9**
plastic *el plástico* **9**
plate *el plato* **5**
play *jugar (ue)* **4**; play an instrument *tocar un instrumento* **2**; play baseball *jugar al béisbol* **2**; play basketball *jugar al básquetbol* **2**; play football *jugar al fútbol americano* **2**; play golf *jugar al golf* **2**; play soccer *jugar al fútbol* **2**; play tennis *jugar al tenis* **2**
Please. *Por favor.* **P**
plural *el plural*
police officer *el policía / la mujer policía* **10**
political party *el partido político* **9**
politics *la política*
poll *la encuesta* **9**
pollute *contaminar* **9**
pollution *la contaminación* **9**
poor *pobre* **1**
population *la población*
post card *la tarjeta postal* **8**
post office *el correo* **4**
potato *la papa; la patata* **5**; potato chips *las papas fritas (pl.)* **5**
poultry *el ave* **5**
prefer *preferir (ie, i)* **4**
prepare *preparar* **2**
preposition *la preposición*
prescription *la receta* **7**
present *el presente;* present progressive *el presente progresivo*
president *el presidente* **9**
preterit *el pretérito*
pretty *bonito / bonita, guapo / guapa* **1**
price *el precio* **8**
print *imprimir* **10**; *estampado / estampada* **6**
printer *la impresora* **10**
professor *el profesor / la profesora* **2**
profit *la ganancia*
promise *prometer* **3**
pronoun *el pronombre*
protect *proteger* **9**
proud *orgulloso / orgullosa* **8**
provide *proveer*
province *la provincia* **9**
psychology *la psicología* **2**
Puerto Rican *puertorriqueño / puertorriqueña* **1**
pure *puro / pura* **9**
purple *morado / morada* **3**
purse *el bolso / la bolsa* **6**
put *poner* **3**; put away *guardar* **3**; put on makeup *maquillarse* **6**

Q

quality *la calidad* **9**
queen *la reina* **10**
question *la pregunta*

R

rabbit *el conejo* **9**
race *la carrera*
radio *la radio* **2**
rain *la lluvia* **3**; *llover (ue)* **3**; acid rain *la lluvia ácida* **9**; It's raining. *Llueve.* **3**
rare (cooking term) *poco hecho* **5**
raw *crudo / cruda* **5**
rat *la rata* **9**
read *leer* **2**; Read. *Lea(n).* **P**
realize *darse cuenta de* **7**
receipt *el recibo* **8**
receive *recibir* **2**
recommend *recomendar (ie)* **4**
recycle *reciclar* **9**
red *rojo / roja* **3**
reflexive verb *el verbo reflexivo*
reforest *reforestar* **9**
refrigerator *el refrigerador* **3**
refuse *rehusar* **9**
region *la región* **9**
remain *quedarse* **6**
remember *recordar (ue)* **4**; *acordarse de (ue)* **6**
repeat *repetir (i, i)* **4**; Repeat. *Repita(n).* **P**
representative (congressional) *el diputado / la diputada* **9**
reserve (a table) *reservar (una mesa)* **5**
resolve *resolver (ue)* **9**
resource *el recurso* **9**
responsible *responsable* **1**
restaurant *el restaurante* **4**
return *regresar* **2**; *volver (ue);* return (an object) *devolver (ue)* **4**
review *repasar; el repaso*
rice *el arroz* **5**
rich *rico / rica* **1**
right: to the right *a la derecha* **3**
ring *el anillo* **8**
river *el río* **9**
roof *el techo* **3**
room *el cuarto* **2**; double room *el cuarto doble* **8**; single room *el cuarto individual* **8**
roommate *el compañero / la compañera de cuarto* **2**
rug *la alfombra* **3**
run *correr* **2**

S

sad *triste* **2**
salad *la ensalada* **5**
sale *la oferta* **8**
salesclerk *el dependiente / la dependiente* **8**
salt *la sal* **5**
same: The same to you. *Igualmente.* **P**
sandals *las sandalias* **6**
Saturday *sábado* **2**
save *salvar; guardar* **10**
say *decir (i)* **3**
schedule *el horario (de clases)* **2**

science *la ciencia* **2**
scientist *el científico / la científica*
screen *la pantalla* **10**
seafood *los mariscos (pl.)* **5**
season *la estación*
secretary *el secretario / la secretaria* **10**
see *ver* **3**; See you later. *Hasta luego.* **P**; See you soon. *Hasta pronto.* **P**; See you tomorrow. *Hasta mañana.* **P**
semester *el semestre* **2**
senate *el senado* **10**
senator *el senador / la senadora* **10**
send *mandar* **4**
September *septiembre* **2**
serve *servir (i, i)* **4**
set the table *poner la mesa* **3**
share *compartir*
shave *afeitarse* **6**
shirt *la camisa* **6**
shoe *el zapato* **6**; shoe store *la zapatería* **8**
short (height) *bajo / baja* **1**; (length) *corto / corta* **6**
shorts *los pantalones cortos* **6**
shot *la inyección* **7**
show *el espectáculo; mostrar (ue)* **4**; *enseñar* **2**
shower *la ducha* **3**; *ducharse* **6**
shrimp *el camarón* **5**
siblings *los hermanos* **1**
sick *enfermo / enferma* **2**
silly *tonto / tonta* **1**
singer *el cantante* **10**
singular *el singular*
sink *el lavabo* **3**
sister *la hermana* **1**
sit *sentarse (ie)* **6**
size *la talla* **8**; *el tamaño* **8**
skirt *la falda* **6**
sky *el cielo* **9**
skyscraper *el rascacielos* **8**
sleep *dormir (ue, u)* **4**
small *pequeño / pequeña* **1**
snack *la merienda* **5**
snake *la serpiente* **9**
sneeze *el estornudo* **7**; *estornudar* **7**
snow *nevar (ie)* **3**; *la nieve* **3**; It's snowing. *Nieva.* **3**
So, so. *Así, así.* **P**; *Más o menos.* **P**
social welfare *el bienestar* **9**
sock *el calcetín* **6**
soft drink *el refresco* **5**
software *el programa de computación* **10**; *el software* **10**
soil *la tierra* **9**
solid-colored *liso / lisa* **6**
some *algún, alguno(a / os / as)* **10**
someone *alguien* **10**
something *algo* **10**
sometimes *a veces* **2**
son *el hijo* **1**; sons and daughters *los hijos* **1**
soup *la sopa* **5**; soup spoon *la cuchara* **5**

Spanish   *español / española* **1**
speak   *hablar* **2**
specialty of the house   *la especialidad de la casa* **5**
speech   *el discurso* **9**
spend   *gastar* **8**
spices   *las especias* **5**
spicy   *picante* **5**
sport   *el deporte*
spring   *la primavera* **2**
stadium   *el estadio* **2**
stair   *la escalera* **3**
stamp   *el sello* **8**; *el timbre* **8**
stand up   *levantarse* **6**
state   *el estado* **9**
station (train, bus)   *la estación (de tren, de autobús)* **8**
stay   *quedarse* **6**
stem-changing verb   *el verbo de cambio radical*
stereo   *el estéreo* **2**
stereotype   *el estereotipo*
still   *todavía*
stockings   *las medias (pl.)* **6**
stomach   *el estómago* **7**
store   *la tienda* **2**
storm   *la tormenta* **9**
stove   *la estufa* **3**
straight ahead   *derecho* **4**
straighten up   *arreglar* **3**
street   *la calle* **8**
stress   *acentuar*
strike   *la huelga* **9**
strong   *fuerte* **1**
student   *el estudiante* **2**; student union   *el centro estudiantil* **2**
study   *estudiar* **2**
subjunctive   *el subjuntivo*
subway   *el metro* **8**
sugar   *el azúcar* **5**
suit   *el traje* **6**
suitcase   *la maleta* **8**
summary   *el resumen*
summer   *el verano* **2**
sun   *el sol* **3**
Sunday   *domingo* **2**
superlative   *el superlativo*
supermarket   *el supermercado* **4**
support   *apoyar* **9**
surf the Net   *navegar por la Internet* **10**
survey   *la encuesta* **9**
sweater   *el suéter* **6**
sweet   *dulce; el dulce* **5**
swim   *nadar* **2**
swimming pool   *la piscina* **2**
swimsuit   *el traje de baño* **6**

T
T-shirt   *la camiseta* **6**
table   *la mesa* **2**
tablecloth   *el mantel* **5**

tablespoon   *la cuchara* **5**
take   *tomar; llevar* **6**; take care of   *cuidar* **9**; take off (one's clothes)   *quitarse (la ropa)* **6**; take out the garbage   *sacar la basura* **3**
tall   *alto / alta* **1**
tasks   *los quehaceres (pl.)*
tax   *el impuesto* **9**
taxi   *el taxi* **8**
tea   *el té* **5**
teach   *enseñar* **2**
team   *el equipo* **2**
teaspoon   *la cucharilla; la cucharita* **5**
television   *la televisión* **3**
temperature   *la temperatura* **3**
tennis court   *la cancha de tenis* **2**
tennis shoe   *los zapatos de tenis* **6**
Texan   *tejano / tejana*
Thank you.   *Gracias.* **P**
theater   *el teatro* **4**
theory   *la teoría*
there is / there are   *hay* **2**
thin   *delgado / delgada* **1**
thing   *la cosa* **3**
think   *pensar (ie)* **4**
throat   *la garganta* **7**
through   *por* **9**
throw away   *botar* **9**
Thursday   *jueves* **2**
ticket   *el boleto* **8**; *la multa* **8**; round-trip ticket   *el boleto de ida y vuelta* **8**
tie   *la corbata* **6**
tight   *estrecho / estrecha* **6**
tip   *la propina* **5**
tire   *la llanta* **8**
tired   *cansado / cansada* **2**
to   *a* **9**
toast   *la tostada* **5**
today   *hoy* **2**
toe   *el dedo del pie* **7**
toilet   *el inodoro* **3**
tomato   *el tomate* **5**; tomato ketchup   *la salsa de tomate* **5**
tomorrow   *mañana* **2**
too   *también*; too much   *demasiado* **2**
tooth   *el diente* **7**
tornado   *el tornado* **9**
tortoise   *la tortuga*
town   *la ciudad;* town square   *la plaza* **4**
traffic   *el tráfico* **8**; traffic light   *el semáforo* **8**
tragedy   *la tragedia* **9**
train   *el tren* **8**; train station   *la estación de tren* **8**
travel   *viajar* **8**; travel agency   *la agencia de viajes* **8**
traveler   *el viajero / la viajera* **8**; traveler's check   *el cheque de viajero* **8**
treatment   *el tratamiento* **7**
tree   *el árbol* **3**
tropical rain forest   *la selva tropical* **9**

truck   *el camión* **8**
trunk   *el baúl* **3**
try   *tratar de* **7**; try on   *probarse (ue)* **8**
Tuesday   *martes* **2**
tuna   *el atún* **5**
turn   *doblar* **8**
typical   *típico / típica*

U
ugly   *feo / fea* **1**
umbrella   *el paraguas* **6**
uncle   *el tío* **1**; aunts and uncles   *los tíos* **1**
underneath   *debajo (de)* **5**
understand   *entender (ie)* **4**, *comprender;* I (don't) understand.   *(No) comprendo.* **P**
unemployment   *el desempleo* **9**
unique   *único / única*
university   *la universidad*
unpleasant   *antipático / antipática* **1**
until   *hasta* **2**
upset   *nervioso / nerviosa* **2**; *molesto / molesta* **8**
use   *usar* **2**
useful   *útil*

V
vacation   *las vacaciones (pl.)* **8**
vacuum   *pasar la aspiradora* **3**
vegetable   *la verdura* **5**
verb   *el verbo*
very   *muy* **1**; very well   *muy bien* **P**
village   *el pueblo*
vinegar   *el vinagre* **5**
virtual reality   *la realidad virtual* **10**
visit   *visitar* **8**
vocabulary   *el vocabulario*
voice mail   *el correo mediante voz* **10**
volcano   *el volcán*
vote   *votar* **9**

W
wait for   *esperar* **2**; wait on   *atender (ie)* **8**
waiter / waitress   *el camarero / la camarera* **5**
wake up   *despertarse (ie)* **6**
walk   *caminar* **2**; *ir a pie* **8**
wall   *la pared* **2**
want   *desear* **3**; *querer (ie)* **3**
war   *la guerra* **9**
wash (oneself)   *lavar(se)* **6**; wash the dishes   *lavar los platos* **3**
waste   *perder (ie)* **8**
watch   *el reloj* **2**; watch television   *mirar la televisión* **2**
water   *el agua* **5**
weak   *débil* **1**
wear   *llevar* **6**
wedding   *la boda* **8**; wedding anniversary   *el aniversario (de boda)* **8**
Wednesday   *miércoles* **2**
week   *la semana;* last week   *la semana pasada* **5**

weekend *el fin de semana* 5
well *bien* P
well-cooked *bien cocido* 5
well-done (cooking term) *bien cocido, bien hecho* 5
whale *la ballena;* blue whale *la ballena azul*
What? *¿Qué?* 2; *¿Cómo?* P; What do you think? *¿Qué te parece?;* What does it mean? *¿Qué significa?* P; What is this? *¿Qué es esto?* P; What is your name? *¿Cómo se llama usted? (formal) ¿Cómo te llamas? (familiar)* P; What time is it? *¿Qué hora es?* 2; What's the weather like? *¿Qué tiempo hace?* 3; What's up? *¿Qué hay?* P
wheel *la rueda* 8
When? *¿Cuándo?* 2

Where? *¿Adónde? ¿Dónde?* 2
Which? *¿Cuál(es)?* 2
white *blanco / blanca* 3
Who(m)? *¿Quién(es)?* P
Why? *¿Por qué?* 2
wide *ancho / ancha* 6
wife *la esposa* 1
wild animal *el animal salvaje* 9
windshield *el parabrisas* 8; windshield wiper *el limpiaparabrisas* 8
wine *el vino* 5
winter *el invierno* 2
with *con* 2
without *sin* 9
woman *la mujer* 1; *la señora* 1; woman police officer *la mujer policía* 10
word *la palabra;* word processor *el procesador de texto* 10

work *trabajar* 2; *funcionar* 8
World Wide Web *la Red* 10
worried *preocupado / preocupada* 2
worry about *preocuparse de* 9
worst *peor* 4; the worst *el peor* 4
wound *la herida* 7
write *escribir* 2; Write. *Escriba(n).* P

Y

year *el año;* last year *el año pasado* 5
yellow *amarillo / amarilla* 3
yes *sí*
yesterday *ayer* 2
you too *igualmente* P
You're welcome. *De nada.* P
young *joven* 1; young man *el joven* 1; young woman *la joven; la señorita* 1

Literary Credits

Bob Vila story printed with his permission, page 193.

Emilina Edwards story printed with her permission, page 194.

Photo Credits

AP/WIDE WORLD PHOTOS, page 1.
AP/WIDE WORLD PHOTOS, page 3 left.
AP/WIDE WORLD PHOTOS, page 3 middle.
AP/WIDE WORLD PHOTOS, page 3 middle left.
AP/WIDE WORLD PHOTOS, page 3 middle right.
AP/WIDE WORLD PHOTOS, page 3 right.
© Ulrike Welsh, page 4.
© Beryl Goldberg, page 5 left.
© Ulrike Welsh, page 5 middle.
Chip and Rosa Maria de la Cueva Peterson, page 5 right.
© Ulrike Welsh, pages 14–15.
© Beryl Goldberg, page 19.
© SUPERSTOCK, page 36 bottom left.
David Heining-Boynton, page 36 bottom middle.
David Heining-Boynton, page 36 top.
© SUPERSTOCK, page 37 bottom left.
Chip and Rosa Maria de la Cueva Peterson, page 37 middle left.
© Beryl Goldberg, page 37 middle center.
Chip and Rosa Maria de la Cueva Peterson, page 37 middle right.
© Beryl Goldberg, page 37 top left.
© Beryl Goldberg, page 37 top center.
Chip and Rosa Maria de la Cueva Peterson, page 37 top right.
© Beryl Goldberg, pages 44–45.
AP/WIDE WORLD PHOTOS, page 70 left.
Byron Augustin/D. Donne Bryant Stock, page 70 right.
© Sophia Elbaz/SYGMA, page 71 left.
© Beryl Goldberg, page 71 right.
© SUPERSTOCK, page 74 bottom left.
© Beryl Goldberg, page 74 bottom middle left.
© Stock Montage, page 74 bottom middle center.
© Archive Photos™, page 74 bottom middle right.
© Stock Montage, page 74 bottom right.
© SUPERSTOCK, page 74 top left.
© Archive Photos™, page 75 bottom.
© Nigel Atherton/Tony Stone Images, page 75 top left.
© Ulrike Welsh, page 75 top right.
© Beryl Goldberg, pages 82–83.
© Archive Photos™, page 95 middle.
Chip and Rosa Maria de la Cueva Peterson, page 97 bottom.
AP/WIDE WORLD PHOTOS, page 97 top.
© SYGMA, page 98 bottom.
AP/WIDE WORLD PHOTOS, page 98 top.
© Ulrike Welsh, page 114 bottom left.
© SUPERSTOCK, page 114 bottom right.
© SUPERSTOCK, page 114 top left.
© Beryl Goldberg, page 114 top right.
© Beryl Goldberg, page 115.

© Europa Press/SYGMA, page 115 bottom.
© Ulrike Welsh, page 115 middle bottom.
© Beryl Goldberg, page 115 middle top.
© SUPERSTOCK, page 115 right.
© Beryl Goldberg, page 115 top.
© Beryl Goldberg, pages 122–123.
Chip and Rosa Maria de la Cueva Peterson, page 134.
© Ulrike Welsh, page 135 left.
David Heining-Boynton, page 135 right.
Alyx Kellington/D. Donne Bryant Stock, page 140 bottom left.
© SUPERSTOCK, page 140 bottom right.
D. Donne Bryant Stock, page 140 top right.
© Beryl Goldberg, page 141.
D. Donne Bryant Stock, page 141 middle left.
AP/WIDE WORLD PHOTOS, page 141 bottom.
D. Donne Bryant Stock, page 141 middle right.
© SUPERSTOCK, page 141 right.
© SUPERSTOCK, pages 148–149.
© SUPERSTOCK, page 160.
© SUPERSTOCK, page 169 left.
© Ulrike Welsh, page 169 middle.
© SUPERSTOCK, page 169 right.
© SUPERSTOCK, page 172 bottom left.
© SUPERSTOCK, page 172 bottom middle.
© Capital Features/The Image Works, page 172 bottom right.
D. Donne Bryant Stock, page 172 top left.
© SUPERSTOCK, page 172 top right.
AP/WIDE WORLD PHOTOS, page 173 bottom left.
© SUPERSTOCK, page 173 bottom left.
© SUPERSTOCK, page 173 top.
© SUPERSTOCK, pages 180–181.
Kjell B. Sandved/Photo Researchers, Inc., page 187 bottom left.
© Ulrike Welsh, page 187 bottom middle.
© Ulrike Welsh, page 187 bottom right.
© Ulrike Welsh, page 187 top left.
© Ulrike Welsh, page 187 top middle.
AP/WIDE WORLD PHOTOS, page 187 top right.
AP/WIDE WORLD PHOTOS, page 193.
David Heining-Boynton, page 194.
David Heining-Boynton, page 195.
© SUPERSTOCK, page 204 left.
© SUPERSTOCK, page 204 right.
© Beryl Goldberg, page 205 bottom left.
AP/WIDE WORLD PHOTOS, page 205 right.
© Andrew Rakoczy/Photo Researchers, Inc., page 205 top left.
© SUPERSTOCK, pages 212–213.
AP/WIDE WORLD PHOTOS, page 223 bottom left.

Index of Culture